Windows Script Host

Tim Hill

Windows Script Host

By Tim Hill

Published by:
Macmillan Technical Publishing
201 West 103rd Street
Indianapolis, IN 46290 USA

03 02 01 00 99 7 6 5 4 3 2 1

Interpretation of the printing code: The rightmost double-digit number is the year of the book's printing; the rightmost single-digit number is the number of the book's printing. For example, the printing code 99-1 shows that the first printing of the book occurred in 1999.

Printed in the United States of America

Library of Congress Catalog Card Number: 99-62129

International Standard Book Number: 1-57870-139-2

Trademark Acknowledgments

All terms mentioned in this book that are known to be trademarks or service marks have been appropriately capitalized. Macmillan Technical Publishing cannot attest to the accuracy of this information. Use of a term in this book should not be regarded as affecting the validity of any trademark or service mark.

Windows 2000 is a registered trademark of Microsoft Corporation.

Warning and Disclaimer

This book is designed to provide information about Windows Script Host. Every effort has been made to make this book as complete and as accurate as possible, but no warranty or fitness is implied.

The information is provided on an "as-is" basis. The authors and Macmillan Technical Publishing shall have neither liability nor responsibility to any person or entity with respect to any loss or damages arising from the information contained in this book or from the use of the discs or programs that may accompany it.

Feedback Information

At Macmillan Technical Publishing, our goal is to create in-depth technical books of the highest quality and value. Each book is crafted with care and precision, undergoing rigorous development that involves the unique expertise of members from the professional technical community.

Readers' feedback is a natural continuation of this process. If you have any comments regarding how we could improve the quality of this book, or otherwise alter it to better suit your needs, you can contact us at `networktech@mcp.com`. Please make sure to include the book title and ISBN in your message.

We greatly appreciate your assistance.

Publisher
David Dwyer

Executive Editor
Linda Ratts Engelman

Managing Editor
Gina Brown

Acquisitions Editor
Karen Wachs

Development Editor
Lisa M. Thibault

Project Editor
Laura Loveall

Copy Editor
Christy Parrish

Indexer
Larry Sweazy

Team Coordinator
Jennifer Garrett

Print Buyer/
Inventory Manager
Chris Moos

Book Designer
Louisa Klucznik

Cover Designer
Aren Howell

Production Team
Scan Communications Group, Inc.

About the Author

Tim Hill is a software and OS developer with more than 20 years experience in systems software and OS architectures. He has designed several real-time operating systems, including RMOS and PKS, the latter of which has been used extensively in mission-critical embedded systems, including ATMs and banking automation systems. After developing millions of lines of system-critical code, Tim is convinced that the best way to develop software is to leave the bugs out. After a number of years consulting on all aspects of Windows NT development and architectural issues, Tim has recently joined Microsoft, where he is working on new systems based upon Windows NT technologies.

Tim is also the author of *Windows NT Shell Scripting* (MTP, 1998), which has received rave reviews from the press as well as from readers and has been a bestseller for many weeks at SoftPro, Barnes and Noble, Borders, and other retailers.

About the Technical Reviewers

These reviewers contributed their considerable practical, hands-on expertise to the entire development process for *Windows Script Host*. As the book was being written, these professionals reviewed all the material for technical content, organization, and flow. Their feedback was critical to ensuring that *Windows Script Host* fits our reader's need for the highest quality technical information.

Gene E. Kellison, Jr. is a computer specialist working at the Bureau of the Public Debt, part of the U.S. Treasury. Gene has 16 years of programming and operating system experience. After earning his two-year degree from West Virginia University at Parkersburg in 1983, he started as a computer consultant. He worked on various minicomputers, programming in UNIX and HP operating system environments. In 1985, he worked for the Wood County Board of Education as a programmer and systems programmer. Three years later, he joined SDS, Inc. doing contract work for DuPont's Washington works plant. He developed a recycling system for the Butacite group that reduced the amount of recycled material created during the Butacity manufacturing process. In 1989, he worked with Ames Company as a systems programmer and assembly language programmer. In 1990, he started his current job with the Bureau of the Public Debt. He built up experience on server operating systems and became an expert in networking technologies. Gene lives with his wife and son in Vienna, West Virginia, where they enjoy walking, golf, and Civil War research.

Robert Marsh has been a Windows NT user and administrator since the NT 3.1 beta in 1993. He is a co-founder and vice president of engineering at Document Technologies, Inc. in Sunnyvale, California. He is the holder of three U.S. patents and is co-inventor of one of the first personal computers, the Processor Tech Sol-20, which debuted in 1976. This machine is now on display in the Smithsonian's Museum of American History in Washington D.C. Bob is also one of the co-founders of the Homebrew Computer Club in Menlo Park and has been featured in two books on the history of personal computing: *Fire in the Valley* and *Hackers*. He is an alumnus of the University of California, Berkeley, (class of 1970) and is a lifelong resident of Berkeley.

Dedication

To my mother and father, who remain stubbornly convinced of my abilities although they freely confess they cannot understand a word of what I write.

Acknowledgments

I've heard it said that writing a book is like having a tooth pulled. It would be more correct to say that it's like pulling your *own* teeth—painful and self-inflicted. Fortunately, the members of the team at Macmillan Technical Publishing are experts at both minimizing the pain and ensuring that the whole process (publishing, not dentistry!) goes as smoothly as possible. My appreciation and thanks go to the entire editorial and production teams for their help and encouragement throughout this project.

My especial thanks go to Linda Engelman, who continues (against all the evidence) to work patiently toward the day when I will actually meet a deadline. Her enthusiasm for this project has been truly outstanding. To Karen Wachs and Lisa Thibault for the excellent editing work, and who, I am sure, now know more about scripting than they ever wished to know. And, to Jennifer Garrett for coordinating everyone and making sure we were all (so to speak) on the same page.

I would also like to thank my friend and colleague, Bob Marsh, for stepping, yet again, into the role of technical editor. Bob's dedication to catching technical errors in the manuscript is second only to his pleasure in pointing them out to me.

Most of all, my thanks and love go to my wife, Donna, and my children, Alex and Becky.

Contents at a Glance

Table of Contents

Introduction

This is a book about *system scripting* for Windows 2000 and Windows NT. A *system script* is a procedure or set of procedures used to automate or simplify an operating system related task. The task might be as simple as copying a single file or as complex as monitoring a set of enterprise servers. Generally, the more complex the task being scripted, the more useful the script because it avoids the need to manually repeat a series of operations, which can be both monotonous and error-prone.

A Short History of Scripting

From their earliest days, operating systems have typically incorporated some sort of *command shell* or command interpreter. This shell allows an interactive user to enter text commands and see the results as textual output. Interaction with these shells always follows the same basic pattern:

1. The operating system prompts the user to enter a command.
2. The user types a line of text (the command) and presses Enter (or some other command termination key).
3. The operating system executes the command and (typically) displays the results of this processing.

By entering sequences of these simple commands, an operator can control all aspects of operating system and computer operation.

Operating system designers were quick to notice that many systems-related tasks involve the repeated execution of specific sequences of commands. To increase efficiency and reduce errors, a system was devised to allow these command sequences to be stored in a file ready for later execution. Upon demand, the operating system reads the file and executes the commands it contains. These simple command lists are called *shell scripts*, *batch files*, or *batch jobs*.

Batch files have been significantly enhanced over the years. One of the first enhancements was *parameterization*, which allows the batch file to be supplied with arguments when it is executed. In addition, various control-flow techniques were borrowed from traditional programming languages. Eventually, batch files reached the point where they could be considered simple programming languages in their own right.

This evolution, however, has led to some significant problems. For example, in my book, *Windows NT Shell Scripting* (by Macmillan Technical Publishing), I described Windows NT batch scripts in detail, including the many script enhancements provided in the Windows NT command shell (CMD.EXE). However, these batch scripts are (at best) awkward to use, and the syntax of the scripts is cumbersome. More importantly, batch scripts are unable to interact with Windows applications to any great extent, which excludes these scripts from many possible uses. Finally, the enhanced Windows NT batch scripts are not cross-platform, and they cannot be run on the Windows 95 and 98 platforms.

These shortcomings have led Microsoft to devise a new set of script technologies that build not upon traditional command-line concepts, but upon modern object-oriented software techniques. These new technologies, collectively referred to here as *system scripting*, are the subject of this book.

Who Should Read This Book

Virtually anyone who wishes to automate a repetitive or awkward operating system task will benefit from the information in this book. However, this book is aimed primarily at Windows 2000 and Windows NT professionals, systems administrators, and power users. Thus, most of the examples and sample scripts deal with system administration and management issues. However, the techniques presented all have much wider applicability, and there is really no limit to the uses for system scripts. To illustrate this, the final sample script in this book presents a simple interactive game.

One area that can be daunting to some potential users of system scripting is that, for the first time, the core of the script system is a true computer language. Previously, Windows NT batch files could be viewed as an extended form of a macro, and therefore, they were just a substitution for directly typing in commands. With system scripting this is no longer the case, which means that many users may be faced with the need to learn a full programming language for the first time.

To ease the trepidation this can cause, I have included in this book a set of sidebars under the heading "Program Guide," which are intended to guide the beginner into the world of software programming with as little pain as possible.

About ActiveX Scripting Technology

This book describes several new system scripting technologies that are available for the Windows 2000 and Windows NT operating systems (as well as Windows 95 and 98). These are:

- *Windows Script Host (WSH)* As a full system-scripting environment, WSH is designed (and almost certainly destined) to replace the old batch scripts that Windows 2000 and Windows NT inherited from MS-DOS. WSH sweeps away the arcane syntax and complexity of these scripts and replaces them with a clean, easy-to-use script environment and a simple, orthogonal object model for accessing application and system functionality.
- *Visual Basic Script Edition (VBScript)* The VBScript language is derived from the popular Visual Basic language, itself a (distant) derivative of the original Dartmouth BASIC developed in the 1970s. The use of VBScript as the core language allows system scripts to take advantage of the robustness and versatility of a modern structured programming language.
- *COM Objects* VBScript has constructs to allow the direct manipulation of COM Objects that expose an automation interface. This allows VBScript to directly control and leverage the object model built into many modern applications, such as Microsoft Office, and system technologies, such as ADSI.
- *Windows Script Components* Windows Script Components (previously known as Server Scriptlets) provide a means to construct COM Objects entirely in script. As such, Windows Script Components are often used to encapsulate reusable script code, which is then referenced from within one or more WSH scripts.

These technologies offer Windows 2000 and Windows NT professionals unprecedented opportunities to automate and control all aspects of client and server computer operations. This book provides all the information needed to effectively use and deploy these technologies on everything from a stand-alone computer to a full enterprise network.

The foundation for all of these new technologies is an architecture known as *ActiveX Scripting*. The ActiveX Scripting architecture, shown in Figure I.1, provides a standard way to separate script *hosts* from script *engines*. The script engines provide the actual script language, whereas the hosts provide an interface between the language and whatever application or facility you plan to script. Because the ActiveX Scripting architecture provides a standard way to connect hosts to engines, any engine can run with any host. Thus, for example, if you obtain a Perl ActiveX Scripting engine and install it, all ActiveX Scripting hosts will automatically be able to execute Perl scripts.

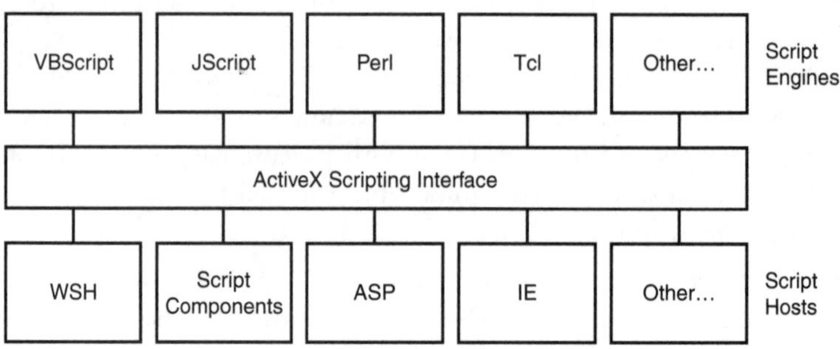

Figure I.1 *ActiveX scripting block diagram.*

Examples of ActiveX Scripting hosts include the popular Internet Explorer web browser, the Microsoft Internet Information Server web server, and the Windows Script Components and WSH technologies described in this book. Examples of ActiveX Scripting engines include the VBScript and JScript languages. There are also third party ActiveX Scripting engine versions of other popular languages, including Perl and Tcl.

Note

This book covers only the VBScript language because this language is in many ways more approachable for newcomers to programming. In addition, the popularity of Visual Basic means that many people will already be familiar with the underlying syntax of VBScript, based as it is upon this language. However, if you prefer to use another language, then you are free to do so—that is one of the advantages of the ActiveX Scripting architecture. However, if you do use a language other than VBScript or JScript, you will have to ensure that the language engine is installed on all machines where your scripts are to be executed. ◆

Organization of This Book

This book is divided into three parts and several appendices.

Part I, "WSH and the VBScript Language"

The first part of the book covers two topics: WSH and the VBScript language (with the exception of objects and classes, which are described in Part II, "Objects and Classes"). As such, the information in this part forms the foundation for using system-scripting technologies.

If you are already familiar with VBScript, you might wish to scan the information on WSH briefly and then skip ahead to Part II. If you have *not* used VBScript before or if you are unfamiliar with computer programming, the material in Part I will provide you with all the core concepts needed to use the VBScript language effectively.

Part II, "Objects and Classes"

Part II of the book covers objects and classes, and it explains the object-oriented paradigm and how this paradigm is used in system scripting. The focus of this part of the book is on the objects and features that are built-in to either WSH or VBScript. You will also find information here on how to construct your own "in-script" objects using VBScript.

Part II also shows how to use *COM Objects*. Many technologies and applications expose their functionality through COM Objects, and therefore, understanding how to access these objects is critical to using system scripting effectively.

Finally, Part II of the book also describes *Windows Script Components*, which is a technology that allows you to create your own COM Objects using VBScript. Windows Script Components provides an excellent way to break up large projects into smaller sub-projects and provides the foundations for dynamic script re-use.

Part III, "Sample Script Solutions"

Part III of the book builds upon the material in the earlier two parts to provide a library of complete, ready-to-use sample scripts. These scripts can be used "as-is" or as a starting point for a custom script project.

Part IV, "Appendices"

Finally, the appendices at the end of the book provide additional information that might be useful to system script authors.

- Appendix A, "Installing Script Components," provides installation instructions for the system scripting components described in this book.
- Appendix B, "Other Scripting Resources," provides information on other script resources available via the Internet.

Conventions Used in This Book

Throughout this book, VBScript source code is shown in a monospace font using a mixed-case convention. However, the VBScript language is not case-sensitive, and source code can be entered as desired. This may *not* be true of third party ActiveX Scripting languages—consult the specific language documentation for information on case sensitivity.

When describing VBScript and other syntax (instead of showing an example), items that must be entered exactly are shown in mixed case. Placeholders that must be replaced by appropriate values are shown in lower case italic. Optional items are shown in brackets, and vertical bar characters separate alternatives, where one item from a list must be selected. For example, the `Do` command syntax is:

```
Do [While expression]
```

This example shows that the `Do` command can be optionally followed by a `While` clause, which consists of the keyword `While` followed by an expression.

Some sample scripts in the book are shown with accompanying line numbers. These line numbers are for reference purposes only—scripts do *not* include line numbers in the program text.

Note

Throughout the book, look out for notes like these, which provide you with useful short cuts and other hints. ◆

Program Guide

If you are new to programming, watch out for the Program Guide tips, which describe core computer programming concepts. ◆

Before You Continue

Before continuing, you might want to take a few minutes to install the latest system scripting components on your computer. Appendix A provides details on where to obtain these components and how to install them. You might also want to look at Appendix B, which provides some links to additional scripting resources, tools, and technologies.

The information in this book is based upon versions 1.0 and 2.0 of Windows Scripting. The VBScript information is based upon version 5.0 of the VBScript engine. Refer to Appendix A for information on obtaining the most recent versions of all these components.

Finally, all the sample scripts shown in this book can be downloaded from the Macmillan Technical Publishing Web site at `www.macmillantech.com`.

Part I

WSH and the VBScript Language

1

Introducing WSH

As explained in the introduction, Windows Script Host (WSH) is an ActiveX Scripting host. This means that, like other ActiveX Scripting hosts, WSH acts as a host environment for the execution of scripts using one or more ActiveX scripting engines, or languages. Most ActiveX Scripting hosts are specific applications (such as Microsoft's Internet Explorer), but with WSH, the host is, in effect, the Windows operating system itself. This is what makes WSH so suitable for system scripting tasks.

WSH has several clear advantages over the more traditional batch scripts previously used for system scripting tasks:

- WSH is available on all 32-bit Windows platforms, which allows the same scripts to be deployed and used across the entire enterprise.
- The ActiveX Scripting technology used by WSH allows any ActiveX Scripting language to be used when authoring scripts.
- ActiveX Scripting languages are generally more expressive and better structured than batch script files, and in many cases, they are already well known in the development community.
- WSH provides access to COM Objects, and thus to any application or facility that exposes its functionality through a COM Automation interface.

Various versions of WSH ship with Microsoft operating systems, however the latest version is available for download for any 32-bit version of Windows. Appendix A, "Installing Script Components," provides additional information on installing WSH, and Chapter 12, "Logon Scripts," provides information on techniques to automate deployment of WSH in enterprise systems.

The *WSCRIPT* and *CSCRIPT* Commands

The WSH host is implemented as two distinct applications: `WSCRIPT.EXE` and `CSCRIPT.EXE`. The WSCRIPT application executes scripts in a GUI environment, whereas the CSCRIPT application executes scripts in a console (command line) environment. However, the differences between the hosts are minimal, and either host can execute any WSH script—scripts rarely contain host-specific code.

The WSH host applications execute scripts by reading these scripts from one or more text files containing the script source code. You can execute one of these script files using any of the following methods:

- Double-click a script file (`.VBS`, `.JS`, `.WSH`, `.WS`, and so on) or icon in an Explorer window, the Find window, or on the Windows desktop.
- Right-click a script file or icon, and select Open from the context menu. This method always uses the WSCRIPT host.
- Right-click a script file or icon, and select Open with Command Prompt from the context menu. This method always uses the CSCRIPT host.
- Enter a script file name in the Run command on the Start menu.
- Enter `WSCRIPT` or `CSCRIPT` and a script file name in the Run command on the Start menu.
- Enter a script file name, including the file extension, in a command prompt window.
- Enter `WSCRIPT` or `CSCRIPT` and a script file name in a command prompt window.
- Enter the script file name only (without the file extension) in a command prompt window. This method only works with Windows 2000 and Windows NT.
- Drag one or more files and drop them onto the script file name, or icon in Windows Explorer. This starts the script and passes the file names as command-line arguments.

If you do not explicitly specify the WSCRIPT or the CSCRIPT host when entering the script command, WSH uses the default host. Initially, the default host is WSCRIPT. However, the default host can be selected using the `//H` switch described in the next section.

Note

When the WSCRIPT host executes a script, the output of `Wscript.Echo` *statements appears in message boxes. Each message box must be dismissed by clicking the OK button before script execution can continue. When the CSCRIPT host executes a script, the output of* `Wscript.Echo` *statements appears in a console window and execution proceeds without user interaction. Because having a series of message boxes appearing one after the other can be distracting, the CSCRIPT host is preferable to the WSCRIPT host if* `Wscript.Echo` *is used extensively.* ◆

Syntax and Command Arguments

The syntax for a `WSCRIPT` or `CSCRIPT` command, when entered into the Run dialog box or a command prompt window, is:

```
[WSCRIPT | CSCRIPT] scriptfile hostoptions arguments
```

If `WSCRIPT` or `CSCRIPT` is specified, that host is used. If not, the default host is used. The *`scriptfile`* argument specifies the name of the text file containing the script to execute (see the *Script File Types* section for more information). The *`hostoptions`*, described in Table 1.1, specifies one or more options that control the WSH host. The *`arguments`* specify zero or more command line arguments that are passed to the script. These are then available to the executing script and can be used in any way desired by the script code. Many of the script examples in this book use script arguments to control their actions.

If a host is *not* specified and the command is entered into a Windows NT or Windows 2000 command prompt window, the file extension of the *`scriptfile`* can be omitted entirely. In this case, Windows uses the `PATHEXT` environment variable to resolve the full name of the script file. Windows searches for matching files by appending to the script file name each of the file extensions specified by `PATHEXT` in the order they are listed. WSH automatically adds the `.VBS`, `.JS`, and `.WS` types to `PATHEXT`, and so Windows searches first for a `.VBS` file, then for a `.JS` file, and finally for a `.WS` file.

For example, the following commands all execute the script `STARTUP.VBS` in a command window, assuming `CSCRIPT` is the default host:

```
cscript startup.vbs
startup.vbs
startup
```

The final example is only applicable to Windows 2000 and Windows NT.

Note

Refer to my book Windows NT Shell Scripting *(from Macmillan Technical Publishing) for full information on how the Windows NT and Windows 2000 command shells resolve command names.*◆

The script file name can be followed on the command line by zero or by more *host options*. All host options begin with two forward slash characters to distinguish them from regular script arguments. Table 1.1 shows the available host options. Note that host options are *not* case-sensitive.

Table 1.1 WSH Host Options

Host Option	Meaning
`//B`	Batch mode. Suppress errors and prompts during script execution.
`//D`	Enable active debugging.
`//E:`*`engine`*	Use the specified *engine* for executing the script.
`//H:Cscript`	Change the default scripting host to `CSCRIPT`.
`//H:Wscript`	Change the default scripting host to `WSCRIPT`.
`//I`	Interactive mode. Opposite of `//B`.
`//Job:`*`id`*	Specifies a specific job ID within a `.WS` file.
`//Logo`	Display the WSH logo (default).
`//NoLogo`	Prevent WSH logo display.
`//S`	Set the specified host options as defaults for this user.
`//T:`*`nn`*	Set script execution time-out to *`nn`* seconds.
`//X`	Execute script in debugger (when active debugging is enabled).
`//?`	Display host options help.

The `//I` and `//B` host options choose between *interactive* and *batch* modes. In interactive mode, messages generated by the host and `Wscript.Echo` commands in the script are displayed (either in dialog boxes or in the command window, depending upon the host used). In batch mode, these messages are suppressed.

The `//D` and `//X` switches control debugging. The `//D` switch enables debugging. If an error occurs and a debugger is active, the script will stop execution at the error within the debugger. If the `//X` switch is also specified, WSH will halt in the debugger at the first line of execution. See Chapter 6, "Introducing Objects," for more information on script debugging.

The `//T` host option can be used to set a time limit on script execution. This can be used as a safeguard against scripts that fail to run as expected. Specify the time-out in seconds. Time-outs are particularly useful with scripts that are run in batch mode.

The `//logo` and `//nologo` host options control the display of the WSH host sign-on banner. This only applies to the CSCRIPT host.

The `//H` host option sets the default host to use if a WSH host is not explicitly specified. Specify either `CSCRIPT` or `WSCRIPT`. Right-clicking on any script file can identify the current default host. If the **`Open`** command is in bold, WSCRIPT is the default host. If the **`Open with Command Prompt`** command is in bold, CSCRIPT is the default host.

The `//S` host option saves host options in the system registry. This makes the specified options the default for subsequent WSH sessions. Options are saved in the per-user portion of the registry, so each user account can maintain different default options. For example, the command:

```
cscript //I //nologo //H:cscript //S
```

This command sets WSH to run the CSCRIPT host as the default, without a sign-on banner, and in interactive mode.

Note

The preceding example, which sets the default host to CSCRIPT with no sign-on banner, is probably the most useful WSH default. The rest of this book assumes the use of the CSCRIPT host with the defaults set as shown in the preceding code. Therefore, take a moment to set up WSH with these defaults now.

This will set up the correct defaults for running all the sample scripts in this book. You can then run the samples (or your own scripts) by opening a command prompt window and using the CD command to navigate to the folder containing the script. Then, run the script by entering the command: ◆

```
cscript scriptname.vbs
```

The `//E` switch allows a specific script engine to be specified. WSH uses the script file type or XML tags to identify which ActiveX Scripting engine to use for the script. However, if you specify a script file that uses a non-standard file type, you can use the `//E` switch to specify the actual engine to use. Note, however, that specifying an engine that does not match the script language actually used in the file can have undesirable results.

The `//Job` switch is used only with WSH version 2.0 script files (that is, `.WS` files). These files can contain multiple script jobs. In this case, the `//Job` switch is used to specify (by job ID) which job is to execute. If no job is specified, the first (or only) job in the script file is executed.

Script File Types

WSH uses of a number of file types. Table 1.2 lists these file types and their uses. For completeness, this table lists file types used by other system scripting components (such as Windows Script Components) that are described later in this book. All the files except `.TLB` files are text files, and so they can be edited with any suitable text editor (for example, Windows Notepad). Appendix B, "Other Scripting Resources," lists several third party text editor tools that are particularly suitable for editing script source files.

Table 1.2 Script File Types

File Type	Meaning
.VBS, .JS, .PL	WSH version 1.0 script source code file. .VBS files contain VBScript scripts, .JS files contain JScript scripts. Other file types (such as .PL for Perl) contain scripts in other languages.
.WS	WSH version 2.0 script source code file. These files can contain scripts in multiple languages. XML elements within the source file indicate the languages used.
.VBE, .JSE	Encoded script code file.
.WSH	WSH property sheet file. Used to store properties for a script source code file.
.WSC	Windows Script Component source code file (the .SCT file type is also available for backward compatibility).
.TLB	COM type library. .TLB files contain type information for server scriptlets and can be accessed by WSH version 2.0 to read types and symbolic constants.

For WSH version 1.0, script source code is stored in files with a file extension that specifies the language of the script code. For example, .VBS files store VBScript scripts, whereas .JS files store JScript scripts. Other third-party script languages might define additional file extensions. When one of these source files is executed, WSH uses the file type to determine the language, loads the appropriate script engine, and passes the script code to the engine for execution.

For WSH version 2.0, script source code can instead be stored in a .WS file. The script language is then specified using XML elements that are embedded within the .WS file itself. Because XML elements specify the script language, it is possible to write a .WS script using more than one script language. For example, VBScript can be used as the main script language, with text processing chores handled by Perl procedures. When a .WS file is executed, WSH uses the XML elements to determine which script engine to load. To ensure backward compatibility, WSH version 2.0 can also process version 1.0 files.

In addition to script source files, WSH also uses files of type .WSH to store script property sheets. These files contain information about a particular script, including what options to use and the path of the script source code files. Property sheet files are described in the next section. When WSH executes a .WSH file, it first reads the property information to set execution options, and then uses the source file property to determine the location of the actual script file, which it then loads and runs.

Windows Script Components (described in Part II, "Objects and Classes") source code is stored in `.WSC` files. These files are similar to `.WS` files, and they contain XML tags that specify the script language. In addition, the XML elements specify information necessary to present the script as a COM Automation object.

Finally, both WSH and Windows Script Components can make use of type libraries, which have a `.TLB` type. Type libraries are a COM standard, and they contain a database describing one or more COM objects, including methods, properties, interfaces, types, and constants. WSH version 2.0 can read a type library and use the symbolic constants defined in that type library. Type library information can also be embedded within `.DLL`, `.OCX` and `.EXE` files.

WSH 1.0 Script File Formats

The original release of WSH supported a simple script scheme that used language specific script files. In this scheme, each script file is a complete, self-contained script authored in a single ActiveX Scripting language. The language is not specified within the script file, but is inferred from the file type of the script file. For example, VBScript scripts are contained in files of type `.VBS`.

This scheme is quite adequate for many scripts and is used in most of the examples in this book. However, it does have a couple of limitations:

- All the script must use the same language, preventing the use of (for example) the superior text capabilities of Perl within a VBScript script.
- The script must be entirely contained within a single source file. This makes script code reuse across projects difficult.

Both of these limitations can be overcome using the more powerful WSH 2.0 script files.

To create a WSH 1.0 script file, simply use a text editor to create a new text file. Enter the script language statements directly into the text file. Save the text file, making sure to use a file type that corresponds to the language used. Then, execute the script using any of the techniques described in "The `WSCRIPT` and `CSCRIPT` Commands" section.

For example, probably the simplest possible WSH script displays the famous `"Hello, World!"` text. This simple script consists of a single line of VBScript code, as follows:

```
Wscript.Echo "Hello, World!"
```

To execute this script, create a new text file called `HelloWorld.vbs` and enter the line shown in the preceding code. Then execute the script. Try executing the script using `WSCRIPT` and `CSCRIPT` to observe the different way in which the output of the `Wscript.Echo` statement is displayed. You will see one of three things:

- If you execute the script using the WSCRIPT host, you will see a dialog box displaying the text `"Hello, World!"`. Click OK to close this dialog box and end the script.
- If you execute the script using the CSCRIPT host by right-clicking and selecting the Open with Command Prompt command in Explorer, you will see a command prompt window open and then almost immediately close again.
- If you execute the script using the CSCRIPT host in an open command prompt window, you will see the text `"Hello, World!"` appear in the command prompt window.

Figure 1.1 shows the output from the `HelloWorld.vbs` script when executed using the last method described.

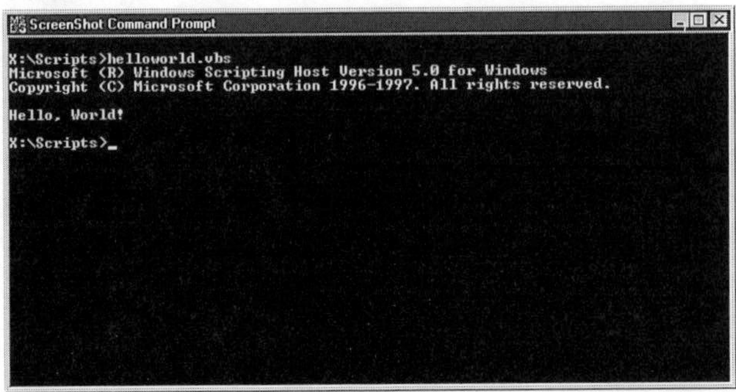

Figure 1.1 `HelloWorld.vbs` *Script Output.*

The `Wscript.Echo` command in this script is known as a *method*. You will learn about methods in some detail in Part II of this book. For the time being, however, it is sufficient to know that the `Wscript.Echo` method simply displays, either in a dialog box or in the command window, whatever arguments are specified. In this case, the script specified the text `"Hello, World!"`. Therefore, this is displayed.

Program Guide

The Famous Hello World Program

Why is the "Hello, World!" program famous? This was the first program shown in the classic text on the C programming language, and it is now almost de rigeur *to include a program that does the same thing in all other texts on programming.*

As you can see, the VBScript version is simple. (The C version was five lines long; the VBScript version is only one line.) ◆

WSH Property Page Files

In addition to setting host options via the switches shown in Table 1.1, the WSCRIPT host provides a property sheet. To access the WSCRIPT property sheet, shown in Figure 1.2, right-click on a script file in Windows Explorer and select the Property command.

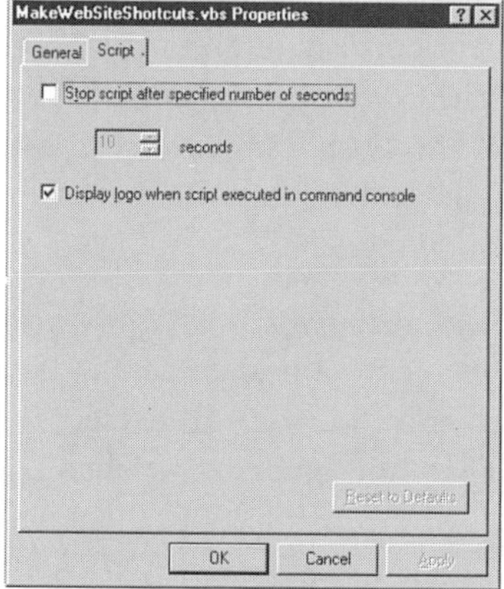

Figure 1.2 *WSCRIPT Property Sheet.*

The property sheet information is stored in a file with the same name as the script file, but with a `.WSH` extension. After a `.WSH` file is created, it can be used to execute the script file. For example, if you create a `.WSH` file for a `.VBS` script, you can then execute the script by double-clicking either the original script file or the `.WSH` file. Selecting the `.WSH` file uses the properties from this file. Selecting the `.VBS` file uses the default properties.

A `.WSH` file contains the full path name to the original script file, so it is possible to copy the `.WSH` file to another location and successfully execute the original script. Therefore, a `.WSH` file also provides a form of shortcut to the original script file.

`.WSH` files are text files, and they can be examined using any standard text editor, such as Windows Notepad.

WSH 2.0 Script File Formats

WSH 2.0 overcomes the limitations of the previous, language-specific, script file format by introducing a new script file type, the `.WS` file. These files, which like WSH 1.0 files are text files, are formatted using XML elements.

The use of XML allows a single script file to contain script written using multiple languages and to contain multiple script "jobs" that can be referenced using the `//Job` host option described in the "Syntax and Command Arguments" section.

XML Element Syntax

A basic `.WS` file contains a sequence of XML elements. The syntax for an XML element is:

```
<element-name [attribute="value" ...]> element-body </element-name>
```

That is, an XML element consists of an opening tag, enclosed in angle brackets, followed by the body of the element, followed by a closing tag, also in angle brackets. The closing tag always consists of the same element name, prefixed with a slash character (`/`). For example, an XML `job` element might consist of the following:

```
<job>job-body</job>
```

Unlike HTML, XML element names are case-sensitive, so `job` and `Job` are considered distinct elements. Some XML parsers relax this constraint for compatibility with HTML and ignore case when considering element names (and attribute names). All the examples in this book use the correct case for elements, allowing the code to pass strict XML syntax checking.

To request strict XML syntax checking on the script file, include the special XML element at the start of script. This element is:

```
<?xml Version="1.0" ?>
```

This element should be entered exactly as shown and be on the very first line of the script for strict XML conformance.

The body of an element can comprise multiple lines as necessary and can start either following the tag, or on the next line. Elements can also be nested one inside another. For example:

```
<animal>
    <giraffe>Has a very long neck</giraffe>
    <lion>Dangerous</lion>
</animal>
```

In this example, the `animal` element encloses both a `giraffe` and a `lion` element. These are shown indented for clarity, but this indentation is purely cosmetic, and is not required.

Each element can also have any number of optional *attributes*. Element attributes are placed in the opening tag following the element name. Each attribute consists of an attribute name and an attribute value. XML attribute values should always be enclosed in double quotes, but many XML parsers relax this constraint for compatibility with HTML (which does not require double quotes). All the examples in this book follow the stricter XML guidelines and enclose attribute values in double quotes. For example:

```
<job id="TestJob4">job-body</job>
```

This example shows a `job` element with a single `id` attribute having a value `TestJob4`. Multiple attributes are separated from one another using spaces.

Some XML elements do not have a body. The syntax of these elements is:

```
<element-name [attribute="value" ...] />
```

In this case, the element name is optionally followed by an attribute list. Notice that the right angle bracket is preceded by a slash character to indicate that no body follows the opening tag, and that there is no closing tag. For example:

```
<species type="animal" name="gazelle" />
```

Here, a `species` element contains two attributes, `type` and `name`.

You can also add comments to XML files using XML comments. These take the form:

```
<!-- comment-text -->
```

All the *comment-text* is ignored by WSH.

Basic .*WS* Files

A basic `.ws` file is always comprised of one or more `job` elements. Each `job` element contains one or more `script` elements. Each `script` element contains a portion of script code, in a specific language. The simplest possible `.ws` file contains a single `job` and `script` element, for example:

```
<job id="HelloWorld">
    <script language="VBScript">
        Wscript.Echo "Hello, world!"
    </script>
</job>
```

The preceding code shows the simple "Hello, World!" program written as a `.ws` file. The `job` element encloses the entire script, and it also specifies an identifier for the job using the `id` attribute. This example can be placed in a file (for example, `HelloWorld.ws`) and executed.

The script code itself is enclosed in a `script` element. The script language contained within the `script` element body is specified using the `language` attribute. In the preceding example, the language specified is VBScript, and so the script body contains VBScript statements. The `language` attribute allows WSH to pass the script to the correct ActiveX Scripting engine for execution.

It is possible for a single `job` element to contain multiple `script` elements. Each script element can have a different `language` attribute, and so multiple languages can be included in one script job. For example, the main script body might be written using VBScript, with some text processing procedures written in Perl. The following script is yet another "Hello, World!" variation written using a Perl procedure to display the actual text.

```
<job id="HelloWorldFromPerl">
    <!-- Here is some VBScript code... -->
    <script language="VBScript">
        PerlHello "Hello, World!"
    </script>

    <!-- Here is some PerlScript code... -->
    <script language="PerlScript">
        sub PerlHello
        {
            my $str1 = @_[0];
            $Wscript->Echo($str1);
        }
    </script>
</job>
```

When this script executes, the VBScript script will call the Perl `PerlHello` procedure to display the `"Hello, World!"` text.

Program Guide

XML, VBScript and Perl

You might find the preceding example, with a combination of XML, VBScript, and Perl, rather complex. Don't worry about the VBScript and Perl code for now, just focus on how it is enclosed within the XML elements. ◆

Although it is somewhat language dependent, script execution typically begins at the first line of the first `script` element in the job.

Include Files

The `script` element can also be used to *include* the source code from a WSH 1.0 script file. This allows a script code to be re-used, and is particularly suitable for the re-use of libraries of procedures and functions (described in Chapter 5, "User-Defined Procedures").

To include an external script file, use the `src` attribute in the `script` element. For example:

```
<job id=CodeReuse>
    <!-- Include MyLib.vbs library -->
    <script language="VBScript" src="MyLib.vbs" />
```

```
    <script language="VBScript">
        LibProc "Hello, World!"
    </script>
</job>
```

In this example, the script file `MyLib.vbs` is included as part of the script. Notice that the `script` element in this case does not have a body, and so it is terminated with a `/>` delimiter.

The source file specified by the `src` attribute can have a full path name or it can be an Internet URL. The script file referenced should be formatted as a WSH 1.0 script file. That is, it should not contain XML elements, just plain script language statements.

Program Guide

Code Re-use

Including the script code from another script file is one method of code re-use. Code re-use, in one form or another, has dominated the development of computer languages since they were initially developed. Other forms of code re-use include procedures, objects (including COM Objects), and external libraries (such as DLLs). In all cases, the objective is to avoid re-inventing the wheel and, instead, to use code that has already been developed and debugged.

The simplest form of code re-use is via cut and paste in a text editor—the script code is simply copied from one file to another. This is considered inferior to other methods, because updates to the shared code must be manually propagated to every file that uses that code, which is an error prone task. ◆

Packages and Jobs

WSH 2.0 script files can contain multiple independent jobs. This allows distinct scripts that are closely related to be contained in a single file. To place multiple jobs in a single script file, enclose the jobs within individual `job` elements, and then enclose all the `job` elements in a single `package` element. For example:

```
<package>
    <job id="HelloWorld">
        <script language="VBScript">
            Wscript.Echo "Hello, world!"
        </script>
    </job>

    <job id="HelloAgain">
        <script language="VBScript">
            Wscript.Echo "Hello again!!!"
        </script>
    </job>
</package>
```

Here, two distinct jobs are enclosed in the single `package` element. Each job must have a unique `id` attribute.

By default, WSH will execute the first job in the `.WS` file. Other jobs will be ignored. To execute a specific job, include the `//Job` switch on the command line and specify the `id` of the job to execute.

A Sample Script

We can make the "Hello, World!" script more interesting by displaying the result as an HTML page in Internet Explorer. Listing 1.1 shows the text of the `HelloWorld2.vbs` script, which does just that.

Listing 1.1 *`HelloWorld2.vbs` Script*

```
'//////////////////////////////////////////////////////////////////////////////
' $Workfile: HelloWorld2.vbs $ $Revision: 3 $ $Date: 12/04/98 3:19p $
' $Archive: /Scripts/HelloWorld2.vbs $
' Copyright (c) 1998 Tim Hill. All Rights Reserved.
'//////////////////////////////////////////////////////////////////////////////

' Simple "Hello World!" WSH Sample

Option Explicit
Wscript.Echo Wscript.ScriptName & " $Revision: 3 $"
Wscript.Echo "Copyright (c) 1998 Tim Hill. All Rights Reserved."

' Open IE and display the about:blank page to give us an empty document
Dim oIE, oIEDoc
Set oIE = Wscript.CreateObject("InternetExplorer.Application")
oIE.Navigate "about:blank"
Set oIEDoc = oIE.Document
oIE.AddressBar = False
oIE.StatusBar = False
oIE.ToolBar = False
oIE.MenuBar = False
oIE.Visible = True

' Now emit the HTML to IE
oIEDoc.WriteLn "<html>"
oIEDoc.WriteLn "<head>"
oIEDoc.WriteLn "<title>HelloWorld2 Sample Script</title>"
oIEDoc.WriteLn "</head>"
oIEDoc.WriteLn "<body>"
oIEDoc.WriteLn "<p><center>Welcome to Windows Script Host.</center></p>"
oIEDoc.Write "<p><center>"
If Hour(Now) < 12 Then
    oIEDoc.Write "Good morning"
ElseIf Hour(Now) < 17 Then
    oIEDoc.Write "Good afternoon"
Else
    oIEDoc.Write "Good evening"
```

```
End If
oIEDoc.WriteLn " world, the time is " & Time & "</center></p>"
oIEDoc.WriteLn "<p><center>Please wait.</center></p>"
oIEDoc.WriteLn "<p><center>This window will close in approx. 10 seconds.</center></p>"
oIEDoc.WriteLn "</body>"
oIEDoc.WriteLn "</html>"

' Wait for 10 seconds
Dim vStart
vStart = Now
Do While DateDiff("s", vStart, Now) < 10
    Wscript.Sleep 1000
Loop
Set oIEDoc = Nothing
oIE.Quit
Set oIE = Nothing
Wscript.Quit 0

'//////////////////////////////////////////////////////////////////////////
```

This script (like all the samples in this book) is available from the Macmillan Technical Publishing web site at `www.macmillantech.com`. Copy the script to a convenient folder and run it in the same way you did the original `HelloWorld.vbs` sample. You should see Internet Explorer open and display a welcome message and the current time. Figure 1.3 shows the script in action.

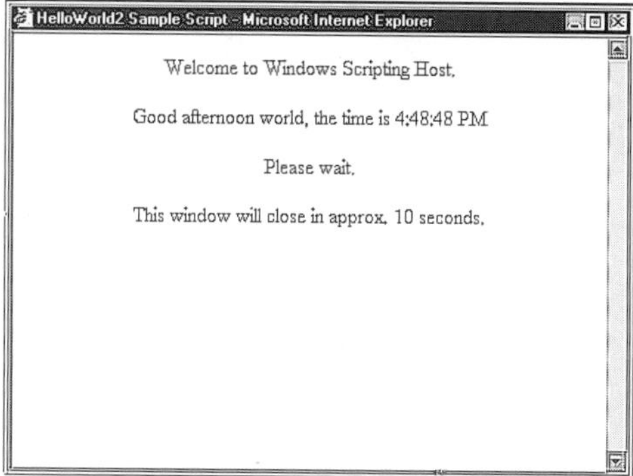

Figure 1.3 *HelloWorld2 Script Output.*

At nearly 60 lines long, the `HelloWorld2.vbs` script is much more complex then the first `HelloWorld.vbs` script. However, it is also somewhat more sophisticated:

- First, the output is valid HTML text.
- Second, the script opens Internet Explorer and displays the text for 10 seconds.

- Third, rather than a plain `"Hello, World!"`, the script displays `"Good morning"`, `"Good afternoon"` or `"Good evening"` depending upon the time of day.

To do these things, the script uses various VBScript features and makes considerable use of Internet Explorer objects. These and other features of WSH are described in detail in the rest of this book. For the time being, you might wish to study the source code in Listing 1.1 and see if you can guess how the script works.

Summary

WSH is an ActiveX Scripting host that uses ActiveX Scripting language engines, such as VBScript or JScript, to execute. These scripts can be used to automate many Windows system management tasks. The WSCRIPT and CSCRIPT applications act as hosts for WSH.

Simple scripts use one script language and specify the language using the file type. More sophisticated scripts use the `.WS` file type and specify the language using XML elements within the file. Both script file types are simple text files and can be edited using any text editor.

2

VBScript Language Essentials

In the early 1960s, John G. Kemeny and Thomas E. Kurtz of Dartmouth College developed a simple computer language for use by their students. This language was named Beginners All-purpose Symbolic Instruction Code, or BASIC, and it was adopted by computer makers and enhanced in various ways, most notably by the Digital Equipment Corporation. It was the DEC version of BASIC that was used as the basis of MBASIC, the dialect developed by Microsoft for 8-bit CP/M computers. MBASIC was enhanced through several major revisions until it became GW-BASIC on the IBM PC. Later, a Windows version of BASIC was developed called Visual Basic, which is now in its sixth major revision. The VBScript language described here, beginning with this chapter, is a subset of the Visual Basic language.

Note

As with all the sample scripts in this book, the scripts in this chapter should be run using the CSCRIPT host unless otherwise noted. The examples shown assume that CSCRIPT is the default WSH host. See Chapter 1, "Introducing WSH," for information on selecting the default WSH host. ◆

Structure of a VBScript Script

As Chapter 1 explained, VBScript scripts are stored in text files with a file extension of `.VBS`, or as XML script elements in `.WS` text files. The script itself consists of a series of statements, with each statement providing a single VBScript instruction. In VBScript, each statement ends at the end of the line—there is no end-of-statement character (unlike, say, JScript). For example, the following are all valid VBScript statements:

```
Rem Don't forget to put the lights out!
Dim a, b, c
a = 14
b = "My first VBScript statement"
c = 3.14159
```

Multiple statements can be placed on one line by separating them with a single colon character. For example, the last three statements in the preceding code can be combined into a single statement as follows:

```
a = 14 : b = "My first VBScript statement" : c = 3.14159
```

Blank lines are allowed in VBScript files, as is whitespace (spaces or tabs) at the beginning or end of the statement, or between individual words and punctuation within a statement. For example, the following are all equivalent:

```
a = 14
a=14
    a    =14
```

Program Guide

Verbs and Nouns in Statements

A VBScript statement describes a specific action to perform. A statement typically consists of a verb that specifies the action and (optionally) one or more nouns that qualify the verb. For example, in the command:

```
Wscript.Echo a, b, c
```

The text `Wscript.Echo` *is the verb, and the three items* `a`, `b`, *and* `c` *are the nouns. In this case, there are three nouns, separated by commas. This arrangement of verbs and nouns is called the syntax of the statement. Syntax is typically represented as a statement template, which shows the form of the statement. For example, the verb/noun form just described can be represented as:*

```
verb [noun, ...]
```

Here, the brackets around the noun indicate that it is optional. The ellipsis indicates a repeating element, so in this case it is possible to have multiple nouns separated by commas. ◆

Line Continuation

Long VBScript statements can be split across multiple lines by including a *continuation character* as the last character on a line. The continuation character is an underscore. For example:

```
a = (a * 14) + 7 / _
        (a * 11)
```

The underscore at the end of the first line in the preceding example causes the statement to continue onto the second line. The second line is indented to show that it is a continuation line, but this indentation is purely cosmetic—it is not required by VBScript. Using indentations in this way can help make your scripts easier to read, particularly if a long statement is broken over many lines.

To be recognized as a continuation character, the underscore must be the very last character on the line. If there are spaces or tabs after the underscore, VBScript will not correctly recognize the continuation, and a syntax error will occur when the script is executed.

Line continuation characters can only be placed *between* individual words and items in a VBScript statement. You cannot place a continuation character within a string constant (described later in the "Numbers, Strings and Variables" section) or in the middle of a variable name. For example, this is *not* legal:

```
a = "This is not the correct way to span a long string of text _
    across several lines"
```

This generates a syntax error when the script is run. The correct way to span long text strings across multiple lines is to concatenate them using the & operator (described in the "Expressions and Assignment" section). For example:

```
a = "To span long strings of text on several lines, " & _
    "concatenate them using the & operator"
```

Case Sensitivity

VBScript is a case-insensitive language. That means that statements have the same meaning regardless of the case used to enter the script text. For example, the following statements are all equivalent:

```
Wscript.Echo MyVariable
WSCRIPT.ECHO MYVARIABLE
wscRIPT.EchO mYVariable
```

Although you can use any case conventions you prefer, by convention VBScript scripts use "capitalized" statements, in which the first letter of each word is in capitals and all other letters are lower case.

Also by convention, long variable names that are a concatenation of multiple words capitalize each word. For example: `MyVariable` and `ThisIsALongVariableName`. Variables are described later in the "Numbers, Strings and Variables" section.

Some Simple Statements

Several common statements in VBScript are used in virtually all scripts. These are:

- Comments, which provide text describing a scripts operation and function.
- The `Wscript.Quit` statement, which terminates script execution.
- The `Wscript.Echo` statement, which displays results in the console window or a message box.

- The `Wscript.Arguments` statement, which provides access to script command line arguments.

Strictly speaking, the previous three `Wscript.xxx` statements are a type of statement known as an *object method call*. However, objects are not discussed until Part II, "Objects and Classes," of this book. Therefore, until Part II, these statements are treated as "magic" operations. The full significance of the `Wscript` object is described in Chapter 7, "Built-In WSH and VBScript Objects."

Comment Statements

The simplest form of VBScript statement is the *comment*. Comments are ignored by VBScript and can be used to place descriptive text within the script, typically to document how the script works. The syntax of a comment statement is:

```
Rem text
```

Follow the keyword `Rem` by any text. VBScript ignores the text and continues to execute the statement following the `Rem` statement. In `Rem` statements a colon character does *not* end the comment and start a new statement. Therefore, all `Rem` statements must be the last or only statement on a line.

VBScript also supports a shorthand notation for comments. Use a *single quote* character anywhere on a line to start a comment. You do *not* need to precede the single quote with a colon. Like the `Rem` statement, the single quote comment continues until the end of the line.

The following are all valid examples of comment statements.

```
Rem This is a comment on a line by itself
' This is also a valid comment, which starts with a single quote
a = 14 : Rem This comment follows another statement on the same line
b = 100 ' So does this, but there is no need to place a colon first
```

The single quote comment is so much more convenient than the `Rem` comment that the `Rem` comment is hardly ever used. The examples and sample scripts in this book use the single quote comment exclusively.

Program Guide

Use Comments Liberally

Although they don't actually do anything, comments are an important part of any script. You should use comments to make clear the intention of each set of statements in the script, or to describe how to use the script. Liberal use of comments can help make your script more understandable to others.

Writing good comments is something of an art, however, because you need to say what a statement's intentions are both clearly and briefly. This is an example of a bad comment:

```
a = 10 ' Set a to 10
```

This comment is a waste of space—it doesn't provide any useful information. This is an example of a useful comment:

```
f = ((c * 9) / 5) + 32 ' Convert Celsius to Fahrenheit
```

This comment describes the intention of the statement, and therefore provides useful additional information. ◆

The *Wscript.Quit* Statement

The `Wscript.Quit` statement ends script execution. No further statements are executed, and the WSH host terminates the operation. The `Wscript.Quit` statement is optionally followed by an integer value (an argument), which specifies the error code to return to the calling process. If the script was run from a command shell, this value is available via the `ERRORLEVEL` environment variable (on Windows NT and Windows 2000) or via the `IF ERRORLEVEL` shell command (on all Windows platforms).

For example, this statement:

```
Wscript.Quit(1)
```

Ends the script and returns the value 1 as an error code.

Note

By convention, scripts return zero to indicate success (normal operation) and nonzero to indicate some kind of error. ◆

Scripts also end execution by reaching the end of the script file, a process sometimes known as "falling off the end" of the script. In this case, the return value of the script is always zero.

The *Wscript.Echo* Statement

The `Wscript.Echo` statement displays all its arguments. `Wscript.Echo` was introduced in Chapter 1 in the `HelloWorld.vbs` script. The operation of this statement depends upon which WSH host is used:

- If the CSCRIPT host is used, the arguments are displayed in the console window. Script execution continues immediately after the results are displayed without a pause. Each `Wscript.Echo` statement generates a single line of output.
- If the WSCRIPT host is used, the arguments are displayed in a message box. Script execution then pauses until the OK button in the message

box is clicked, or the Enter key pressed. Subsequent `Wscript.Echo` statements generate additional message boxes.

If a `Wscript.Echo` statement does not have any arguments, an empty line or message box is displayed. Otherwise, all the arguments are displayed in the order listed, separated by a single space. For example, these `Wscript.Echo` commands:

```
Wscript.Echo "This is sample output..."
Wscript.Echo "The results are",10,11,12
```

Generate this output in the console window:

```
This is sample output...
The results are 10 11 12
```

All the scripts in this book assume that the CSCRIPT host is used. `Wscript.Echo` is used extensively in this book to display script output and results.

The *Wscript.Arguments* Statement

The `Wscript.Arguments` statement is not actually a statement at all. Technically, `Wscript.Arguments` provides access to an object collection. However, because object collections are not discussed until Part II of this book, this "statement" is treated, for the time being, as magic.

`Wscript.Arguments` can be used in one of two ways:

- To access the number of command line arguments supplied to the script.
- To access individual command line arguments.

To obtain the number of command line arguments, use `Wscript.Arguments.Count`. To access individual command line arguments, use `Wscript.Arguments(n)`, where *n* specifies the argument *index*. The first command line argument has an index of zero, the next has an index of one, and so on.

Both forms of `Wscript.Arguments` return values to the executing script. Therefore, `Wscript.Arguments` is always used as part of an *expression*. Expressions are described in the "Expressions and Assignment" section.

Command line arguments allow a script to change its behavior based upon the arguments supplied, in the same way as built-in commands, such as `COPY` or `DEL`. Although the CSCRIPT and WSCRIPT hosts both support command line arguments, the CSCRIPT host and the command window interface are easier to use for command-line driven scripts.

The *ShowArgs1.vbs* Script

The `ShowArgs1.vbs` sample script, shown in Listing 2.1, illustrates the use of the `Wscript.Arguments` statement.

Listing 2.1 *`ShowArgs1.vbs` Script*

```
'//////////////////////////////////////////////////////////////////////////
' $Workfile: ShowArgs1.vbs $ $Revision: 1 $ $Date: 12/02/98 11:34a $
' $Archive: /Scripts/ShowArgs1.vbs $
' Copyright (c) 1998 Tim Hill. All Rights Reserved.
'//////////////////////////////////////////////////////////////////////////

' Display first four command line arguments

Wscript.Echo "You entered", Wscript.Arguments.Count, "arguments"
On Error Resume Next
Wscript.Echo "Argument 0:", Wscript.Arguments(0)
Wscript.Echo "Argument 1:", Wscript.Arguments(1)
Wscript.Echo "Argument 2:", Wscript.Arguments(2)
Wscript.Echo "Argument 3:", Wscript.Arguments(3)

'//////////////////////////////////////////////////////////////////////////
```

`ShowArgs1.vbs` begins with a `Wscript.Echo` statement that displays a count of the number of arguments entered on the command line. The `On Error Resume Next` statement (described in Chapter 7) is necessary in cases where fewer than four arguments are entered. Without this statement a subscript error could occur. Next, individual arguments are accessed using four distinct `Wscript.Arguments` calls, each with a different argument index. The results of these calls are then displayed using `Wscript.Echo` statements.

Figure 2.1 shows the results of executing `ShowArgs1.vbs` twice with different command lines. You might want to take a moment to experiment with `ShowArgs1.vbs` by passing different command line arguments and see what the results are. Try placing arguments in double quotes on the command line, or including spaces within the argument. You can also try extending `ShowArgs1.vbs` to display additional arguments beyond four.

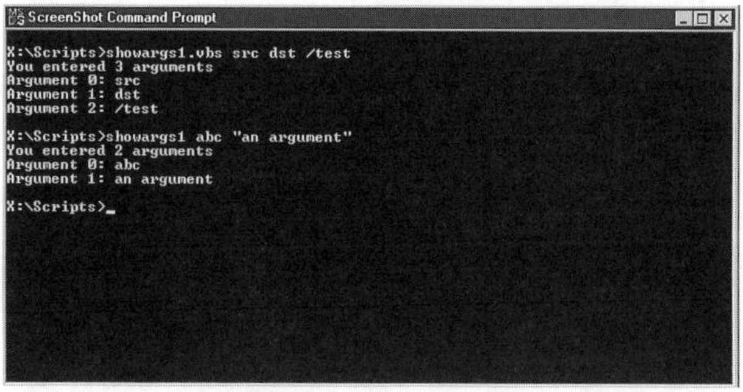

Figure 2.1 *`ShowArgs1.vbs` sample output.*

Numbers, Strings and Variables

Although VBScript supports many different data types, there are actually two fundamental data types that support most programming tasks: *numbers* and *strings*.

Numbers are regular numeric quantities, expressed using normal numeric syntax, such as decimal points and exponential notation. For example, the following are all valid numbers:

```
100
45.2
17000.56
0.005
900
12.5E3
```

The last line of the preceding example shows the use of exponential notation. The integer value following the letter `E` specifies the exponent (power of ten) for the number. Note that while it is possible to include a decimal point in a number, it is *not* permissible to include thousands separators (such as commas).

Strings are arbitrary sequences of characters. To place a string literally within a VBScript program, place the string within double quote characters. Any characters are allowed within the string. For example, the following are all valid strings:

```
"This is a string"
"You can also use any special characters %$**## in a string"
"to place a double quote within a ""string"", use two double quotes"
""
```

The last line of the preceding example represents the *empty string*, that is, a string containing no characters.

VBScript strings can be *very* long—up to 2 billion characters. In practice, this means that the length of a string is limited only by available memory.

The *Dim* Statement

In VBScript, a *variable* is used to store a data value that can change during script execution. Each variable is given a name, which typically describes the meaning of the value stored in the variable.

Program Guide

Understanding Variables

Variables are similar to the memory buttons available on most pocket calculators. You can store numbers in a variable, and then use the contents of the variable later. In addition, like a calculator, when you store a new value into a variable, any previous value is lost. However, unlike a calculator you are not restricted in the number of variables you can use within a script. Instead, you can create as many variables as you wish. In addition, variables can contain non-numeric values, such as text strings.

In most calculators, you must recall the memory's contents before you can use that number in a calculation. In VBScript, this is not required, and variable values can be used directly within a calculation. ♦

Before a variable can be used, it must be *declared*. Declaring a variable *creates* the variable and causes VBScript to assign storage memory for use by the variable. There are two basic methods used to declare a variable: *explicit* and *implicit* declarations.

In *implicit* declarations, the variable is "declared by use." That is, VBScript automatically declares the variable when it first encounters the variable's name within the script. Implicit declaration is easy to use because VBScript does the work behind the scenes.

In *explicit* declarations, the variable is declared using a `Dim` statement. The syntax of the `Dim` statement is:

```
Dim var [,...]
```

Follow the `Dim` keyword by a list of one or more variable names. Separate the variable names with commas. For example:

```
Dim a, b, c, nMyVar, nTotal, sUserName
```

After a variable is declared using a `Dim` statement, it can be used within other script statements. You can place `Dim` statements anywhere within a script and use as many as necessary to declare all your variables. However, with explicit declaration you *must* place a `Dim` statement for a particular variable *before* the variable is first used in any other statement.

The *Option Explicit* Statement

Implicit declaration might appear more attractive than explicit declaration because it is automatic and does not involve the use of the `Dim` statement. However, implicit declaration has one significant drawback; it makes it easy to miss-type variable names. For example, consider these two lines of VBScript source code:

```
nViewable = 10                ' Set viewable count to 10
nViewable = nVievable + 1     ' Increase viewable count by 1
```

The comments in this example make the *intention* clear, but in the second line, the `nViewable` variable is accidentally misspelled as `nVievable`. If you use implicit declaration, this misspelling will *not* generate an error, because VBScript automatically creates a new variable called `nVievable` and then uses its default value (0) in the calculation. This kind of error can be time-consuming to find when debugging a script. However, if explicit declaration is used instead, this kind of error is avoided because VBScript flags the `nVievable` variable as an undeclared variable before the script is even executed.

For this reason, explicit declaration is strongly recommended. Unfortunately, by default VBScript allows implicit declaration. Therefore, to disable this and *force* all declarations to be made explicitly, use the `Option Explicit` statement. This statement has the following syntax:

```
Option Explicit
```

Place this statement, as shown, at the start of all scripts. It must be the *first* executable statement (with the exception of comments) within the script file. Almost all the sample scripts in this book use the `Option Explicit` statement to force explicit variable declaration.

Expressions and Assignment

An *expression* is a calculation that combines numbers, strings, and variables, using *operators*, to yield a *result*. One form of expression, the numeric expression, uses the familiar arithmetic operators (such as addition and subtraction) to yield a final numeric value as the result. However, VBScript supports other expressions, such as string expressions that operate on string (text) data.

An *assignment* statement is a statement that assigns a new value to a variable. The syntax of the assignment statement is:

```
variable = expression
```

Replace *`variable`* with the name of a variable, and *`expression`* with a valid expression. The variable specified is assigned the result of the expression. The following are all valid assignment statements.

```
nCount = 100
sFilename = "c:\temp\mydata.txt"
nTotalCount = 100 - 40
```

In an assignment statement, the `=` sign does not signify mathematical equality, instead it means "becomes." Thus the assignment statement `x = 10` means that the variable `x` *becomes* the value 10, (that is, the value of the variable is changed to 10).

Assignment statements are among the most common statements used in scripts, and expressions are even more common. In addition to assignment statements, expressions are used in function and procedure calls and several other VBScript statements. For example, the `Wscript.Echo` statement, described in the "Some Simple Statements" section, accepts a list of expressions as arguments. Thus, the following script fragment displays the value 500 when executed:

```
Wscript.Echo 200 + 200 + 100
```

In this example, the + signs are *operators*, whereas the numbers are *operands*. Operands can be numbers, strings, or variables. (Operands can also be functions, which are described in the "Functions" section and in Chapters 4, "Built-In Functions," and 5, "User Defined Procedures.") For example, the following are also valid numeric expressions:

```
PI * fRadius ^ 2.0
(nCount * 10) / 5
```

When a variable is used in an expression, VBScript uses the current value of the variable. The value of a variable is never changed by an expression, only by an assignment statement.

There is no limit to the complexity of an expression, which can contain dozens of operands and operators. However, complex expressions can be difficult to read and understand. It is, therefore, considered good practice to break complex expressions into simpler ones and to assign intermediate results to temporary variables.

VBScript supports many different operators. Some of these operators work with numeric data, whereas others work with other types of data (such as strings). In general, VBScript can automatically convert data to the type required by the operator. For example, if a string is used where a number is required, VBScript converts the string to a number.

Numeric Operators

The numeric operators include the familiar arithmetic operations, such as addition, subtraction, and multiplication. For example, the following are all valid numeric expressions:

```
1 + 2 - 5
14 * 3 + 7
11 * (5 + 3)
```

VBScript uses the * sign to represent multiplication and the ^ sign to represent exponentiation. Table 2.1 lists the arithmetic operators.

***Table 2.1** Arithmetic Operators*

Operator	Meaning
`a ^ b`	Exponentiation. Raises `a` to the power `b`.
`-b`	Unary negation. Changes the sign of `b`.
`a * b`	Multiplication.

continues ▶

Operator	Meaning
`a / b`	Division. Divides `a` by `b`.
`a \ b`	Integer division. Divides `a` by `b` to yield an integral result.
`a Mod b`	Modulus. Computes the remainder when `a` is divided by `b`.
`a + b`	Addition.
`a - b`	Subtraction. Subtracts `b` from `a`.

VBScript supports two division operators. The normal `/` operator performs a normal division that can yield a non-integral result. The `\` operator performs an integer division that always yields an integer result. For example, `5 / 2` yields 2.5, whereas `5 \ 2` yields 2.

The `Mod` operator computes the integral remainder of the integer division of two numbers. For example, `5 Mod 2` yields 1.

Program Guide

Assigning Variables to Themselves

The following assignment statement is quite common in VBScript:

```
x = x + 1
```

The same variable (in this case `x`*) is used on both sides of the = sign. Because this is a mathematical assertion, this equation can only be (loosely) true when* `x` *is infinity. However, in VBScript, the = sign means "becomes," so this statement is evaluated as follows: First, VBScript evaluates the expression on the right side of the = sign. Assuming that* `x` *is currently 10; the result of the expression is obviously 11. After the expression is evaluated, the result is assigned back into the variable* `x`*, replacing the original value 10 with 11. Thus, this statement simply adds 1 to the existing value of the variable x, and the statement is sometimes called the increment statement because it increments the value of a variable.* ◆

String Operators

VBScript only supports one string operator: `&` (ampersand). Other string operations are handled via the string functions described in Chapter 4. The `&` operator is the *concatenation* operator. It takes two strings as operands and generates a result that is the concatenation of the two strings (with the left string first). For example, this assignment statement assigns the value `c:\temp\myfile.txt` to the variable `sName`:

```
sName = "c:\temp\" & "myfile.txt"
```

Notice that the two strings are simply spliced together with no intervening characters or spaces. This property of the `&` operator is often used in

`Wscript.Echo` statements. For example, these two statements produce slightly different output:

```
Wscript.Echo "Filename=",sFilename
Wscript.Echo "Filename=" & sFilename
```

The first statement includes two arguments, and so the `Wscript.Echo` statement places a space between the first and second argument when they are displayed. The second statement only has one argument, a string expression, and so no extra space is introduced in the output. For example, assuming `sFilename` contains `c:\temp`, the resulting output from the preceding two lines is:

```
Filename= c:\temp
Filename=c:\temp
```

Comparison Operators

Comparison operators compare two operands and yield a boolean result. For example, the `=` comparison operator compares two values and generates a `True` result if the values are equal, and a `False` result if the values are different. Table 2.2 lists the comparison operators.

Table 2.2 Comparison Operators

Operator	Meaning
`a = b`	Equality. True if `a` is equal to `b`.
`a <> b`	Inequality. True if `a` is not equal to `b`.
`a < b`	Less Than. True if `a` is less than `b`.
`a > b`	Greater Than. True if `a` is greater than `b`.
`a <= b`	Less Than Or Equal. True if `a` is less than or equal to `b`.
`a >= b`	Greater Than Or Equal. True if `a` is greater than or equal to `b`.

The comparison operators can operate on almost all data types. For numeric data types, the operators compare the numeric values and generate a `True` or `False` result accordingly. For date and times (described in detail in Chapter 3, "VBScript Data Storage") the operators compare the time and date and generate a result accordingly. For string data types, the operators work as follows:

- The two strings are scanned from left to right for the first character in the strings that do not match. Determination of less than/greater than is made by comparing these two characters.
- If the end of either string is reached before a non-matching character is found, the shorter string is "less than" the longer string.

- If both strings are the same length *and* consist of the same sequence of characters, the strings are considered equal.

For example, the following comparison operations all return a `True` result.

```
100 = 100                      ' Values are equal
1500 >= -5                     ' 1500 is greater than -5
"abcdefg" = "abcdefg"          ' Both strings are identical
"abc" < "abcd"                 ' "abc" is shorter than "abcd"
"abc" > "aad"                  ' "b" is greater than "a"
```

The following comparison operations all return a `False` result.

```
90 = 91                        ' Values are NOT equal
"aaaa" = "aaa"                 ' Strings are different
"abc" >= "abcd"                ' Shorter string is less than longer
```

The equality operator uses an = sign. The = sign is also used in the assignment statement, but the meaning is different. As previously explained, the = sign in the assignment statement means *becomes*, whereas the = sign as an equality operator means *is equal to*. It is always clear from the context which meaning to assign to the = sign.

Because the = sign is used in the assignment statement and is used as an operator, it is possible to write a statement, such as the following:

```
bReady = nCount = 10           ' Is nCount equal to 10?
```

In this statement, the first = sign is part of the assignment statement and can be read as "becomes." The second = sign is the equality comparison operator. Therefore, when this statement is executed, the expression `nCount = 10` is evaluated. If `nCount` is equal to 10, then `bReady` is set to `True`. Otherwise, `bReady` is set to `False`.

Logical Operators

Logical operators perform logical operations on boolean values and return a boolean result. Boolean values are described in more detail in Chapter 3. They are frequently used to combine several comparison operations into a single test. Table 2.3 lists the logical operators.

Table 2.3 Logical Operators

Operator	Meaning
`Not a`	Logical Negation. `True` becomes `False` and vice-versa.
`a And b`	Conjunction. `True` only if `a` and `b` are both `True`.
`a Or b`	Disjunction. `True` if either `a` or `b` are `True`.
`a Xor b`	Exclusion. `True` if exactly one of `a` or `b` is `True`.

Operator	Meaning
a Eqv b	Equivalence. True if a is the same as b.
a Imp b	Implication. True unless a is True and b is False.

When used with boolean values (True and False), the logical operators return boolean values. When used with integer values, the logical operators perform a *bitwise* operation. In a bitwise operation, each binary bit of the operands is treated as an individual boolean value (with 0 corresponding to False). For example, 5 And 12 yields a result of 4. This is because in binary, 5 is 0101 and 12 is 1100. The only bit that is 1 in both operands is the third bit (reading from the right). So the result is 0100, which is 4 in decimal.

Logical operators are frequently used with comparison operators to check to see if a value is within a certain range. For example:

```
bInRange = (a > 1) And (a < 10)
```

Here, the bInRange variable is only set to True if a is both greater than 1 and less than 10, that is, it is between 2 and 9 inclusive.

Miscellaneous Operators

The Is operator is used to test for object equivalence. The expression a Is b will return True only if both a and b reference the same object. Because this is only used with objects, the use of this operator is discussed in Part II.

Precedence and Parentheses

As previously explained, a VBScript expression can be any combination of operands and operators. For example, the following are all valid expressions:

```
nCount + nStart * nFactor
2 * PI * nSquare < 1000
bSomeArgs And bDebug And Not bTrace
nStart > 10 And nStart < 1000
```

To evaluate a complex expression, VBScript first evaluates individual operators and their operands. This evaluation yields intermediate results that are then used with remaining operators until the entire expression is evaluated and a final result obtained. VBScript applies a series of rules to control the order in which the individual operators are applied. These rules are:

- Parts of the expression that are in parentheses are evaluated first.
- Higher precedence operators are evaluated before lower precedence operators.
- Operators of equal precedence are evaluated from left to right.

The first rule allows parentheses to be used to control the order of evaluation. For example, these two expressions yield different results:

```
(10 + 2) * 5
10 + (2 * 5)
```

The first expression yields the value 60, and the second yields the value 20.

In the absence of parentheses, VBScript uses *operator precedence* to decide how to evaluate the expression. All operators have a precedence level assigned to them. Operators with higher precedence are evaluated first (unless parentheses are used). Table 2.4 shows all the VBScript operators in order of precedence, with the highest precedence operators listed first.

Table 2.4 *Operator Precedence*

Operator	Meaning
^	Exponentiation.
-	Unary Negation.
*	Multiplication.
/	Division.
\	Integer Division.
Mod	Integer Modulus.
+	Addition.
-	Subtraction.
&	String Concatenation.
=, <>, <, >, <=. >=	Comparison Operators.
Is	Object Equivalence.
Not	Logical Negation.
And	Conjunction.
Or	Disjunction.
Xor	Exclusion.
Eqv	Equivalence.
Imp	Implication.

In the absence of parentheses, the highest precedence operator, ^ (exponentiation), is always evaluated first, followed by the other arithmetic operators in the order shown. All the comparison operators have the same precedence, followed by the logical operators in the order shown in the table.

Because multiplication is higher in precedence than addition, the expression:

```
10 + 2 * 5
```

Is evaluated as:

```
10 + (2 * 5)
```

Therefore, the result is 20, not 60. As a more complex example, the expression:

```
nCount < cMax * 100 And Not bDone
```

Is evaluated as:

```
(nCount < (cMax * 100)) And (Not bDone)
```

The preceding expression evaluates to `True` only if `bDone` is `False` *and* `cMax * 100` is less than `nCount`.

Note

The evaluation order in an expression can always be forced by using parentheses. In fact, the use of parentheses is useful even when they are not strictly required. In the last example, the parenthesized expression is more easily understood. It is generally a good idea to use parentheses in more complex expressions. ◆

The final rule used to control expression evaluation handles operators of equal precedence. In the absence of parentheses, if an expression contains one or more operators of equal precedence in succession, those operators are evaluated from left to right. For example, the expression:

```
nCount / nMax / 4
```

Is evaluated as:

```
(nCount / nMax) / 4
```

As with all other expression rules, the order of evaluation can be forced using parentheses. For example:

```
nCount / (nMax / 4)
```

Functions

In addition to numbers, strings, and variables, an expression operand in VBScript can also be a *function*. A function is an operation that yields a result, often called a *return value*, which can be used in an expression. Functions, like variables, are typically given descriptive names, and VBScript supplies many built-in functions.

As an example function, the `Rnd` function yields a return value that is a random number between 0 and 1. Each time the `Rnd` function is used in an expression it yields a new random value. For example:

```
x = Rnd
```

This example assigns a new random number (between 0 and 1) to the variable `x`.

Program Guide

Functions Behind the Scenes

In the previous example, the function `Rnd` *might look like a variable, but it is quite different. First, a variable will always provide the same value when it is used in an expression. In contrast, a function can provide a different value each time it is used, even in the same expression.*

Internally, a variable is associated with storage, *where its value is stored. A function, however, is associated with executable code, which is executed each time the function is used. It is this code that computes the value that the function returns.* ◆

Functions can also use one or more *arguments*. These arguments are used as input values for the function. The actual meaning of each argument is specific to the function. For example, the `Sqr` function takes a single argument, a number, and then returns the square root of that number.

Function arguments are placed in parentheses following the name of the function. For example:

```
x = Sqr(16)
```

This will assign the value 4 (the square root of 16) to the variable `x`.

If more than one argument is required by the function, they are separated by commas. For example:

```
x = Left("Fred Brown", 4)
```

Here, the `Left` function (described in Chapter 4) takes two arguments, a string and a number.

Each individual argument to a function is itself an expression. Therefore, you can use the full set of expression operators within a function argument, *including other functions*. For example:

```
x = (-b + Sqr(b ^ 2 - (4 * a * c))) / (2 * a)
```

This complex expression (which computes one of the roots of a quadratic equation), includes the expression `b ^ 2 - (4 * a * c)` as the argument to the `Sqr` function. When VBScript evaluates such an expression, it evaluates the function arguments before it evaluates the rest of the expression. For example:

```
x = Sqr(8 * 2) + 5
```

When this assignment statement executes, VBScript first evaluates the expression `8 * 2` and then executes the `Sqr` function to compute the square root of 16, which is 4. Then this result is added to 5, yielding a final result of 9, which is assigned to the variable `x`.

The VBScript language has many built-in functions for performing a variety of data-manipulation tasks. Chapter 4 provides details on all these functions. In addition, it is possible to define your own functions in VBScript and information on this is provided in Chapter 5.

The *SphereStats.vbs* Script

The `SphereStats.vbs` sample script, shown in Listing 2.2, illustrates the use of the `Dim` statement, simple variables, and expressions. The script reads the radius of a sphere as a single command line argument, and then computes the volume and surface area of the sphere.

Listing 2.2 `SphereStats.vbs` *Script*

```
'//////////////////////////////////////////////////////////////////////////////
' $Workfile: SphereStats.vbs $ $Revision: 2 $ $Date: 4/18/99 3:39p $
' $Archive: /Scripts/SphereStats.vbs $
' Copyright (c) 1998 Tim Hill. All Rights Reserved.
'//////////////////////////////////////////////////////////////////////////////

' Compute surface area and volume of sphere given radius

Option Explicit

Dim fRadius, fSurface, fVolume, PI
PI = 3.1415926
fRadius = Wscript.Arguments(0)
fSurface = 4 * PI * fRadius^2
fVolume = (4 * PI * fRadius^3) / 3

Wscript.Echo "Radius:", fRadius, "Surface area:", fSurface, "Volume:", fVolume

'//////////////////////////////////////////////////////////////////////////////
```

`SphereStats.vbs` begins with an `Option Explicit` statement. This means that (as recommended) all variable declarations must be made explicitly using `Dim` statements. Immediately following this is a single `Dim` statement that declares all the variables used by the script.

The `PI` variable is then set to the approximate value of the transcendental constant Pi. Next, the radius of the sphere is stored in the `fRadius` variable. The radius is obtained from the first command line argument using the `Wscript.Arguments(0)` value.

Next, two assignment statements calculate the surface area and volume of the sphere and store the results in the `fSurface` and `fVolume` variables. Finally, the `Wscript.Echo` statement is used to display the results of the calculations.

To exercise this script, run the script from the command line. Enter the radius of the sphere following the name of the script.

Simple Arrays

The section "Numbers, Strings and Variables" described how simple variables are named and used. An *array* is a type of variable that can hold multiple values *at the same time*. Each individual value in an array is called an array *element*, and each element stored in an array variable is distinct from all other elements in that array.

Each element in an array is accessed using an integer *index*. (The index is also sometimes called an array subscript.) The index is a numeric "address" that uniquely identifies each element in an array. The first element in an array always has an index of 0, the second an index of 1, and so on. The last element (the *n*th) always has an index of *n*-1. This maximum index is called the *upper bound* of the array. The *lower bound* of the array is always 0. Specify the index by placing it in parentheses immediately after the variable name. For example:

```
x = a(1)
```

This example assigns the variable `x` the contents of the second element of array `a`. Figure 2.2 illustrates an example array `a` containing 4 elements, each containing data of a different type. If this array was used with the preceding statement, the `x` variable would be assigned the string `Foo`.

Array Index	Element Contents
a(0)	1000
a(1)	"Foo"
a(2)	True
a(3)	14.5

Figure 2.2 *A simple array.*

Arrays *must* be explicitly declared before they are used (even if you are using implicit declaration). Like simple variables, arrays are declared using the `Dim` statement. Follow the name of the array by the *upper bound* of the array in parentheses. For example:

```
Dim a(10)
```

This statement declares an array of eleven (not ten) elements with indices from 0 to 10. To declare an array with *n* elements, specify *n*-1 as the upper bound in the `Dim` statement. Like simple variables, each element of an array is initialized with the special `Empty` value.

Program Guide

Counting to Ten

In general, programmers prefer to start counting with the value 0 instead of the value 1. When a programmer thinks of the fingers of his hands, he might think "I have ten fingers, numbered 0 to 9." This is actually more mathematically correct than counting from 1 to 10 because 10 is really in the second decade, not the first. It also simplifies many programming tasks. For example, to determine which "decade" (block of ten elements) an array index is in, simply divide the index by 10. This would not work if the elements were numbered starting at 1.

Technically this is expressed as the difference between "ordinal" and "cardinal" numbers. Ordinal numbers indicate the position of something in a sequence (first, second, third, and so on), whereas cardinal numbers are used to count items. It is technically correct to say that the cardinality of fingers on your hands is ten, with ordinals from 0 to 9.

For example, the third Millennium does not start until the year 2001 (celebrations notwithstanding) because years are counted from 1 and not 0, and the Twentieth Century did not begin until January 1, 1901. ◆

Multiple arrays can be declared with a single `Dim` statement, and regular variables and arrays can be mixed in a single `Dim`. For example:

```
Dim nCount, nTotalCount, sList(10), bDone(100)
```

After an array has been declared using `Dim`, its elements can be used in the same way as a simple variable. For example:

```
a(2) = a(3)                    ' Copy element 3 to element 2
a(3) = "Assign a string to an element"
a(4) = nCount + a(8)          ' Element 4 becomes nCount + element 8
```

The element index does not have to be a constant value. In fact, the element index can be any valid VBScript expression. For example:

```
a(nCount - nMax) = a(nCount - nMax) + 1
```

This assignment statement adds 1 to the value of the element of `a`, whose index is `nCount - nMax`.

Program Guide

Arrays as Data Structures

Arrays are a useful form of data structure. The power of the array lies in the fact that the element index is computed at run-time, rather than when the script is created. This index might read from a file, be the result of a calculation, or even obtained interactively from the user. In some situations, array elements can even contain indices of other elements in the same (or another) array.

For example, an array of strings can contain an entire text file, with each element containing a single line from the file. The element index thus corresponds to the line number in the file. Because file line numbers start with 1 and not 0, element 0 of the array is not used for storing a line of text. Instead, this element could (for example) be used to store the name of the file on disk. ◆

Because element indices are computed at run-time, it is possible for a script to attempt to access an element that does not exist. For instance, it might attempt to access element 100 in an array that is declared only to have 10 elements. Such an access attempt indicates a bug in the script code. VBScript detects these conditions and terminates script execution with an error.

It is possible to determine the size of an array at run time using the `UBound` function. This function takes the name of an array as an argument and returns the upper bound (that is, the index of the last element) of the array. For example:

```
Dim a(100)
x = UBound(a)
Wscript.Echo "The array a has",x + 1,"elements."
```

Because all arrays have a lower bound of zero, the number of elements is always one greater than the upper bound of the array, as shown in the previous example.

Control Flow

When VBScript executes a script file, the statements within the script are executed one by one in sequence. Each statement completes execution before VBScript begins executing the next. Statements are executed in the order they are listed within the script file, starting with the first line and ending with the last line. Script execution ends after the last statement in the file is executed.

Multiple statements on a single line (separated by colons) are also executed in sequence, starting with the left-most statement and working from left to right within the line. After the last statement on the line completes, execution continues with the first statement on the next line.

This flow of script execution, from the first to the last statement, is called *control flow*, and it is fundamental to almost all computer languages. However, if control flow only consisted of starting at the top and proceeding to the end of the script, scripts would have limited functionality.

Fortunately, VBScript includes a set of statements that allow the default control flow to be modified in various ways. These statements are described in this section.

Conditional Statements

The simplest form of control flow modification is the *conditional statement*, or `If` statement. The conditional statement only executes if a certain condition is met. The syntax of a simple conditional statement is:

```
If expression Then statements
```

Execution of a simple conditional statement proceeds as follows:

1. The `expression` following the `If` keyword is evaluated.
2. If the value of the expression evaluated in step 1 is `True` or non-zero, the `statements` following the `Then` keyword are executed.
3. If the value of the expression is `False` or zero, the `statements` are skipped.

The statements that are executed (or not) by the conditional statement can be any valid VBScript statements, even another conditional statement (although this is not common). For example:

```
If a = 10 Then Wscript.Echo "a is 10"
If nCount > 100 Then nCount = 0
```

The second statement has the effect of setting the value of `nCount` to zero if it is greater than 100.

It is possible to "nest" two conditional statements. For example:

```
If a >= 10 Then If a <= 20 Then Wscript.Echo "a is between 10 and 20"
```

In this example, the `Wscript.Echo` statement only executes if both `If` statements evaluate to `True`, that is, if `a` is both greater than and equal to 10 and less than or equal to 20. However, it is more efficient (and clearer) to combine these tests into a single expression using the `And` logical operator, as follows:

```
If a >= 10 And a <= 20 Then Wscript.Echo "a is between 10 and 20"
```

This statement is equivalent to the previous one, but it is more compact, easier to understand, and will also typically execute slightly faster.

It is permissible to follow the `Then` keyword with multiple statements, separated as usual by colon characters. Either all the statements are executed (if the expression is `True` or non-zero) or none of the statements are executed (if the expressions is `False` or zero). For example:

```
If Wscript.Arguments.Count < 1 Then Wscript.Echo "Missing arguments" : Wscript.Quit(1)
```

This statement first checks to see if there are fewer than one (that is, zero) arguments on the command line. If that is the case, the `Wscript.Echo` statement issues an error message and the `Wscript.Quit` statement ends script execution.

The *Else* Clause

Simple `If` statements can also contain an *else* clause. The syntax for these `If` statements is:

```
If expression Then true-statements Else false-statements
```

The behavior of this statement is similar to the more basic `If` statement. If the *`expression`* evaluates to `True` or non-zero, then the *`true-statements`* are executed. In addition, however, if the expression evaluates to `False` or zero, then the *`false-statements`* are executed. For example:

```
If x < 100 Then x = x + 1 Else Wscript.Echo "x out of range" : Wscript.Quit(1)
```

In this statement, if the variable `x` is less than 100, its value is incremented by 1. Otherwise, an error message is displayed and the script terminates.

Multiple statements (separated by colons) are allowed for both the *`true-statements`* and *`false-statements`* clauses.

Multi-Line Conditional Statements

The simple conditional statement can become cumbersome if there are more than one or two statements in the *`true-statements`* or *`false-statements`* clauses. To overcome this, VBScript supports a second form of conditional statement, the multi-line conditional. The syntax for this statement is:

```
If expression Then
    statements
    .
    .
End If
```

This conditional statement is evaluated in the same manner as the simple conditional statement. However, if the *`expression`* evaluates to `True` or non-zero, then all the statements enclosed between the `Then` and `End If` keywords are executed. If the expression is `False` or non-zero, then all the statements are skipped. This allows an entire block of statements to be executed conditionally.

The multi-line conditional statement also supports an `Else` clause. The syntax for this statement is:

```
If expression Then
    true-statements
    .
    .
Else
    false-statements
    .
    .
End If
```

The following example re-formats the previous example as a multi-line conditional statement.

```
If x < 100 Then
    x = x + 1
Else
    Wscript.Echo "x out of range"
    Wscript.Quit(1)
End If
```

Notice that although this format is less compact than the single line form shown previously, the statement is easier to read. The use of indentation also assists with readability, although this indentation is optional.

Multi-way Conditional Statements

The multi-line conditional statement also supports an extended form of conditional execution that is not available with the single line form. This is called the multi-way conditional statement. Its syntax is as follows:

```
If expression1 Then
    statements1
ElseIf expression2 Then
    statements2
[...repeat ElseIf as needed]
Else
    false-statements
End If
```

This statement operates as follows:

1. The *expression1* expression is evaluated.
2. If the expression is `True` or non-zero, *statements1* executes, and evaluation of the entire `If` statement is then complete (that is, the next statement to execute is the one following the `End If` keyword).
3. Otherwise, *expression2* is evaluated, and if it is `True` or non-zero, then *statements2* executes, and evaluation of the entire `If` statement is then complete.
4. Otherwise, additional `ElseIf` expressions (if present) are evaluated, until one is found that evaluates to `True` or non-zero.
5. Otherwise, if none of the expressions evaluate to `True` or non-zero, the statements in the `Else` clause (if present) are executed.

In other words, each conditional expression is evaluated until one is found that evaluates to `True` or non-zero. The corresponding set of statements is then executed. If no expression evaluates to `True` or non-zero, the `Else` clause statements, if present, are executed.

For example:

```
If a < 10 Then
    Wscript.Echo "a is less than 10"
ElseIf a < 100 Then
    Wscript.Echo "a is less than 100"
ElseIf a < 1000 Then
    Wscript.Echo "a is less than 1000"
Else
    Wscript.Echo "a is not less than 1000"
End If
```

In this example, one of the `Wscript.Echo` statements will execute depending upon the value of the variable `a`. In this particular case, there is also a subtle interaction between the individual expressions. If the example is re-written using a different order, it will *not* work. For example:

```
If a < 1000 Then
    Wscript.Echo "a is less than 1000"
ElseIf a < 100 Then
    Wscript.Echo "a is less than 100"
ElseIf a < 10 Then
    Wscript.Echo "a is less than 10"
Else
    Wscript.Echo "a is not less than 1000"
End If
```

Although similar, this example fails to operate as expected. The reason is that the first test, `a < 1000`, fully includes the other tests, `a < 100` and `a < 10`, within its result domain. In other words, there cannot be a value of `a` where the first test is `False` and the second (or third) tests are `True`. Hence, neither the second nor the third `Wscript.Echo` statement will ever execute. This illustrates the need to construct multi-way conditional statements carefully so that earlier test expressions do not mask later ones.

Loops

Loop statements in VBScript cause a group of statements to execute repeatedly until some condition is satisfied. Without loops, a script composed of *n* statements would execute, at most, *n* statements during its execution (it could execute fewer depending upon the results of conditional statements). With loops, the number of statements that a script executes, regardless of its length, is essentially unlimited. This re-use of statements is one of the ways computer programs achieve their goals.

The *Do While* Loop

The most common loop statement in VBScript is the `Do While` loop, the syntax of which is:

```
Do While expression
    statements
    .
    .
Loop
```

The `Do While` loop operates as follows:

1. The *expression* is evaluated. If the expression evaluates to `False` or non-zero, the execution of the `Do While` loop ends and execution of the script continues with the statement following the `Loop` keyword.
2. The *statements* are executed once in sequence up to the `Loop` keyword.
3. Control transfers back to the start of the `Do While` statement and operation continues at step 1.

In other words, the block of statements enclosed in the `Do While` loop (sometimes called the loop body) is executed repeatedly until the *expression* evaluates to `False`. For example:

```
x = 0
Do While x < 100
    Wscript.Echo "The square root of",x,"is",Sqr(x)
    x = x + 1
Loop
```

When the `Do While` loop is first entered, the variable `x` is zero (as a result of the first assignment statement). Thus, the expression `x < 100` is true and the loop body executes. Within the loop body, the `Wscript.Echo` statement displays the value of `x` and its square root (in this case, 0 and 0).

The assignment statement following the `Wscript.Echo` statement increments the value of `x`; in this case, changing it from 0 to 1. The loop then restarts and the expression `x < 100` is again true; the loop body executes again, displaying the square root of 1, and `x` increments to 2. This continues until `x` reaches 100, at which point the loop terminates.

Thus, this loop displays a list of numbers from 0 to 99 and their square roots. Several things should be noted about this example:

- The variable `x` is used to control execution of the loop. This is sometimes called the *loop control variable.*
- The *expression* used to control the loop is only checked once for each execution of the loop body, just before the loop body executes. Thus, changes made within the loop body that alter the result of the *expression* do not cause the loop body to stop execution until the next "pass" through the loop is about to begin.
- The loop control variable is preset to 0 before the loop begins. It is important to ensure that the initial conditions that control the loop are correct before the loop begins.

- The *expression* is `x < 100`, therefore the loop terminates if `x` is greater than or equal to 100.
- The statement `x = x + 1` causes the loop control variable to increment by 1. It is vital that one or more of the statements in the loop can alter the *expression*, because otherwise the loop will never end, creating a condition called an *infinite loop*.

Program Guide

Loop Boundary Conditions

Take a moment to look carefully at the previous example. What is the first square root displayed? What is the last? The last value displayed is the square root of 99, not 100. That is, the loop executes with values of `x` *from 0 to 99, inclusive. Walk through the operation of the loop in your head as it approaches the end. Let's assume that* `x` *is currently 98. The* `Do` *condition is obviously true (98 is less than 100), so the loop body executes and the square root of 98 is displayed. Next, the variable* `x` *is incremented to 99 and the loop starts over. Again, 99 is less than 100 so the loop body executes again, ending up by incrementing* `x` *to 100. This time, however, the* `Do` *condition is no longer true, because 100 is not less than 100. Therefore, the loop ends at this point.*

This is an example of a boundary condition. Errors in boundary conditions are common, typically by having a loop execute one too many or one too few loops. Another common error involves not considering the case where the loop body never executes at all (which may or may not be valid depending upon the circumstances). ◆

The *Do Until* Loop

The second loop type in VBScript is the `Do Until` loop. The syntax of the `Do Until` loop is:

```
Do Until expression
    statements
    .
    .
Loop
```

The execution of the `Do Until` loop is identical to the `Do While` loop except that the test applied to the *expression* is reversed. That is, execution of the loop continues while the expression is `False`, rather than `True`. In fact, the `Do Until` loop is identical in operation to the following `Do While` loop:

```
Do While Not (expression)
    statements
    .
    .
Loop
```

The difference is primarily readability. It is sometimes more natural to construct a loop using a `Do Until` loop rather than a `Do While` loop. For example:

```
sCmdLine = ""
x = 0
Do Until Wscript.Arguments(x) = "--"
    sCmdLine = sCmdLine & Wscript.Arguments(x)
    x = x + 1
Loop
```

This example concatenates command line arguments until an argument consisting of -- is encountered.

Post Test Loops

Both the `Do While` and the `Do Until` loops are called *pre-test* loops. That is, the conditional expression that controls the looping operation is tested at the start of the loop, before the loop executes. One result of this pre-testing is that it is entirely possible that the loop body *never* executes. This happens in a `Do While` loop if the conditional expression evaluates to `False` on the first test.

VBScript offers a second form of loop in which the tests are performed *after* the loop statements have executed for the first time. These are called *post-test* loops and are known as `Loop While` and `Loop Until`. They have the following syntax:

```
Do
    statements
Loop While expression

Do
    statements
Loop Until expression
```

The `Loop While` loop operates as follows:

1. The *`statements`* are executed in sequence up to the `Loop` keyword.
2. The *`expression`* is evaluated. If the expression evaluates to `False` or non-zero, execution of the `Loop While` loop ends and execution of the script continues with the statement following the `Loop` keyword.
3. Control transfers back to the start of the `Do` statement and operation continues at step 1.

Because the conditional test is performed after the *statements* in the loop body are executed, a `Loop While` or `Loop Until` loop will always execute the loop body at least once. `Loop While` and `Loop Until` loops are occasionally useful, but they are far less common than pre-test loops.

The *Exit Do* Statement

Occasionally it might be necessary to terminate a loop while executing the statements in the loop body. The `Exit Do` statement is used for this purpose. Its syntax is:

```
Exit Do
```

Executing an `Exit Do` statement causes the execution of the current loop to terminate immediately (including any remaining statements in the loop body). The next statement to execute will be the first statement following the `Loop` keyword.

The `Exit Do` statement is almost always used in a conditional statement. For example:

```
Dim a(99)
x = 0
Do While x < 100
    If a(x) = 0 Then Exit Do
    x = x + 1
Loop
If x = 100 Then Wscript.Echo "zero element not found"
```

This `Do While` loop executes until either the variable `x` reaches 100, or an element in the array `a` is located that is zero. Thus, this example loop can search an array for a specific value (in this case, zero).

Program Guide

Testing Loop Termination

In the preceding example, there are two ways for the loop to terminate.

- *The variable x might reach 100, in which case the Do While loop terminates normally.*
- *The array element a(x) might be zero, in which case the Exit Do statement terminates the loop early.*

Because there are two different ways that the loop can terminate, an `If` *statement is often used following the loop to distinguish between each possible reason. In the preceding example, the variable* `x` *is checked. If it is 100, the loop terminated "normally;" if not, then the loop must have terminated via the* `Exit Do` *statement.*

It might appear that the final `If` *statement could be rewritten to check the value of* `a(x)`*. This is not correct, however, because, if the loop ends normally, the variable* `x` *contains 100. This is not a valid element index for* `a`*.* ◆

Nesting Loop Statements

Loop statements can be nested. That is, the loop body can contain another loop or loops. In this case, the innermost loop executes completely for *each* pass through the outermost loop. For example:

```
x = 0
Do While x < 10
    y = 0
    Do While y < 10
        Wscript.Echo "(", x, ":", y, ")"
        y = y + 1
    Loop
    x = x + 1
Loop
```

This double loop will display all combinations of `x` and `y` between 0 and 9 (that is, 100 combinations). Notice that the `y` variable processing is enclosed completely within the outer `Do While` loop, including initializing `y` on each pass through the loop.

There is no limit imposed by VBScript on the depth of loop nesting. However, depending upon the number of iterations of each loop, very deeply nested loops might take a long time to execute. For example:

```
x = 0
Do While x < 100
    y = 0
    Do While y < 100
        z = 0
        Do While z < 100
            Wscript.Echo "(", x, ":", y, ":", z, ")"
            z = z + 1
        Loop
        y = y + 1
    Loop
    x = x + 1
Loop
```

This example extends the previous example to three nested loops. Each loop executes 100 times, but the innermost loop is itself executed 100 times for *each* of the enclosing loops executions; and this loop in turn executes for 100 times for each pass through the outermost loop. Thus, this loop will actually cause the `Wscript.Echo` statement to execute 1,000,000 times!

While Wend Loops

VBScript offers one additional loop type, called the `While Wend` loop. The syntax of this loop is:

```
While expression
    statements
    .
    .
Wend
```

The `While Wend` loop operates as follows:

1. The *`expression`* is evaluated. If the expression evaluates to `False` or non-zero, execution of the `While Wend` loop ends and execution of the script continues with the statement following the `Wend` keyword.
2. The *`statements`* are executed once in sequence up to the `Wend` keyword.
3. Control transfers back to the start of the `While Wend` statement and operation continues at step 1.

This loop is identical in operation to the `Do While` loop. It is present in VBScript primarily for backward compatibility with earlier versions of Visual Basic. You should use the `Do While` loop in all new scripts, and none of the example scripts in this book use the `While Wend` loop.

Simple Iteration

Several of the previous examples covering `Do` loops shared a common structure. In each case, the loop was something like this:

```
x = 0
Do While x < 100
    statements
    x = x + 1
Loop
```

In this type of loop, the loop body is executed repeatedly while a variable (in this case `x`) is swept through a range of values (in this case, 0 to 99). The loop body executes exactly once for each value of `x`, and the values are always executed in order (that is, 0, 1, 2, 3, and so on).

This common loop type is called an *iteration loop*, and it is so common that VBScript provides a special statement specifically for executing iterated loops. This statement is the `For` statement. The syntax of a `For` statement is:

```
For variable = start To end [Step increment]
    statements
    .
    .
Next
```

The `For` loop operates as follows:

1. The *`variable`* is initialized to the value of *`start`*, which can be any numeric expression.
2. If *`variable`* is greater than *`end`*, execution of the `For` loop is complete and the statement following the `Next` statement executes.
3. The *`statements`* in the loop body are executed once.

4. The *increment* value is added to the *variable*. If the `Step` clause is not present, the *variable* is incremented by one.
5. Execution continues at step 2.

The values *start*, *end,* and *increment* can be any valid numeric expression. The *variable* must be a simple variable (array elements are not allowed). *statements* can be any valid statements, including other loop types or even additional `For` loops.

The `For` statement is essentially equivalent to the following `Do While` loop:

```
variable = start
Do While variable <= end
    statements
    .
    .
    variable = variable + increment
Loop
```

Several important points should be noted about `For` loops:

- The *start* expression is evaluated once when it is used to initialize the iterator variable.
- The *end* expression is also only evaluated once. This is slightly different to the similar `Do While` loop, which evaluates the expression for each iteration.
- The loop executes while the variable is less than *or equal to* the value of the *end* expression. This means that `For` loops are *inclusive* loops.
- VBScript permits statements inside the loop body to alter the value of the *variable*. However, this is generally considered bad programming practice and it should be avoided.
- If the *increment* is negative, the *variable* will actually decrease in value with each iteration of the loop. In this case, the completion test in step 2 of the procedure is modified so that iteration ends when *variable* is less than, instead of greater than, *end*.

Here is an example `For` statement:

```
For x = 0 to 99
    Wscript.Echo "The square root of",x,"is",Sqr(x)
Next
```

This example provides the same functionality as the first example `Do While` loop shown in the "Loops" section. However, it is only three lines instead of five, and the operation of the loop, as an iteration, is clearer. Also, notice that the *end* value is 99, not 100. As previously explained, the loop will continue while the variable `x` is less than or equal to 99.

The following example will count down from 10 to 0 in steps of 2:

```
For x = 10 To 0 Step -2
    Wscript.Echo "x=",x
Next
```

`For` loops are extremely useful when processing arrays. For example, this loop will clear all the elements of an array to zero:

```
Dim a(100)
For x = 0 To 100
    a(x) = 0
Next
```

This loop executes 101 times (0 to 100 inclusive). Each time the loop body executes one of the elements of the array `a` (selected by the variable `x`) is cleared to zero. This loop can be improved by using the `UBound` function. For example:

```
Dim a(100)
For x = 0 To UBound(a)
    a(x) = 0
Next
```

Here the value 100 has been changed to `UBound(a)`. This change means that the `For` loop will clear the array `a` whatever size it happens to be.

Program Guide

Defensive Coding

Why is this trivial change so important? In this particular example, the size of the array is evident from the `Dim` *statement, but in a real script, the* `Dim` *statement might be far from the loop and the correct size of the array difficult to determine. If someone alters the size of the array, they might not check through the code to update all the* `For` *and* `Do` *loops. By using the* `UBound` *function, the code corrects itself!*

In addition, Chapter 3, "VBScript Data Storage," introduces arrays that can have different sizes at different times. For these arrays, the `UBound` *function is the only way to determine the correct size of the array.*

This is an example of defensive coding—writing script code that is robust even when the script changes. In general, defensive coding is usually a matter of examining the assumptions made by the code and then trying to rewrite the code in such a way that it still works even if those assumptions are no longer valid. In this case, the assumption was that the size of the array was known and would never change. ◆

Like `Do` loops, VBScript provides a statement to exit a `For` loop early. The syntax is:

```
Exit For
```

The `Exit For` statement is typically placed in a conditional statement to terminate loop execution if a certain condition is met.

For statements can also be nested. For example, the following code performs the same function as the nested Do While loop example in the previous section, but it is more compact:

```
For x = 0 To 9
    For y = 0 To 9
        Wscript.Echo "(", x, ":", y, ")"
    Next
Next
```

Collection Iteration

One common use of the For statement is processing the elements in an array. For example:

```
Dim a(100)
sum = 0
For x = 0 To UBound(a)
    sum = sum + a(x)
Next
```

This example computes the sum of all the elements in the array a, by adding each element, one by one, to the sum variable. This particular type of For loop can be re-written in a slightly different form, as follows:

```
Dim a(100)
sum = 0
For Each e In a
    sum = sum + e
Next
```

This type of For statement is called a *collection iteration*, and it is designed specifically to iterate collections. (Arrays are one type of collection, others are described in Part II.) The general syntax of a collection iteration is:

```
For Each variable In collection
    statements
    .
    .
Next
```

The For Each loop iterates the *statements* in the loop body for each element in the *collection*. The elements are iterated in order (that is, from the lowest to highest array index). For each iteration, the *variable* is assigned the value of one of the array elements.

The For Each statement can be more convenient than a regular For or Do loop, but it has several disadvantages:

- The index of the current array element is not available—there is no equivalent to the x variable used in the previous examples.
- The array elements in the *collection* cannot be altered by the loop. Only the *value* of the current element is available.

These restrictions make the `For Each` loop useful only when the items in an array are being read, rather than altered.

As with regular `For` loops, the `Exit For` statement can be used to terminate the loop early.

The *ShowArgs2.vbs* Script

The `ShowArgs2.vbs` sample script, shown in Listing 2.3, illustrates the use of all three loop types described in this chapter. The script is an enhanced version of the `ShowArgs1.vbs` script (shown in Listing 2.1) presented earlier in this chapter. Unlike `ShowArgs1.vbs`, this script displays all the arguments entered on the command line, no matter how many are present.

Listing 2.3 *`ShowArgs2.vbs` Script*

```
'//////////////////////////////////////////////////////////////////////////////
' $Workfile: ShowArgs2.vbs $ $Revision: 4 $ $Date: 4/24/99 11:20a $
' $Archive: /Scripts/ShowArgs2.vbs $
' Copyright (c) 1998 Tim Hill. All Rights Reserved.
'//////////////////////////////////////////////////////////////////////////////

' Display all command line arguments

Option Explicit
Dim nIndex, sArg

Wscript.Echo "You entered",Wscript.Arguments.Count,"arguments"

' Use looping to display all args
nIndex = 0
Do While nIndex < Wscript.Arguments.Count
    Wscript.Echo "Argument " & nIndex & ":", Wscript.Arguments(nIndex)
    nIndex = nIndex + 1
Loop

' Use iteration to display all args
For nIndex = 0 To Wscript.Arguments.Count - 1
    Wscript.Echo "Argument " & nIndex & ":", Wscript.Arguments(nIndex)
Next

' Use collection iteration to display all args
For Each sArg In Wscript.Arguments
    If sArg = "ghost" Then
        Wscript.Echo "The ghost in the machine!"
    Else
        Wscript.Echo "Argument :", sArg
    End If
Next

'//////////////////////////////////////////////////////////////////////////////
```

As with `ShowArgs1.vbs`, the new `ShowArgs2.vbs` script begins by displaying a count of arguments entered on the command line. The script then uses three loops, each of which displays all the command line arguments. The three loops illustrate the use of `Do While`, `For`, and `For Each` statements.

The first loop uses a `Do While` statement to display the arguments. In this loop, the variable `nIndex` is used as an index into the `Wscript.Arguments` collection. The `Wscript.Echo` statement then displays both the index itself and the value of the argument. The `nIndex` variable is incremented in the loop body, so that each argument is displayed.

The second loop uses a `For` statement to display the arguments. In this loop, the `nIndex` variable is handled entirely by the `For` statement, making this loop more compact than the `Do While` loop.

The final loop uses a `For Each` statement to display the arguments. This loop uses a new variable, `sArg`, to contain the command line argument. Recall that in a `For Each` loop the variable contains the actual value of each array or collection element; therefore, indexes are not required. This does mean, however, that this loop cannot display the index of the argument in its `Wscript.Echo` statement. (This can be corrected by adding code to manipulate the `nIndex` variable, but this is left as an exercise for the reader.)

The `For Each` loop also contains an example of an `If` statement. Before displaying the argument, the `If` statement checks the value of the argument to see if it is equal to "ghost." If it is, then an alternate `Wscript.Echo` statement executes. Try executing the script with one or more arguments with a value of "ghost" to see the results.

Program Guide

Choosing a Loop Statement

Of all three loop examples in this script, the `For` *loop is the simplest and it is probably the best loop to use for this case. Choosing the correct loop form for a given script scenario is an acquired skill, but there are several rules that will help you choose.*

- Use a `For Each` loop only if you are iterating an array and wish to access, but not change, the values in the array. Otherwise, use one of the other loop statements.
- Use a `For` loop if you are iterating through a fixed sequence of values or array indices. Try to avoid using too many `Exit For` statements—using several of these in a `For` loop is typically an indication that you should be using a `Do` loop.
- Use a `Do` loop in all other cases. Use the pre-test loops (`Do While` and `Do Until`) unless you are certain that you want the loop body to always execute once under *all* circumstances. In this case, use the post-test loops.

Statement Selection

The following `If` statement illustrates a common programming scenario. The statement is checking the value of a command line argument (in `Wscript.Arguments(0)`) against a number of possible values.

```
If Wscript.Arguments(0) = "-d" Then
    Wscript.Echo "debug enabled"
ElseIf Wscript.Arguments(0) = "-?" Or Wscript.Arguments(0) = "-help" Then
    Wscript.Echo "help enabled"
ElseIf Wscript.Arguments(0) = "-v" Then
    Wscript.Echo "verify enabled"
Else
    Wscript.Echo "unknown argument:", Wscript.Arguments(0)
End If
```

Each `If` or `ElseIf` clause checks the `Wscript.Arguments(0)` value against a particular string. If the value matches, a `Wscript.Echo` statement executes. If none of the values match, an error message is displayed instead. Notice that, because of the syntax of the `If` statement, only one of the `Wscript.Echo` statements will execute.

This form of `If` statement is so common that VBScript includes a special statement just for this special case. The statement is called the `Select Case` statement. Its syntax is:

```
Select Case testexpression
    Case expression [,...]
        statements
        .
        .
    Case expression [,...]
        statements
        .
        .
    [...repeat Case as needed]
    [Case Else
        statements
        .
        .
    ]
End Select
```

The entire `Select Case` statement begins with a `Select Case` clause and ends with an `End Select` keyword. Within these clauses are one or more `Case` clauses. Each `Case` clause consists of one or more *expressions* (separated by commas) and a series of *statements*.

The `Select Case` statement operates as follows:

1. The *testexpression* is evaluated to yield a test value.
2. Each *expression* in each `Case` clause is evaluated and its value is compared to the value of the *testexpression*. If the values are not equal,

comparison continues with the next *expression*, either in the current `Case` clause or in the next `Case` clause.

3. When a match is found, the *statements* following the `Case` clause for the matching *expression* are executed, and execution of the entire `Select Case` statement then ends.

In other words, the `Select Case` statement looks for a match between the value of the *testexpression* and the value of one of the *expressions* in the `Case` clauses. If a match is found, the *statements* following the `Case` clause execute.

There are several points to note about the `Select Case` statement:

- The *testexpression* is only evaluated once. This is slightly different to the multiple `If` statement approach, which evaluates the *testexpression* multiple times. This might be important if the expression calls user defined functions (described in Chapter 5).
- Only one set of *statements* (at most) is executed. After a match is found and the *statements* execute, execution of the `Select Case` statement is complete and no further *statements* execute, *even if additional matches could occur on subsequent* `Case` *clauses.*
- The set of statements to execute starts at the statement following the matching `Case` clause and ends at the beginning of the next `Case` clause or the `End Select` clause.
- The `Case Else` clause can be used to execute a default set of statements if none of the *expressions* yield a match. If present, the `Case Else` clause must be the last `Case` clause in the `Select Case` statement.
- If a `Case Else` clause is *not* present and none of the *expressions* match the *testexpression*, none of the *statements* in the `Select Case` statement execute.

To illustrate `Select Case`, here is the previous `If` statement re-written as a `Select Case` statement:

```
Select Case Wscript.Arguments(0)
    Case "-d"
        Wscript.Echo "debug enabled"
    Case "-?", "-help"
        Wscript.Echo "help enabled"
    Case "-v"
        Wscript.Echo "verify enabled"
    Case Else
        Wscript.Echo "unknown argument:", sArg
End Select
```

Rewriting this example as a `Select Case` statement increases the readability of the statement considerably; it also makes adding additional test values much easier. In addition, the repeated use of `Wscript.Arguments(0)` is eliminated, making the statement less cluttered. It is also easier to modify, because the *`testexpression`* appears in only one place, rather than scattered throughout the `If` statement.

Run-Time Script Evaluation

VBScript is an *interpreted* language. This means that the script code is decoded "on the fly" as control flow passes through the script. (Actually, the engine performs some internal preprocessing, but this is transparent to the user.) In addition to this normal script interpreting, VBScript exposes the interpreter functionality for use by scripts. The interpreter can be accessed in one of three ways:

- Using the `Execute` statement.
- Using the `ExecuteGlobal` statement.
- Using the `Eval` function.

The *Execute* and *ExecuteGlobal* Statements

The `Execute` and `ExecuteGlobal` statements have the following syntax:

```
Execute expression
ExecuteGlobal expression
```

Here, *`expression`* can be any string expression that forms a syntactically valid VBScript statement. `Execute` and `ExecuteGlobal` differ depending on the context in which the expression is executed. `Execute` runs the expression in the current context, whereas `ExecuteGlobal` runs the expression in the global context. This is only significant if the statement is inside a function or procedure. For more information on this difference, refer to Chapter 5.

When the `Execute` or `ExecuteGlobal` statement is executed, VBScript executes whatever statement is contained within the *expression*. For example:

```
a = 10
Execute "a = a + 10"
Wscript.Echo "a=", a
```

In the preceding example, the string expression `"a = a + 10"` is executed by the `Execute` statement. As expected, this results in the variable `a` having the value 20, which is displayed in the following `Wscript.Echo` statement.

At first reading, this might seem pointless. After all, the preceding example could easily be rewritten as follows:

```
a = 10
a = a + 10
Wscript.Echo "a=", a
```

This will yield the same result as the first example. However, there is a subtle but important difference between these two examples. In the first example, the assignment statement is expressed as *string data*, whereas in the second example, the assignment statement is expressed as regular script code. Script code can only come from one place—the script file itself. However, string data can come from many sources, including text files, database fields, input devices (such as keyboards), or the Internet.

What this means is that the `Execute` statement (and the other evaluation statements previously mentioned) can execute code that is known *only* when the script is executed, and this code can vary from execution to execution. In other words, it is possible to use VBScript as an engine that executes script code obtained from any convenient source when the script is run.

The *Eval* Function

The `Eval` function takes a single string expression as an argument and evaluates the text of the string as a VBScript expression. The result of this expression is then returned by the `Eval` function. For example:

```
a = Eval("12 + 5")
```

This statement assigns the integer value 17 to the variable `a`.

Notice the difference between `Execute` and `Eval`. `Execute` is a *statement*, and it evaluates the string expression as a statement. `Eval` is a *function*, and it evaluates the string expression as an expression. This means that the following are *not* valid:

```
Execute "a + 10"              ' Cannot execute an expression
a = Eval("Dim c")             ' Cannot evaluate a statement
```

In the first example, the value `"a + 10"` is an expression, and it is not valid for the `Execute` statement. In the second example, the value `"Dim c"` is a statement, and it is not valid for the `Eval` function.

When the string `a=b` is executed by an `Execute` statement, the `=` sign is interpreted as an assignment statement, and so the value of `b` is assigned to `a`. When the same string is executed by the `Eval` function, the `=` sign is interpreted as the comparison equality operator, and the `Eval` function returns `True` or `False` depending upon the values in the variables `a` and `b`.

As an example use of `Eval`, consider a database of employee records. Each record contains information for an employee, including a salary. Typically, an employee's bonus is computed based upon the salary of the employee using some sort of formula. However, that formula might vary from employee to employee. The problem, then, is how to specify that formula.

One possibility (which is quite common) is to add a new field to the employee's record that contains a code value indicating which of the various formulae is to be used when computing the bonus. This can then be used in a `Select Case` statement to compute the bonus. For example:

```
' Assume that salary=employees salary and bonuscode=code specifying bonus (0, 1, 2
etc.)
Select Case bonuscode
    Case 0                      ' 0 code means no bonus!
        bonus = 0
    Case 1                      ' 1 code means 5% bonus
        bonus = salary * 0.05
    Case 2                      ' 2 code means 10% bonus
        bonus = salary * 0.1
    Case 3                      ' 3 code means fixed $1000 bonus
        bonus = 1000
    Case Else                   ' All other codes mean no bonus
        bonus = 0
End Select
```

This code is quite clean and efficient. However, if a policy change alters the bonus structure the script code must be re-written.

An alternative to this approach is to store the actual VBScript expression that computes the bonus within the employee record in the database instead. The preceding `Select Case` statement can then be replaced as follows:

```
' Assume salary=employees salary and bonuscode=expression used to compute bonus
If bonuscode <> "" Then bonus = Eval(bonuscode) Else bonus = 0
```

This one line replaces the entire `Select Case` statement. The actual bonus that is computed is dependent upon the value in the `bonuscode` variable. For example, if this contains "salary * 0.1," then a 10% bonus is granted; if it contains "1000," then a fixed $1000 bonus is granted; and so forth. New bonus formulae can be added simply by adding the new formulae directly to the database records, without changing the script code.

The *QuickCalc.vbs* Script

The `QuickCalc.vbs` sample script, shown in Listing 2.4, illustrates the use of the `Eval` function. The script evaluates the entire command line as an expression and displays the result. The result is also passed back (using `Wscript.Quit`) as the return value from the script to the command shell.

Listing 2.4 *`QuickCalc.vbs` Script*

```
'//////////////////////////////////////////////////////////////////////////////
' $Workfile: QuickCalc.vbs $ $Revision: 3 $ $Date: 4/18/99 7:18p $
' $Archive: /Scripts/QuickCalc.vbs $
' Copyright (c) 1998 Tim Hill. All Rights Reserved.
'//////////////////////////////////////////////////////////////////////////////

' Evaluate all command line argument as expression and display result
```

```
Option Explicit
Dim sCmdLine, sArg, sResult

' First, assemble the complete command line
sCmdLine = ""
For Each sArg In Wscript.Arguments
    If sCmdLine = "" Then
        sCmdLine = sArg
    Else
        sCmdLine = sCmdLine & " " & sArg
    End If
Next

' Now evaluate the command line
sResult = Eval(sCmdLine)
Wscript.Echo sCmdLine & "=" & sResult
Wscript.Quit(CInt(sResult))

'//////////////////////////////////////////////////////////////////////////////
```

Before the script can evaluate the command line, the command line arguments must be assembled into a single string argument. To do this, the arguments are concatenated together using the `&` string operator. A `For Each` loop is used to add each argument to the end of the variable `sCmdLine`, which will therefore eventually contain the entire command line. In addition, each argument is separated by a single space character. To avoid the first character in the command line being a space, an `If` statement in the `For Each` loop processes the first argument as a special case.

The `QuickCalc.vbs` script is simple, and yet it provides full access to the VBScript expression engine. Try experimenting with different command arguments and expressions. Use double quotes if the argument contains any of <, >, &, ^ or |, because these are special command-line characters. Here is a sample `QuickCalc.vbs` session:

```
C:\>quickcalc 1+2
1+2=3

C:\>quickcalc 2.3 * 18.4 -3
2.3 * 18.4 - 3=39.32

C:\>quickcalc 12/5
12/5=2.4
```

Summary

VBScript scripts are text files stored in `.VBS` files that consist of *statements*. Multiple statements on a single line are separated by colon characters, and statements can be continued onto multiple lines be ending a line with an underscore character. Comments are delimited by a single quote character, and they continue to the end of the current line.

The `Dim` statement is used to declare variables, which can store numbers and strings. The `Option Explicit` statement is used to force explicit declaration of all variables, which is strongly recommended.

An expression is a calculation that yields a numeric or string result. Expressions are composed of values in the form of numbers, strings, variables, functions, and operators that combine the values to form the final result. One common use of expressions is the assignment statement, which assigns the result of the expression to a variable.

An array is a variable that can store multiple values simultaneously. Each individual value, called an element, is accessed by specifying a numeric index. In VBScript, the index of the first element of the array is always 0.

The `If` and `Select Case` statements execute statements conditionally, depending upon the results of a test expression. The various loop statements allow a set of statements to be executed repeatedly.

The `Execute` and `ExecuteGlobal` statements provide run-time execution of arbitrary VBScript statements, and the `Eval` function provides run-time evaluation of arbitrary VBScript expressions.

3

VBScript Data Storage

The previous chapter provided most of the essential elements of VBScript. This chapter drills down into some of the details of data storage and manipulation available in VBScript, such as constants and additional array features.

Note

As with all the sample scripts in this book, the scripts in this chapter should be run using the CSCRIPT host unless otherwise noted. The examples shown assume that CSCRIPT is the default WSH host. See Chapter 1, "Introducing WSH," for information on selecting the default WSH host. ◆

VBScript Data Types

So far in this book, the data manipulated by scripts have been characterized as either *numeric* or *string*. However, VBScript supports a number of additional data types, as well as several different flavors of numeric data. Table 3.1 shows the various data types.

Table 3.1 *VBScript Data Types*

Type	Meaning
Boolean	Logical value, either `True` (0) or `False` (-1)
Byte	Unsigned integer in the range 0 to 255
Integer	Signed integer in the range -32,768 to 32,767
Long	Signed integer in the range -2,147,483,648 to 2,147,483,647
Single	Single precision floating-point number in the range -3.402823E38 to -1.401298E-45 for negative values and 1.401298E-45 to 3.402823E38 for positive values

continues ▸

Type	Meaning
Double	Double precision floating-point number in the range -1.79769313486232E308 to -4.94065645841247E-324 for negative values and 4.94065645841247E-324 to 1.79769313486232E308 for positive values
Currency	Fixed-point numbers designed for exact financial computations in the range -922,337,203,685,477.5808 to 922,337,203,685,477.5807
Date/ Time	A value representing a date and time between January 1, 100 to December 31, 9999
String	A variable length sequence of text characters up to 2 billion characters long
Object	An object reference (described in Part II, "Objects and Classes")
Error	An error code or number

Boolean Data

Boolean data can be one of two values: `True` or `False`. As such, boolean data represents logical values (on/off, yes/no, and the like). The boolean constants `True` and `False` can be entered directly into VBScript scripts.

VBScript supports a variety of operators that work with boolean data (see Table 2.3 in Chapter 2, "VBScript Language Essentials"). For example, the `And` operator takes two boolean values and returns `True` only if both the values are `True`. In addition, all the comparison operators (such as `<=`) return a boolean result.

Boolean data is frequently used implicitly within conditional statements and loops. For example:

```
If x = 100 Then Wscript.Echo "x is 100"
```

In this example, the expression `x = 100` uses the comparison operator to compare the variable `x` to 100. The result of this comparison is either `True` or `False`. The `If` statement executes the `Wscript.Echo` statement if the expression evaluates to `True`.

For loops like `Do While`, the loop executes only while the test expression evaluates to `True`. For example:

```
Do While x < 100 And sArg <> "end"
    Wscript.Echo "Arg=", sArg
Loop
```

This loop executes only while the variable `x` is less than 100 *and* the variable `sArg` does not contain the text "end."

In VBScript, the value True is numerically equivalent to -1, and False is equivalent to 0. However, VBScript treats any non-zero numeric value as meaning True. This means that numeric data can be used anywhere that boolean data is expected by VBScript. For example:

```
x = 10
If x Then Wscript.Echo "x is true"
```

Here, the variable x contains the value 10. The If statement evaluates this to mean True because the value is non-zero, and so the Wscript.Echo statement executes. If x had instead been zero, the statement would not execute.

Although VBScript treats non-zero numeric data as equivalent to True, the actual value of True is -1. For example:

```
x = 10
If x Then Wscript.Echo "This will be displayed"
If x = True Then Wscript.Echo "This will not"
```

In this example, the first Wscript.Echo statement executes, as before. However, the second Wscript.Echo will *not* execute. This is because the numeric = comparison compares the value of x, which is 10, to the value of True, which is -1. Obviously these are not equal, and so the result is False.

In cases such as these, numeric data can be converted to boolean data using the CBool function, described in the "Conversion Functions" section.

Byte, Integer, and Long Data

Integer data is data that represents discrete quantities, or "whole" numbers (2, 4, -14, and so forth). Integer constants are entered in a script without a decimal point or a thousands separator. The following are all valid integer constants:

```
0 1 1000 -56 455 2388383
```

Integer constants can also be entered in hexadecimal (base 16) or octal (base 8) notation. To enter a hexadecimal number, precede the number with &h or &H. To enter an octal number, precede the number with &o or &O (the letter O, not zero). For example, the following constants are all equal to 1000 decimal:

```
1000 &H3E8 &o1750
```

VBScript supports three types of integer data:

Byte Bytes are unsigned integer values that range from 0 to 255, inclusive. A byte corresponds to an 8-bit unsigned binary number.

Integer Integers are signed integer values that range from -32768 to 32767. An integer corresponds to a 16-bit signed binary number.

Long Longs are signed integer values that range from -2147483648 to 2147483647. A long corresponds to a 32-bit signed binary number.

Integers are the most common data type used in VBScript scripts. All arithmetic using integer data is exact—no rounding errors occur as long as computations do not cause values to overflow the range of a Long value.

The boolean operators, such as `And`, `Or`, and `Xor`, have a special function when applied to integer data. They process the integer data as a set of discrete binary bits, and then they apply the boolean operation to each bit in the data independently. This is described in the "Logical Operators" section in Chapter 2.

Non-Integral Numeric Data

VBScript supports several flavors of non-integral numeric data. The single and double data types, also known as *floating-point* numbers, provide an approximation of real numbers. Single values are stored as 32-bit values, and double values are stored as 64-bit values. Double values provide higher precision than single values, and they provide a greater magnitude range. Internally, VBScript stores all non-integral data as double. All arithmetic using the single or double types is limited in accuracy by the precision of the data type, and hence rounding errors can occur.

Currency data is a special form of numeric data designed primarily for computations involving monetary amounts. The currency format provides exact arithmetic with 4 decimal places, which allows financial computations to be made exactly without loss of precision.

Floating-point and currency constants should be entered with a decimal point and (for floating-point numbers) an optional exponent using the familiar "E" notation to represent the exponent (power of ten). The following are all valid floating-point constants or currency constants:

```
0.5 .0001 1.45E7 14.2E-6 1.0
```

Date and Time Data

Date and time information represents dates and times starting at January 1, 100 C.E. and extending to December 31, 9999 C.E.

In VBScript scripts, enter the date and/or time information between # characters. A single date/time constant represents a time, a date, or both a time and a date. The following are valid date/time constants:

```
#12/01/1998#
#11:45 pm#
#09/05/1999 1:04am#
#3 April 1999#
```

VBScript accepts a variety of date and time representations. However, the date locale for date literals is fixed as US-English ("mm/dd/yy") regardless of the current locale settings in Windows Control Panel.

String Data

As described in Chapter 2, strings are character text sequences. Strings can be of any desired length up to a maximum of 2 billion characters. A string can also be empty, or zero characters long (represented by a pair of double quotes with nothing between them).

Enclose all string constants in double quotation marks. The double quotes that enclose a string are *not* part of the string themselves. To include a double quote *within* a string constant, place *two* double quote marks one after the other within the string. For example:

```
"Here, ""this"" is in double quotes"
```

VBScript is able to automatically convert string data to numeric data, and vice versa, depending upon the context in which the data is used. For example:

```
Wscript.Echo 50 + 50
Wscript.Echo 50 + "50"
```

In the second example, the string constant 50 is converted to a numeric value because it is being used with addition, which only makes sense for numbers, not strings.

VBScript can also convert all non-string data types to strings if necessary. This allows non-string data to be used with string functions. String functions are described in Chapter 4, "Built-In Functions."

Object Data

The object data type is used to represent objects. Objects and the object data type are described in Part II of this book.

VBScript Variables

Chapter 2 introduced variables and the `Dim` statement that can be used to declare a variable. This section describes some additional properties of variables.

Although a variable can store many different types of data, variables themselves all have the same data type, which is known as *variant*. Variants are able to store any of the data types previously described in *VBScript Data Types*. This means that *any* variable in a script can hold data of *any* type. In fact, the same variable can be used to store data of different types at different times in the same script. For example, a variable might initially be assigned an integer value, later assigned a text string, and finally assigned a date. The section "Data Type Functions" describes a number of functions that can be used to determine the type of the data that is stored in a variable.

Normally, VBScript can automatically convert between data types as necessary. For example, if during a computation an integer value overflows it is automatically converted to a long. In addition, VBScript provides a variety of functions to convert between data of different types. These functions are described in "Conversion Functions."

Variable Name Restrictions

Variable names must follow these naming rules:

- The name must not be the same as any of the built-in keywords used in VBScript, such as `For`, `Loop`, `To`, and so forth.
- The name can consist of letters, digits, and underscore characters only. The name cannot contain spaces.
- The name must begin with a letter, not a digit or an underscore.
- The name can be up to 255 characters long.
- The name must not conflict with other constant or variable names within the scope in which it is declared. (Scoping rules are discussed in Chapter 5, "User Defined Procedures.")
- The name is *not* case-sensitive: `FRED`, `Fred`, and `fred` and all considered identical by VBScript.

These restrictions apply to simple variables and array names. The following are all valid variable names:

```
x
e400
averylongvariablename
aMixedCaseName
Underscores_Are_Allowed_In_Names
```

Program Guide

Naming Variables

It is generally considered good practice to assign suggestive names to variables, to assist in documenting the operation of a script. In fact, just thinking about what to name a variable can often assist you in understanding the operation of a script. ◆

Variable Naming Conventions

As previously explained, any VBScript variable can contain data of any type. However, it is considered good programming practice to restrict the type of data in a variable to a specific type unless there is a particular need for the data type to alter during script execution. It is also useful to adopt a naming convention so that the intended data type of the variable is encoded within the variable name.

There are many different naming conventions in use. The convention suggested here, and used throughout this book, is based upon the so-called Hungarian notation used by C programmers. This is, however, only a convention and you are free to use any naming convention that suits your taste.

The Hungarian notation uses a short lower case prefix to the variable name to indicate the data type of the variable. For example, the prefix `s` indicates string data, so the variable `sArg` indicates a variable used to store string data. Table 3.2 shows suggested prefixes to use with variables.

Table 3.2 *Recommended Variable Name Prefixes*

Prefix	Meaning
`b`	Boolean (either `True` or `False`)
`c`	Constant (not a variable)
`d`	Date (a date, time or date and time)
`f`	Single or double precision floating-point number
`n`	Long (long signed integer)
`o`	Object (reference to an object, described in Part II)
`s`	String (text data)
`v`	Variant (variable can contain different types at different times)
`g_`	Global scope prefix

The following examples illustrate the use of the recommended variable prefixes:

```
bNetworkDrive            ' True if drive is a network mapped drive
Const cMaxFolders        ' Maximum number of folders (constant)
dLastAccessTime          ' Time of last access to file
fTotalMass               ' Total mass of all parts
nPartCount               ' Count of all parts required
sFolderName              ' Name of destination folder
```

It should be understood that the name prefixes are merely *conventions*. VBScript does not know about or enforce naming conventions and merely views the prefix as additional letters of the variable name. It is perfectly possible to store, for example, a number in a variable called `sFileName`. However, the use of a convention does assist in providing additional documentation about the *intended* use of the variable.

The `v` prefix can be used if a variable really will contain data of different types at different times. However, as previously noted, this is not advisable.

The final prefix in Table 3.2, `g`, is used in addition to the data type prefixes to indicate the *scope* of a variable. Scopes, and the use of these prefixes, are discussed in Chapter 5 and in Part II. Until then, all variables used in sample scripts have *global* scope (that is, they can be used anywhere within the script after they are declared using a `Dim` statement).

Empty and Null Variables

When a variable is created, either implicitly or explicitly, it is initially set to the special `Empty` value. `Empty` variables have the value `0`, `False`, or `""` (the empty string), depending upon the context in which they are used. After a variable is assigned a value, it is no longer considered empty. A variable can be explicitly emptied of its current contents by assigning it the special `Empty` value. For example:

```
a = Empty
```

A variable can also contain the special `Null` value. Unlike `Empty` variables, `Null` variables have no default value. If a `Null` variable is used in an expression, the result of the expression is always `Null`. A variable can be set to `Null` by assigning it the special `Null` value. For example:

```
a = Null
```

`Null` values are sometimes used to indicate that a variable is "off limits" and should not be used in calculations. If the variable is accidentally used, the result is `Null`, and a `Null` result typically generates an error. In contrast, an empty variable will not generate an error if it is used in a calculation. For example:

```
a = Empty
b = Null
c = a + 10
d = b + 10
```

Because the variable `a` is empty, the expression `a + 10` results in 10, due to the fact that the empty value is treated as 0 in expressions. Thus, the variable `c` is assigned the value 10. However, the variable `b` is `Null`, and the result of the expression `b + 10` is also `Null`. Thus, the variable `d` is assigned the value `Null`.

The "Data Type Functions" section describes functions that can distinguish the type of a variable, including if the variable is `Empty` or `Null`.

Symbolic Constants

If a constant value (such as a number or string) is entered directly into a script, it is known as a *literal* constant. In addition to literal constants, VBScript also provides *symbolic* constants. A symbolic constant is a name (sometimes known as a symbol) that is used as an alias for the actual constant value. For example, you could create a symbolic constant called `PI` with a value of 3.1415926, and then use this symbolic constant instead of the actual value of Pi. You can use symbolic constants in a script anywhere that a normal constant can be used.

Symbolic constants are declared using the `Const` statement. The syntax for this statement is:

```
Const name = literal
```

In the `Const` statement, the *name* specifies the name of the symbolic constant being defined. This name must follow the previously given rules. The *literal* is any literal constant. The following are all valid `Const` statements:

```
Const PI = 3.1415926           ' The constant Pi
Const TEN = 10                 ' Probably not necessary
Const MAXIMUM_LINES = 100      ' Maximum number of lines
Const cStartDate = #01/01/1990#
Const cTempFolder = "d:\temp" ' Temporary file folder
```

There are two common conventions for naming symbolic constants. In one convention, shown in the first three examples above, the names are placed in all upper case. In another convention, shown in the last two examples, the names are preceded by a lower case prefix, which is either `c` or `con`. In addition, VBScript has a number of built-in constants which all begin with the prefix `vb`. One good reason for using a naming convention is to easily distinguish symbolic constants from variables when used within scripts. However, these are only conventions, and you are free to use whatever naming system you think best.

As the name implies, a symbolic constant is a *constant*. Once it has been defined by a `Const` statement, its value cannot be changed (for example, by an assignment statement).

Symbolic constants are used extensively in scripts for several reasons.

- They allow you to assign descriptive names to otherwise opaque literal constants.
- They help avoid the errors that can occur when the constant must be entered many times in the same script.
- They provide a single central location where a literal constant can be changed.

For example, it's far better to use the symbolic constant `PI` than 3.1415926, although most people can recognize this universal constant. However, it is even more important if the literal constants are more obscure. For example, the natural logarithm function E has the approximate value 2.71828. Defining a symbolic constant `E` is far better than using the literal constant.

If a constant is used repeatedly throughout a script the chances of mis-typing one of the values increases. Bugs like these can be hard to find because they might only appear as subtle numerical errors. One way to avoid this kind of problem is to use a symbolic constant and enter the value once in the `Const` statement. If the symbolic constant is mis-typed, the VBScript engine will flag the mis-typed value before the script executes (assuming the `Option Explicit` statement is used).

Built-In Symbolic Constants

In addition to symbolic constants defined using the `Const` statement, VBScript has a number of symbolic constants pre-defined for use in scripts. Most of these constants are used with specific VBScript functions, and they are described with these functions in Chapter 4. Table 3.3 shows the general-purpose constants defined by VBScript. These can be used anywhere within a script file as necessary.

Table 3.3 General Purpose Predefined Constants

Name	Value	Meaning
`vbBlack`	`&h000000`	RGB value for black
`vbRed`	`&h0000FF`	RGB value for red
`vbGreen`	`&h00FF00`	RGB value for green
`vbYellow`	`&h00FFFF`	RGB value for yellow
`vbBlue`	`&hFF0000`	RGB value for blue
`vbMagenta`	`&hFF00FF`	RGB value for magenta
`vbCyan`	`&hFFFF00`	RGB value for cyan
`vbWhite`	`&hFFFFFF`	RGB value for white
`vbCr`	`Chr(13)`	ANSI carriage-return string
`vbCrLf`	`Chr(13) & Chr(10)`	ANSI carriage-return and line-feed string
`vbFormFeed`	`Chr(12)`	ANSI form-feed string
`vbLf`	`Chr(10)`	ANSI line-feed string
`vbNewLine`	`Chr(13) & Chr(10)` *or* `Chr(10)`	ANSI new line. Either carriage-return and line-feed, or just line-feed (depending upon platform)
`vbNullString`	`0`	Special null string value (not the same as the empty string `""`)
`vbNullChar`	`Chr(0)`	ANSI null string
`vbTab`	`Chr(9)`	ANSI tab string
`vbVerticalTab`	`Chr(11)`	ANSI vertical tab string

The various RGB color constants are not frequently used in VBScript programs. They are present mainly for compatibility with other versions of Visual Basic. The various predefined strings (such as `vbCr`) define ANSI control sequences. For example, insert `vbNewLine` in a string to break the text in the string into two lines (when displayed). Each ANSI string is defined in terms of its ANSI control character codes using the `Chr` function, which is described in Chapter 4.

Data Type Functions

In VBScript, any variable can contain data of any type. This can mean that in some circumstances the type of data in a variable is not known when the script is written, but only when the script is run. In these cases, VBScript has a set of functions that allow a script to discover the type of data in a variable at run time. Table 3.4 lists these functions.

Table 3.4 Data Type Functions

Function	Description
`IsArray(`*var*`)`	Returns `True` if variable is an array or contains an array.
`IsDate(`*expr*`)`	Returns `True` if variable or expression is a valid date or time.
`IsEmpty(`*expr*`)`	Returns `True` if variable or expression is empty.
`IsNull(`*expr*`)`	Returns `True` if variable or expression is Null.
`IsNumeric(`*expr*`)`	Returns `True` if variable or expression is numeric.
`IsObject(`*var*`)`	Returns `True` if variable is a reference to an object (see Part II).
`TypeName(`*expr*`)`	Returns a string describing the type of a variable or expression.
`VarType(`*expr*`)`	Returns a numeric code describing the type of a variable or expression.

The `Is`*`Xxx`* functions in Table 3.3 all return a boolean value. They return `True` if the variable or expression supplied as an argument matches the specified data type. For example, the `IsDate` function returns true if the expression is a valid date or time, as follows:

```
d = #12/1/1999#
If IsDate(d)Then Wscript.Echo "Date is valid"
```

The IsEmpty and IsNull functions only return True if the expression or variable evaluate to the special Empty or Null values described in the "Empty and Null Variables" section. For example:

```
x = Empty
y = Null
If IsEmpty(x) Then Wscript.Echo "var x is empty"
If IsEmpty(x + 10) Then Wscript.Echo "This cannot happen"
If IsNull(y + 10) Then Wscript.Echo "This can happen"
```

The second IsEmpty test in the preceding example cannot evaluate to True. This is because, even though x is empty, the expression x + 10 is *not* empty—it's simply the value 10. However, the IsNull test *will* be True, since the Null value in y propagates through the expression.

The IsArray function returns True if the specified variable is an array or contains an array (arrays in variables are explained in the "Advanced Arrays" section that follows). Specify the name of the array without an element index. For example:

```
Dim x, a(10)
If IsArray(x) Then Wscript.Echo "this will not display"
Is IsArray(a) Then Wscript.Echo "but this will"
```

Finally, the IsNumeric function returns True if the expression is a valid numeric data type, such as integer or currency. Note also that there is *no* IsString function. Fortunately, this can be simulated using the VarType function described next.

Decoding Data Types

The Is*Xxx* functions previously described provide a way to confirm the type of data in a variable or expression. The TypeName and VarType functions provide actual type information. The TypeName function provides a text description of the data type, whereas the VarType function provides a numeric code indicating the type.

For example:

```
x = #12/23/1992#
Wscript.Echo TypeName(x)
```

When executed, the Wscript.Echo statement displays the text "Date." The TypeName function is valid with any variable type or expression.

The VarType function returns a numeric code indicating the type of the variable passed as an argument. Table 3.5 shows a list of these codes and their meanings. The codes also have predefined symbolic constants, also shown in the table.

Table 3.5 VarType Function Predefined Constants

Name	Value	Meaning
`vbEmpty`	0	Empty variable or expression
`vbNull`	1	Null variable or expression
`vbInteger`	2	Integer (16-bit) variable or expression
`vbLong`	3	Long (32-bit) variable or expression
`vbSingle`	4	Single precision variable or expression
`vbDouble`	5	Double precision variable or expression
`vbCurrency`	6	Currency variable or expression
`vbDate`	7	Date or time variable or expression
`vbString`	8	String variable or expression
`vbObject`	9	Object reference
`vbError`	10	Error code
`vbBoolean`	11	Boolean variable or expression
`vbVariant`	12	Variant variable or expression (used with arrays)
`vbByte`	17	Byte (8-bit) variable or expression
`vbArray`	8192	Array variable

The special `vbArray` value is returned by the `VarType` function if the variable is an array. However, the `VarType` function also indicates the type of each element in the array by *adding* the type of the element to the value 8192 (the value of `vbArray`). In other versions of Visual Basic, array elements can have many different types, but in VBScript, all array elements are of type *variant*, so for arrays the return values is always `vbArray + vbVariant`, or 8204.

In binary notation, the value 8192 has a single bit set. Therefore, the following two expressions are identical:

```
IsArray(a)
(VarType(a) And vbArray) <> False
```

The first expression obviously returns `True` if the variable `a` is an array. The second example also does this. As explained in the "Expressions and Assignment" section in Chapter 2, the `And` operator performs a bit-wise logical `And` operation when used with numeric values. In this case, the result of the expression `VarType(a) And vbArray` is either 0 or 8192. By then *comparing* this result to `False`, the value 0 (which is equal to `False`) converts to the value `False`, and the value 8192 (which is not equal to `False`) converts to `True`.

The *VarType1.vbs* Script

The `VarType1.vbs` sample script, shown in Listing 3.1, illustrates the use of the `TypeName` and `VarType` functions.

Listing 3.1 *`VarType1.vbs` Script*

```
'//////////////////////////////////////////////////////////////////////////////
' $Workfile: VarType1.vbs $ $Revision: 1 $ $Date: 4/28/99 8:40p $
' $Archive: /Scripts/VarType1.vbs $
' Copyright (c)1998 Tim Hill. All Rights Reserved.
'//////////////////////////////////////////////////////////////////////////////

' Display the types of variables WSH Sample

Option Explicit

' Declare some variables and assign various values and types
Dim A(10), B(2), x
A(0) = Empty                ' Empty value
A(1) = Null                 ' Null value
A(2) = 10                   ' An integer
A(3) = 14.5                 ' Floating point value
A(4) = #14/3/1952#          ' A date
A(5) = "Hi there"           ' A string
A(6) = False                ' A boolean
A(7) = B                    ' An array

' Now display the variables types
For x = 0 To UBound(A)
    Wscript.Echo "Type of A(" & x & ") is " & TypeName(A(x)) _
            & " (" & VarType(A(x)) & ")"
Next

    '//////////////////////////////////////////////////////////////////////////////
```

The `VarType1.vbs` script first assigns various different data type values to the elements of the array `A`, and then displays, for each element, the name of the type (from `TypeName`) and the numeric code for the type (from `VarType`).

Note that uninitialized entries in the array (in this case, elements 8 through 10) are all shown as having the `Empty` type when this script executes. Also, element 7 of the array receives an array as its value. Storing arrays in array elements is covered in "Advanced Arrays."

Conversion Functions

The functions described in the previous section provide a way to determine the type of data in a variable or expression. In contrast, Conversion Functions explicitly convert data from one type to another. Table 3.6 lists all the conversion functions.

Table 3.6 Conversion Functions

Function	Description
`CBool(expr)`	Converts *expr* to boolean type
`CByte(expr)`	Converts *expr* to byte (8-bit integer) type
`CCur(expr)`	Converts *expr* to currency type
`CDate(expr)`	Converts *expr* to date or time type
`CDbl(expr)`	Converts *expr* to double precision floating-point type
`CInt(expr)`	Converts *expr* to integer (16-bit) type
`CLng(expr)`	Converts *expr* to long (32-bit) type
`CSng(expr)`	Converts *expr* to single precision floating-point type
`CStr(expr)`	Converts *expr* to string type
`Hex(expr)`	Converts *expr* to hexadecimal string
`Oct(expr)`	Converts *expr* to octal string

All the conversion functions are locale-aware. Therefore, these functions, such as `CInt`, can convert string data containing locale specific data formats. For example:

```
a = CInt("10,000")
b = CInt("10.000")
```

In the U.S., the first expression yields the integer 10,000, whereas the second yields the integer 10. In many parts of Europe, where the comma is used as the decimal separator, the results of these two expressions are reversed.

The conversion functions can also be used to coerce the type of an expression where VBScript would otherwise use an inappropriate type. For example:

```
a = "$100" : b = "$200"
Wscript.Echo a + b, CCur(a) + b, CStr(CCur(a) + 10)
```

When executed, this example yields the following results:

```
$100$200 300 $110
```

Normally, VBScript can convert a string, such as `"100"`, into a numeric value. However, VBScript is not automatically aware of locale-specific currency information, and so cannot convert the string `"$100"` into a currency value. Instead, VBScript treats the value as a 4 character string, and the result of the expression `a + b` is simply the concatenation of the two string values, or `$100$200`. However, the `CCur` function *is* locale aware and recognizes the string as a valid currency value. Therefore the result of the expression `CCur(a) + b` is 300. It is not necessary to convert both the `a` and the `b` variables—as soon as the data type of the expression is coerced to currency, any additional conversions are automatic. This behavior is summarized in Table 3.7.

Table 3.7 String to Number Conversions

Expression	Result (Type)
`100 + 200`	`300 (numeric)`
`"100" + "200"`	`300 (numeric)`
`CStr("100" + "200")`	`"300" (string)`
`"$100" + "$200"`	`"$100$200" (string)`
`CCur("$100") + CCur("$200")`	`$300 (currency)`
`CStr(CCur("$100") + 200)`	`"$300" (string)`

The final expression in the last example also illustrates using the `CStr` function to provide data type aware conversions to string form. In the second expression, the `CCur(a) + b` expression yields a currency result, but this is displayed as a simple numeric value. The `CStr` function is data type aware and can convert the currency data type into a locale correct form for display.

Individual Conversion Operations

The results of each individual conversion function depend upon the data values passed to the function. Note that as usual VBScript converts string data to numeric data if necessary (and possible) before passing the data to the conversion function.

- `CBool` Any non-zero numeric value converts to True, whereas zero converts to False. Non-numeric data generates a run-time error.
- `CByte` Numeric data in the range 0 to 255 converts to the 8-bit integral byte type. Non-integral values are rounded using the same rules as the `CInt` function. Numeric values outside the range 0 to 255 and non-numeric data generate a run-time error.
- `CCur` Numeric data is converted to the currency type, which allows fixed precision arithmetic to occur without the rounding errors associated with floating-point data types. Non-numeric data generates a run-time error.
- `CDate` String data containing a locale specific date and/or time is converted to a date or time. Numeric data is assumed to be a serial number representing a date and/or time, using the same format as Microsoft Excel. The integer part of the serial number specifies the date

as a day offset, where 1 corresponds to 12/31/1899 and 0 means "no date." The fractional part of the serial number specifies the time since midnight as a proportion of the 24-hour period, so 0.5 represents midday. A fractional part of zero means "no time." Data that is non-numeric or cannot be converted to a time/date string generates a run-time error.

- `CDbl` Numeric data is converted to the double-precision floating-point format. Very large currency values can lose some precision when converted to this data type. Non-numeric data generates a run-time error.
- `CInt` Numeric data in the range -32,768 to 32,767 converts to the 16-bit integral type. Non-integral values are rounded to the nearest integral value. For example, 14.4 rounds to 14, whereas 14.6 rounds to 15. If the fractional part is exactly 0.5, the value is rounded to the nearest *even* integral value. Therefore, 14.5 rounds to 14, whereas 15.5 rounds to 16 (not 15). This rounding method ensures that the average value of a large number of samples remains numerically consistent. Numeric values outside the range -32,768 to 32,767 and non-numeric data generate a run-time error.
- `CLng` Numeric data in the range -2,147,483,648 to 2,147,483,647 converts to the 32-bit integral type. Non-integral values are rounded using the same rules as the `CInt` function. Numeric values outside the -2,147,483,648 to 2,147,483,647 and non-numeric data generate a run-time error
- `CSng` Numeric data is converted to the single-precision floating-point format. Double precision and currency values might experience some loss of precision. Double precision values with exponents outside the range for single precision floating point number, and non-numeric data generate a run-time error.
- `CStr` Converts the data to a string (character) representation. The conversion is locale aware. Therefore, the correct currency symbol (if appropriate) and decimal point characters are used. This function is valid for all data types (even object types described in Part II) and never generates a run-time error.
- `Hex` Converts numeric data to a string containing the hexadecimal (base 16) representation of the integral value of the data. Non-numeric data generates a run-time error.
- `Oct` Same as Hex, except generates an octal (base 8) representation. For example, Oct(10) generates the string "12." Non-numeric data generates a run-time error.

Advanced Arrays

Chapter 2 introduced arrays as variables that can hold multiple data values simultaneously. This section describes additional array facilities in VBScript.

As explained in Chapter 2, arrays are declared using the `Dim` statement and specifying the upper bound of the array. For example:

```
Dim a(100)
```

The `UBound` function returns the upper bound of the array. For example:

```
x = UBound(a)
```

This sets the variable `x` to 100 (assuming the previous declaration of the array `a`). VBScript also provides the `LBound` function, which returns the *lower* bound of the array. In VBScript, all arrays have a lower bound of 0, and so `LBound` always returns zero. However, other versions of Visual Basic support different lower bound values. For this reason, you should use `LBound` to ensure that script code is portable to other implementations of Visual Basic. For example:

```
Dim a(10)
For x = LBound(a) To UBound(a)
    Wscript.Echo a(x)
Next
```

This example displays the entire contents of the array, regardless of the upper and lower bounds of the array.

Finally, the number of elements in the array can be computed from the difference between `UBound` and `LBound` and adding 1. For example:

```
Dim a(25)
Wscript.Echo "a has", UBound(a) - LBound(a) + 1, "elements"
```

Erasing Arrays

The `Erase` statement erases the contents of an array. Its syntax is:

```
Erase array-name
```

Specify the array name only—do not include an element index.

The `Erase` statement sets each element in the array to `Empty`. If the array element contained an object, VBScript first sets the element to `Nothing` to release the object reference. See Part II for more information on objects.

Dynamic Arrays

After an array is declared with the `Dim` statement, its upper bound (that is, the number of elements in the array) is fixed for the duration of the script. Such an array is called a *static array*. It is also possible to declare *dynamic* arrays. A dynamic array can be resized during script execution, allowing the number of elements to be increased (or decreased) as necessary.

A dynamic array is initially declared using either a `Dim` statement or a `ReDim` statement. The initial declaration does *not* specify the upper bound of the array. Instead, use a pair of parentheses with nothing between them. For example:

```
Dim d()
ReDim d()
```

To use the array, specify an upper bound using the `ReDim` statement. The syntax of the `ReDim` statement is:

```
ReDim [Preserve] var(UBound) [,...]
```

var is the name of the array to resize (which must have previously been declared using `Dim` or `ReDim`), and *UBound* is the new upper bound for the array. Unlike the `Dim` statement, the `ReDim` statement accepts any expression for *UBound*. (The `Dim` statement only accepts literal or symbolic constants for *UBound*.) For example:

```
Dim d()                     ' Declare dynamic array "d"
ReDim d(100)                ' Resize to 101 elements, don't preserve contents
ReDim Preserve d(200)       ' Resize to 201 elements, preserve contents
```

Multiple dynamic arrays can be resized using a single `ReDim` statement. If a dynamic array is enlarged when it is resized, additional elements are created and assigned the special `Empty` value. If a dynamic array is reduced in size, elements beyond the new upper bound are discarded, and the data they contained is lost.

If the `Preserve` keyword is not used in the `ReDim` statement, the content of the array is lost and *all* elements are assigned the special `Empty` value. If the `Preserve` keyword is used, elements that exist both before and after the resize operation retain their values. However, using `Preserve` can slow script execution.

Program Guide

Why Use Dynamic Arrays?

Dynamic arrays are very important in VBScript, because they solve a real problem with static arrays—the fixed size of the array. There are many occasions when the amount of data that a script needs to process is not known before script execution. For example, a script might wish to sort all the files in a folder by date. If static arrays are used, it is necessary to decide upon a fixed maximum number of files the script can sort, which could cause the script to fail if a folder contains a large number of files. Dynamic arrays solve this problem by allowing the array to be sized to fit the size of the data set.

The `UBound` function is particularly useful with dynamic arrays because the size of dynamic arrays is typically not known until the script executes. However, using the `UBound` or `LBound` functions on a dynamic array that has not yet been allocated elements (using `ReDim`) causes a run-time error.

Using `UBound` is also a convenient way to incrementally increase the size of a dynamic array. For example:

```
ReDim Preserve t(UBound(t) + 100)
```

This `ReDim` statement first computes the value `UBound(t) + 100` and then resizes the dynamic array `t` to this size. The effect of this statement is to increase the size of the dynamic array `t` by 100 elements.

The `Erase` statement can also be used with dynamic arrays. If used with a dynamic array, the `Erase` statement *deletes* the entire array and recovers the storage allocated for the array by `ReDim`. As a result, the dynamic array cannot be accessed until a new `ReDim` statement allocates some elements for the array. This differs from the operation of `Erase` for static arrays, where only the contents of individual elements are erased.

Growing Dynamic Arrays Efficiently

There are many occasions when a dynamic array is used in a script to store a data set whose size is unknown until run-time. Sometimes the required size of the array can be determined before the data set is loaded. For example, when loading file names from a folder, it is possible to determine the number of files in the folder, to use a `ReDim` statement to correctly size the array, and then to load the file names into the dynamic array (presumably using a loop of some kind). In general terms, the algorithm is:

- Determine the size of the data set (number of elements required).
- Use `ReDim` to size a dynamic array to this size.
- Copy the data set into the array elements.

For example:

```
Dim a(100)                      ' Source of data set
Dim d(), size                   ' Destination dynamic array
size = UBound(a)                ' Step 1: Determine required size
ReDim d(size)                   ' Step 2: Set the size of the dynamic array
For x = LBound(d)To UBound(d)
    d(x) = a(x)                 ' Step 3: Copy the elements
Next
```

This example copies one array, `a`, into a new dynamic array, `d`. Because the array `d` is sized dynamically from the array `a`, the script code works regardless of the size of the array `a`. In this example, the expression `UBound(a)` determines the size of the dynamic array.

However, there are many times when a script has to load a data set where the size of the set cannot be determined until the set is loaded. For example, to load a text file into an array one line at a time involves reading the text file until the end of file is reached. It is not possible until *after* the data is loaded to determine how much space to allocate for the dynamic array. In this case, it is necessary to resize the dynamic array each time a new data item is loaded into the array. The algorithm is:

1. Set the current size of the array to zero elements.
2. Loop through the following steps (3 to 5) for each data item.
3. Resize the dynamic array to the current size.
4. Add the data item to the array.
5. Increment the array size.

For example:

```
Dim a(100)                      ' Source of data set
Dim d(), size                   ' Destination dynamic array
size = 0                        ' Step 1: Set current size to 0
For Each x In a                 ' Step 2: Loop for each data item
    ReDim Preserve d(size)      ' Step 3: Resize the dynamic array
    d(size) = x                 ' Step 4: Add the data item
    size = size + 1             ' Step 5: Increment the array size
Next
```

There are several things to note about this example:

- The `size` variable contains a count of the items in the array. After the `For` loop exits, `size` is valid *even* if the array was empty.
- The `ReDim` statement occurs *before* the first data assignment. This ensures that at least one element exists before an assignment occurs.
- The `Preserve` keyword is necessary to preserve previous data elements already in the `d` array.

The array index is specified by `size`. If the array contains (for example) four items already, then `size` is (by definiton) 4. Because array indices start at zero, the elements containing these four items are numbered 0 to 3, and so element index 4 (that is, the same value as `size`) is the next free element in the array.

The script code shown in the previous example works, but code such as this should not be used in production scripts. The reason is that it is inefficient. The `Preserve` keyword is necessary to preserve the array contents when the array is enlarged, but this keyword slows down execution of the `ReDim` statement considerably. Because the array is resized for *every* data item read, this might result in thousands of resize operations, slowing script execution to a crawl.

The solution to this is to use a more sophisticated approach. The basic idea is to resize the array less frequently by allocating new elements, not one at a time but in batches of (say) 100. This reduces the number of ReDim operations required by a factor of 100. For example:

```
Dim a(1000)                     ' Source of data set
Dim d(), size, asize            ' Destination dynamic array
size = 0 : asize = 0            ' Set current size and array size to 0
For Each x In a                 ' Loop for each data item
    If size >= asize Then       ' Do we need more dyanmic array elements?
        asize = asize + 100     ' Compute new array size
        ReDim Preserve d(asize)    ' Enlarge the array
    End If
    d(size) = x                 ' Add the data item
    size = size + 1             ' Increment the array size
Next
ReDim Preserve d(size - 1)      ' Trim the array to exact size
```

If the new If statement is ignored, this loop simply copies the contents of the array a into the array d, one element at a time. The size variable tracks the element index to copy. However, as before, d is a dynamic array and must be enlarged as new elements arrive. This is the function of the If statement. The new variable, asize, tracks the *allocation* size of the array d. If the required size of the array (indicated by the size variable) reaches the allocation size, more elements are needed. In this case, the asize variable is increased by 100, and the array is enlarged by this amount. This means that the ReDim statement is only executed on 1 out of every 100 loops, which greatly improves the performance of this loop.

For clarity, the preceding example used a variable, asize, to track the current size of the dynamic array. However, it is possible to discard this variable entirely and instead use the UBound function to check the size of the dynamic array directly.

There is one other issue arising from this optimization. After the loop has completed, typically there are array elements allocated in d that are past the end of the actual data stored in the array. This is a direct consequence of allocating elements in blocks of 100. Therefore, after the loop a final ReDim statement trims the array to the exact size of the data set, discarding these excess elements. If this step is not performed, any subsequent script code that uses the UBound function will process too many elements.

Multiple Array Dimensions

The simple arrays described so far have used a single element index. Arrays that use a single element index are sometimes called *vectors*. However, arrays in VBScript can have more than one index. An array with two independent indices is called a *matrix* and is similar in structure to a table or spreadsheet. To declare a matrix, specify two upper bounds, separated by commas, when declaring the array with a `Dim` statement. For example:

```
Dim v(10), m(10,20)
```

This statement declares a vector (single element index) array of 11 elements, and a matrix array of 11 by 21 elements. The matrix `m` thus has a total of 231 individual elements.

Once declared, matrix elements are accessed in a similar manner to vector elements, except that two element indices must be specified. For example:

```
nTotal = m(5,7)
```

It is sometimes useful to imagine a matrix as a table of rows and columns. The two indices then specify a specific cell in the table by indicating the row and column of the table. The first index specifies the row, and the second index specifies the column.

The number of independent indices in an array is called the *dimensionality* of the array. A vector, with one index, is a one-dimensional array. A matrix, with two indices, is a two-dimensional array. VBScript supports arrays of *any* dimension, limited only by available resources (such as memory). For example, the following `Dim` statement declares a three-dimension array:

```
Dim x(5,10,20)
```

In this example, the array `x` contains 1,386 elements (the product of 6, 11, and 21). The number of elements in an array grows rapidly as the dimensionality increases. For example, this array contains 1,771,561 elements:

```
Dim VeryBigArray(10,10,10,10,10,10)
```

Note

Arrays with greater than two dimensions are only rarely used. In fact, even two-dimensional arrays (matrices) are only occasionally used, the most common use being in spreadsheet type programs and graphics applications that store bitmaps as two-dimensional arrays. By far the most common array type is the simple one-dimensional vector. Frequently, using an array of higher dimensionality indicates a problem in the design of the script or the data structures. In addition, arrays beyond three dimensions are difficult to visualize, because they have no counterpart in our everyday three-dimensional world.

Dynamic arrays can also have multiple dimensions. For example:

```
Dim d()
ReDim d(10,12)
ReDim Preserve d(10,15)
ReDim d(10,15,2)
```

As the last example shows, the `ReDim` statement can be used to change the dimensionality of a dynamic array (in this case, from two to three dimensions). However, there are restrictions on when the `Preserve` keyword is allowed with multiple dimensions. Specifically, `Preserve` is allowed *only* if the dimensionality is *not* changed, *and* only the last upper bound is altered in size. The second `ReDim` statement in the preceding code is valid because the dimensionality (two) remains the same, and only the last upper bound is changed (from 12 to 15).

The `UBound` and `LBound` functions can also be used with multiple dimension arrays. Supply the dimension to be returned using an additional argument. For example:

```
Dim a(5,10)
Wscript.Echo UBound(a, 1), UBound(a, 2)
```

Storing Arrays in Variables

As explained in the "VBScript Variables" section, all variables in VBScript have the *variant* data type. This means variables can contain data of any type, *including arrays*. For example, consider the following code:

```
Dim x, a(10)                    ' Declare variable and vector
x = 10                          ' Assign a simple integer value
a(1) = 100                      ' Ditto for an array element
x = a                           ' Assign an array
Wscript.Echo x(1)               ' Will display 100
```

The `Dim` statement in the preceding code declares a simple variable `x` and a static vector array `a`. The first assignment statement assigns an integer value to `x`, and the second assignment assigns an integer value to an element of `a`. The third assignment statement is more interesting. It assigns the *entire array* `a` to the simple variable `x`. This means that `x` then contains an entire array. Because `x` contains an array, it is now legal to access the individual elements of the array using normal element indexing, as shown in the final `Wscript.Echo` statement in the preceding code. This is legal—although the original `Dim` statement declared `x` as a simple variable.

If an array is assigned to a variable in this manner, VBScript copies the entire contents of the array as well as information on the size and dimensionality of the array. Thus, after the assignment shown in the preceding code, the contents of `x` and `a` are independent—changing an element of `a` has no effect on the contents of `x`.

A variable that contains an array can still be re-assigned a simple data value. As usual, this reassignment deletes the old contents of the variable (in this case, an array). However, it is *not* possible to convert an array variable declared as such using a `Dim` statement into a simple variable.

Continuing with the previous example, the first assignment in the following code is valid, whereas the second causes an error:

```
x = 1                        ' Revert x to simple variable (array discarded)
a = 10                       ' Not legal! a is declared an array and cannot change.
```

Variables can contain arrays of any dimensionality. They can also contain dynamic arrays. After a variable contains a dynamic array, it can be used in a `ReDim` statement just like any other dynamic array variable. For example:

```
Dim x, d()                   ' Declare variable and dynamic array
ReDim d(10)                  ' Change size of dynamic array
x = d                        ' Copy dynamic array to simple variable
ReDim x(100)                 ' Change size of dynamic array in variable
```

In the preceding example, the variable `x` is assigned a copy of the dynamic array `d`. The `ReDim` statement is then used to enlarge this dynamic array. This does not alter the original `d` variable, which retains an upper bound of 10.

Note

Technically, there are internal differences between a "genuine" array variable declared with `Dim` *and a simple variable that contains an array as a result of an assignment statement. However, these differences are handled internally by VBScript. Consequently, arrays and variables containing arrays can be used interchangeably in most cases.*

The *Array* Function

Dynamic vector (that is, one dimensional) arrays can also be constructed "on-the-fly" from a list of individual expressions using the `Array` function. For example:

```
Dim x                        ' Declare simple variable
x = Array(10,11,12)          ' Create a 3 element dynamic array and assign to x
```

In this example, the `Array` function creates a three element dynamic array. Element 0 is assigned the value 10, element 1 the value 11, and element 2 the value 12. Because the array stored in the variable `x` is dynamic, it can later be resized using the `ReDim` statement.

Each item in the element list of the Array function can be an expression of any type. For example:

```
x = Array(10 + 2, "one" & "two",  #12/05/87#)
```

This example creates a three element dynamic array containing an integer, a string, and a date.

The `Array` function can be used to simulate structured data. See "Using Arrays as Structures" for more information.

Storing Arrays in Array Elements

Simple variables can store arrays because they are *variants*, and variants can hold data of any type, including arrays. Array elements are *also* variants. Therefore, an *array element* can also store an *entire array*. This is quite powerful. For example:

```
Dim a(2), b(10)                 ' Declare two arrays
b(5) = "one"                    ' Element 5 of b becomes "one"
a(0) = "two"                    ' Element 0 of a becomes "two"
a(1) = b                        ' Element 1 of a becomes array b contents
Wscript.Echo a(0), a(1)(5)      ' Should display "one two"
```

In the fourth line of the preceding code, the array `b` is assigned to the array element `a(1)`. This means that this element of `a` now contains a copy of the entire array `b`. To access an element of the array contained within this element, it is necessary to use two sets of parentheses, as shown in the `Wscript.Echo` command in the preceding code. The first set of parentheses, `a(1)`, access the element of `a` that contains the array. The second set of parentheses, `a(1)(5)`, specifies the element of the array to access.

This technique is applicable to arrays of any dimension, and static and dynamic arrays can be mixed as desired. For example:

```
Dim m(10,10), b(5)              ' Declare matrix m and vector b
b(3) = "one"                    ' Element 3 of b becomes "one"
m(1,4) = Array(10, "two", b)    ' Assign dynamic array to m
Wscript.Echo m(1,4)(2)(3)       ' Should display "one"
```

In this example, the element `(1,4)` of matrix `m` is assigned a dynamic array created using the `Array` function. The last item of this dynamic array is *itself* the static array `b`. To access an element of this array, as shown in the `Wscript.Echo` statement, it is necessary to first access the element `(1,4)` of the matrix `m`, then access the appropriate element of the dynamic array created by the `Array` function (in this case, 2), and then access the appropriate element of the copy of the `b` array (in this case, 3). Thus, this is an example of a static vector array contained within a dynamic vector array contained within a matrix.

Program Guide

Don't Panic

The preceding example is complex. Don't be worried if you don't fully grasp what is going on the first time you read the code. In fact, none of the scripts in this book uses structures that are as complex as this. However, if you can understand this, you can almost be sure that you will have no trouble with the rest of this book, or most other programming books!

The capability of storing an array in a dynamic array element can be used to overcome the limitations of dynamic matrices. In a two-dimensional dynamic array (a matrix), only the last upper bound (the number of columns) can be altered using a `ReDim` statement if the `Preserve` keyword is used. To overcome this limitation, use a one-dimensional dynamic array and store vectors in each element. For example:

```
Dim d(), a(3)                ' Declare dynamic vector and static vector
ReDim d(2)                   ' Allocate 3 elements to d
d(1) = a : d(2) = a          ' Assign array to d(1) and d(2)
ReDim Preserve d(10)         ' Enlarge d but preserve contents of all array
```

From the perspective of VBScript, the array `d` is a simple one-dimensional array. Therefore, the `Preserve` keyword is valid and can be used when enlarging (or reducing) the array size. However, the array actually has all the properties of a matrix because each element itself contains a vector.

Using Arrays as Structures

Many programming languages support data constructs called *structures* (also known as *records* or *aggregates*). A structure is a collection of simple data types that can be processed as a whole. For example, a personnel database might contain information about employees, including an employee ID, the employee's name, and the date employment commenced. These three items (an integer, a string, and a date) can be combined to form an employee record.

The VBScript language does not support structures directly (although they can be represented with classes, which are described in Chapter 9, "Creating VBScript Classes"). Instead, structures can be simulated using small vector arrays, with each element representing an item in the structure. If an array is used in this manner, it is sometimes called a *record array*, or just *record*. For example, the employee record previously described can be represented as a three-element record array, in which element 0 contains the ID, element 1 the employee name, and element 2 the date of employment. These items can then be placed in a dynamic array and be assigned to a variable. For example:

```
Dim Employee
Employee = Array(1, "John Doe", #04/02/92#)
```

Here, the variable `Employee` is assigned a dynamic record array that is initialized with the details of employee John Doe (employee ID 1, date of employment April 2, 1992). Array indexing is then used to access individual data items. For example, to print the employees name:

```
Wscript.Echo Employee(1)
```

If an array is used as a record array, it is convenient to define symbolic constants for the element indices. For example:

```
Const cEmployeeID = 0         ' Index for employee ID
Const cEmployeeName = 1       ' Index for employee name
Const cEmployeeDate = 2       ' Index for employee date of employment
```

These constants can then be used when indexing the array. For example:

```
Wscript.Echo "Employee ID=", Employee(cEmployeeID)
```

In addition to accessing elements in the record array, the ability to copy dynamic arrays by assignment allows the entire employee record to be copied from one variable to another. For example:

```
Dim Employee2
Employee2 = Employee          ' Copy employee details to Employee2
```

It is also possible to declare a vector array, `Employees`, which contains a list of employee records. For example:

```
Dim Employee, Employees(100)  ' Employee record and Array of employee data
Employee = Array(2, "Bert Whistle", #02/01/90#)
Employees(2) = Employee       ' Save employee details in element of array
Wscript.Echo Employees(2)(cEmployeeName)    ' Display employee name
```

The `Employees` vector is, in effect, a table of employee data. Each element of the array either is empty, or contains an employee record. Notice the use of the "double index" in the `Wscript.Echo` statement to display the employee's name. The first element index, 2, specifies the entry in the `Employees` vector (and hence which employee to access), whereas the second element index, `cEmployeeName`, specifies the item index for that employee's record.

Program Guide

Planning Data Structures

Structuring data as records and arrays of records is used in virtually all non-trivial programming projects. In fact, the most important part of many projects is planning how data is to be represented within the program or script. A well structured set of data often results in compact, efficient, and clear script code, whereas badly structured data can lead to complex and opaque code.

Unfortunately, there are no known rules that allow you to find the best structure for data automatically. This skill can only come through experience and trial and error. One good place to start, however, is to mentally picture how you would organize the data manually, or perhaps in a spreadsheet program. Think about how the data can be decomposed into simpler items and how each of the items is related.

Part II of this book introduces object-oriented techniques that can further assist in organizing data into well-understood forms.

Summary

VBScript contains a rich set of data types that can represent numeric, boolean, string, and date/time values. The language automatically converts between these data types where this is appropriate. In addition, functions are available to identify the type of data stored in a variable and to change that data type explicitly.

In addition to explicit literal constants, VBScript supports symbolic constants, which allows meaningful names to be given to opaque data values. The language also predefines a number of symbolic constants.

All variables in VBScript can contain data of any type, including arrays. In addition to simple arrays, VBScript supports arrays of multiple dimensions and arrays that are sized (and resized) dynamically. Entire arrays can be manipulated as single data items and assigned to variables or array elements. This allows complex data types to be represented using arrays within other arrays.

4

Built-In Functions

This chapter describes in detail the various VBScript built-in functions. As previously described in the "Functions" section in Chapter 2, "VBScript Language Essentials," a *function* is a transformation operation that takes zero or more input data values (called *arguments*) and produces a new output data value (called the *function result*, or *return value*). If used as part of an expression, the functions described in this chapter allow many complex data transformations to be efficiently performed. For example, the string functions can manipulate text data in a variety of ways, and the date/time functions allow dates and times to be managed effectively.

If a function has one or more arguments, these are separated by commas and enclosed in parentheses following the function name. For example:

```
a = Left("12345", x + 2)
```

In this example, the `Left` function takes two arguments: the string literal `"12345"` and the expression `x + 2`.

Each argument is an expression that should evaluate to an appropriate data type. For example, if the function expects a string argument, the argument expression should yield a string. This is shown in the descriptions of the functions as *`string`* for string expressions, *`number`* for numeric expressions, and so on. However, the usual VBScript auto-conversion rules described in Chapter 3, "VBScript Data Storage," apply, and so typically VBScript can convert (for example) strings to numeric values and vice versa as necessary.

VBScript also supports *optional* arguments for some functions. If an optional argument is not supplied, a default action is taken by the function. In the syntax description of functions in this chapter, optional arguments are shown in square brackets. For example:

```
UBound(arrayname [,dimension])
```

This example shows that the `UBound` function takes an optional second argument specifying the dimension for which to return the upper bound. For example:

```
Dim a(10,12)
Wscript.Echo UBound(a), UBound(a, 1), UBound(a, 2)
```

In this example, the first two `UBound` functions display `10`, the upper bound of the first dimension. The final `UBound` function returns `12`.

In general, it is not possible to "skip" optional function arguments: If you supply the value for an optional argument, you must also supply values for all optional arguments that appear before (to the left of) that argument. For example, if a function takes three arguments, the last two of which are optional, then the second argument must be supplied if the third argument is supplied.

The various functions to manipulate arrays, convert data types, or examine the data type of a variable were described in Chapter 3.

String Functions

The string functions manipulate string data. String functions are very common in system scripts because they can be used to analyze and process file names, text files, registry keys, and command arguments. Many of the string functions take one string as an argument and return a modified string as a result. Table 4.1 lists the string functions available in VBScript.

Table 4.1 *VBScript String Functions*

Function	Description
`Asc(`*`string`*`)`	Returns the ANSI code for the first character in *`string`*.
`Ascb(`*`string`*`)`	Returns the numeric value of the first byte of *`string`*.
`Ascw(`*`string`*`)`	Returns the Unicode code for the first character in *`string`*.
`Chr(`*`number`*`)`	Returns a single character string specified by the ANSI code of *`number`*.
`Chrb(`*`number`*`)`	Returns a single character string encoding *`number`*.
`Chrw(`*`number`*`)`	Returns a single character string specified by the Unicode code *`number`*.
`Filter(`*`array`*`, `*`search`*` [,`*`include`*`] [,`*`mode`*`])`	Returns an array of strings for each element of *`array`* matching search.
`InStr([`*`start`*`,] `*`string`*`, `*`search`*` [,`*`mode`*`])`	Returns the index of the first occurrence of *`search`* in string.

Function	Description
`InStrRev([start,] string, search [,mode])`	Returns the index of the last occurrence of *search* in string.
`Join(array [,delim])`	Returns the elements of array concatenated together.
`LCase(string)`	Returns *string* converted to lower case.
`Left(string, length)`	Returns up to *length* characters from the start of the *string*.
`Len(string)`	Returns the length (number of characters) of the *string*.
`Lenb(string)`	Returns the byte size of the *string*.
`LTrim(string)`	Returns *string* with leading spaces (if any) removed.
`Mid(string, start [,length])`	Returns a sub-string from *string*.
`Midb(string, start, [,length])`	Returns a sub-string of bytes from *string*.
`Replace(string, substr, repl [,start] [,count] [,mode])`	Returns *string*, with occurrences of *sub str* replaced with *repl*.
`Right(string, length)`	Returns up to *length* characters from the end of the *string*.
`RTrim(string)`	Returns *string* with trailing spaces (if any) removed.
`Space(number)`	Returns a *string* of *number* spaces.
`Split(string, [,delim] [,count] [,mode])`	Returns an array of strings derived from *string*.
`StrComp(string1, string2 [,mode])`	Compares *string1* to *string2* using the specified *mode*.
`String(number, character)`	Returns a string comprising *number* repeats of *character*.
`StrReverse(string)`	Returns *string* with the order of characters reversed.
`Trim(string)`	Returns *string* with leading and trailing spaces (if any) removed.
`UCase(string)`	Returns *string* converted to upper case.

Character Code Functions

The `Ascx` and `Chrx` functions convert between single character strings and character codes (that is, integers that represent the coding for a particular character).

The `Asc` and `Chr` functions are complementary. The `Asc` function returns the ANSI numeric code for the first character of the specified string expression. Any value from 0 to 255 might be returned. The `Chr` function converts an ANSI character code into a single character string. For example, `Chr(97)` returns the string `"a"`. The `Chr` function is commonly used to encode the various ANSI control characters in the range 0 to 31. For example, `Chr(10)` returns a string containing a single line feed character. VBScript predefines some of the more common `Chr` encodings of control characters. See Table 3.3 in Chapter 3 for more information.

The `Ascw` and `Chrw` functions are the Unicode equivalents of the `Asc` and `Chr` functions. Although the `Asc` and `Chr` functions are restricted to ANSI character codes in the range 0 to 255, the Unicode functions support the full Unicode character space. For example:

```
Wscript.Echo Chrw(2000)
```

The `Ascb` and `Chrb` functions process byte data in strings. The `Ascb` function returns the byte value of the first byte in the specified string, whereas the `Chrb` function encodes a byte as a single character string.

To understand the difference between the different flavors of `Asc` and `Chr` functions, consider this example:

```
a = Chrw(2000)
Wscript.Echo Ascw(a), Ascb(a)
```

When this code executes, the output is:

```
2000 208
```

The `Chrw` function encodes the number 2000 as a single character string. The Unicode encoding for this string consists of the integer value 2000 stored as a 16-bit Unicode value, which is &H07D0 in hexadecimal. VBScript stores this value as two bytes in "little-endian" order on Intel platforms; therefore, the first byte of the string is &HD0 and the second byte is &H07. The `Ascw` function converts the Unicode value back to a number and displays 2000. The `Ascb` function, however, only converts the first *byte* of the string. In this case, the first byte is &HD0, which is 208 in decimal.

In the preceding example, the `Asc` function is not valid because the first character of the string lies outside the legal range for ANSI characters (0 to 255). Attempting to use `Asc` will generate a run-time error.

String Size Functions

The `Len` function returns the length of the string specified as an argument. An empty string returns zero. The length of the string is measured in character units, for example the length of the string `"macmillan"` is nine.

The `Lenb` function returns the length of the string in bytes (sometimes called the *size* of the string). Because each Unicode character in a string occupies two bytes, the result returned by `Lenb` is always double that of `Len` for any given string.

As noted in Chapter 3, VBScript strings are always Unicode. However, it is possible that other versions of Visual Basic will support ANSI strings that have only one byte per character. By using `Len` and `Lenb`, it is possible to detect this difference, for example:

```
If Len("a") = Lenb("a") Then
    Wscript.Echo "ANSI strings"
Else
    Wscript.Echo "Unicode strings"
End If
```

String Editing Functions

The `Left` and `Right` functions trim a string to a specified maximum length. The first argument specifies the string to trim, and the second argument specifies the length. If the string is shorter than or equal in length to the length argument, the string is returned unchanged. If the string is longer than the specified length, characters are trimmed from the string to make it the specified length. The `Left` function trims characters from the right, whereas the `Right` function trims characters from the left. This results in the `Left` function returning the left-most *`length`* characters and the `Right` function returning the right-most *`length`* characters.

For example:

```
a = "Stravinsky"
b = "Tallis"
c = "Vaughan Williams"
Wscript.Echo Right(a, 3), Left(b, 8), Left(c, 7)
```

This example generates the following output:

```
sky Tallis Vaughan
```

Note that the string `b` is six characters long, and the result of `Left(b, 8)` is still a six character (unchanged) string. The `Left` and `Right` functions never *extend* a string—the *`length`* argument specifies only a maximum length, not a minimum.

The *Mid* Function

The `Mid` function extracts a sub-string from a string. The *`start`* argument specifies the character index within the string of the start of the sub-string. The first character in a string is numbered 1. If the optional *`length`* argument is omitted, all characters from *`start`* up to the end of the string are returned. For example:

```
a = "123456789"
x = Mid(a, 3)
```

This assigns the string `"3456789"` to the variable `x`.

If the `length` argument is present, it specifies a maximum length for the sub-string so that the `Mid` function will return a string of up to `length` characters starting at the specified start index. Fewer than `length` characters are returned if the string is shorter. For example:

```
a = "123456789"
x = Mid(a, 5, 2)
y = Mid(a, 5, 10)
```

This assigns the string `"56"` to the variable `x` and `"56789"` to the variable `y`.

If the `Mid` function is called with a `start` index that lies beyond the end of the string, an empty string is returned. This is also the case if the specified `length` value is zero.

Note

Unlike array indices, which start with zero, string indices start with one. Therefore, the following `Right` *and* `Mid` *examples return the same result:*

```
a = "abcdef"
x = Right(a, 3)
y = Mid(a, Len(a) - 3 + 1)
```

The variable `x` *contains* `"def"`, *the last three characters in the variable* `a`. *To simulate this with* `Mid`, *it is necessary to compute a* `start` *index that yields the last three characters. This index is not the expression* `Len(a)-3`, *because this yields a value of 3, which is the index of the letter* `"c"` *and not* `"d"` *as desired. Thus, we need to add 1 to this result to compensate for the use of a start index of 1.*

The use of string indices that start at 1 instead of 0 (as with arrays) is unfortunate and inconsistent. However, this use was inherited from earlier versions of the BASIC language, and it is certainly far too late to change. ◆

The `Midb` function is similar in operation to the `Mid` function, except that the function works with bytes within a string rather than characters. Both the `start` and `length` values specify a byte offset into the `string` argument. This allows individual byte values within a string to be extracted. For example:

```
x = Ascb(Midb(a, 14, 1))
```

This example assigns the byte value (0 to 255) from index 14 in the string `a` into the variable `x`.

The *Replace* Function

The `Replace` function replaces one or more occurrences of a sub-string with another. The function can take up to six arguments to control the replacement operation. The simplest form takes three arguments: a `string` containing text to search, a *substr* string that specifies a sub-string for which to search, and a *repl* string that specifies the replacement string. For example:

```
a = "12345678934"
x = Replace(a, "34", "XX")
```

This assigns the string `"12XX56789XX"` to the variable `x`. The `Replace` function replaces each occurrence of the string `"34"` with the string `"XX"`.

The *substr* and *repl* strings do not need to be the same length. For example:

```
a = "Converting &amp; replacing"
x = Replace(a, "&amp;", "&")
```

This assigns the string `"Converting & replacing"` to the variable `x`. If the replacement string *repl* is empty, all occurrences of *substr* are deleted from the *string*. For example:

```
a = "123456789"
x = Replace(a, "6", "")
```

This assigns the string `"12345789"` to the variable `x`. If the *substr* string is empty, no replacements occur regardless of the *repl* string, and the original *string* is returned unaltered.

By default, `Replace` scans the entire *string* and replaces all occurrences of *substr* with *repl*. By specifying a *start* argument, the replace operation begins at a specified start index. Like the `Mid` function, indices start at one. Characters in *string* before the *start* index are neither scanned for replacement *nor copied* to the return result. For example:

```
a = "123456789"
x = Replace(a, "8", "-", 3)
```

This assigns the string `"34567-9"` to the variable `x`. If the *start* index specified a starting position past the end of the *string*, `Replace` returns an empty string.

The optional *count* argument specifies the number of occurrences of *substr* to replace. After *count* replacements have been made, additional characters in *string* are returned unaltered. Specify a *count* of -1 to replace all occurrences, or omit the argument entirely.

The optional *mode* argument specifies how the *substr* string is compared to characters in the *string*, and it can be either `vbBinaryCompare` (the default) or `vbTextCompare`. See the discussion of `StrComp` in the "Other String Functions" section for more details.

Search Functions

The `InStr` function locates a sub-string within a string. The function can take up to four arguments to control the search operation. The simplest form takes two arguments: a *string* to search and a *search* string containing the string for which to search. If the *search* string is located within the *string*, the InStr function returns the index of the location of the search string within *string*. For example:

```
a = "the quick brown fox"
x = InStr(a, "qu")
```

This example assign the value 5 to the variable x. The InStr function searches from the start (left) of the string and stops when it finds the first occurrence. If the *search* string is not found, the function returns 0. If the *search* string is empty, the function returns 1 because an empty search string matches the imaginary emptiness at the very start of all strings. If the *string* is empty, the function returns 0 (even if *search* is also empty).

By default, the InStr function always starts searching from the start of the *string* argument. If the optional *start* argument is specified, searching begins at this index in the *string*. As usual, the index of the first character in the *string* is 1. The *start* argument must be the first argument to the Instr function. For example:

```
a = "what goes around comes around"
x = InStr(15, a, "around")
```

This assigns the value 24 to the variable x (the start index of the second instance of the search string "around").

If a *start* argument is specified, the optional *mode* argument can also be included as the fourth and last argument. The *mode* argument specifies how the *search* string is compared to characters in the *string* and can be either vbBinaryCompare (the default), or vbTextCompare. See the discussion of StrComp in "Other String Functions" for more details.

VBScript also provides the InStrRev function. This is identical to the InStr function except that searching occurs backwards from the end (right) of the *string*, and so the function finds the *last* occurrence of the *search* string. In addition, the *start* argument, if present, specifies the index of the first (right-most) character to search, or it can be -1 to specify searching from the far right of the *string*.

Array Functions

The Filter function filters a one-dimensional string array based upon a search string. The simplest form of this function takes two arguments. The first argument must be a one-dimensional array of strings. The second argument specifies a *search* string. The return value of the Filter function is another one-dimensional array of strings. The function scans each element of the input array to see if it contains the *search* string. If it does, the element is included in the returned array. If it does not, the element is excluded from the returned array. For example:

```
a = Array("tim", "tom", "bat")
x = Filter(a, "m")
```

This example returns a new dynamic array containing two elements: "tim" and "tom". The third element of the input array is not included in the returned array because it does not contain the string "m". The *search* string can be longer than one character if required.

The optional third argument for the Filter function specifies if matching elements should be excluded or included in the return result. If this argument is True (the default value), matching elements are returned and non-matching elements are excluded. If this argument is False, matching elements are excluded and non-matching elements are returned.

The optional *mode* argument specifies how the *search* string is compared to elements in the *array* and can be either vbBinaryCompare (the default), or vbTextCompare. See the discussion of StrComp in "Other String Functions" for more details.

The *Join* Function

The Join function returns a single string created by concatenating the elements of a one-dimensional string array. All the elements of the array are concatenated, in element order. By default, each element is separated from the next by a single space character. For example:

```
x = join(array("Tom", "Dick", "Harry"))
```

This example assigns the string "Tom Dick Harry" to the variable x.

If the optional *delim* argument is present, this string is used as the separator instead of a space. For example:

```
x = join(array("bob", "sue", "karen"), ",")
```

This example assigns the string "bob,sue,karen" to the variable x.

delim can be the empty string, in which case all the elements of the array are concatenated without any intervening delimiter characters.

The *Split* Function

The Split function is the opposite of the Join function. It takes a single *string* argument and breaks the string up into sub-strings, which are then returned as elements of a one-dimensional array. The simplest form of Split takes a single *string* argument and breaks the string using spaces as delimiters. For example:

```
a = Split("tom dick harry")
```

This example assigns the variable a an array containing three string elements: "tom", "dick" and "harry".

Multiple space delimiters (including leading and trailing delimiters) will generate additional empty elements within the array. For example:

```
a = Split(" tom dick  harry")
```

This example assigns the variable `a` an array containing five string elements: `""`, `"tom"`, `"disk"`, `""` and `"harry"`.

The optional second *`delim`* argument can specify an alternate delimiter to the default space character. The delimiter can be more than one character long. For example:

```
a = Split("tom//dick//harry", "//")
```

This example also assigns the variable `a` an array containing three string elements: `"tom"`, `"dick"` and `"harry"`. If the *`delim`* string is the empty string, the result of the `Split` function is an array with a single element that contains all of *`string`*.

By default, the `Split` function processes the entire *`string`* for array elements. The optional third *`count`* argument specifies the maximum number of elements to place in the array. If there are fewer than *`count`* delimited strings, each string is placed in an array element as usual. If the number of strings reaches one less than *`count`*, then the entire rest of the *`string`*, including any delimiters, is placed in the last element of the array. For example:

```
a = Split("tom,dick,harry", ",", 2)
```

This example assigns the variable `a` an array containing only two string elements: `"tom"` and `"dick,harry"`.

The final optional fourth argument specifies the comparison *`mode`* used when comparing characters in *`string`* to those specified by the delimiter argument. See the discussion of `StrComp` in the "Other String Functions" section for more details.

Other String Functions

The three functions `Trim`, `LTrim` and `RTrim` strip leading and trailing spaces from strings. `LTrim` trims leading spaces (that is, spaces to the left of the string) and `RTrim` trims trailing spaces (that is, spaces to the right of the string). The `Trim` function trims both leading and trailing spaces. None of the functions trims spaces embedded *within* a string. For example:

```
a = Trim("   VBScript is great   ")
```

This code assigns the string `"VBScript is great"` to the variable `a`.

Space trimming is typically used when processing command line arguments and file names to ensure that extraneous leading and trailing spaces are discarded.

The `Space` function returns a string composed entirely of spaces. The single argument specifies the number of spaces (and hence the length of the string returned). If the argument is zero, an empty string is returned. The

`Space` function is often used with the `Left` function to pad a string with spaces to a fixed width. For example:

```
a = "A String"
b = Left(a & Space(20), 20)
```

This example assigns the string `"A String            "` to the variable `b`. First, the string `a` is padded with 20 extra spaces. This ensures that the string is *at least* 20 characters long. Next, the `Left` function trims the string to exactly 20 characters. A similar construct can be used to pad fixed width strings on the left:

```
a = "A String"
b = Right(Space(20) & a, 20)
```

The `String` function returns a string composed of a single character repeated multiple times. The first argument specifies the repeat count; the second argument specifies the character to repeat. If this argument is numeric, the `String` function uses the `Chr` function to convert the number to a string. If the argument is a string, the first character from the string is repeated. For example:

```
x = String(10, "x")
```

This assigns the string `"xxxxxxxxxx"` to the variable `x`. Note that the `Space` function is simply a special case of the `String` function with the second argument assumed to be the space character.

The `LCase` and `UCase` functions convert the case of letters within a string. The `UCase` function converts lower case letters to upper case, and the `LCase` function converts upper case letters to lower case. Non-alphabetic characters in the string are not altered by the functions.

The `StrReverse` function reverses the order of characters in a string and returns the mirror image of the string passed as an argument. For example:

```
x = StrReverse("Mahler")
```

This example assigns the string `"relhaM"` to the variable `x`.

The `StrComp` function compares two strings for equality. The return value of `StrComp` indicates the result of the comparison. If the strings are identical, the result is 0. If the first string is less than the second string, the result is -1. If the first string is greater than the second string, the result is 1. For example:

```
a = "123" : b = "46"
Select Case StrComp(a, b)
    Case -1
        Wscript.Echo "a is less than b"
    Case 0
        Wscript.Echo "a is equal to b"
    Case 1
        Wscript.Echo "a is greater than b"
End Select
```

`StrComp` accepts an optional third argument that controls the mode of comparison. If the argument is omitted or is the constant `vbBinaryCompare` (which has the value 0), characters are compared using their character code values. This is identical to the comparisons made using the comparison operators described in Chapter 2.

If the third argument to `StrComp` is the constant `vbTextCompare` (which has the value 1), characters are compared lexically. Lexical comparison treats upper and lower case letters as identical, for example:

```
If StrComp("abc", "ABC", vbTextCompare) = 0 Then Wscript.Echo "They are the same"
```

The *ParseArgs1.vbs* Script

The `ParseArgs1.vbs` sample script, shown in Listing 4.1, illustrates using string functions to parse command line arguments.

Listing 4.1 `ParseArgs1.vbs` *Script*

```
'//////////////////////////////////////////////////////////////////////////////
' $Workfile: ParseArgs1.vbs $ $Revision: 1 $ $Date: 5/08/99 3:21p $
' $Archive: /Scripts/ParseArgs1.vbs $
' Copyright 1999 Tim Hill. All Rights Reserved.
'//////////////////////////////////////////////////////////////////////////////

' Parse command arguments of the form <name>=<value>

Option Explicit
Dim sArg, sName, sValue, ix, a, sChar, bInValue

' Parse the arguments char-by-char
Wscript.Echo "Parsing character by character..."
For Each sArg In Wscript.Arguments
    sName = "" : sValue = ""
    ix = 1 : bInValue = False
    Do While ix <= len(sArg)
        sChar = Mid(sArg, ix, 1)
        ix = ix + 1
        If bInValue Then
            sValue = sValue & sChar
        ElseIf sChar = "=" Then
            bInValue = True
        Else
            sName = sName & sChar
        End If
    Loop
    Wscript.Echo "Name=" & sName, "Value=" & sValue
Next

' Parse the arguments using Instr etc
Wscript.Echo "Parsing using InStr/Left/Mid..."
For Each sArg In Wscript.Arguments
    ix = InStr(sArg, "=")
```

```
    If ix <> 0 Then
        sName = Left(sArg, ix - 1)
        sValue = Mid(sArg, ix + 1)
    Else
        sName = sArg
        sValue = ""
    End If
    Wscript.Echo "Name=" & sName, "Value=" & sValue
Next

' Parse the arguments using Split function
Wscript.Echo "Parsing using Split..."
For Each sArg In Wscript.Arguments
    a = Split(sArg, "=", 2)
    sName = a(0)
    If UBound(a) >= 1 Then
        sValue = a(1)
    Else
        sValue = ""
    End If
    Wscript.Echo "Name=" & sName, "Value=" & sValue
Next
    '//////////////////////////////////////////////////////////////////////////////
```

This sample parses command line arguments of the form *name=value*. For example:

```
a=14 fred=brown tim=tom a=a-very-long-argument a=b=c
```

The problem here is to break apart each argument into a distinct string that represents the *name* and *value* part of each argument on the left and right sides of the = character. This lexical analysis is known as *parsing*. Even this simple syntax has several issues that must be handled by the script code:

- The argument may be empty (a zero length string).
- The argument may not contain an = character.
- The argument may have no text following the = character (an empty *value*).
- The argument may have no text before the = character (an empty *name*).
- The argument may consist only of an = character (an empty *name* and *value*).
- The argument may contain multiple = characters.

When looking at the sample code in this script, consider how the script handles each of these possible conditions and whether the results are correct. In particular, look at how the code reacts to values of `ix` that are 0, 1 or the length of `sArg`. Test the script with different argument values.

The `ParseArgs1.vbs` script parses each command line argument using three different techniques:

- Using a `Do Loop` statement to process each argument, character by character.
- Using `InStr`, `Left`, and `Mid` to manually decompose each argument.
- Using `Split` to automatically decompose each argument.

In all cases, a `For Each` loop is used to process each individual command line argument. The argument to parse is initially placed in the `sArg` variable by the `For Each` loop. The results of the parse are then placed in the `sName` and `sValue` variables, which contain the *`name`* and *`value`* components of the argument respectively.

State Machine Parsing

The first `For Each` loop uses a manual character-by-character parser. A `Do Loop` processes each character in the argument by index. The `Mid` function is then used to extract the individual character into the variable `sChar`. A construct known as a *state machine* is then used to process the characters. The state machine uses the variable `bInValue` to control the operation of the machine. It does this by observing the following rules:

1. Initially, all characters from the argument form the *name* part of the argument.
2. An `"="` character indicates that all subsequent characters form the *value* part of the argument.

The `bInValue` variable is initialized to `False`, indicating that the state machine is currently not in the value part of the argument. Then, for each character, an `If` statement handles all the possible states, as follows:

1. If `bInValue` is `True`, we are processing the *value* part of the argument. In this case, add the character to the `sValue` string.
2. Otherwise, we are processing the *name* part of the argument. However, if the character is `"="`, then we need to switch to processing the *value* part, so we set `bInValue` to `True` to indicate this.
3. Finally, if `bInValue` is `False` and the character is not `"="`, then we simply add the character to the `sName` string.

State machines are frequently used to process text data in this manner. Take a moment to try to follow how the script code processes a typical argument. Notice how the `"="` character “triggers” the state machine to switch from adding characters to `sName` to adding characters to `sValue`.

Program Guide

State Machines

The state machine derives its name from pioneering computer science work done by Alan Turing. Despite its forbidding name, state machines are quite simple, and we use them every day. For example, when you drive to work each morning, you first have to change the state of the car engine from off to on, then switch the transmission to drive, and then press the gas pedal. One way to state this is as a sequence of VBScript functions. For example:

```
Engine(True)
Transmission(Drive)
GasPedal(Down)
```

A hypothetical smart car, however, might be clever enough to figure out that when you press the gas pedal, what you really want is the engine started and the transmission in drive. So you can just say:

```
GasPedal(Down)
```

Now, our hypothetical `GasPedal` *function has to know to start the engine and put the transmission in drive. However, it cannot do this every time. What if the car was just idling at a red light? Therefore, the* `GasPedal` *function has to remember if the engine is started and the transmission is in drive using state information. This is achieved using a state machine inside the* `GasPedal` *function like this:*

```
If Not bEngine
    Engine(True)
    bEngine = True
End If
If Not bInDrive
    Transmission(Drive)
    bDrive = True
End If
```

Here we use two variables, `bEngine` *and* `bDrive`, *to track the state of the engine and transmission. If the engine isn't started, we start the engine* and record that information *in* `bEngine` *so that we don't mistakenly start it again later.*

Similarly the `bInValue` *variable in the script tracks if we have located an* `"="` *sign and have transitioned from processing characters that are part of the name to characters that are part of the value.*

String Function Parsing

The second `For Each` loop uses the `InStr` function to locate the index of the first `"="` character in the `sArg` argument. This index is stored in the `ix` variable. The script then has to consider two possible outcomes: the `sArg` argument *does* contain an `"="` character, and the argument *does not* contain an

`"="` character. This test is made using an `If` statement, by comparing the index `ix` to zero.

If `ix` is zero, then the `sArg` string does *not* contain an `"="` character. (This is the return value of `InStr` if no matching string is located.) In this case, the `Else` clause of the `If` statement executes, the variable `sName` is assigned the entire value of `sArg`, and the variable `sValue` is set to the empty string.

If `ix` is non-zero, an `"="` character was found. The script code must now split the `sArg` variable into the two strings: `sName` and `sValue`. The `ix` variable indicates where in the string (by index) we wish to split the string. The *name* is all the text from the start of the string up to the `"="` character. If the `"="` character were the second character in the string, `ix` would be 2, and the number of characters in the name would be 1, that is one less than `ix`. Therefore, we need to extract `ix-1` characters from `sArg`. This is done using the `Left` function.

The *value* part of the argument is the rest of the `sArg` string following the `"="` character. Obviously, the character actually *at* the index `ix` in `sArg` is the `"="` characters, and so the *value* is all of `sArg` starting at index `ix + 1`. The `Mid` function is used to extract this data.

Split Function Parsing

The final `For Each` loop processes each argument using the `Split` function. This function does all the hard work of breaking the argument up into a *name* and *value* part, and conveniently places each part into an array element for easy access. Therefore, the `sName` variable can be immediately assigned the value of the first array element. However, the code must still handle the case where there is no "=" character in the argument. In this case, the `Split` function returns an array with a single element, and attempting to access the second element to access the *value* part generates an error. Therefore, an `If` statement checks for this case using the `UBound` function, and then assigns the correct value to `sValue`.

Note

The `Split` *function uses an optional third argument to limit the maximum number of array elements to two. This conveniently takes care of the case where the value part of the argument also contains an* `"="` *character. Without the limit on the array size the* `Split` *function would treat this additional* `"="` *character as an additional delimiter and would add an additional element to the array.* ◆

Finally, the `ParseArgs1.vbs` script does not contain any code to handle leading or trailing spaces in the *name* or *value*. Depending upon the application, it might be desirable to trim leading and trailing space from these values using the `Trim` function.

Formatting Functions

The formatting functions format specific VBScript data types as strings. These functions allow the programmer more precise control over the format of the string than that provided by the default conversions built into VBScript. Table 4.2 lists the formatting functions available in VBScript.

Table 4.2 VBScript Formatting Functions

Function	Description
`FormatCurrency(`*`expr`* `[,`*`numdigits`*`] [,`*`leadingdigits`*`] [,`*`useparens`*`] [,`*`groupdigits`*`])`	Returns a string with *`expr`* formatted as a currency value.
`FormatDateTime(`*`date`* `[,`*`format`*`])`	Returns a string with *`date`* formatted as appropriate.
`FormatNumber(`*`expr`* `[,`*`numdigits`*`] [,`*`leadingdigits`*`] [,`*`useparens`*`] [,`*`groupdigits`*`])`	Returns a string with *`expr`* formatted as a numeric value.
`FormatPercent(`*`expr`* `[,`*`numdigits`*`] [,`*`leadingdigits`*`] [,`*`useparens`*`] [,`*`groupdigits`*`])`	Returns a string with *`expr`* formatted as a percentage value.

Many of the formatting functions use arguments that are expressed as *tri-state* values. A tri-state value can have one of three possible values:

- `TristateTrue` has the value -1 and indicates a tri-state true value.
- `TristateFalse` has the value 0 and indicates a tri-state false value.
- `TristateUseDefault` has the value -2 and indicates that the appropriate value (true or false) should be obtained from the locale settings for the computer.

The functions `FormatCurrency`, `FormatNumber`, and `FormatPercent` format numeric values. They differ as follows:

- `FormatCurrency` includes the locale-specific currency symbol as part of the return string. The `FormatCurrency` function is typically used with the currency data type, but it can be used with any numeric type.
- `FormatNumber` returns the numeric value formatted as a numeric string.
- `FormatPercent` adds a percent suffix to the return string, and multiplies the value of *`expr`* by 100.

For example:

```
a = 1.4
Wscript.Echo FormatNumber(a), FormatCurrency(a), FormatPercent(a)
```

This example displays the following:

```
1.40 $1.40 140.00%
```

The three number formatting functions can have several optional arguments, as follows:

- *numdigits* Specifies the number of digits to include after the decimal point. If this argument is -1, the default value from the operating system is used.
- *leadingdigits* A tri-state value. If `TristateTrue` and the value is fractional (between -1.0 and +1.0 exclusive), a leading zero is included before the decimal point.
- *useparens* A tri-state value. If `TristateTrue` and the value is negative, the entire value is enclosed in parentheses.
- *groupdigits* A tri-state value. If `TristateTrue`, group delimiter characters (for example, thousands separators) are included as appropriate.

For example:

```
Wscript.Echo FormatNumber(14000.53, 3)
```

This displays the following:

```
14000.530
```

The `FormatDateTime` function formats a *date* value. The date is formatted according to the optional *format* argument. This argument can be one of the following:

- `vbGeneralDate` Display the date part (if present) as a short date, and the time part (if present) as a long time. This is the default if *format* is omitted.
- `vbLongDate` Display a date only, in long format.
- `vbShortDate` Display a date only, in short format.
- `vbLongTime` Display a time only, in long format.
- `vbShortTime` Display a time only, in short format.

For example:

```
Wscript.Echo FormatDateTime(Now, vbLongDate)
```

Date and Time Functions

The date and time functions manipulate date and time data. Some functions create date and time data, whereas others decompose this data into individual fields (such as a month or a year). Table 4.3 lists the date and time functions available in VBScript.

Table 4.3 VBScript Date and Time Functions

Function	Description
`Date`	Returns the current system date.
`DateAdd(type, value, date)`	Adds the specified interval to the given *date*.
`DateDiff(type, date1, date2 [,firstday] [,firstweek])`	Computes the difference (interval) between two dates.
`DatePart(type, date [,firstday] [,firstweek])`	Returns specified part of the date.
`DateSerial(year, month, day)`	Returns a date value representing the specified *year*, *month*, and *day*.
`DateValue(string)`	Returns the locale specific date *string* as a date value.
`Day(date)`	Returns the day of the month (1 to 31) for the given *date*.
`Hour(date)`	Returns the hour of the day (0 to 23) for the given *date*.
`Minute(date)`	Returns the minute of the hour (0 to 59) for the given *date*.
`Month(date)`	Returns the month of the year (1 to 12) for the given *date*.
`MonthName(month [,short])`	Returns the localized name of a month (1 to 12).
`Now`	Returns the current system data and time.
`Second(date)`	Returns the seconds count (0 to 59) for the given *date*.
`Time`	Returns the current system time as a date value.
`Timer`	Returns number of seconds since midnight.
`TimeSerial(hour, minute, second)`	Returns a date value representing the specified *hour*, *minute*, and *second*.
`TimeValue(string)`	Returns the locale specific time *string* as a date value.
`Weekday(date [,firstday])`	Returns the day of the week (1 to 7) for the given *date*.
`WeekdayName(weekday [,short] [,firstday])`	Returns the localized name of a weekday (1 to 7).
`Year(date)`	Returns the year for the given *date*.

Date and Time Creation Functions

The `Date`, `Time`, and `Now` functions return the current system date or time. These functions obtain this information from the computer's internal clock. The functions all return the information as a date/time data type (see "Date and Time Data" in Chapter 3 for more information).

The `Date` function returns the current system date, whereas the `Time` function returns the current system time. Finally, the `Now` function returns the current system date and time. For example:

```
dStart = Now
Wscript.Echo "The time is", Time
```

The `DateSerial` and `TimeSerial` functions create a date value from individual date or time elements. The `DateSerial` function creates a date from the specified year, month, and day. For example:

```
dMillenium = DateSerial(2001, 1, 1)
```

The `TimeSerial` function creates a date value from the specified hour, minute, and second. The hour value should use 24-hour notation. For example:

```
dLunchTime = TimeSerial(13, 0, 0)
```

The `DateValue` and `TimeValue` functions convert a localized date or time string into a date value. For example:

```
dWifesBirthday = DateValue("April 24 1957")
```

Both the `DateValue` and `TimeValue` functions provide locale aware conversions. The `DateValue` function ignores any time information present in the string, and the `TimeValue` function ignores the date information present in the string.

Date and Time Part Functions

The `Day`, `Month`, and `Year` functions return the numeric value of the day, month, or year from a date value. For example:

```
Wscript.Echo "It's day", Day(Now), "of the month."
```

Similarly, the `Hour`, `Minute` and `Second` functions return the numeric value of the hour, minute or second from a date value. The `Hour` function returns a 24-hour time value. For example:

```
Wscript.Echo "It's hour", Hour(Now), "of the day."
```

The `Weekday` function returns the day of the week for a date value. The function returns 1 for the first day of the week, 2 for the second, and so forth. By default, the `Weekday` function assumes that Sunday is the first day of the week. To change this, use the optional second *`firstday`* argument to specify a starting day of the week. This can be either `vbUseSystem` to use the value supplied by the operating system, or `vbSunday` through `vbSaturday` to specify a particular first day of the week. The return value is then simply the day offset from that particular day. For example, if `vbWednesday` is used, a weekday of Wednesday is returned as the value 1.

Date Computation Functions

The `DateAdd` function adds an interval to a date value, returning a new date value offset by that interval. The interval can be either positive to advance the date into the future, or negative to retard the date into the past.

The interval to add to the date is specified as a combination of an interval *`type`* and an interval *`value`*. The interval type is a string specifying the units of the value. Interval type strings are shown in Table 4.4. Note that the string `"n"` is used to indicate an interval of minutes, and `"m"` an interval of months.

Table 4.4 `DateAdd` *and* `DateDiff` *Function Interval Type Strings*

Type String	Description
"yyyy"	Interval is expressed in years.
"q"	Interval is expressed in calendar quarters.
"m"	Interval is expressed in months.
"y"	Interval is expressed in days of the year.
"d"	Interval is expressed in days.
"w"	Interval is expressed in weekdays.
"ww"	Interval is expressed in weeks of the year.
"h"	Interval is expressed in hours.
"n"	Interval is expressed in minutes.
"s"	Interval is expressed in seconds.

For example, this adds 11 days to the current date:

```
wscript.echo DateAdd("d", 11, Now)
```

For the `DateAdd` function, the `"d"`, `"w"`, and `"y"` interval types have the same effect.

The `DateDiff` function computes the interval between two dates. The interval can be expressed in different units as specified by the *`type`* argument. The *`type`* argument can have any of the values shown in Table 4.4. For example:

```
nDays = DateDiff("d", #1/1/98#, #1/4/99#)
```

This example computes the number of days between the two dates.

The `DateDiff` function has an optional fourth *`firstday`* argument that has the same use as the *`firstday`* argument to the `Weekday` function. This is only necessary when using the `"w"` or `"ww"` interval types.

The final (optional) argument to `DateDiff` is used to specify how the first week of the year is determined, as follows:

- `vbUseSystem` The `DateDiff` function uses the locale settings of the operating system.
- `vbFirstJan1` The first week is whichever week in which January 1 occurs. This is the default for `DateDiff`.
- `vbFirstFourDays` The first week is the first week that has at least four days in the new year.
- `vbFirstFullWeek` The first week is the first complete week in the year.

If the interval type is `"w"`, the `DateDiff` function computes the number of complete seven-day intervals between the two dates, starting on the day specified by the first date. If the interval type is `"ww"`, the `DateDiff` function computes the number of calendar weeks between the two dates, using the *`firstday`* argument to identify the starting day of the week.

The `DatePart` function returns the specified part of a date. The part to return is specified by the *`type`* argument. The *`type`* argument can have any of the values shown in Table 4.4. For example:

```
nMonth = DatePart("m", Now)
```

The `DatePart` function is similar to the various individual date part functions (such as `Year` and `Second`), but it has additional capabilities. For example, the `"ww"` type returns the week of the year, and the `"y"` type returns the day of the year (sometimes known as the Julian day). The `DatePart` function has optional *`firstday`* and *`firstweek`* arguments. The function of these arguments is identical to the corresponding arguments in the `DateDiff` and `Weekday` functions.

Other Date and Time Functions

The `Timer` function returns the number of seconds that have elapsed since midnight. It can be used to time short operations, provided these operations do not span across multiple days.

The `MonthName` function returns the name of a month. For example:

```
Wscript.Echo "The month is", MonthName(Month(Now))
```

The names returned by `MonthName` are locale specific. The optional second argument to `MonthName` controls the name format. If this argument is `True`, the month name is abbreviated to a shorter form. For example:

```
Wscript.Echo "The short month is", MonthName(Month(Now), True)
```

The `WeekdayName` function returns the name of a day of the week. For example:

```
Wscript.Echo "Today is", WeekdayName(Weekday(Now))
```

Like `MonthName`, the `WeekdayName` function takes an optional second argument that can be used to generate an abbreviated weekday name. For example:

```
Wscript.Echo "Today is", WeekdayName(Weekday(Now), True)
```

The `WeekdayName` function can also take an optional third argument that specifies the first day of the week. See the previous discussion of the `Weekday` function for more details on this argument.

GUI Functions

VBScript also provides several GUI functions. These can be used for simple interaction with the user. Table 4.5 lists the GUI functions available in VBScript.

Table 4.5 VBScript GUI Functions

Function	Description
`InputBox(prompt [,title] [,default] [,xpos] [,ypos] [,helpfile, context])`	Returns text entered into dialog box edit control.
`MsgBox(prompt, [,buttons] [,title] [,helpfile, context])`	Returns button clicked in a message box.

The `MsgBox` function displays a message box containing one or more buttons. When the user clicks one of these buttons, the function returns a value indicating which button was clicked. The *`prompt`* text is displayed in the message box. For example:

```
bContinue = MsgBox("Ready to continue")
```

By default, the `MsgBox` function displays a message box containing only one button, the OK button. To display other buttons and features, use the optional *`buttons`* argument. Choose one of the following constants to specify the buttons to display:

- `vbOKOnly` Display the OK button only. This is the default.
- `vbOKCancel` Display OK and Cancel buttons.
- `vbAbortRetryIgnore` Display Abort, Retry and Ignore buttons.
- `vbYesNoCancel` Display Yes, No and Cancel buttons.
- `vbYesNo` Display Yes and No buttons.
- `vbRetryCancel` Display Retry and Cancel buttons.

For example, this message box will contain Yes and No buttons only:

```
bYes = MsgBox("Do you want to create this account?", vbYesNo)
```

If an OK or Yes button is displayed, pressing the Enter key is the same as clicking the button. If a Cancel or No button is displayed, pressing the Esc key is the same as clicking the button.

In addition to the button constants in the preceding list, the *buttons* argument can also specify an icon to display in the dialog. Choose one of the following constants:

- `vbCritical` Displays the critical message icon.
- `vbQuestion` Displays the question mark (query) icon.
- `vbExclamation` Displays the warning message icon.
- `vbInformation` Display the information message icon.

By default, the first button displayed in the dialog is the default button. To make another button the default, specify one of the following constants for the *buttons* argument:

- `vbDefaultButton1` First button is the default (this is the default).
- `vbDefaultButton2` Second button is the default.
- `vbDefaultButton3` Third button is the default.
- `vbDefaultButton4` Fourth button is the default.

By default, the current script will wait for the message box to complete before continuing. Other applications are not affected. To make all applications wait until the message box is acknowledged, specify `vbSystemModal` as the *buttons* argument.

The *buttons* argument can specify a button set, icon, default button, and modal behavior in any desired combination. Simply combine the various constants using the `Or` or `+` operators. For example:

```
bOK = MsgBox("Confirm account deletion?", vbYesNo + vbQuestion)
```

This example displays a message box with Yes and No buttons and a question mark icon.

The return value from the message box indicates which button was clicked. This can be one of the following constants:

- `vbOK` The OK button was clicked, or the Enter key pressed.
- `vbCancel` The Cancel button was clicked, or the Esc key pressed.
- `vbAbort` The Abort button was clicked.
- `vbRetry` The Retry button was clicked.
- `vbIgnore` The Ignore button was clicked.
- `vbYes` The Yes button was clicked.
- `vbNo` The No button was clicked.

The optional third *title* argument to `MsgBox` can be used to provide a title for the message box. If not supplied, the default title `VBScript` is used.

Finally, a help context can be supplied using the optional *helpfile* and *context* arguments. Both must be supplied together. If present, the user can press the F1 key to obtain context sensitive help from the specified help file.

The `InputBox` function displays a simple dialog box containing a prompt and a single-input text box. The user can enter text into the text box and click OK. The function then returns the text that was entered into the text box as a string. For example:

```
sFilename = InputBox("Enter file name to delete:")
```

The dialog box displayed by the `InputBox` function always contains an OK and a Cancel button. If the Cancel button is clicked or the Esc key pressed, the `InputBox` function returns an empty string.

The optional second *title* argument to `InputBox` can be used to provide a title for the input box. If not supplied, the default title VBScript is used.

The optional *default* argument is used to supply a default value for the text box. This value is placed in the text box when the dialog box is first displayed.

The optional *xpos* and *ypos* arguments position the dialog box on the display. If this argument is absent, the dialog box is centered on the screen. Otherwise, the dialog is positioned as indicated. The coordinates are specified in units called *twips*, which are 1/1440″.

Finally, a help context can be supplied using the optional *helpfile* and *context* arguments. Both must be supplied together. If present, the user can press the F1 key to obtain context sensitive help from the specified help file.

Math Functions

VBScript provides a complete set of mathematical functions. Most of these functions perform familiar mathematical transforms, such as computing the natural logarithm of a numeric expression. Almost all the functions take a single numeric argument and return a numeric result. Table 4.6 lists the math functions available in VBScript.

Table 4.6 VBScript Math Functions

Function	Description
`Abs(`*number*`)`	Returns absolute value (positive magnitude) of *number*
`Atn(`*number*`)`	Returns arctangent, in radians, for *number*
`Cos(`*number*`)`	Returns cosine for *number* (in radians)

continues ▸

Function	Description
`Exp(number)`	Returns e raised to the power of *number* (natural anti-logarithm)
`Fix(number)`	Returns the integer part of *number*, discarding any fractional part
`Int(number)`	Returns the rounded integer part of *number*
`Log(number)`	Returns the natural logarithm of *number*
`Randomize number`	Initializes random number generator (this is a statement)
`Rnd[(number)]`	Returns a random number
`Round(number [,places])`	Rounds *number* to the number of decimal places specified by places
`Sgn(number)`	Returns the sign of *number*
`Sin(number)`	Returns sine for *number* (in radians)
`Sqr(number)`	Returns the square root of *number*
`Tan(number)`	Returns the tangent for *number* (in radians)

Rounding Functions

The `Int`, `Fix`, and `Round` functions round or truncate numeric values. Both `Int` and `Fix` truncate values to integers. Any fractional part is discarded. Unlike the `CInt` function (described in Chapter 3), which rounds the fractional part, the `Int` and `Fix` functions simply discard it, so `Int(8.7)` returns 8. The `Int` function always truncates toward negative infinity, so `Int(4.2)` returns 4 and `Int(-4.2)` returns -5. The `Fix` function truncates towards zero, so `Fix(4.2)` returns 4 but `Fix(-4.2)` returns -4.

The `Round` function rounds a value to the specified number of decimal places. For example:

```
x = Round(14.152, 1)
```

This sets the variable `x` to 14.2. The `Round` function performs normal mathematical rounding with digits less than five rounding down and digits five and greater rounding up. If the second expression (specifying the number of decimal places) is zero or absent, the `Round` function rounds to the nearest integer value. Like `Fix`, `Round` rounds toward zero, so `Round(-14.15)` returns -14.

Random Number Generation

The `Rnd` function returns a pseudo-random number between 0 and 1 (including 0 but excluding 1). The `Rnd` function uses a mathematical simulation of random numbers that follows a predefined pseudo-random sequence. This sequence is controlled by a *seed* value, a number that controls the sequence.

The expression used with the Rnd function controls how random numbers are generated:

- If the expression is positive, or not present, the next number in the pseudo random sequence is returned. For example:

  ```
  Wscript.Echo Rnd, Rnd, Rnd
  ```

  This example displays three different random values.
- If the expression is zero, the last random number to be generated is returned.
- If the expression is negative, the value of the expression is treated as a seed value, and the first random number generated from that seed is returned.

By default, VBScript uses a fixed built-in seed value to start the random number sequence when a script executes. This means that the same sequence of numbers is used each time the script executes. To change this behavior, use the Randomize statement. Its syntax is:

```
Randomize [expr]
```

If the optional expression is not present, the Randomize statement uses the operating system timer to initialize the random number seed. This typically generates random numbers that vary from run to run because the system timer returns unpredictable values.

If the expression is present, the Randomize statement uses the value and the current seed to generate a new seed. Thus, this starts a new random number sequence. However, because the previous seed is used to generate a new seed, the new sequence is only predictable if either of the following occur.

- Randomize is used before Rnd is used for the first time.
- Rnd is used with a negative value *before* calling Randomize, thus fixing the previous seed to a known value.

Other Math Functions

The trigonometric functions Sin, Cos, Tan, and Atn (arctangent) all use *radians* as their unit of angular measure. In this system, 360 degrees is equivalent to 2 * Pi radians. To convert radians to degrees, multiply by 180/Pi.

The Log and Exp (or anti-log) functions use *natural*, or base *e*, logarithms. To generate the base 10 logarithm of an expression, divide the result of the Log function by Log(10).

The Abs function returns the absolute value of an expression. That is, the function returns the positive magnitude of the expression. For example,

`Abs(5)` returns 5 and `Abs(-12.5)` returns 12.5. The `Sgn` function returns the sign of the expression. Negative values return -1, positive values return 1, and zero values return 0.

Miscellaneous Functions

Table 4.7 lists various miscellaneous functions provided by VBScript.

Table 4.7 VBScript Miscellaneous Functions

Function	Description
`ScriptEngine`	Returns text string describing current script engine.
`ScriptEngineBuildVersion`	Returns build version of current script engine.
`ScriptEngineMajorVersion`	Returns major version of current script engine.
`ScriptEngineMinorVersion`	Returns minor version of current script engine.

The `ScriptEngine` function returns a string indicating the script engine currently executing the script. For VBScript, this string is always `"VBScript"`. The function might also return `"VBA"` if the script is being executed by Visual Basic for Applications. The JScript script engine (for JavaScript or ECMAScript scripts) also has an equivalent function that returns `"JScript"`.

The `ScriptEngineBuildVersion` function returns the current build of the script engine. This is generally used for informational purposes only because there is no direct correspondence between build numbers and VBScript features.

The `ScriptEngineMajorVersion` and `ScriptEngineMinorVersion` functions return the major and minor versions of the VBScript engine. For example, if the version is 4.1, `ScriptEngineMajorVersion` returns 4 and `ScriptEngineMinorVersion` returns 1.

The `ScriptEngineMajorVersion` and `ScriptEngineMinorVersion` functions can be used to verify that the correct version of VBScript is available. This allows a script that uses a language feature introduced at a particular version of VBScript to check that the feature is available. For example:

```
If ScriptEngineMajorVersion < 5 Then Wscript.Echo "VBScript 5.0 or later required."
```

In VBScript, this kind of version checking has limited functionality, however. VBScript pre-compiles scripts before they execute, and pre-compiling (say) a V5.0 script on a V3.x script engine typically generates a compile error *before* any script code executes.

When performing version checking, never check *only* the minor version—this is meaningless unless the major version is always checked. Also, always check that the version numbers are greater than a particular value, not equal to. Finally, take care to correctly check version numbers. For example, the following code does *not* work as expected:

```
If ScriptEngineMajorVersion >= 5 And ScriptEngineMinorVersion >= 1 Then
    Wscript.Echo "Version > 5.1"
End If
```

This code might appear to check that the version number is 5.1 or greater. However, it does not work as expected because the second clause in the `If` statement fails for a version of 6.0. The correct statement is:

```
If ScriptEngineMajorVersion > 5 Or _
        (ScriptEngineMajorVersion = 5 And ScriptEngineMinorVersion >= 1) Then
    Wscript.Echo "Version >= 5.1"
End If
```

Summary

VBScript contains a rich set of built-in functions that manipulate all types of data. The string functions are particularly useful in system scripts because these scripts typically deal with textual data, such as file names or registry keys.

Other useful function groups include: the date/time functions, which are particularly useful when working with files and folders; the formatting functions, which allow reports to be laid out accurately in columns; and the random number functions. Other math functions are less frequently used in system scripts.

5

User-Defined Procedures

This chapter describes the various forms of *procedures* provided by VBScript. Procedural programming is the key to writing almost all non-trivial scripts, and it is the foundation for *structured programming*, which allows a complex programming problem to be broken down into a set of simpler sub-problems.

VBScript supports two types of procedures:

- *Subroutines* These encapsulate and group together a set of statements that define a specific task.
- *User-defined functions* These encapsulate a computation that returns a value to an expression.

Note

As with all the sample scripts in this book, the scripts in this chapter should be run using the CSCRIPT host unless otherwise noted. The examples shown assume that CSCRIPT is the default WSH host. (See Chapter 1, "Introducing WSH," for information on selecting the default WSH host.)

Subroutines

Chapter 2, "VBScript Language Essentials," described the various forms of *control flow*, such as the `If` and the various `Do Loop` statements. Many simple scripts can be constructed using just these flow statements, but trying to develop more complex scripts in this way can lead to difficulties, such as:

- The script is limited to flowing from the first line to the last (perhaps with some intermediate loops). This flow might not be suitable for some tasks.
- Long, continuous scripts are difficult to understand. It's hard to see the overall design and goals of a script by looking at all the individual detailed statements.

- If a set of statements needs to repeat in different parts of the script, these statements must be explicitly entered in the script each time they are needed.

Subroutines solve all these problems (and several others). A *subroutine* is simply a named collection of VBScript statements that can be invoked, or "called," from anywhere within the script. Invoking the subroutine executes the statements within the subroutine as if they had been entered in-line at the location in the script where the subroutine was invoked.

To create a subroutine, enclose the statements for the subroutine within a `Sub` and `End Sub` statement pair. The syntax is:

```
Sub name
        statement
        .
        .
End Sub
```

The `Sub` and `End Sub` statement pair is said to *declare* the subroutine. Declaring a subroutine does *not* execute the statements within the subroutine. The *`name`* following the `Sub` keyword names the subroutine, and it is used to reference the subroutine elsewhere in the script. The *`statements`* are any valid VBScript statements, and they are sometimes known as the *procedure body*, or *subroutine body*. It is valid for the procedure body to be empty (that is, contain no statements).

To execute the statements in the procedure body, simply enter the name of the subroutine as a statement anywhere within the main script. This is known as *invoking,* or *calling,* the subroutine. When a subroutine is invoked, VBScript performs the following actions:

1. The location of the subroutine invoking statement is recorded.
2. VBScript searches the script for a `Sub` statement with a matching name. (This actually happens very quickly because VBScript pre-processes scripts to identify all subroutines before beginning script execution).
3. Statement execution then continues at the first statement in the procedure body of the subroutine.
4. When the end of the subroutine is reached (the `End Sub` statement), VBScript resumes executing statements following the statement that originally invoked the subroutine, using the location information recorded in step 1.

These concepts are most easily understood with an example. Listing 5.1 shows a simple script that displays the day of the week for each date entered as a command-line argument.

Listing 5.1 `DayOfWeek1.vbs` *Script*

```
'//////////////////////////////////////////////////////////////////////////
' $Workfile: DayOfWeek1.vbs $ $Revision: 1 $ $Date: 5/22/99 3:39p $
' $Archive: /Scripts/DayOfWeek1.vbs $
' Copyright (c) 1998 Tim Hill. All Rights Reserved.
'//////////////////////////////////////////////////////////////////////////

' Display day of the week

Option Explicit
Wscript.Echo String(40, "-")
Wscript.Echo "DayOfWeek version 1.0"
Wscript.Echo "Copyright (c) 1999 The Acme Software Co."
Wscript.Echo String(40, "-")

Dim sArg

For Each sArg In Wscript.Arguments
    If IsDate(sArg) Then
        Wscript.Echo sArg, "is a", WeekdayName(Weekday(DateValue(sArg)))
    End If
Next

'//////////////////////////////////////////////////////////////////////////
```

The `DayOfWeek1.vbs` script shown in Listing 5.1 actually consists of two distinct parts. The first part displays a sign-on banner message, and the second part processes the command-line arguments, displaying a day of the week for each valid date entered. The second part uses a `For Each` iterator loop to process each command-line argument via the `sArg` variable. Listing 5.2 shows the same program re-written to use two procedures.

Listing 5.2 `DayOfWeek2.vbs` *Script*

```
'//////////////////////////////////////////////////////////////////////////
' $Workfile: DayOfWeek2.vbs $ $Revision: 1 $ $Date: 5/22/99 3:39p $
' $Archive: /Scripts/DayOfWeek2.vbs $
' Copyright (c) 1998 Tim Hill. All Rights Reserved.
'//////////////////////////////////////////////////////////////////////////

' Display day of the week

Option Explicit
ShowBanner
ProcessArgs

Sub ProcessArgs
    Dim sArg
```

continues ▶

Listing 5.2 *continued*

```
12     For Each sArg In Wscript.Arguments
13         If IsDate(sArg) Then
14             Wscript.Echo sArg, "is a", WeekdayName(Weekday(DateValue(sArg)))
15         End If
16     Next
17 End Sub

18 Sub ShowBanner
19     Wscript.Echo String(40, "-")
20     Wscript.Echo "DayOfWeek version 1.0"
21     Wscript.Echo "Copyright (c) 1999 The Acme Software Co."
22     Wscript.Echo String(40, "-")
23 End Sub

24 '///////////////////////////////////////////////////////////////////////////
```

Examining the `DayOfWeek2.vbs` script reveals a couple of changes from the first version of this script:

- The two distinct parts of the script have been moved into two subroutines, named `ProcessArgs` and `ShowBanner`.
- Two new statements have been added to the main script (lines 8 and 9). These statements invoke the two new subroutines by name.

When this script executes, the following events occur:

1. The first statement (line 7), `Option Explicit`, executes.
2. The next statement (line 8), `ShowBanner`, is the name of one of the subroutines. VBScript thus invokes the subroutine, and control flow moves to the first line of the `ShowBanner` subroutine, line 19.
3. The statements in the `ShowBanner` subroutine (lines 19 to 22) execute normally.
4. At line 23, the subroutine ends. VBScript then *returns* from the subroutine to its original location and continues with the next statement following the subroutine invocation, in this case line 9.
5. Line 9 invokes the `ProcessArgs` subroutine. Again, control flow moves to the first line of this subroutine at line 11.
6. The statements in the `ProcessArgs` subroutine (lines 11 to 16) execute normally, including the `For Each` loop.
7. At line 17, the subroutine ends and VBScript returns from the subroutine to its previous location and continues executing at the statement following line 9.
8. The next line is line 10, which is the start of the `ProcessArgs` subroutine. VBScript does *not* execute this subroutine again, nor does it

execute the `ShowBanner` subroutine following this at line 18. In fact, there are *no* more statements to execute in this script following line 9, and so the script ends at this point.

VBScript does *not* execute subroutine statements if it encounters a `Sub` statement somewhere within the script. Statements within subroutines are *only* executed when a subroutine is explicitly invoked, not when it is declared. This means that `Sub` statements and procedure bodies can be placed anywhere within a script, either before or after the main script statements. It also means that the ordering of individual subroutines is unimportant. This is shown in `DayOfWeek2.vbs`, which actually places the two subroutines in the reverse of the order in which they are invoked.

The process of decomposing a script into individual subroutines is somewhat arbitrary. Here is an excerpt from another variation on the `DayOfWeek1.vbs` script:

```
Sub ShowValidDate
    If IsDate(sArg) Then
        Wscript.Echo sArg, "is a", WeekdayName(Weekday(DateValue(sArg)))
    End If
End Sub

Dim sArg
For Each sArg In Wscript.Arguments
    ShowValidDate
Next
```

In this version, the `For Each` iterator loop remains outside the subroutines and in the main script body. Instead, it invokes a new subroutine called `ShowValidDate` for each individual argument.

This variation also illustrates another important feature of subroutines. All the variables declared in the main script body are available for access by the subroutine. In this case, the `sArg` variable is available within the `ShowValidDate` subroutine. Detailed rules for variable access are described later in the "Local Procedure Variables" section.

The *Call* Statement

Subroutines are normally invoked simply by using the subroutine name as a statement. However, VBScript also supports the `Call` statement to invoke a subroutine explicitly. The syntax of the `Call` statement is:

```
Call subroutine
```

Replace *`subroutine`* with the name of the subroutine to invoke. For example, the following two statements are identical:

```
ShowValidDate
Call ShowValidDate
```

The `Call` statement has an identical effect to the direct "invocation by name" method of subroutine invocation. However, this book uses the direct invocation method exclusively—the `Call` statement is provided primarily for backward compatibility with earlier versions of Visual Basic.

The `Call` statement differs slightly from direct subroutine invocation if one or more arguments are supplied to the procedure. In this case, the arguments must be enclosed in parentheses if the `Call` statement is used. For more information, see the "Procedure Arguments" section later in this chapter.

The *Exit Sub* Statement

Subroutines return when control flow reaches the `End Sub` statement. This is sometimes known as "falling off the end" of the subroutine. Occasionally, however, it is desirable to terminate subroutine execution before the end of the subroutine is reached. The `Exit Sub` statement is used to terminate subroutine execution. The syntax is:

```
Exit Sub
```

When an `Exit Sub` statement executes, no further statements in the subroutine are executed and control flow returns to the statement following that which invoked the subroutine, just as if the `End Sub` statement had been reached.

The `Exit Sub` statement is typically used in an `If` statement. For example:

```
Sub WeeklyBackup

    If Weekday(Date) <> 1 Then Exit Sub
    ' It's Sunday, time for a weekly backup...
End Sub
```

Here, a subroutine called `WeeklyBackup` is (presumably) only supposed to run on Sundays. The subroutine, therefore, checks to see if it is indeed Sunday, and it exits if it is any other day of the week.

User-Defined Functions

Chapter 4, "Built-In Functions," described the various built-in functions available in VBScript in detail. In addition, VBScript allows the definition of additional functions within the script itself. These are called *user-defined functions*.

Declare a user-defined function using a `Function` and `End Function` statement pair. The syntax is:

```
Function name
    statement
    .
    .
End Function
```

This syntax is similar to that used to declare subroutines, and user defined functions share most of the features of subroutines. There are, however, several slight differences:

- User defined functions are invoked by including the name of the function as part of an expression.
- A user-defined function always returns a value.
- A used-defined function includes a special return-value variable.

Just like built-in functions, user defined functions are used within expressions. The function is invoked during the evaluation of the expression. When the function is invoked, the statements that comprise the procedure body are executed. These statements then determine the return value of the function. When the function returns, the return value is then used within the expression. For example:

```
Function TodayIs
    TodayIs = WeekdayName(Weekday(Date))
End Function
```

This example declares a user-defined function called `TodayIs`. This function returns a string giving the weekday name for today's date, using the `WeekdayName`, `Weekday`, and `Date` built-in functions.

Within a user-defined function, VBScript automatically declares a special variable that has the same name as the function. When the function returns, the value of this variable is used as the return value of the function. In the example `TodayIs` function, the variable is assigned the result of the `WeekdayName` function, which is the name of the day of the week for the expression `Weekday(Date)`.

The special return-value variable is only available within the function body. While in the function, the variable can be assigned different values or even used in expressions. However, the return value from the function is always the *final* value that the variable has when the function returns.

To invoke a user-defined function, include the function name anywhere that a variable or constant can be used within an expression. For example:

```
Wscript.Echo "Today is " & TodayIs
```

This example displays the result of the string expression `"Today is " & TodayIs`, which is the literal text concatenated with the return value of the `TodayIs` function. For example:

```
Today is Monday
```

User-defined functions also support an `Exit Function` statement that is similar in operation to the `Exit Sub` statement for subroutines. When executed, the `Exit Function` statement causes the function to immediately return, and whatever value is currently assigned to the special return value variable is then used as the return value.

Invoking Procedures from Procedures

Although procedure declarations can be placed anywhere within the main script body, you *cannot* declare a new procedure *within* the body of another. For example, the following is *not* valid:

```
Sub MySub1
    ' Cannot declare one Sub within another!
    Sub MySub2
    End Sub
End Sub
```

However, it *is* legal to *invoke* one procedure from within another. For example:

```
Wscript.Echo "Starting"
Sub2 : Sub1
Wscript.Echo "Ending"

Sub Sub2
    Wscript.Echo "In Sub2"
End Sub
Sub Sub1
    Wscript.Echo "In Sub1"
    Sub2
End Sub
```

When these statements execute, they generate the following output:

```
Starting
In Sub2
In Sub1
In Sub2
Ending
```

The `Sub2` subroutine executes twice: once from the main script body, and once from within the body of `Sub1`.

Program Guide

Tracing Nested Subroutines

If you are unfamiliar with procedural programming, you might want to take a moment to follow the control flow in the preceding example. Pay close attention to the order in which the two subroutines are invoked and the order in which they return.

When a subroutine returns, either as a result of falling off the end of the subroutine body, or because of an `Exit Sub` *statement, control flow always continues with the statement following the original subroutine invocation. This is true even when subroutine invocations nest one inside another.*

When `Sub2` *is invoked from within* `Sub1`, *it first executes the* `Wscript.Echo` *statement, and then falls off the end of the subroutine body. This causes VBScript to continue with the next statement following the invocation of* `Sub1`. *In this case, this statement is the* `End Sub` *statement in* `Sub1`, *so* `Sub1` *also falls off the end of the subroutine body.*

Invoking procedures from within other procedures is called *procedure nesting* and is common in scripts that are more complex. VBScript places no fixed limits on the depth of procedure nesting—the only limit placed on how deeply procedures can nest is available memory because each procedure invocation has an associated (although small) memory overhead.

User-defined function invocations can also be nested, allowing an expression within a user-defined function to invoke another user-defined function. In fact, VBScript allows any combination of subroutine and user-defined function nesting. A subroutine may contain an expression that invokes a user-defined function, and that function may invoke one or more subroutines, which may, in turn, invoke other subroutines or user-defined functions.

The most complex scenarios occur when a procedure (subroutine or user-defined function) invokes *itself*. This is a condition known as recursion, which is explained later in the "Recursion" section.

Data Storage in Procedures

Chapter 2 described the `Dim` and `Const` statements that are used to declare variables and constants. Variables and constants that are declared within the main body of a script are available within procedures that are called by that script. For example:

```
Sub ShowValue
    Wscript.Echo "x=", x
End Sub

Dim x
x = 12
ShowValue
```

In this example, the `ShowValue` procedure can access the variable `x` that is declared in the main body of the script.

Variables used in subroutines must be declared before the subroutine is invoked; although the declaration does *not* need to physically precede the subroutine within the script file. This is shown in the preceding example, where the variable `x` is declared physically below the `ShowValue` subroutine. However, the variable is declared *before* the `ShowValue` subroutine is actually invoked because the `Dim` statement executes first.

All variables and constants declared using `Dim` and `Const` statements in the main body of the script (outside of any procedures) are said to have *global scope*, and they are known as *global* variables and constants. This is because after the variable or constant is declared, it is available throughout the rest of the script, including within all procedure bodies.

In addition to global variables and constants, it is also possible to declare variables and constants within a procedure body. For example:

```
Sub TodaysDate
    Dim dDate
    dDate = Date
    Wscript.Echo "Today is", dDate
End Sub
```

In this example, the variable `dDate` is declared *inside* the `TodaysDate` subroutine. The usual `Dim` statement is used—the difference is that the statement is within the subroutine.

Variables and constants declared within a procedure are said to have *local scope*, and they are known as *local* variables and constants.

Namespaces and Shadowing

Variables and constants declared within a procedure (that is, local variables) are totally independent of all other variables and constants. They can even have the same names as global variables, constants, or local variables and constants declared in other procedures. For example:

```
Sub Test1
    Dim nCount
End Sub

Sub Test2
    Dim nCount
End Sub

Dim nCount
```

In this example, there are three distinct variables all named `nCount`. Two of these exist locally in two distinct procedures, and a third is declared globally. As previously explained, all three variables are distinct, so changing the value or data type of one variable does *not* alter the other two in any way.

The use of distinct variables with the same name is an expression of an idea known as a *namespace*. VBScript has a single public namespace in which all global variables reside, and each procedure has its own private namespace for its local variables. *Within* a namespace, each variable or constant must have a unique name, but two distinct variables can share the same name if they are in different namespaces.

Statements within a procedure actually have access to both the global namespace and their own local namespace. This is why these statements can access global variables as well as their own local variables. However, if a global and local variable have the same name, a process known as *shadowing* occurs. In this case, the global variable is *shadowed* by the local variable, and *only* the local variable is accessible. For example:

```
Sub Shadow
    Dim x
    Wscript.Echo "Shadow x=", x
End Sub

Dim x
x = 10
Shadow
Wscript.Echo "Main x=", x
```

In this example, the main script body and the `Shadow` subroutine have a variable named `x`. Within the main script body, references to `x` access the global variable. Within the `Shadow` procedure, references to `x` access the local variable. This means that for the duration of the `Shadow` procedure the global variable `x` is hidden—there is no way for the `Shadow` procedure to access the global `x` although the variable still exists and will "emerge from the shadows" after the `Shadow` procedure returns.

Scope and Lifetime

The previous sections described two possible variable scopes: global and local. The *scope* of a variable is a static indication of which statements are allowed to access that variable. The indication is static because it can be determined if the reference to a variable is legal simply by examining the script code. For example:

```
Option Explicit
Sub NoWay
    Dim nLocal
End Sub

Dim x
x = nLocal
```

Here, the main body of the script attempts to access a local scope variable called `nLocal`. This is invalid, and VBScript will not even begin execution of such a badly formed script. In fact, the VBScript language is such that the VBScript interpreter can detect *all* scope errors such as these before script execution begins.

In addition to scope, all variables also have a lifetime. The *lifetime* of the variable is a dynamic indication of when the variable exists during the script execution. In all cases, scope can be determined by the examination of a script's statements. Lifetime, however, can sometimes only be determined by tracing the dynamic execution of the script.

Simple global variables declared with `Dim` statements have a scope and lifetime that starts when the variable is declared and ends when the script terminates. Local variables in a procedure have a scope and lifetime that encompasses the procedure body. This has several consequences:

- As previously explained, local variables are only accessible within the procedure in which they are declared.
- Local variables are created when the procedure is invoked and destroyed when the procedure returns. They do *not* continue to exist between procedure invocations.

The second rule means that it is not possible to use a local variable to maintain information *between* invocations of a procedure. For example, the following does *not* work:

```
Sub WontWork
    Dim nInvokeCount
    nInvokeCount = nInvokeCount + 1
End Sub
```

Here, the code attempts to track how many times a subroutine is invoked by incrementing the local variable `nInvokeCount`. However, this variable is created each time the subroutine is invoked; so, the result of the increment is always one (because the initial value of `nInvokeCount` is always zero), no matter how often the subroutine is invoked. The only way to do this kind of operation is to use a global variable, which has a lifetime that spans invocations of the procedure.

In most cases, the scope and lifetime of a variable are similar. For example, a global variable has a lifetime that begins when a `Dim` statement declaring the variable executes, and then the global variable continues until the script terminates. The *scope* of such a variable includes all statements in the main body of the script and all statements in procedures, except those procedures that shadow the global variable with a local variable of the same name. While such a procedure executes, a global variable is within its lifetime but is out of scope.

Other variables also have scopes and lifetimes that differ. For example:

```
Dim a()
ReDim a(100)
a(2) = 1000
If Wscript.Arguments.Count > 0 Then Erase a
Wscript.Echo a(2)
```

In this example, the variable a holds a dynamic array. The array is declared using the `Dim` statement and has a scope that starts with this statement and continues until the end of the script. The final `Wscript.Echo` statement is therefore a valid script. However, the *lifetime* of the variable is more complex. First, the lifetime only begins with the `ReDim` statement that allocates 101 elements to the array. Second, if one or more command line arguments are present, the `Erase` statement executes, which deletes the dynamic array and thus ends its lifetime. Therefore, the lifetime of the array contents is determined *at run time* as a result of script execution. In fact, if a command argument is present, the `Wscript.Echo` statement fails with an error because in this case `a(2)` is no longer valid.

Balancing Global and Local Variable Use

In general, a procedure should use local variables for *all* its data storage requirements, unless it *must* use global variables. Reasons for accessing global variables within a script include:

- *Initializing Global Variables* Frequently a script contains an `Init` or `Setup` procedure that performs internal set up operations for the script. Such a procedure can be responsible for the initialization of various global variables.
- *Accessing Standard Global Values* Many scripts maintain well-defined state information in global variables, and then make this state information directly available to procedures.
- *Maintaining State* Some procedures might need to maintain data or state information across individual invocations. Global variables are the only way this can be done without using objects (described in Part II, "Objects and Classes").

Procedures that make copious use of global variables are difficult to maintain and should be avoided. In particular, such practices frequently lead to subtle errors where one procedure alters a variable unexpectedly. If a procedure *does* alter or use global variables, it is always a good idea to describe clearly within the script (using comments) which global variables are used and why. In fact, it is possible to categorize procedures by the way they use global variables:

- The best procedures make *no* use of global variables. These procedures are totally self-contained, and they can be reused in other scripts simply by cutting and pasting the procedure code into the new script.
- Poorer procedures use the values in global variables, but do not alter them (that is, assign new values to one or more global variables). Before these procedures can be used, it is necessary to make sure that the global variables in question are declared and initialized with appropriate values.

- The poorest procedures use and alter the values of global variables. Unless carefully documented and used, these procedures can have unexpected side effects.

It might also appear that global variables are the only way to pass information and data into a procedure for processing. However, this is better handled by procedure arguments, which are described in the next section.

Global and Local Variable Naming

Chapter 3, "VBScript Data Storage," introduced the concept of a naming convention for variables, whereby a short prefix to the name indicated the type of data stored in the variable. Table 3.2 lists the various recommended prefixes. This table also lists a *global scope prefix*, which can be used to indicate in a script that a variable has global scope. The global scope prefix is `g_`, and it is prefixed to the variable name before the type prefix. For example:

```
Dim g_sArg, g_dToday
```

This `Dim` statement declares two global variables, presumably a string and a date respectively.

There are several advantages to using this prefix convention:

- The prefix makes all global variable names unique, and avoids the possibility of a global variable being shadowed by a local variable.
- Global variables are easily identified within procedures. This makes it easier to determine which global variables are used by a procedure.

However, note that the global scope prefix, like the data type prefixes, is merely a convention, and VBScript does not enforce this name system in any way. As previously noted, however, using such a convention can help to document the relationships between global variables and procedures.

Procedure Arguments

Procedures—both subroutines and user-defined functions—can also be supplied with one or more *arguments*. These arguments allow data to be passed to the procedure for processing.

To specify that a procedure takes one or more arguments, follow the name of the procedure with a list of variable names in parentheses. For example:

```
Function ZeroPad(nValue, nWidth)
    ZeroPad = Right(String(nWidth, "0") & CStr(nValue), nWidth)
End Function
```

This function converts a data value to a string and pads it on the left with one or more leading zeroes. The function takes two arguments: `nValue`, which is the value to convert to a string, and `nWidth`, which specifies the width of the formatted string.

Arguments that are specified in this way are sometimes called *parameters*, or *formal parameters*. A procedure parameter is a special type of local variable, and placing the name of the parameter in parentheses after the procedure name declares the variable for use within the procedure body. Parameters can be used within the script body like normal local variables. Because parameters are a form of local variable, they follow the same scope and lifetime rules as normal local variables.

Normal local variables are declared using a `Dim` statement and are initialized to `Empty` when the procedure body begins execution. Parameters are initialized by the arguments that are specified when the procedure is invoked. To specify one or more arguments when invoking a function, enclose the arguments in parentheses after the function name, separated by commas. For example:

```
Wscript.Echo ZeroPad(4, 2)
```

Notice that the syntax for invoking user-defined functions is identical to the syntax for calling built-in functions.

Subroutines can also use parameters. For example:

```
Sub ShowVarType(vVar)
    Wscript.Echo "The type is", TypeName(vVar)
End Sub
Dim a
a = #1/1/98#
ShowVarType a
```

If a subroutine is invoked simply by using its name as a statement, the argument list should follow the subroutine name *without* any enclosing parentheses. If the `Call` statement is used, the argument list *must* be enclosed in parentheses. For example, the following two invocations are identical:

```
ShowVarType x
Call ShowVarType(x)
```

Regardless of the procedure type (subroutine or function) or the invocation method, the number of arguments passed to a procedure must always be the same as the number of parameters specified by the procedure declaration.

Associating Argument and Parameters

When a procedure is invoked, VBScript must associate the arguments specified in the procedure invocation with the corresponding parameters specified in the procedure body. It can do this in one of two different ways:

- *By value*—If an argument is associated with a parameter by value, before the procedure body executes, VBScript copies the current value of the argument to the parameter.

- *By reference*—If an argument is associated with a parameter by reference, VBScript treats the parameter as an *alias* for the argument during the execution of the procedure body.

By value association is actually quite simple. When a procedure is invoked and before the first statement of the procedure body executes, VBScript executes a hidden assignment statement for each "by value" parameter. For example:

```
Sub Showxy(x, y)
    Wscript.Echo x, y
End Sub

Showit 14 + 5, 1000 * 2
```

In this example, when the `Showxy` subroutine is invoked, VBScript executes two hidden assignment statements that, in effect, simulate the following statements:

```
x = 14 + 5
y = 1000 * 2
```

Thus, when the subroutine body executes, each "by value" parameter contains the result of the corresponding argument expression.

The "by reference" association is slightly more complex. When a procedure is invoked, any "by reference" parameters are, in effect, replaced with the variable specified as an argument throughout the procedure body. For example:

```
Sub Addxy(x, y)
    x = x + y
End Sub

Dim a, b
a = 10 : b = 20
Addxy a, b
Wscript.Echo a
```

In this example, when the `Addxy` subroutine is invoked, VBScript in effect re-writes the subroutine to look like this:

```
Sub Addxy(x, y)
    a = a + b
End Sub
```

Because both `a` and `b` are global variables, the assignment statement changes the value of the global variable `a`.

The "re-writing" operation illustrated in the preceding example is efficient. VBScript does not actually alter the script text in any way. Instead, it uses a technique that is virtually instantaneous, so passing arguments by reference is as efficient as passing them by value.

VBScript chooses the argument association method as follows:

- If the argument is a simple variable, array, or array element, VBScript uses the "by reference" method.
- If the argument is an expression, VBScript uses the "by value" method.

The method to use can also be specified explicitly when the procedure is declared. To specify the argument association method, prefix a procedure parameter with the `ByVal` or `ByRef` keywords. For example:

```
Sub Addxy(ByRef x, ByVal y)
    x = x + y
End Sub
```

Here, the `Addxy` procedure specifies that the first argument should be passed by reference, and the second argument should be passed by value.

The presence of the `ByVal` or `ByRef` keywords modifies the way VBScript chooses the argument association method as follows:

- If the parameter corresponding to an argument specifies `ByVal`, VBScript passes the argument by value.
- If the argument is an expression, VBScript passes the argument by value *even* if the `ByRef` keyword is specified in the corresponding parameter.
- If the argument is a variable, array, or array element and the corresponding parameter does *not* specify `ByVal`, VBScript passes the argument by reference.

One of the most important things to understand about passing arguments by reference is that *the value of the corresponding argument variable can be altered*. When an argument is passed by value, the procedure parameter behaves like a normal local variable. Any changes made to the parameter are entirely local to the procedure and do not affect the argument used to initialize the parameter. This is a direct result of the way VBScript passes arguments by value via a hidden assignment statement.

However, arguments passed by reference are aliases for variables outside the procedure body. Thus, altering a parameter value within the procedure body *also* alters the value of the variable specified as an argument.

Sometimes this can be desirable, for example, to update a global variable or to pass back several values as results. Sometimes, however, this is *not* desirable. In this case, it is important to declare the parameter as `ByVal` to prevent the procedure from accidentally altering the argument variable.

The argument association rules can be illustrated as follows:

```
Sub PassArgs(ByRef x, ByVal y, z)
    x = 10
    y = 11
    z = 12
End Sub

Dim a, b, c
PassArgs a, b, c
PassArgs 1, 2, 3
PassArgs (a), (b), (c)
```

Here, the `PassArgs` subroutine has three parameters. The first, `x`, is explicitly passed by reference; the second, `y`, is explicitly passed by value; and the third, `z`, uses the default passing convention.

In the first invocation of `PassArgs`, three global variables are used as arguments. The first parameter is declared `ByRef`, and so the variable `a` becomes 10 when the assignment statement `x = 10` executes. The second parameter is declared `ByVal`, and so the variable `b` is unaltered by the `PassArgs` procedure. The third parameter uses default parameter passing. Because the argument is a variable, the argument is passed by reference, and the assignment statement `z = 12` *does* alter the value of the variable `c`.

In the second invocation of `PassArgs`, three expressions (actually just numbers) are used as arguments. Using expressions as arguments forces VBScript to pass the arguments by value regardless of the procedure declaration.

In the third invocation of `PassArgs`, it might appear that three global variables are again passed as arguments. However, enclosing a variable in parentheses makes VBScript treat the variable as an expression. Therefore, in this case, the arguments are again passed by value, although the arguments are variables. Enclosing a variable name in parentheses like this will always ensure that the argument is passed by value, regardless of the procedure declaration. This ensures that the variable value is never altered by the procedure.

Passing Arrays as Arguments

Chapter 3 introduced many of the features of arrays, including the use of dynamic arrays and the technique of storing an array inside a normal variable. These same techniques can be used to pass arrays as arguments to procedures. For example:

```
Function SumOfElements(a)
    Dim x
    SumOfElements = 0
    If Not IsArray(a) Then Exit Function
    For x = LBound(a) To UBound(a)
        SumOfElements = SumOfElements + a(x)
    Next
End Function

Dim w(1000), x
For x = 0 To 1000
    w(x) = x
Next
Wscript.Echo SumOfElements(w)
```

In this example, the `SumOfElements` function takes a single argument `a` and returns the arithmetic sum of all the elements in the array. To make the function robust, the function checks that the passed argument is indeed an array using the `IsArray` function (described in Chapter 3). If it is not, the function returns 0. Otherwise, the function sums the elements one by one and returns the result.

In the preceding example, the global array variable `w` is used as an argument. Because this is a variable and not an expression, the argument is passed by reference and not by value. To pass the array by value, either enclose the argument `w` in an extra set of parentheses, or specify `ByVal` in the declaration of `SumOfElements`.

Program Guide

Parentheses Overload

VBScript uses parentheses for three quite distinct purposes:

- *To indicate the order of evaluation within an expression*
- *To enclose the list of arguments passed to a function*
- *To enclose the list of array element indices*

Because of the structure of the VBScript language, the meaning of parentheses is never ambiguous. However, it is sometimes confusing to figure out what each set of parentheses mean. In the invocation of the preceding `SumOfElements` *function, the array* `w` *is passed as an argument. The parentheses around the argument* `w` *are present because function arguments are always enclosed in parentheses. Therefore, the argument that is passed to the* `SumOfElements` *function is simply* `w`*, which is a variable. Following the normal rules for argument passing, this means that the* *array is passed by reference. To pass the array by value, enclose it in an additional set of parentheses, as follows:*

```
Wscript.Echo SumOfElements((w))
```

Here, the outermost parentheses are still the parentheses used to enclose the argument list of the function. Within them, the `(w)` *argument is now seen as an expression by VBScript, and so the argument is passed by value, not by reference.*

The most extreme case can be illustrated as follows:

```
Wscript.Echo SumOfElements((w(1)))
```

This expression can be decoded as follows: The innermost set of parentheses specifies an element index for the array `w`, *and so the result is a simple variable,* `w(1)`. *The next set of parentheses encloses the variable as before, making it an expression. The final, outermost, parentheses delimit the argument list of the function* `SumOfElements`.

Both by reference and by value argument passing operate in the same manner for arrays as they do for simple variables. If by value argument passing is used, a hidden assignment is performed as usual. If by reference argument passing is used, the parameter name is aliased to the array. For example:

```
Sub Extend(ByRef a)
    ReDim a(UBound(a) + 100)
End Sub

Dim x(), y()
ReDim x(100)
ReDim y(100)
Extend x
Extend (y)
Wscript.Echo UBound(x), UBound(y)
```

In this example, the subroutine `Extend` enlarges a dynamic array by 100 elements each time it is called. To work correctly, this subroutine *must* use by reference passing. Otherwise, the `ReDim` statement just enlarges the local variable copy of the passed array, not the original array. Thus, the second invocation of `Extend` does not work and the array `y` is not extended as desired.

As previously noted, passing arguments by value is safer than passing them by reference because it prevents the procedure from unexpectedly altering the value of variables used as arguments. This is also true for arrays. However, it is sometimes desirable to pass arrays by reference even when the procedure should not alter the array. The reason is that the hidden assignment statement used to pass an argument by value can be very time consuming with large arrays. Assigning the value of a 250,000-element array, for example, might take several seconds. It also requires that two copies of the array data exist in memory simultaneously, which causes the script to consume more system memory.

Passing large arrays by reference has neither of these disadvantages. The aliasing process, used when an argument is passed by reference, is as fast for an array as it is for a simple variable, regardless of the size of the array. Furthermore, the alias process does not create an additional copy of the array in memory. Only one copy of the array exists, and this copy is shared between the invoking script code and the procedure.

Advanced Procedure Techniques

As noted in the introduction to this chapter, procedures play an important role in all non-trivial script projects. The ability to encapsulate blocks of functionality within a procedure "envelope" is the first step towards structured design.

The primary advantage of procedural programming is the ability to separate *interface* from *implementation*. The interface to a procedure consists of the arguments to the procedure, any global variable requirements, and a description of the actions performed by the procedure. What the interface does *not* specify is *how* the procedure actually implements the functionality implied by the interface. That is purely an implementation detail. This means that a procedure's implementation (that is, the procedure body) can be totally re-written or modified in any way without affecting the rest of the script as long as the interface remains unaltered.

Without the separation of interface and implementation that is possible with procedures, any changes to implementation could have a ripple-through effect to any other parts of a script. This would make script modification nearly impossible, even with quite short scripts.

Designing effective procedures involves following several basic design rules:

- Use parameters to pass all data to procedures. Don't use global variables. Add comments to the procedure to describe each parameter, the expected data type, and any special considerations.
- Restrict the use of global variables within a procedure as much as possible. Never alter global variables within a procedure, unless that procedure is specifically designed to set up the script.
- If a procedure *must* alter a global variable, use by reference argument passing to alter that variable indirectly. Avoid referencing the global variable directly.

- Use by value argument passing wherever possible, unless the passed argument must be modified or the argument is expected to be a large array.
- Use comments to carefully document all uses of by reference argument passing.

Structured Program Design

The concept of replacing a block of statements with a name that describes the result of executing those statements is the cornerstone of *structured program design*. This technique allows complex programming problems to be decomposed into a set of smaller, but simpler, problems or tasks. Each of these tasks is in turn reduced still further until the individual tasks become trivial. This decomposition process is called *top-down design*. Structured programming expresses this design methodology by using procedures to represent each task.

As an example, consider a script that must copy a list of files. The list of files to copy is maintained in another file (sometimes called a *response* file), and the name of this file is passed to the script as a command line argument.

The first attempt at designing this script produces the following script code:

```
Init
ProcessCommandLine
CopyAllFiles
```

Here, the initial problem has been broken into three procedures.

1. The `Init` procedure provides general script set up and initialization (for example, it might display a sign-on banner).
2. The `ProcessCommandLine` procedure handles the chores associated with parsing the command line and extracting the name of the response file. This procedure should also check that the command line syntax is valid.
3. The `CopyAllFiles` procedure performs the actual file copy operations.

This first attempt is only a small step toward the final script because the bodies for the three procedures have not been written. However, it does clearly define three tasks that must be processed for the script to perform its function.

The second attempt further decomposes the three procedures, producing the following script code:

```
Dim g_sResponseFilename
Init
ProcessCommandLine Wscript.Arguments, g_sResponseFilename
CopyAllFiles g_sResponseFilename
```

```
' Note: This procedure initializes all script globals
Sub Init
    g_sResponseFilename = ""
    ShowSignonBanner
End Sub

Sub ProcessCommandLine(ByVal Args, ByRef sResponseFilename)
    CheckArgumentCount Args
    sResponseFilename = GetResponseFilename (Args)
    CheckResponseFileExists sResponseFilename
End Sub

Sub CopyAllFles(ByVal sResponseFilename)
    Dim ResponseFile, sFile
    ResponseFile = OpenResponseFile (sResponseFilename)
    For Each sFile In ResponseFile
        CopyFile sFile
    Next
    CloseResponseFile ResponseFile
End Sub
```

In this attempt, the details of how each of the three tasks are to be carried out have themselves been defined, along with some variables to hold core data values.

The `Init` procedure only performs two actions. It initializes global variables, and it displays the sign-on banner. Altering global variables within this procedure is legitimate as long as this is clearly documented in the script. In this case, the only global variable is `g_sResponseFilename`, a string that holds the name of the response file.

The `ProcessCommandLine` procedure has three tasks:

1. Check that at least one argument (the response file name) is present.
2. Get that argument and store it as the response filename.
3. Check that the response file exists.

To do this, the procedure requires access to the command line, and so the `Wscript.Arguments` array is passed to the procedure. This argument is passed by value because the arguments are not altered by the procedure. The procedure also takes a second argument, which is used to pass back to the caller the response filename. Thus, by reference argument passing is used so that the global variable `g_sResponseFilename` is updated by the procedure.

The `CopyAllFiles` procedure also has three tasks:

1. Open the response file ready to read the file names from the list.
2. For each name in the list, copy the file.
3. Close the response file.

Some of the tasks previously described are sufficiently trivial to be written as final VBScript statements. For example, the `CheckArgumentCount` task can be written as:

```
If Wscript.Arguments < 1 Then
    Wscript.Echo "Filename required"
    Wscript.Quit(1)
End If
```

This code is sufficiently simple to add in-line within the `ProcessCommandLine` subroutine, replacing the `CheckArgumentCount` task. Other tasks, such as `CopyFile`, remain more complex and probably need to be decomposed further. In addition, the `For Each` loop is not yet valid VBScript code because the meaning of `ResponseFile` is unclear. However, the *overall structure* of the script should be becoming clear. This structure should also be readily apparent to anyone looking at the script for the first time.

Recursion

As explained in "Nesting Procedures," invocations of procedures can be nested to any desired depth and complexity. Large, complex scripts can often nest procedures 5, or even 10, layers deep. One special case of procedure nesting occurs when a procedure invokes *itself*. This self-referential process is known as *recursion*. Recursion is an advanced technique and is not frequently used in small scripts. However, there are several places where it is useful in scripting, and so an understanding of the process is useful.

The concept of recursion is not limited to computer programming. For example, if two mirrors are placed directly facing one another, each mirror reflects an image of the other mirror. Inside the image of that mirror, is the image of the other mirror, slightly smaller. Inside *that* image of a mirror is another mirror, and another, and another. The sequence continues (at least in theory) infinitely, with smaller and smaller images of mirrors.

Another example of recursion occurs in certain acronyms. An acronym is a name that is derived from the first letters of a phrase. For example, the acronym BASIC stands for Beginners All-purpose Symbolic Instruction Code. The acronym GNU stands for "GNU's Not Unix." In this case, the expansion of the acronym has yielded a phrase that contains the original acronym. If we expand the acronym again, we have "GNU's Not Unix Not Unix," which can be expanded repeatedly.

A more familiar example of recursion can be found on every computer's hard disk. A hard disk is organized into a set of *folders*. Each folder contains one or more *elements*. Each element is either a *file* or a *folder*. This definition is recursive: a folder contains elements. Some of those elements can themselves be folders, and so these folders can in turn contain other elements, which can also be folders, which can also contain elements, and so on.

The common theme to each of these examples is that an element is defined in such a way that the definition of the element contains the element itself as part of the definition. The equivalent of this process in programming is a procedure that invokes itself. The first time the procedure is called, it performs some work, and then it invokes itself again to perform additional work, then again, and again, and again. For example:

```
Sub Forever
    Wscript.Echo "Forever..."
    Forever
End Sub
```

This procedure is a recursive procedure. After executing the `Wscript.Echo` statement, it invokes itself again. If this procedure were invoked from a script (which is *not* advised), the result would be a rapid scrolling display of the text `Forever...`, followed by a successively slower display of the text as the computer ran low on memory, followed by VBScript terminating as a result of low memory conditions.

The reason for this behavior is the recursive nature of the procedure. Each invocation causes another invocation, and another, and another. None of the invoked procedures ever exits because before it does so it invokes yet another instance of itself.

Obviously, useful recursive procedures cannot exhibit such run-away behavior, and so these procedures provide a way to limit the recursion—typically by making the recursion conditional on some set of conditions. For example:

```
Sub NotForever(ByVal nLimit)
    Wscript.Echo "Not forever..."
    If nLimit > 0 Then NotForever nLimit - 1
    Wscript.Echo "Done"
End Sub

NotForever 10
```

In this example, the recursion is controlled by an `If` statement. Initially, the `NotForever` procedure is invoked with an argument of 10, which is passed into the `nLimit` argument. The first invocation displays the `Wscript.Echo` text, and then executes the `If` statement. In this case, `nLimit` is 10, and so the `If` test is true and the `NotForever` procedure is invoked again.

For the second invocation of `NotForever`, the argument is `nLimit -1`; therefore, in this case, the procedure is invoked with an argument of 9. Again, the `If` statement is true, and so a third invocation of `NotForever` occurs, this time passing a value of 8 as the argument.

This cycle repeats until `NotForever` is invoked with an argument of 0. When this happens the `If` statement evaluates to false, and the recursion ends. The current `NotForever` invocation exits, and control returns to the next most recent invocation of NotForever. This also ends, and this ripple effect continues until all the invocations exit. As each invocation exits, it displays the text Done to indicate its progress.

The same scope and lifetime rules that apply to normal procedures also apply to recursive procedures. Each invocation of a recursive procedure gets its own set of local variables that are independent of the other invocations of the same procedure. Invocations do *not* share local variables; therefore, data must be passed from one invocation to another using normal arguments.

The *VarType2.vbs* Script

The VarType2.vbs sample script, shown in Listing 5.3, illustrates one use of recursion.

Listing 5.3 VarType2.vbs *Script*

```
'//////////////////////////////////////////////////////////////////////////////
' $Workfile: VarType2.vbs $ $Revision: 2 $ $Date: 5/29/99 5:31p $
' $Archive: /Scripts/VarType2.vbs $
' Copyright (c) 1998 Tim Hill. All Rights Reserved.
'//////////////////////////////////////////////////////////////////////////////

' Display the types of variables WSH Sample

Option Explicit

' Declare some variables and assign various values and types
Dim a(5), b(5), c(5), x
For x = 0 To UBound(a)
    a(x) = 0
    b(x) = x
    c(x) = x * x
Next
c(5) = Array(#1/1/99#, 12.5, True)
c(4) = "This is a string"
b(2) = c
a(4) = b
a(2) = Empty
a(3) = Null
x = 100
ShowVar 0, "x", x
ShowVar 0, "a", a

' ShowVar: Show type of variable, with array element type support
' Arguments: nLevel=recursion level, sName=var name, X=variable
Sub ShowVar(ByVal nLevel, ByVal sName, ByRef x)
    Dim s, ix
    s = space(nLevel * 4) & "Type of " & Chr(34) & sName & Chr(34) & ": " & TypeName(x)
    If IsObject(x) Then
        Wscript.Echo s & "   (object)"
```

```
    ElseIf IsNull(x) Then
        Wscript.Echo s & "    (null)"
    ElseIf IsEmpty(x) Then
        Wscript.Echo s & "    (empty)"
    ElseIf IsArray(x) Then
        Wscript.Echo s & "    (array)..."
        For ix = 0 to Ubound(x)
            ShowVar nLevel + 1, sName & "(" & ix & ")", x(ix)
        Next
    Else
        Wscript.Echo s & "    value=", x
    End If
End Sub

'//////////////////////////////////////////////////////////////////////////
```

The VarType2.vbs script is a more sophisticated version of the VarType1.vbs script from Chapter 3. The script displays type information for a variable, and it is enhanced from the previous version in two ways. First, the code to display the type of a variable is encapsulated in a subroutine, ShowVar. This allows the script to display information on any variable simply by calling this subroutine and passing the appropriate parameters. Second, the subroutine has been enhanced to support the display of array element types.

The first enhancement allows the ShowVar subroutine to be used in any script simply by adding the subroutine to the script and then calling it. It does not use any global variables and, therefore, is easy to add to new scripts.

The second enhancement is more interesting because it requires the subroutine to be recursive. The reason for this lies in the definition of an array. (See Chapter 3.) An array is composed of individual elements. Each element can contain a variable of any type, including another array. This definition is recursive, and so the most natural procedure to handle this is also one that is recursive.

The ShowVar subroutine takes three arguments. The first argument specifies the current recursion. The second is the name of the variable to be displayed, and the third is the actual variable.

The core of the ShowVar subroutine simply displays a description of the type of the variable. The TypeName function is used to extract the type name information for the variable. This is then displayed along with the name of the variable (one of the original arguments to the subroutine). The various IsArray, IsNull, and similar functions are used to decode the type and display additional information based upon the type of the variable. If the variable is a simple data type, the value is also displayed.

If the variable is identified as an array, the information on the array is displayed. Then the ShowVar subroutine processes each individual array element. For each element, the `ShowVar` subroutine is invoked recursively, and the individual array element is passed, along with the name of the element.

Each time the `ShowVar` subroutine is invoked recursively, the first argument is incremented by one. This argument indicates the level of recursion. This is used by the subroutine to indent the display of variable information, thus providing a graphical representation of the recursive calls to the `ShowVar` subroutine.

Stateless and Stateful Procedures

Procedures (both subroutines and functions) can be categorized into two distinct types: *stateless* and *stateful*.

- A *stateless* procedure is one where the outcome of executing the procedure is solely dependent upon the arguments passed to the procedure. Stateless procedures never depend upon the values of global variables, and they are entirely self-contained.
- A *stateful* procedure is one where the outcome of executing the procedure depends upon the arguments passed to the procedure *and* upon the values of one or more global variables. These global variables are said to define the *state* for the procedure.

Stateless procedures are easier to maintain and use than stateful procedures for several reasons:

- There is no need to set up global variables before a stateless procedure can be safely called.
- The results of a stateless procedure can always be predicted if the arguments are known.
- A stateless procedure can be reused in another script simply by cutting and pasting the procedure text.

Here is an example stateless procedure:

```
Function IsUNCName(sPath)
    If Left(sPath, 2) = "\\" Then
        IsUNCName = True
    Else
        IsUNCName = False
End If
```

This simple function determines if a pathname passed as an argument is a UNC name or not (it does this by checking to see if the first two characters are `"\\"`). The function is stateless because it does not reference any global variables (that is, *state*) in any way. Because the function is stateless, it is entirely self-contained, and it can be re-used in multiple scripts easily.

Here is an example stateful procedure:

```
Sub CountUNCNames(sPath)
    If IsUNCName(sPath) Then g_nUNCCount = g_nUNCCount + 1
End Sub
```

This subroutine provides an incremental counter of UNC path names. Each time the subroutine is called, a counter is incremented if the path is a UNC path (as defined by the `IsUNCName` function). This procedure is stateful because it must maintain a counter, `g_nUNCCount`, across invocations of the procedure, and this counter *must* be a global variable. Using this subroutine is more complex than the stateless `IsUNCName` function. For example:

```
Dim g_nUNCCount, sArg
g_nUNCCount = 0
For Each sArg In Wscript.Arguments
    CountUNCNames(sArg)
Next
Wscript.Echo g_nUNCCount
```

This example contains numerous references to the `g_nUNCCount` variable in the main script text. It must be declared, initialized before each batch of names is counted, and directly accessed to display the results of the count.

The `CountUNCNames` procedure can be improved somewhat by using a "by reference" parameter to refer to the counter. This de-couples the name of the global variable from the script code. For example:

```
Sub CountUNCNames(By Ref nTotal, sPath)
    If IsUNCName(sPath) Then nTotal = nTotal + 1
End Sub
```

Here, the direct reference to the global variable is replaced by a "by reference" parameter. This not only de-couples the procedure from the global variable, but it also allows the `CountUNCNames` subroutine to maintain multiple independent counters. For example:

```
Dim g_nOddCount, g_nEvenCount, sArg, ix
g_nOddCount = 0 : g_nEvenCount = 0
For ix = 0 To Wscript.Arguments.Count
    sArg = Wscript.Arguments(ix)
    If (ix & 1) Then
        CountUNCNames g_nOddCount, sArg
    Else
        CountUNCNames g_nEvenCount, sArg
    End If
Next
Wscript.Echo g_nOddCount, g_nEvenCount
```

Although they are more difficult to maintain, stateful procedures are used because it is often impossible to describe the required functionality in a purely stateless way. However, a better way to script stateful procedures is using objects, which are the subject of Part II of this book.

Summary

Procedures are the primary means to break long complex scripts into units that are more manageable. They also allow blocks of script code to be developed that can then be re-used in different scripts. This reduces script development time and allows the development of libraries of pre-built functionality that can be added to scripts simply by cutting and pasting the script text.

Procedures come in two variations: *subroutines* that are invoked via statements, and *functions* that return values and that are invoked as part of expressions. Both types support local variables, arguments, passing parameters (by value or reference), and recursion.

Part II

Objects and Classes

6

Introducing Objects

This chapter, along with the other chapters in this part of the book, describes the concepts behind *object-oriented* programming, and it describes how VBScript can be used with these concepts.

The material in this chapter describes the mechanisms available in VBScript to create and manipulate objects, including *Common Object Model (COM) Objects*, which provide scripts with access to system resources and applications. Chapter 7, "Built-In WSH and VBScript Objects," and Chapter 8, "File System Objects," provide details on various built-in objects available via VBScript and WSH. Chapter 9, "Creating VBScript Objects," shows how to create objects within a script, and Chapter 10, "Windows Script Components," details how to create a COM object using VBScript.

VBScript is not a full object-oriented language, and it only supports a subset of the object-oriented paradigm. However, this subset is adequate for all normal scripting needs, and in general, the features that are not available in VBScript (such as inheritance) are not important in typical system scripts.

The object features of VBScript are the conduit through which scripts can access and manage operating system functionality and third party applications. In fact, the capability of accessing external COM objects makes the combination of WSH and VBScript a true system-scripting environment. Most of the sample scripts in Part III, "Sample Script Solutions," use COM Objects to access system and application functionality. Then, they use the various VBScript language features described in Part I, "WSH and the VBScript Language," to manipulate these objects.

Note

As with all the sample scripts in this book, the scripts in this chapter should be run using the CSCRIPT host unless otherwise noted. The examples shown assume that CSCRIPT is the default WSH host. (See Chapter 1, "Introducing WSH," for information on selecting the default WSH host.) ◆

The Object Paradigm

The object-oriented paradigm was originally developed as an extension to procedural programming. In *procedural programming* (as described in Chapter 5, "User-Defined Procedures"), blocks of statements are encapsulated within a procedure—either a subroutine or a function. This procedure provides an *interface,* which describes its functionality, and an *implementation,* which actually implements the functionality. The interface to a procedure consists of the procedure parameters, any global variables required by the procedure, a description of the operations performed by the procedure, and (for functions) a description of the return value. The implementation of a procedure consists of the actual script code used to implement the functionality that is implied by the interface.

The separation of interface and implementation is the primary advantage of procedural programming. As long as the interface to a procedure is unaltered, the implementation can be changed without this change affecting other portions of the script. Furthermore, the procedure can be used in a script without any need to study the implementation. As long as the interface properly describes the procedure, the implementation can remain essentially hidden, and the procedure can be treated as a "black box." Finally, this separation ensures a high degree of *code re-use*, allowing procedures to be re-used in other scripts simply by copying them into the new script.

Program Guide

Interfaces in the Real World

The concept of distinct interfaces and implementations is common in the real world. Probably the most common example is the automobile. Driving an automobile requires knowledge of how to use the controls (the interface), but it does not require detailed knowledge of the workings of the engine or the transmission (the implementation). Because all automobiles use essentially the same interface, it is not necessary to relearn how to drive each time we buy a new car. ◆

However, procedural programming does have one drawback: It only encapsulates *behavior*. That is, it can hide the details of how an action is performed, but it cannot hide the details of the data required to manage that action. This is particularly true with *stateful procedures*, in which data (state) must be maintained across procedure invocations. For example, here is the `CountUNCNames` subroutine from Chapter 5:

```
Sub CountUNCNames(ByRef nTotal, sPath)
    If IsUNCName(sPath) Then nTotal = nTotal + 1
End Sub

Dim g_nOddCount, g_nEvenCount, sArg, ix
g_nOddCount = 0 : g_nEvenCount = 0
For ix = 0 To Wscript.Arguments.Count
```

```
    sArg = Wscript.Arguments(ix)
    If (ix & 1) Then
        CountUNCNames g_nOddCount, sArg
    Else
        CountUNCNames g_nEvenCount, sArg
    End If
Next
Wscript.Echo g_nOddCount, g_nEvenCount
```

In this example, the behavior of the UNC counter is correctly encapsulated in the `CountUNCNames` procedure, but the state information (in this case, a counter) is visible to the main script.

To extend the encapsulation of the UNC counter, a mechanism is required that wraps the `CountUNCNames` procedure *and* the global counter variable into a single package. This package, which contains both the counter functionality and the counter itself (the state), is called an *object.*

An object that represents a UNC counter needs three distinct procedures:

- A procedure to initialize the counter to zero
- A procedure to increment the counter if a name is a UNC name
- A procedure to fetch the current count for display purposes

The `CountUNCNames` example can now be restructured using this hypothetical object, as follows:

```
Dim oOddCount, oEvenCount, sArg, ix
oOddCount.Reset : oEvenCount.Reset
For ix = 0 To Wscript.Arguments.Count
    sArg = Wscript.Arguments(ix)
    If (ix & 1) Then
        oOddCount.AddName sArg
    Else
        oEvenCount.AddName sArg
    End If
Next
Wscript.Echo oOddCount.Count, oEvenCount.Count
```

In this theoretical example (which is not yet valid VBScript code) we use two objects, oOddCount and oEvenCount, to maintain the two counters. The objects use the three procedures previously noted to process the count of UNC names:

- A `Reset` subroutine to clear the counter to zero
- An `AddName` subroutine to add a UNC name to the count
- A `Count` function to return the current count

The syntax used to access these procedures is described in more detail in the next section; however, it should be clear that encapsulating the counter functionality has hidden the actual count global variable within the object.

All the manipulations of the counter state that were visible in the non-object version of the code have been hidden within the object procedures. Therefore, the state associated with counting items has disappeared, along with the behavior, into the counter object.

Thus, the encapsulation of the counter as an object has wrapped both the functionality (behavior) and the data (state) into a single package. This encapsulation is the core of object-oriented programming.

Program Guide

Objects, Instances, and Classes

Object-oriented literature often talks about the terms object, instance, *and* class. *These terms are borrowed from the everyday world, but they have a slightly more precise meaning in object-oriented programming.*

A class *is a set of behaviors that is shared amongst one or more* instances *of that class. An* object *is an instance of a class. For example, the term Dolphin describes a certain type of marine mammal, whereas Flipper is a specific* instance *of the* class *Dolphin. Dolphins all share certain behaviors (swimming, eating, and so on), but each individual Dolphin has his or her own "state" (for example, size, weight, and age). Similarly, all Excel spreadsheets are instances of the general class "Excel spreadsheet," but each individual spreadsheet contains its own distinct formulae and values. Thus in the object-oriented world a particular Excel spreadsheet is actually an object. In general, an object is typically referred to using "the," and a class is referred to using "a." For example:* the *Titanic is* a *ship.*

Although object-oriented programming is less than 20 years old, the study of objects dates back to classical Greece, and it is tied closely to modern knowledge theory, in which classes are known as universals *and objects are known as* particulars. ♦

Methods and Properties

Procedures that are encapsulated within an object are referred to as *methods* of the object, and state information (data) is referred to as the *properties* of the object. In the previous example, the hypothetical UNC counter can be viewed as having two methods, `Reset` and `AddName`, and one property, `Count`.

Object methods include both subroutines and functions. They are identical in operation to regular procedures and functions except that they are packaged within an object.

Object properties are slightly more complex. First, an object property can be read-only (or, less frequently, write-only). That is, the current value of the property can be read, but the value cannot be altered (or vice-versa for write-only properties). Second, the property can be implemented within the object as a procedure.

Consider an object that represents a simple text edit box in Windows. Such an object might have several properties, including a `Text` property that represents the current text in the text box, a `Color` property that specifies the color of the text, and a `Bold` property that specifies the use of a bold font. Changing the `Color` property involves repainting the text box with the new text color. Thus, when the `Color` property changes value, the text box object must execute whatever code is necessary to repaint the text. This is also true for the `Bold` and `Text` properties. Changing any of these properties causes the text box object to invoke internal procedures to update the text box appearance. These procedures are invoked automatically whenever the property value is altered.

Thus, both methods and properties execute code within an object. Therefore, the distinction between the concepts of behavior and state is somewhat blurred in the object paradigm—invoking a method can change an object's state, and changing a property can internally invoke procedures. In general, however, the following are true:

- The internal state of an object is the sum of its properties. However, the internal representation of these properties within the object can differ considerably from the way the object presents the properties in its interface.
- Methods represent actions that can be carried out on the object.
- Properties are generally commutative (that is, properties are independent of the sequence of operations). For example, changing the font and then color of text in a text box has the same effect as changing the color and then the font.
- Methods are generally *not* commutative. For example, printing the contents of a document and then deleting the contents does not have the same effect as deleting the contents and then printing the document.
- Methods and properties in combination are not commutative. In general, properties of an object need to be set properly before methods of an object can be used.

Manipulating Objects in VBScript

VBScript can access and manipulate two different types of objects:

- Objects authored within the script. (These are described in detail in Chapter 9.)
- External COM objects, including several built into VBScript or WSH, and Windows Script Component objects (which are described in Chapter 10).

Although there are slight differences in the way these objects are created, using objects in VBScript always involves the following steps:

1. An object variable is declared.
2. The object is created.
3. The object variable is assigned an object reference.
4. The object is used by changing its properties and invoking its methods.
5. The object is deleted.

Notice that the object has a script controlled *lifetime*, which begins when the object is created in step 2, and ends when the object is deleted in step 5. The following sections describe each of these steps in more detail.

Declaring Objects

In VBScript, all objects are represented as variables. Variables that represent objects are identical in most respects to other VBScript variables. They are declared using a `Dim` statement and can have either global or local scope. Objects can also be represented in array elements, passed to procedures as arguments, and returned from functions. Finally, they can also be used as arguments to other object's methods or properties.

The `IsObject` function can be used to check a variable. If the variable represents an object (even the special `Nothing` object described later), the function returns `True`. Otherwise, the function returns `False`. The `VarType` and `TypeName` functions also return information that describes an object variable. These are described in Chapter 3, "VBScript Data Storage."

To declare an object, use the `Dim` statement. For example:

```
Dim oFile, oFolder
```

This example declares two objects, `oFile` and `oFolder`. The naming convention introduced in Chapter 3 is used, which uses the prefix "o" to indicate an object variable. However, objects can be stored in *any* variable, as previously noted—the naming convention is, as usual, merely a mnemonic for the script author.

Creating Objects

Objects can be created in many different ways. The most common way to create an object is via the `CreateObject` function (other ways are discussed later in the "Other Ways to Create Objects" section). The return value of this function is an *object reference*. The `CreateObject` function takes one argument, a string value that specifies the class of object to create. All the objects that are created using the `CreateObject` function are Microsoft COM objects. This is discussed further in the "Using COM Objects" section.

WSH also supplies one object that is created automatically whenever a script executes. This object is called `Wscript`. The `Wscript` object provides a variety of WSH related information, including access to the command line and script output. The `Wscript.Echo` "statement" introduced in Chapter 2, "VBScript Language Essentials," is in fact an object method, the object being `Wscript` and the method being `Echo`. Other `Wscript` "statements," such as `Wscript.Quit`, are also object methods of the `Wscript` object. The `Wscript` object is described fully in the next chapter.

Note

Don't confuse the `Wscript` *object with the WSCRIPT.EXE command (and WSCRIPT host). The two are distinct, and the* `Wscript` *object is available in both the WSCRIPT and CSCRIPT hosts. See Chapter 1 for more information on the WSH hosts.* ◆

Assigning Objects to Variables

The return value of the `CreateObject` function is an object reference. To use an object reference, it must be assigned to an object variable using the `Set` statement. For example:

```
Dim oFSO
Set oFSO = CreateObject("Scripting.FileSystemObject")
```

Here, a new object variable, `oFSO`, is initialized with an object reference using the `Set` statement. The syntax of the `Set` statement is:

```
Set variable = object-reference-expression
```

Here, *`variable`* can be any variable or array element, and *`object-reference-expression`* must be an expression that yields an object reference. The `Set` statement sets the specified variable to refer to the object specified by the object reference expression.

The `Set` statement is similar in syntax to the assignment statement. However, the regular assignment statement *cannot* be used to assign an object reference to a variable. For example, the following will *not* work as expected:

```
Dim oFSO
oFSO = CreateObject("Scripting.FileSystemObject")
```

The reason the `Set` statement is used instead of the assignment statement is that the `Set` statement manipulates *object references*, while the assignment statement manipulates regular data items. Maintaining these references correctly requires additional work by VBScript, and the `Set` statement performs this work.

The Set statement must also be used if a function returns an object reference. For example:

```
Function StartExcel
    Set StartExcel = CreateObject("Excel.Application")
End Function
```

One consequence of using object references is that multiple variables can refer to the *same* object. For example:

```
Dim oFS01, oFS02
Set oFS01 = CreateObject("Scripting.FileSystemObject")
Set oFS02 = oFS01
```

In this example, the oFS02 variable is assigned (via the Set statement) the same object reference as the oFS01 variable. At this point, both variables contain references to the *same* object, and the variables can be used interchangeably to refer to the same object. This is quite different from normal assignment statements, which create *copies* of data. For example:

```
Dim a(10), b
b = a
```

Here, after the assignment statement, the variable b will contain a new array that contains the same data as the array a. However, this is a copy of the data, and changing the elements in b will not alter the elements in a, or vice-versa.

Program Guide

More About Dolphins

As noted above, we can think of the term "Dolphin" as a class, and "Flipper" as an individual dolphin (an instance of the class). In fact, this is only true in a casual sense because the word *"Flipper" is really a name for a specific dolphin. The actual dolphin is distinct from its name. Thus, using this name, we can refer to the same actual dolphin in many places (books, movies, conversation, and so on), by using the same name. Each utterance of the name is a distinct reference to the same dolphin.*

This is, in effect, how object references work. The object reference is the "name" of the object (though it's not in a textual form). Each object reference (in a variable) refers to the same "real" object.

Thus, you can have multiple object references that refer to the same object. That object is, in turn, an instance of a class. ◆

If an object variable is passed by value to a procedure, the same reference copy semantics are used. For example:

```
Sub Doit(ByVal oData)
End Sub
```

```
Dim oFSO
Set oFSO = CreateObject("Scripting.FileSystemObject")
Doit oFSO
```

In this example, the `oData` parameter is assigned a reference to the same object as the `oFSO` variable.

Variables that refer to the same object are sometimes called *aliases* for that object because all the variables are different ways to refer to the same object. Aliases are always interchangeable within script code. For example:

```
Dim oWS
Set oWS = Wscript
oWS.Echo "hello world"
Wscript.Echo "hello world"
```

In this example, the `oWS` variable is set to refer to the `Wscript` object. Because both `Wscript` and `oWS` refer to the same object, `oWS` can now be used anywhere that `Wscript` is used. The final two statements in the example thus have identical effect.

Note

Using a regular assignment statement instead of a `Set` *statement is probably the most common mistake made when authoring scripts. When you are copying or manipulating object references, always use the* `Set` *statement. When you are copying or manipulating other data (even data generated by object methods or properties), use a regular assignment statement.*

Unfortunately, it is *legal to assign an object reference to a variable; therefore, VBScript will not indicate an error if you mistakenly use a regular assignment instead of the* `Set` *statement. For example:*

```
Dim oVar1, oVar2
Set oVar1 = CreateObject("Excel.Application")
oVar2 = oVar1
```

In this example, the second assignment statement is probably a mistake, and it was probably meant to be a `Set` *statement. However, VBScript will not stop with an error. Instead, any attempts made later to use the* `oVar2` *variable as an object will cause an error.*

When an object reference is assigned to a variable in this way, the variable is set to a string that describes the type of the object. ◆

Accessing Methods and Properties

After an object is created and one or more variables are set to refer to it, the methods and properties of the object can be accessed. To access an object method, use this syntax:

```
objectref.method [arglist]
```

Here, `objectref` is the name of a variable containing an object reference, and *`method`* is the name of the method being invoked. The period is a special VBScript operator that links an object to its methods and properties. As with regular subroutines, the method invocation can be followed by zero or more arguments, as specified by the method. For example:

```
Dim oWS
Set oWS = Wscript
oWS.Echo "a=", a
```

In this example, the `oWS` variable is assigned an object reference to the built-in WSH `Wscript` object. The `.Echo` method is then invoked on this object with two arguments.

Methods that return values (that is, object functions) use the same syntax except that, like regular functions, the argument list should be enclosed in parentheses and the method should be used as part of an expression.

Some object methods return object references. In this case, as usual, the `Set` statement must be used to assign these references to variables. For example:

```
Dim oFSO, oDrives
Set oFSO = CreateObject("Scripting.FileSystemObject")
Set oDrives = oFSO.Drives
```

Here, the `.Drives` method of the file system object is used to retrieve an object that represents all the disk drives in the system.

Properties are accessed using a similar syntax to methods. However, a property typically does not take arguments. In addition, assignment statements can alter property values (that is, a property can appear on the left side of the = sign in an assignment statement). For example:

```
Dim oTextBox
Set oTextBox = CreateObject("TextBox.Object")
oTextBox.Bold = True
oTextBox.Text = "Hello"
If oTextBox.Bold Then oTextBox.Text = oTextBox.Text & "!!!"
```

In this example, a hypothetical text edit box has two properties, `.Bold` and `.Text`. The properties are assigned initial values, and then the `If` statement tests the `.Bold` property and alters the `.Text` property accordingly.

Note

In the previous example, the properties are assigned new values using regular assignment statements. Do not *use the* `Set` *statement with property assignments* unless *the value being assigned is an object reference.*

If you are confused about the use of the `Set` *and assignment statements, focus on the* `"="` *sign in the statement. Think about the data that is flowing across the sign, from the expression on the right to the variable or property on the left. Is this data an object reference? If the answer to this question is "yes," use the* `Set` *statement. If the answer is "no," use the assignment statement.*

In the preceding example, the left side of the assignment statements are object properties, but the data *flowing across the* `"="` *sign is regular data: a boolean value for the* `.Bold` *property and a string value for the* `.Text` *property. Hence, in this case, regular assignment statements are required.* ◆

In the preceding syntax for accessing object methods, the *`objectref`* is typically an object variable. However, it can be any valid *expression* that returns an object variable. For example:

```
Dim oArgs
Set oArgs = Wscript.Arguments
Wscript.Echo Wscript.Arguments.Count, oArgs.Count
```

The `Wscript.Arguments` property of the `Wscript` object returns an object that represents all the command line arguments. This object, in turn, includes a `.Count` property that returns a count of the command line arguments. The example shows two different ways to access this property, either indirectly via an intermediate `oArgs` variable, or directly via the `Wscript.Arguments.Count` property.

The final example shows how multiple period operators are allowed. The first period accesses the `Arguments` property of the `Wscript` object. This yields a new object reference, and this reference is then used to access the `Count` property.

Deleting Objects

When access to the object is complete, the object should be deleted. This is done by assigning the object variable the special `Nothing` value. For example:

```
Set oFSO = Nothing
```

This special assignment (which, as usual, must use the `Set` statement) deletes the object reference stored in the variable. The object is then no longer accessible via this variable.

Variables that contain the special `Nothing` value are still considered object references, and the `IsObject` function will still return `True` in this case. Object references are also deleted under several other circumstances:

- If a variable containing an object reference is assigned a reference to a different object via a `Set` statement.
- If a variable containing an object reference is assigned data via a regular assignment statement.
- When a procedure returns, all object references in local scope variables are automatically deleted. The same also happens for procedure arguments that contain object references.

- When the script exits, all global variables that contain object references are automatically deleted.

Deleting an object may or may not delete the actual item to which the object refers. For example, if the object represents a dialog box, the dialog box is typically removed from the screen and destroyed when the object is deleted. However, if the object represents an Excel document, the document file on disk is typically *not* deleted when the object is deleted. The actual semantics involved with object deletion are specific to each class of object.

If multiple variables reference an object, VBScript does not delete the object until *all* the variable references to the object are deleted. For example:

```
Sub Doit(ByVal oTest)
    Set oTest = Nothing
End Sub

Dim oFSO
Set oFSO = CreateObject("Scripting.FileSystemObject")
Doit oFSO
Set oFSO = Nothing
```

In this example, the `Doit` function deletes the reference to the file system object. However, the `oFSO` variable also refers to the object at this time, so the object is not deleted until the `oFSO` object deletes *its* reference to the object. Only then will VBScript delete the underlying object.

Collections

Collections are special object types that are similar to arrays. In addition to methods and properties, a collection object also contains a set of data elements that can be accessed individually. The `Wscript.Arguments` object is an example of a collection.

Collection methods and properties are accessed as usual, using the period operators. For example, most collections contain a `.Count` property that indicates how many data elements are stored within the collection. This can be accessed as follows:

```
Dim nArgCount
nArgCount = Wscript.Arguments.Count
Wscript.Echo "You entered", nArgCount, "arguments"
```

Individual data elements in a collection are accessed by specifying an element identifier in parentheses. For example:

```
Dim sArg, oArgs
Set oArgs = Wscript.Arguments
If oArgs.Count > 0 Then sArg = oArgs(0)
```

Here, the first command line argument is accessed via the `Wscript.Arguments` collection. In this case, the collection is accessed indirectly via the `oArgs` variable. The assignment statement in the `If` statement accesses the collection element:

```
sArg = oArgs(0)
```

The syntax is similar to the syntax for accessing arrays. In this case, the element identifier accesses the first data element, which is the first command line argument.

In VBScript arrays, the element index is always numeric, and the first element of the array always has an index of zero. In collections, however, the meaning of the element identifier is defined entirely by the collection itself. In some collections (such as the `Wscript.Arguments` collection), the first data element has an index of zero. In others, the first data element might have an index of one. In some collections, the element index might not be numeric, and might instead be a string or some other data type. To determine the correct indexing method for a collection, refer to the documentation for that collection object. For example, in Microsoft Excel, the set of worksheets open in a workbook is represented as a collection object. Individual worksheets are accessed either by index, with the first worksheet numbered 1, or by the name of the worksheet.

By convention, collection objects are given names that are plural, to indicate that they contain multiple data elements. Variables that contain references to collections also typically follow this convention.

As described in Chapter 2, collections are frequently used with the `For Each` loop statement. This statement automatically iterates through each individual element in a collection. For example:

```
For Each oBook in oExcel.Workbooks
    Wscript.Echo oBook.Name
Next
```

Default Properties and Methods

Many objects have a *default* property or method. The default property or method is accessed whenever the object variable is used within a script without an explicit property or method. Using the default property is a shorthand way to access the property or method. For example:

```
Dim oExcel
Set oExcel = CreateObject("Excel.Application")
Wscript.Echo oExcel.Name
Wscript.Echo oExcel
```

The Excel application object has a `.Name` property that accesses the name of the application. This is the default property for this object, and so both `Wscript.Echo` statements display the same result.

Many collections have a `.Item` property that accesses an individual item within the collection. This property is typically the default property for the object. For example:

```
Dim oArgs
Set oArgs = Wscript.Arguments
Wscript.Echo oArgs(0)
Wscript.Echo oArgs.Item(0)
```

The `Wscript.Arguments` collection has a default `.Item` property; thus, the last two statements in the preceding example display the same result. In fact, the most common use of default properties is when accessing individual elements within a collection.

Default properties can only be used within expressions. They cannot be used on the left side of an assignment statement. For example:

```
Dim oSheet
Set oSheet = (some code to access an Excel worksheet)
oSheet.Name = "Summary"
Wscript.Echo oSheet
oSheet = "New Summary"
```

Here, the `.Name` property of an Excel worksheet is explicitly altered to change the name of the worksheet. The `.Name` property is the default property, and so the `Wscript.Echo` statement will display the name of the worksheet, which in this case is `"Summary"`. The final assignment statement, however, does *not* change the `.Name` property to a new value. Instead, the variable `oSheet` is assigned the string value and the reference to the Excel worksheet object is deleted.

The *With* Statement

Some objects have many properties and methods. For example:

```
Dim oSheet
Set oSheet = (some code to access an Excel worksheet)
oSheet.Cells(1,1).Font.Bold = True
oSheet.Cells(1,1).Font.Italic = Not oSheet.Cells(1,1).Font.Italic
oSheet.Cells(1,1).Font.Size = 12
```

This example accesses a worksheet in Microsoft Excel and changes the font information for the top left cell. The `.Cells` method returns an object that represents the specified cell. This object, in turn, has a `.Font` property that returns an object that represents the font information for that cell. Finally, this object has various properties, such as `.Bold` and `.Size`, which define the font for the cell.

Repeating the expression `oSheet.Cells(1,1).Font` four times is cumbersome. It's easy to make a typing mistake, particularly if the expression is repeated dozens of times. It's also inefficient because VBScript must evaluate the expression four times instead of once. The following example rewrites this example to avoid these problems:

```
Dim oSheet, oCell
Set oSheet = (some code to access an Excel worksheet)
Set oCell = oSheet.Cells(1,1)
oCell.Font.Bold = True
oCell.Font.Italic = Not oCell.Font.Italic
oCell.Font.Size = 12
Set oCell = Nothing
```

This example calls the `.Cells` method only once and uses the result via an intermediate `oCell` variable. This example can be further enhanced by eliminating the multiple references to the `.Font` property. For example:

```
Dim oSheet, oFont
Set oSheet = (some code to access an Excel worksheet)
Set oFont = oSheet.Cells(1,1).Font
oFont.Bold = True
oFont.Italic = Not oFont.Italic
oFont.Size = 12
Set oFont = Nothing
```

The preceding example is more efficient that the previous examples. However, to obtain this efficiency, the extra `oFont` variable has been introduced.

In VBScript, the `With` statement provides a way to provide the same code efficiency without adding additional temporary variables. The syntax of the `With` statement is:

```
With object
    statements
End With
```

Here, *`object`* is any valid object reference, such as an object variable or a function, method, or property that returns an object reference. *`statements`* are any valid VBScript statements. However, the *`statements`* within the `With` statement can refer to the methods and properties of the specified *`object`* without explicitly naming the object. For example:

```
Dim oSheet
Set oSheet = (some code to access an Excel worksheet)
With oSheet.Cells(1,1).Font
    .Bold = True
    .Italic = Not .Italic
    .Size = 12
End With
```

Here, the preceding example is re-written using the `With` statement. The `With` statement has all the advantages of the previous example (efficiency and only one reference to the complex `oSheet` expression), but it does not need the addition of a temporary object variable.

Any statements are allowed within a `With` statement, including another `With` statement. For example:

```
Dim oSheet
Set oSheet = (some code to access an Excel worksheet)
With oSheet.Cells(1,1)
    .Value = "A Sample Spreadsheet"
    With .Font
        .Bold = True
        .Italic = Not .Italic
        .Size = 12
        Wscript.Echo "Value is", oSheet.Cells(1,1).Value
    End With
End With
```

Here, there are two `With` statements nested one inside the other. When a `With` statement is nested in another `With` statement like this, the inner `With` statement temporarily over-rides the outer `With` statement. Within the outer `With` statement, the `oSheet.Cells(1,1)` object can be accessed implicitly (that is, without expressly naming the object). However, within the *inner* `With` statement, the `oSheet.Cells(1,1).Font` object is accessed implicitly and the `oSheet.Cells(1,1)` object is only accessible explicitly.

The *Is* Operator

As described in the "Assigning Objects to Variables" section, it is possible for several variables to contain references to the same object. It is sometimes necessary to determine if two distinct object variables refer to the same object. The `Is` operator can be used to determine this. For example:

```
Dim oWS
Set oWS = Wscript
If oWS Is Wscript Then oWS.Echo "Yes, they are the same"
```

An object that has been assigned the special `Nothing` value can be compared to `Nothing` using the `Is` operator. For example:

```
Dim oWS
Set oWS = Nothing
If oWS Is Nothing Then Wscript.Echo "It's nothing"
```

It is sometimes necessary to check in a script to see if a variable contains a valid object. The preceding comparison is insufficient in this case, because it will also fail if the variable simply contains non-object data or is empty. The `IsValidObject` function shown in the following example returns `True`, if the specified variable contains a valid object reference, and `False` in all other cases.

```
Function IsValidObject(ByRef oObj)
    IsValidObject = False
    If IsObject(oObj) Then
        If Not oObj Is Nothing Then
```

```
            IsValidObject = True
        End If
    End If
End Function
```

Because each invocation of the CreateObject function creates a *new* object, the object reference returned by each invocation is unique. For example:

```
Dim oFS01, oFS02, oFS03
Set oFS01 = CreateObject("Scripting.FileSystemObject")
Set oFS02 = CreateObject("Scripting.FileSystemObject")
Set oFS03 = oFS01
Wscript.Echo oFS01 Is oFS02, oFS01 Is oFS03
```

Here, the three variables oFS01, oFS02, and oFS03 all refer to objects of the same class (in this case, the file system object that is described in Chapter 7). The oFS01 and oFS02 variables each receive object references from the CreateObject function, and therefore refer to distinct file system objects. The oFS03 variable receives a copy of the oFS01 variable, and therefore refers to the same file system object as oFS01. The variables oFS01 and oFS03 refer to one object, whereas the variable oFS02 refers to another object. Thus, the result of the final Wscript.Echo method is zero and –1.

Using COM Objects

As explained in the preceding section, "Creating Objects," the CreateObject function is used to create objects. This function takes one argument and returns an object reference. The argument is a string that specifies the type (or *class*) of object to create. These object classes are not built into WSH or VBScript. Instead, the object classes are specified outside the WSH/VBScript environment via the Microsoft Common Object Model, or COM.

COM specifies a standard way in which an application (that is, an .EXE file) or a library (that is, a .DLL file) can present its functionality as a series of one or more object classes. For example, a database application, such as Microsoft Access, might provide an object class that represents a database and another class that represents a table in that database. Each class then provides the methods and properties appropriate for manipulating that class of object. For example, the Access database object might have a method for adding a new table to the database.

When a COM compatible application is installed on a computer, it advertises, via a process known as *registration*, the various object classes that it has available. After these classes are correctly advertised, any COM aware application can make use of the objects provided by the application. Thus COM provides a standard bridge between an application that uses COM objects, which is known as a COM *client*, and an application or library that provides COM objects, which is known as a COM *server*. WSH and VBScript are COM clients, and the objects they can create and access via the `CreateObject` function are all COM objects.

Note

Not all COM objects registered on a computer are available to a VBScript script. Technically, for a COM object to be accessible from a script, it must provide an interface known as `IDispatch`*. This interface qualifies the object as an Automation object, and only Automation objects are accessible from VBScript.* ◆

The registration process that advertises installed COM objects uses a database of installed objects. This database is stored in the HKEY_CLASSES_ROOT of the system registry. The database contains a lot of information that the system uses to activate COM objects, but the most important item is known as the *Programmatic Identifier*, or *ProgID*.

The ProgID is a short text string that identifies, by name, each object class that an application supports. Additional information in the registry allows the operating system to associate the ProgID with the executable application or library that provides the objects of that class.

It is the ProgID that is specified as the only argument to the `CreateObject` function, and thus this string provides the bridge connecting the VBScript language, the WSH environment, and all COM objects installed on a computer.

How Objects Are Created

When `CreateObject` creates an object, a complex process is set in motion whereby an object of the specified class is created. Many of the steps in the creation process involve reference to the object database stored in HKEY_CLASSES_ROOT. In outline, this process works as follows:

1. The string expression passed as the only argument to `CreateObject` is evaluated. This string is then passed to an internal COM API that carries out the rest of the processing outlined in the following steps.
2. The HKEY_CLASSES_ROOT key is searched for a key whose name matches the string expression. If a key is not found, `CreateObject` fails with an error.
3. The located registry key is checked for a key named `CLSID`. If this key is not found, `CreateObject` fails with an error.
4. The default value is taken from the `CLSID` registry key. This yields an entry called a *GUID*, which is a long, unique string of hexadecimal digits.
5. The HKEY_CLASSES_ROOT\CLSID key is searched again, this time for a key whose name matches the GUID obtained in step 4. If this key is not found, `CreateObject` fails with an error.

6. The sub-keys in this key are then used to locate an appropriate executable application or library to load.
7. After the library or application is loaded, the COM library calls APIs within the application to create the requested object.
8. The application or library creates the object and returns a reference to that object. This reference is returned to the `CreateObject` function, which in turn, returns it to the executing script.

It's not necessary to fully understand this process to effectively use objects in VBScript and WSH. However, several points should be understood:

- Objects created with `CreateObject` are not part of the VBScript/WSH environment. They are simply general-purpose COM objects. Because almost all new operating system and application functionality is now delivered in the form of COM objects, VBScript can leverage this functionality in system scripts.
- The link between the script and the object, in the form of the ProgID passed to `CreateObject`, is resolved when the script executes. This is known as *late binding*. Late binding makes linking the script to the object easy—all that is necessary is that the application or library providing the object be installed on the computer.

  However, late binding can mean that a script that executes satisfactorily on one computer can fail on another if that computer does not have the same object classes installed. Therefore, when using objects, take care to document which objects are used and which applications or libraries must be loaded for the script to function.
- Applications (or libraries) control the selection of ProgID names. The documentation supplied with the application or library will provide information on the ProgIDs for each object, as well as on the methods and properties supported by the object.
- Creating an object with `CreateObject` can load an application or library. If an application is loaded, a new process is created for that application. If a library is loaded, the library is loaded within the current process.

The last point in this list means that, for example, if an object is created that represents a Microsoft Excel spreadsheet, Microsoft Excel is loaded as a side effect of creating that object. However, the operating system starts Excel in a special mode, called *Embedded* or *Server* mode. In this mode, the application will not create any windows on the desktop and, in fact, runs invisibly. When the object is deleted, the application will terminate automatically.

Some objects are not associated with applications, but with libraries (that is, .DLL files). These objects are known as *in-process servers* because they do not load a new application, but instead are loaded as part of the current application (that is, as part of the WSH process). However, the same general rules apply as for application-created objects: The library is loaded when objects are created and unloaded when objects are deleted.

A Simple Example

To illustrate object creation in more detail, Listing 6.1 shows the HelloWorld2.vbs script first introduced in Chapter 1.

Listing 6.1 *HelloWorld2.vbs Script*

```
'//////////////////////////////////////////////////////////////////////////
' $Workfile: HelloWorld2.vbs $ $Revision: 3 $ $Date: 12/04/98 3:19p $
' $Archive: /Scripts/HelloWorld2.vbs $
' Copyright (c)1998 Tim Hill. All Rights Reserved.
'//////////////////////////////////////////////////////////////////////////

' Simple "Hello World!" WSH Sample

Option Explicit
Wscript.Echo Wscript.ScriptName & " $Revision: 3 $"
Wscript.Echo "Copyright (c)1998 Tim Hill. All Rights Reserved."

' Open IE and display the about:blank page to give us an empty document
Dim oIE, oIEDoc
Set oIE = CreateObject("InternetExplorer.Application")
oIE.Navigate "about:blank"
oIE.AddressBar = False
oIE.StatusBar = False
oIE.ToolBar = False
oIE.MenuBar = False
oIE.Visible = True

' Now emit the HTML to IE
Set oIEDoc = oIE.Document
oIEDoc.WriteLn "<html>"
oIEDoc.WriteLn "<head>"
oIEDoc.WriteLn "<title>HelloWorld2 Sample Script</title>"
oIEDoc.WriteLn "</head>"
oIEDoc.WriteLn "<body>"
oIEDoc.WriteLn "<p><center>Welcome to Windows Scripting Host.</center></p>"
oIEDoc.Write "<p><center>"
If Hour(Now) < 12 Then
    oIEDoc.Write "Good morning"
ElseIf Hour(Now) < 17 Then
    oIEDoc.Write "Good afternoon"
Else
    oIEDoc.Write "Good evening"
End If
```

```
oIEDoc.WriteLn " world, the time is " & Time & "</center></p>"
oIEDoc.WriteLn "<p><center>Please wait.</center></p>"
oIEDoc.WriteLn "<p><center>This window will close in approx. 10 seconds.</center></p>"
oIEDoc.WriteLn "</body>"
oIEDoc.WriteLn "</html>"

' Wait for 10 seconds
Dim vStart
vStart = Now
Do While DateDiff("s", vStart, Now) < 10
    Wscript.Sleep 1000
Loop
Set oIEDoc = Nothing
oIE.Quit
Set oIE = Nothing
Wscript.Quit 0

    '///////////////////////////////////////////////////////////////////////////
```

The `HelloWorld2.vbs` script begins by declaring two object variables, `oIE` and `oIEDoc`, to hold object references. It then creates a new object using a ProgID of `"InternetExplorer.Application"`. This ProgID creates a new instance of the Microsoft Internet Explorer application and returns an object reference that represents that instance.

The goal of the script is to display a welcome message in the Internet Explorer window. The first step to this is to create an empty document into which the HTML text can be entered. This is done using the `.Navigate` method, which is passed a single argument that specifies the URL to display. In this case, the special `"about:blank"` string is used to display an empty document.

Next, a series of properties are set to adjust the appearance of the Internet Explorer application. The `.AddressBar`, `.StatusBar`, `.ToolBar`, and `.MenuBar` properties are set to `False` so that none of these UI features are displayed. Finally, the `.Visible` property is set to `True`. As previously explained, applications started as a result of creating COM objects are not normally visible. After the `.Visible` property is set to `True`, the Internet Explorer window instantly becomes visible on the desktop.

The next set of statements in the `HelloWorld2.vbs` script displays the message using HTML. The HTML text must be placed in the document created previously by the `.Navigate` method. This document is itself an object, and a reference to this object can be obtained via the `.Document` property of the Internet Explorer application object. This object reference is assigned to the `oIEDoc` variable (although a `With` statement could have been used here).

The Internet Explorer document object supports `.Write` and `.WriteLn` methods to add text to the current document (the latter also appends a new line to the document). These are used to construct the HTML text in the document, which is then displayed by Internet Explorer.

Finally, after a short time-out, the `.Quit` method is used to terminate the Internet Explorer application, and all object references are assigned `Nothing` to delete the objects.

To use an application or library in VBScript two sets of information are needed:

- The ProgIDs of all the objects made available by the application or library.
- The methods and properties supported by each COM object provided by the application or library.

In both cases, this information is typically made available in the documentation accompanying the application or library. This documentation typically describes an *object hierarchy*.

Object Hierarchies

Although `CreateObject` provides the primary means to create an object, many objects are created or accessed via the methods and properties of other objects. Sometimes, these subsidiary objects have methods or properties that support additional objects, and these secondary objects can have methods and properties that return objects, and so on. Thus, by starting with an initial object created by the `CreateObject` function, it is possible to create or access numerous additional associated objects.

Such a collection of objects is called an *object hierarchy*. Object hierarchies are very common in large applications like Microsoft Word or Excel. For example:

```
Dim oExcel, oBook, oSheet, oCell, oFont
Set oExcel = CreateObject("Excel.Application")
Set oBook = oExcel.Workbooks.Add
Set oSheet = oBook.Worksheets(1)
Set oCell = oSheet.Cells(1,1)
Set oFont = oCell.Font
```

This code initially creates a new Microsoft Excel application object. This object represents a running instance of Excel and will, as usual, start a copy of Microsoft Excel (although it will not be visible). The `oExcel` object contains a collection object, `oExcel.Workbooks`, which contains all the workbooks currently open in Excel. The `.Add` method of this collection adds a new workbook to the collection and returns a new object that represents this new workbook. The `oBook` object that refers to this workbook itself contains a collection object, `oBook.Worksheets`, which contains all the worksheets in the workbook. New workbooks are always created with three worksheets, and so `oBook.Worksheets(1)` returns an object that represents the first worksheet in the collection (Excel numbers worksheets starting with 1). The `.Cells` method returns an object that represents one or more cells in the spreadsheet, and the `.Font` property of this object returns an object that represents the formatting of that cell.

In general, an object hierarchy starts with a high-level object (in the previous example, an Excel application object) and drills-down to subsidiary objects that represent more specific items of information (in the previous example, a workbook, then a worksheet, then a cell, and finally the formatting for that cell). At each level, the particular object provides methods and properties to access objects that are lower down the hierarchy and other methods and properties that are appropriate to that particular object.

Some properties and methods of objects can create and return *new* objects. For example, the `oExcel.Workbooks.Add` method creates a new workbook in Excel and a new object for that workbook; therefore, each invocation returns a new object. The `Wscript.Arguments` property, however, always returns the same object: a collection representing the command line arguments. Repeatedly referencing this property always returns the same object. In general, object *properties* return existing objects, whereas object *methods* create new objects, although there are exceptions to this rule. Consult the documentation for the application or library to obtain information on which methods and properties create new objects.

The object hierarchy is typically provided as part of the documentation for an application or COM library. The sample scripts in Part III provide several examples of access to an application's object hierarchy.

Other Ways to Access Objects

The `CreateObject` function is one way to create objects. However, there are several other methods supported by VBScript, and these are described in this section with the exception of the `New` operator, which is described in Chapter 9.

Accessing Existing Objects Using *GetObject*

The `CreateObject` function always creates a new object. The `GetObject` function is used to access existing objects or to create an object from a file.

When `CreateObject` creates a new object, it will also create a new running instance of the COM server application if necessary. For example:

```
Dim oExcel1, oExcel2
Set oExcel1 = CreateObject("Excel.Application")
Set oExcel2 = CreateObject("Excel.Application")
```

This example creates two new Excel application objects. Each object represents a new instance of Microsoft Excel, and so two distinct copies of Excel are loaded and executed as a result of the two invocations of `CreateObject`. This occurs because the objects being created represent a complete application. If the objects are not applications, only one application instance can be created. For example:

```
Dim oSheet1, oSheet2
Set oSheet1 = CreateObject("Excel.Sheet")
Set oSheet2 = CreateObject("Excel.Sheet")
```

Here, two Excel spreadsheet objects are created. Because a single instance of Microsoft Excel can handle multiple spreadsheets, only one instance of Excel is executed.

Note

Some objects are single instance objects. For these objects, only one instance of the object is created no matter how many times `CreateObject` *is invoked. In this case, all invocations of* `CreateObject` *return the same object reference.* ◆

Thus, the `CreateObject` function will create application instances as necessary to create the requested object. Sometimes, however, it is desirable to retrieve an object reference for an object that already exists. For example, a script may know that a copy of Excel is already running and wish to use that instance rather than create a new one using `CreateObject`. This can be done using the `GetObject` function. For example:

```
Dim oExcel1, oExcel2
Set oExcel1 = CreateObject("Excel.Application")
Set oExcel2 = GetObject(,"Excel.Application")
If oExcel1 Is oExcel2 Then Wscript.Echo "They are the same object"
```

In this example, the `CreateObject` invocation creates a new instance of Excel. The `GetObject` function then retrieves a second reference to the same object. Because both objects reference the same object, the final `If` statement will evaluate to `True`.

Notice the syntax of the `GetObject` function. The function takes two arguments. However, in this case, the first argument is not used and is left blank, hence the comma before the second argument, which is a ProgID.

In the preceding example, the script creates the initial instance of Excel. This need not be the case for `GetObject` to succeed. As long as there is an instance of Excel running (even an interactive copy invoked normally via the Start menu), the `GetObject` function will retrieve an object reference for that instance. However, if there is *no* copy of Excel running, the `GetObject` function will fail with an error. When used in this manner, `GetObject` does not *create* new objects—it only returns references to existing objects.

Accessing Persistent Objects via *GetObject*

As previously noted, `GetObject` does not normally create new objects, but it is used to return references to existing objects. In the object-oriented world, a document file, such as an Excel spreadsheet, can actually be thought of as an object. The state of this object is the data in the document file, and the behavior of the object is the set of methods and properties for the document provided by the Excel application.

An object that is stored in a file is an example of a *persistent* object. A persistent object is one that has an existence that extends beyond the lifetime of the application or library that manipulates it. For example, Excel might be used to create a new spreadsheet, which exists only in system memory as an object. To make this object persistent, it is necessary to save the object (the spreadsheet) as a `.XLS` file. Then, at some future time, the object can be recreated by loading the `.XLS` file and regenerating the spreadsheet object.

Because a document is an object, the `GetObject` function can be used to return an object reference to that document. To do this, specify the path to the document file as an argument to `GetObject`. For example:

```
Dim oSheet
Set oSheet = GetObject("c:\my documents\testdata.xls")
```

This example creates a spreadsheet object from the specified `.XLS` document file.

Note

Using `GetObject` *is typically not the only way to load a document file. Most application objects support some sort of* `.Load` *or* `.Open` *method that opens a document file and returns an object for that file.* ◆

Sometimes, two distinct COM objects can load a document file. In this case, specify an additional argument to `GetObject` to specify the ProgID of the COM object. For example:

```
Dim oSheet
Set oSheet = GetObject("c:\my documents\testdata.xls", "Excel.Sheet")
```

`GetObject` also supports one special case when the filename is the empty string. In this case, `GetObject` actually creates a *new* object, just like `CreateObject`. For example:

```
Dim oExcel1, oExcel2
Set oExcel1 = CreateObject("Excel.Application")
Set oExcel2 = GetObject("", "Excel.Application")
```

In this example, both statements are equivalent. They both create new Excel application objects, and in this case, they both create a new instance of

Microsoft Excel. In fact, the `CreateObject` function is really a shorthand way of invoking the `GetObject` function with an empty filename argument.

Accessing Monikers via *GetObject*

The `GetObject` function can also be used to access objects via *monikers*. A moniker is itself an object that acts as an intermediary between VBScript and the actual object to be accessed. Monikers are typically used when the objects to be accessed exist in a namespace other than the file system. For example, the ADSI (Active Directory System Interface) facility provides COM object access to the user account database on a Windows NT or Windows 2000 computer. Access to individual items in this database is specified via a moniker.

A moniker is specified as a string; the first part of which specifies the moniker class, and the second part of which specifies the moniker data or item. These parts are separated by a colon character. For example:

```
Dim oUser
Set oUser = GetObject("WinNT://DOMAIN/Users/John")
```

Here, the moniker string is `"WinNT://DOMAIN/Users/John"`. The `"WinNT"` part of the string is the moniker class, which in this case, is the ADSI provider for the Windows NT domain directory. The remaining portion of the moniker specifies an individual user record within this domain. The returned object is an ADSI object that contains all the user account information for the specified user. The ADSI technology is explored in more detail in Chapter 12, "Logon Scripts."

Internally, VBScript uses COM to convert the moniker string into an object reference. The portion of the moniker string before the colon is used to load a special moniker object. This object then uses the rest of the string (the portion after the colon) to create the requested object. Thus, the meaning and syntax of the portion of the string after the colon is dependent upon which moniker name is used before the colon character. Other monikers can have different string formats from that shown for the ADSI preceding example.

Additional examples of moniker access to objects are provided in Part III.

The XML *object* Element

Another way to create an object is to use an XML `object` element in a `.WS` style script file. This element must appear within the `job` element but outside of any other elements. The element defines an object in a manner similar to the `CreateObject` function of VBScript, but the object is defined outside of any script language blocks and is, therefore, available to all language blocks regardless of the chosen script language. Objects created with the `object` element have global scope.

The `object` element supports two attributes: an `id` attribute that specifies the ID of the object, and a `progid` attribute that specifies the ProgID of the object. For example:

```
<job id="Job1">
    <object id="oExcel" progid="Excel.Application">
    <script language="VBScript">
        oExcel.Workbooks.Add
    </script>
</job>
```

The `object` element in the preceding example is equivalent to:

```
Dim oExcel
Set oExcel = CreateObject("Excel.Application")
```

The primary difference between the `object` element and the `CreateObject` function is that WSH creates all objects specified with `object` elements before any script code executes. Thus, all objects created in this manner have global scope and are available in all `script` elements, regardless of the language used in each element.

Creating Remote Objects

The `CreateObject` function can take an optional second parameter that allows objects to be created on a remote computer using DCOM (*Distributed COM*, a way to access objects over the network). An object created on a remote computer looks and acts like an object created locally, except that the object has access to the remote computer's resources (because it is running on that computer). There is also a performance overhead associated with a remote object, because each method or property request to the object involves a round-trip across the network to the remote computer.

To create a remote object, specify the computer name as the second argument to `CreateObject`. For example:

```
Dim oExcel
Set oExcel = CreateObject("Excel.Application", "Server1")
```

This example creates an instance of the Excel application running on the computer Server1.

Setting up and using DCOM is complex, and it requires the use of the `DCOMCNFG.EXE` tool on both the client and remote computers. Refer to Appendix B, "Other Scripting Resources," for references on using DCOM.

Creating Objects with Event Handlers

Objects that are manipulated by invoking methods and changing properties are essentially *passive* objects. They only perform operations in response to requests from the script that created them. Some objects, particularly those in libraries (that is, .DLL files) always operate in this manner. Other objects, however, can be contained in active applications (that is, .EXE files) that are capable of independent operations. These objects are *active* objects in that they can change state without that state change being initiated by the script.

When an object changes state without prompting from the script, it is sometimes useful for the script to be informed of these changes of state. This informing occurs through a mechanism known as *events*. If an object changes state, it can "fire" an event. This event then triggers execution of a procedure, known as an *event handler*, within the script. This procedure can then perform any actions that are associated with the event. Thus, event handlers provide a way for an object to "reach back" into the calling script to inform the script of internal actions and state changes as they occur.

For an object to fire an event and trigger an event handler, the object must be created using the `Wscript.CreateObject` or `Wscript.GetObject` methods. These methods are similar to the built-in `CreateObject` and `GetObject` functions of VBScript, but they both support an additional argument. This argument specifies a string prefix that is used to map events to procedures. For example:

```
Dim oExcel
Set oExcel = Wscript.CreateObject("Excel.Application", "Excel_")

Sub Excel_Quit
End Sub
```

The second argument to the `Wscript.CreateObject` method is a string that is used as a prefix when binding events to procedures. When the Excel object fires an event, the name of the event is concatenated to the string prefix, and this combined string is then used as the name of the procedure. If a procedure with this name exists within the script, the procedure is invoked. Therefore, in the preceding example, a `Quit` event causes the `Excel_Quit` procedure to execute.

A different string prefix can be specified for each instance of an object. This allows multiple instances of the same class to trigger different procedures for the same event, simply by specifying a different string prefix when the object is created by `Wscript.CreateObject`.

Additional examples of event handlers are provided in Part III. However, event handlers are less common in system scripts than in web page scripts.

Summary

The object-oriented paradigm provides a way to encapsulate both state and behavior into a single package, called an object. The object is then accessed via the methods and properties defined for that object.

Objects are typically created using the `CreateObject` function. Once created, an object is accessed via a variable, which stores a reference to an object. This variable provides access to the methods and properties of the object in VBScript.

The objects that are manipulated by VBScript are all COM objects, which can reside in external applications or libraries. Almost all application and operating system functionality can be accessed via one of these COM objects.

7

Built-In WSH and VBScript Objects

The previous chapter introduced objects and the object-oriented paradigm. This chapter details some objects that are supplied as part of either VBScript or Windows Script Host, and that are, therefore, available to system script authors.

Objects that are supplied by WSH are available to all system scripts, regardless of the language used. Objects that are supplied by VBScript are only available if the VBScript language is used for scripting. Therefore, if you use another script language, you will not have access to the VBScript objects.

The file system object is also supplied as part of the VBScript. This object is described in Chapter 8, "File System Objects."

Note

As with all the sample scripts in this book, the scripts in this chapter should be run using the CSCRIPT host unless otherwise noted. The examples shown assume that CSCRIPT is the default WSH host. (See Chapter 1, "Introducing WSH," for information on selecting the default WSH host.) ◆

VBScript Objects

VBScript provides the following objects to scripts:

- The `Err` object, which provides access to run-time error information.
- The `RegExp` object, which matches strings against special text patterns, called regular expressions.
- The `Dictionary` object, which provides an item indexing facility.

The *Err* Object

The `Err` object encapsulates errors for a VBScript script. So far in this book, all the sample scripts have used default error handling. By default, if an error occurs, VBScript terminates script execution and WSH reports the error back to the user. Sometimes however, this default error processing is not desirable. In this case, the `Err` object and the `On Error` statement can be used to let scripts perform their own error handling.

The `Err` object is a predefined global object—it does not need to be declared before it can be used. The object is used to encapsulate all the information relating to an error condition. This information is presented as a series of properties, as follows:

- The `.Number` property is the error number (or code) for the error. This is the default property of the `Err` object.
- The `.Source` property contains a string that specifies the source of the error, typically the ProgID (Programmatic Identifier) of the object that generated the error.
- The `.Description` property contains a string describing the error.
- The `.HelpFile` and `.HelpContext` properties store information to reference a help topic in a help file. This allows the error to refer the user to information on possible causes of the error.

To generate a user-defined run-time error, first clear the `Err` object using the `.Clear` method, and then raise the error using the `.Raise` method. This method takes up to five arguments that correspond, in order, to the properties previously listed. For example:

```
Err.Clear
Err.Raise 1000, "This is a script-defined error", "Test Script"
```

This example displays a message showing the description string followed by a colon and the source string.

To intercept run-time errors and process them in scripts, use the `On Error` statement. The syntax of this statement is:

```
On Error Resume Next
```

After this statement executes, subsequent run-time errors do *not* cause script execution to terminate. Instead, the `Err` object properties are set to reflect the error information and processing continues with the next statement. For example:

```
Err.Clear
On Error Resume Next
Err.Raise 100,"Script Error"
If Err.Number Then Wscript.Echo "Error=", Err.Number
```

In this example, the `Err.Raise` method is used to raise a run-time error. Normally, this would terminate script execution. However, the earlier `On Error` statement allows script execution to continue, and so the `If` statement executes and displays the error number.

In the preceding example, the error was generated by the `Err.Raise` method. However, the same processing applies to *any* run-time error, regardless of how it is generated. For example:

```
On Error Resume Next
Err.Clear
x = CInt("foo")
If Err.Number <> 0 Then Wscript.Echo Err.Number, Err.Description, Err.Source
```

Here, an attempt is made to convert the string `"foo"` into an integer. Because this is an invalid conversion, a run-time type mismatch error is generated. The information on this error is placed in the `Err` object, and this is then processed by the `If` statement.

After an `On Error` statement executes, it remains in effect for the remainder of the procedure in which it executes. If the `On Error` statement executes in global scope, it remains in effect until the script terminates. Nested procedures can each have their own `On Error` statement. For example, subroutine `A` can execute an `On Error` statement and then execute subroutine `B`, which in turn, executes an `On Error` statement.

If an error occurs while an `On Error` statement is active, execution continues with the following statement *in the same scope as the most recently executed* `On Error` *statement*. For example:

```
On Error Resume Next
Wscript.Echo "Begin"
Sub1
Wscript.Echo "End"

Sub Sub1
    Wscript.Echo "Enter Sub1"
    Err.Raise 100
    Wscript.Echo "Leave Sub1"
End Sub
```

In this example, an `On Error` statement executes at global scope, and then the `Sub1` procedure executes. Within this procedure, an `Err.Raise` method is used to generate an error. Because the most recently executed error is at global scope, the next statement to execute is the `Wscript.Echo` statement at *global* scope, and *not* the `Wscript.Echo` statement following the `Err.Raise` statement. In fact, the error causes VBScript to abandon further execution of the statements in `Sub1` and continue execution at global scope. Thus, the output of this script is:

```
Begin
Enter Sub1
End
```

Notice that the final `Wscript.Echo` statement in `Sub1` never executes. When an error occurs, VBScript immediately abandons execution of whatever running procedures are necessary in order to resume with the correct statement after an error. For example:

```
On Error Resume Next
Wscript.Echo "Begin"
Sub1
Wscript.Echo "End"

Sub Sub1
    Wscript.Echo "Enter Sub1"
    Sub2
    Wscript.Echo "Leave Sub1"
End Sub

Sub Sub2
    Wscript.Echo "Enter Sub2"
    Err.Raise 100
    Wscript.Echo "Leave Sub2"
End Sub
```

Here, the `Err.Raise` method invocation is nested even more deeply. In this case, when the error occurs, VBScript abandons further execution of both `Sub1` and `Sub2` in order to continue execution at the global level.

Because VBScript abandons execution of procedures only until it finds the most recently executed `On Error` statement, it is possible to capture an error within a procedure simply by placing an `On Error` statement in that procedure. For example:

```
On Error Resume Next
Wscript.Echo "Begin"
Sub1
Wscript.Echo "End"

Sub Sub1
    Wscript.Echo "Enter Sub1"
    On Error Resume Next
    Sub2
    Wscript.Echo "Leave Sub1"
End Sub

Sub Sub2
    Wscript.Echo "Enter Sub2"
    Err.Raise 100
    Wscript.Echo "Leave Sub2"
End Sub
```

This example modifies the previous example by adding an `On Error` statement to the `Sub1` procedure. Thus, when the `Err.Raise` method in `Sub2` executes, execution continues with the next statement in `Sub1`. Notice that the `Leave Sub2` line never executes. The output from this example is:

```
Begin
Enter Sub1
Enter Sub2
Leave Sub1
End
```

Program Guide

Structured Exception Handling

The `On Error` *statement is a simple form of a technique known as structured exception handling. The basic idea behind this technique is to centralize all the error handling code in a single location outside of the main "flow" of the program. This is the reason for the apparently complex behavior of the* `On Error` *statement.*

The assumption is that a large script might contain many procedures that interact in complex ways. It is possible that an error will occur when procedures are nested very deeply. Without the `On Error` *statement, each procedure must return some form of error code to the procedure from which it was called. In turn, this procedure must do the same thing, and so on for all the nested procedures. This can add greatly to the complexity of the script.*

With the `On Error` *statement, this complexity can be avoided. When an error occurs, VBScript automatically takes care of unwinding out of the complex nest of procedures back to the statement following the original procedure invocation.*

The *RegExp* Object

The `InStr` function described in Chapter 3, "VBScript Data Storage," can be used to search a string to see if it contains another string. The `RegExp` object provides a far more sophisticated string searching facility by using regular expressions.

A *regular expression* is a string that describes a *match pattern*. The match pattern provides a template that can be used to test another string, the *search string*, for a matching sub-string. In its simplest form, the match pattern string is just a sequence of characters that must be matched. For example, the pattern `"fred"` matches this exact sequence of characters and only this sequence. More sophisticated regular expressions can match against items such as file names, path names, and Internet URLs. Thus, the `RegExp` object is frequently used to validate data for correct form and syntax.

To test a search string against a match pattern, create a `RegExp` object and set the match pattern. Then use the `.Test` method to test for a match. For example:

```
Dim oRE, bMatch
Set oRE = New RegExp
```

```
oRE.Pattern = "fred"
bMatch = oRE.Test("His name was fred brown")
```

Regular expression objects are created using the `New` keyword, which is described in Chapter 9, "Creating VBScript Classes." This is an anomaly of VBScript, because it is the only object, apart from user-defined objects, that is created in this manner. Once created in this way, the methods and properties of the object are accessed normally.

The `.Pattern` property defines the match pattern, and the `.Test` method tests the supplied string against this match pattern, returning `True` if the match pattern is found within the supplied string. In the preceding example, `bMatch` is set to `True` as there is clearly a match.

The `.Execute` method of the `RegExp` object also checks for a pattern match, but it returns a `Matches` collection object that contains detailed information on each pattern match. The `Matches` object is a normal collection object containing a `.Count` property and a default `.Item` property. Each item in the `Matches` object is a `Match` object that describes a specific pattern match. After the `.Execute` method is invoked, the returned `Matches` object contains a `Match` object for each match located in the search string.

Each `Match` item has three properties. The `.Value` property contains the actual text in the search string that was matched. The `.FirstIndex` property contains the index of the first character of the match in the search string. The `.Length` property contains the length of the matched string. Unlike other VBScript string indexes, the `.FirstIndex` property uses 0 as the index of the first character in the string. Therefore, always add one to this value before using it with other VBScript string functions.

By default, the `.Execute` method only matches the first occurrence of the pattern. If the `.Global` property is set to `True`, the method matches *all* the occurrences in the string and returns a `Match` object for each match. For example:

```
Dim oRE, oMatches
Set oRE = New RegExp
oRE.Pattern = "two"
oRE.Global = True
Set oMatches = oRE.Execute("two times three equals three times two")
For Each oMatch In oMatches
    Wscript.Echo "Match:", oMatch.Value, "At:", oMatch.FirstIndex + 1
Next
```

This example lists all the matches against the pattern `"two"` in the specified string.

Simple match patterns, such as those shown in the previous example, provide no additional functionality over that provided by the `InStr` function. Much more powerful searches are available, however, by using the special regular expression features of the search pattern. These are most easily explored using the `RegExp.vbs` sample script shown in Listing 7.1.

Listing 7.1 *`RegExp.vbs` Script*

```
'//////////////////////////////////////////////////////////////////////////
' $Workfile: ShowArgs2.vbs $ $Revision: 5 $ $Date: 4/24/99 11:36a $
' $Archive: /Scripts/ShowArgs2.vbs $
' Copyright (c) 1999 Tim Hill. All Rights Reserved.
'//////////////////////////////////////////////////////////////////////////

' Process a regular expression pattern match
' First arg=regexp match pattern, second arg=search string

Option Explicit

' Check for sufficient command line arguments
Dim sPattern, sSearch
If Wscript.Arguments.Count < 2 Then
    Wscript.Echo "usage: regexp <match-pattern> <search-string>"
    Wscript.Quit(1)
End If
sPattern = Wscript.Arguments(0)
sSearch = Wscript.Arguments(1)

' Do the regular expression match
Dim oRE, oMatches
Set oRE = New RegExp
oRE.Global = True
oRE.IgnoreCase = True
oRE.Pattern = sPattern
Set oMatches = oRE.Execute(sSearch)

' Now process all the matches (if any)
Dim oMatch
Wscript.Echo "Pattern String: " & Chr(34) & sPattern & Chr(34)
Wscript.Echo "Search String: " & Chr(34) & sSearch & Chr(34) & vbCRLF
Wscript.Echo oMatches.Count, "Matches:"
Wscript.Echo "    " & sSearch
For Each oMatch In oMatches
    Wscript.Echo "    " & String(oMatch.FirstIndex, " ") & String(oMatch.Length, "^")
Next

    '//////////////////////////////////////////////////////////////////////////
```

To use the `RegExp.vbs` script, execute the script with two command line arguments. Enter a match pattern as the first argument and a search string as the second argument. If either argument contains spaces or special shell characters, enclose the argument in double quotes. The script uses the `.Execute` method of the `RegExp` object to locate all matches and then displays these matches graphically. Use this script to experiment with the various advanced regular expression features described in the following paragraphs. (Several of the preceding `Wscript.Echo` statements use the expression `Chr(34)`. This simply evaluates to a double quote character.)

Regular Expression Syntax

Within the match pattern, letters, digits, and most punctuation simply match a corresponding character in the search string. A sequence of these characters matches the equivalent sequence in the search string. However, some characters within the match pattern have special meaning. For example, the `"."` (period) character matches any character except a new-line character. Thus, the match pattern `"a.c"` matches `"abc"` or `"adc"` or `"a$c"`. The match pattern `".."` matches any sequence of two characters.

The special character `"^"` matches the *start* of the string. Thus, the match pattern `"^abc"` matches the string `"abc"`, but not `"123abc"` because this string does not begin with `"abc"`. Similarly, the special character `"$"` matches the *end* of the string, and so the pattern `"red$"` matches the search string `"fred"`, but not `"fred brown"`.

Using both these characters allows a regular expression to match complete strings. For example, the pattern `"abc"` matches `"123 abc that"` and any other string *containing* `"abc"`, whereas the pattern `"^abc$"` only matches the exact string `"abc"`.

The three characters `"*"`, `"+"`, and `"?"` are called *modifiers*. These characters modify the preceding character. The `"*"` modifier matches the preceding character zero or more times, the `"+"` modifier matches the preceding character one or more times, and the `"?"` modifier matches the preceding character zero or one time. For example, the pattern `"a+"` matches any sequence of one or more `"a"` characters, whereas the pattern `"ab*c"` matches `"abc"`, `"abbbbbc"`, and `"ac"`, but not `"adc"` or `"ab"`.

A list of characters enclosed in brackets is called a *range* and matches a single character in the search string with any of the characters in brackets. For example, the pattern `"[0123456789]"` matches any digit character in the search string. Ranges such as this, where the characters are sequential, can be abbreviated as `"[0-9]"`. For example, the pattern `"[0-9a-zA-Z_]"` matches a digit, letter (either upper or lower case), or the underscore character. If the first character of the range is `"^"`, the range matches all those characters that are *not* listed. For example, `"[^0-9]"` matches any non-digit character.

Ranges can be combined with modifiers. For example, the pattern `"[0-9]+"` matches any sequence of one or more digit characters. The pattern `"[a-zA-Z][a-zA-Z_0-9]*"` matches a valid VBScript variable name, because it only matches sequences that start with a letter and are followed by zero or more letters, digits, or underscore characters.

To match a character an exact number of times, follow the character in the pattern by a count of matches required enclosed in braces. For example, the pattern "a{3}" matches exactly three "a" characters, and it is equivalent to the pattern "aaa". If a comma follows the count, the character is matched *at least* that number of times. For example, "a{5,}" matches five or more "a" characters. Finally, use two counts to specify a lower and upper bound. For example, the pattern "a{4,8}" matches between four and eight "a" characters.

As with other modifiers, the pattern count modifier can be combined with ranges. For example, the pattern "[0-9]{4}" matches exactly four digits.

Use parentheses in the match pattern to group individual items together. Modifiers can then be applied to the entire group of items. For example, the pattern "(abc)+" matches any number of repeats of the sequence "abc". The pattern "(a[0-9]c){1,2}" matches strings such as "a0c" and "a4ca5c".

There is a difference between matching the pattern "abc" and the pattern "(abc)+" using the RegExp object. Matching the pattern "abc" against the search string "abcabcabc" generates three individual matches and results in three Match objects in the Matches collection. Matching the pattern "(abc)+" against the same string generates one match that matches the entire string.

The "|" vertical bar character separates lists of alternate sub-expressions. For example, the pattern "ab|ac" matches the strings "ab" or "ac". The vertical bar separates entire regular expressions. The pattern "^ab|ac$" matches either the string "ab" at the start of the search string or the string "ac" at the end of the search string. Use parentheses to specify alternates within a larger pattern. For example, the pattern "^(ab|ac)$" matches the exact strings "ab" or "ac" only.

To match any of the special characters literally in a pattern, they must be preceded by a back-slash character, which is known as an *escape*. For example, to match a literal asterisk, use "*" in the pattern. To match a back-slash itself, use two back-slash characters in the match pattern. The following characters must be escaped when used literally within a match pattern:

. (period) * + ? \ ( ) [ ] { } ^ $

There are also several additional escape sequences that provide useful shorthand for more complex patterns:

- The "\d" escape matches any digit, and it is equivalent to "[0-9]". The "\D" escape matches any non-digit, and it is equivalent to "[^0-9]".
- The "\w" escape matches any word character and is equivalent to "[0-9a-zA-Z_]", and the "\W" escape matches any non-word character.

- The `"\b"` escape matches a word boundary, which is the boundary between any word character and a non-word character, whereas `"\B"` matches a non-word boundary.
- The `"\s"` escape matches any whitespace character, including space, tab, new-line, and so on, whereas the `"\S"` escape matches any non-whitespace character.

Finally, certain escapes can match non-printing characters, as follows:

- The `"\f"` escape matches a form-feed character.
- The `"\n"` escape matches a new-line character.
- The `"\r"` escape matches a carriage-return character.
- The `"\t"` escape matches a tab character.
- The `"\v"` escape matches a vertical tab character.
- The `"\onn"` escape matches a character whose octal code is *nn*.
- The `"\xnn"` escape matches a character whose hexadecimal code is *nn*.

The special escape `"\n"`, where *n* is a digit, matches the search text previously matched by a sub-expression in parentheses. Each sub-expression in a match pattern is numbered from left to right, and the escape `"\n"` matches the *n*th sub-expression. For example, the pattern `"(..)\1"` matches any two character sequence that repeats twice, such as `"abab"`. The first sub-expression matches the first two characters, `"ab"`, and the `"\1"` escape then matches these same two characters again.

Regular Expression Examples

Regular expression match patterns provide a powerful way to validate the syntax of strings. For example, a script can obtain a command line argument that is the name of a file to create. Before creating the file, a script might want to validate that the command line argument is a valid file name. A regular expression can be used for this purpose.

The `ParseArgs.vbs` script in Chapter 3 processed command line arguments of the form *`name=value`*. This script is simplistic in that it simply breaks apart each argument at the `"="` sign—no attempt is made to check if the name and value parts are valid. The following regular expression matches these command line arguments:

```
[^=]+=.*
```

This match pattern is interpreted as follows: The range `"[^=]"` matches any character that is *not* an `"="` sign. The `"+"` modifier following the range means that the pattern matches any set of one or more characters that are not "=" signs. The next "=" sign in the pattern matches a literal "=" sign (that is, the separator between the name and value parts). Finally, the ".*" pattern matches any sequence of zero or more characters.

Parentheses can be used to make the meaning more clear. For example:

```
([^=]+)=(.*)
```

This example is identical to the previous example, but the parentheses help make the individual parts of the pattern more understandable.

Typically, the *name* in the previous example should be restricted to a valid name. We define valid names as a letter followed by zero or more letters, digits, or underscores. This yields a new regular expression as follows:

```
([a-zA-Z]\w*)=(.*)
```

Here, the pattern "[a-zA-Z]" matches any single letter. Then the pattern "\w*" matches zero or more letters, digits, or underscores, using the "\w" escape as a shorthand for "[0-9a-zA-Z_]".

The previous regular expression does not allow spaces before or after the *name*. For example, only the first of these strings matches the expression:

```
account=123456
account = 575888
 account  = 5544
```

The following regular expression corrects this by adding optional leading and trailing whitespace around the name:

```
(\s*)([a-zA-Z]\w*)(\s*)=(.*)
```

The new addition, "\s*", matches zero or more whitespace characters.

Here is a sample script that uses this expression to validate command line arguments:

```
Dim oRE, oMatches, oMatch, sArg
Set oRE = New RegExp
oRE.Global = True
oRE.IgnoreCase = True
oRE.Pattern = "(\s*)([a-zA-Z]\w*)(\s*)=(.*)"
For Each sArg In Wscript.Arguments
    Set oMatches = oRE.Execute(sArg)
    If oMatches.Count > 0 Then
        Wscript.Echo "Valid argument: " & sArg
    Else
        Wscript.Echo "Invalid argument: " & sArg
    End If
Next
```

As another example, we can define a command line *switch* to be an argument of the form:

```
/name[:¦=value]
```

Another way to define a command line switch is an argument that begins with a slash character and ends with a name. The name can be followed by an optional value that is delimited with either a colon or an equal sign character. The following are valid example switches:

```
/b
/file=c:\myfile.txt
/debug:on
```

Here is the regular expression that matches a command line switch:

```
(\s*)/([a-zA-Z]\w*)((=|:)(.*)|)
```

This complex expression breaks down as follows:

- The `"(\s*)/"` pattern matches any leading whitespace followed by the slash character.
- The `"([a-zA-Z]\w*)"` pattern matches the name, as in the previous example.
- The `"(=|:)(.*)"` pattern matches either an equal sign or a colon, followed by any sequence of characters.
- The `"((=|:)(.*)|)"` pattern makes the `"(=|:)(.*)"` optional, by matching either this pattern or nothing.

Using the *.Replace* Method

Matching patterns against strings allows a script to determine if a string follows a specific syntax, as shown in the previous examples. The `RegExp` object can also be used to assist in *modifying* the search string. This facility is provided by the `.Replace` method, which takes two arguments: the search string and a replacement string, and returns a new string in which all matches in the search string are replaced by the replacement string. For example:

```
Set oRE = New RegExp
oRE.Global = True
oRE.Pattern = "a"
Wscript.Echo oRE.Replace("all a's are replaced", "X")
```

In this example, any `"a"` character in the search string is replaced by an `"X"` character. The pattern and replacement strings do not need to be the same length. For example:

```
oRE.Pattern = "\s+"
Wscript.Echo oRE.Replace("compress  all      whitespace    ", " ")
```

Here, all sequences of whitespace are replaced by a single space character.

Within the replacement string, the special character sequence `"$n"` is allowed. If present, this sequence is replaced by the text matched by the *n*th sub-expression in the pattern. For example:

```
oRE.Pattern = "^\s*(\w+)\s*=\s*(\w+)\s*$"
sSearch = "    this    = that"
Wscript.Echo oRE.Replace(sSearch, "$1,$2")
```

This example works as follows:

- The pattern contains both the start of string `"^"` and end of string `"$"` characters. This means that the pattern either matches the *entire* search string or not at all.
- The pattern matches any whitespace and sequence of one or more word characters, more whitespace, an `"="` sign, more whitespace, another set of word characters, and finally more whitespace.
- Both the word patterns are in parentheses, marking them as sub-expressions 1 and 2 respectively.
- When the `.Replace` method is invoked, it matches successfully against the entire search string. This means that the replacement string replaces the entire contents of the search string, because this entire string matched the regular expression. Thus, the string returned by `.Replace` is simply the replacement string.
- The replacement string is `"$1,$2"`. As noted, the two sub-expressions in the pattern contain the two words matched in the search string, which in this case are `"this"` and `"that"`. Thus, the replacement string becomes `"this,that"`, and this is the value returned.

The result of this processing is that the `RegExp` object has validated the search string against the match pattern and extracted the required elements from the search string. Additional examples of this use of the `RegExp` object are found in Chapter 11, "A Script Developer's Toolkit."

The *Dictionary* Object

The `Dictionary` object is used to hold a set of data values in the form of (*key*, *item*) pairs. A dictionary is sometimes called an *associative array* because it associates a key with an item. The keys behave in a way similar to indices in an array, except that array indices are numeric and keys are arbitrary strings. Each key in a single `Dictionary` object must be unique.

The ProgID for a `Dictionary` object is `"Scripting.Dictionary"`, and so the following example creates a `Dictionary` object:

```
Dim oDict
Set oDict = CreateObject("Scripting.Dictionary")
```

`Dictionary` objects have one property that should be set before any data values are stored in the dictionary. There are two modes for the `.CompareMode` property which control how individual keys are compared. If the mode is `vbBinaryCompare` (the default), upper and lower case letters in keys are considered distinct. If the mode is `vbTextCompare`, upper and lower case letters in keys are considered identical. This means that a `Dictionary` object in binary mode can contain two keys `"Key"` and `"key"`, whereas these would be considered the same key in text mode.

To add a value to a `Dictionary`, use the `.Add` method. For example:

```
Dim oDict
Set oDict = CreateObject("Scripting.Dictionary")
oDict.CompareMode = vbBTextCompare
oDict.Add "Pastrami", "Great"
oDict.Add "Roast Beef", "OK on Sunday"
oDict.Add "Salami", "Not so good"
```

The first argument to the `.Add` method is the key value and the second argument is the item value. There is no limit to the number of values that can be added to a dictionary. To remove a value from a dictionary, use the `.Remove` method and specify the key to remove. For example:

```
oDict.Remove "Salami"
```

To remove all values and clear the dictionary, use the `.RemoveAll` method. Use the `.Count` property to obtain a count of values in the dictionary.

The `.Exists` method returns `True` if the specified key exists within the dictionary. For example:

```
If oDict.Exists("Pastrami") Then Wscript.Echo "Pastrami is available today."
```

To retrieve the item value for a given key, use the `.Item` property. This is the default property for a `Dictionary` object. For example:

```
If oDict.Exists("Salami") Then Wscript.Echo oDict("Salami")
```

Here, the `Wscript.Echo` statement displays the item value stored in the dictionary for the `"Salami"` key.

Use the `.Key` property to change the key value for a given key. For example:

```
oDict.Key("Salami") = "Italian Salami"
```

The `.Keys` and `.Items` methods return an array containing all the keys or items from the dictionary. For example:

```
aMeats = oDict.Keys
aComments = oDict.Items
```

Dictionaries are frequently used when some items need to be stored and recovered by name. For example, a dictionary can hold all the environment variables defined by the system or all the values associated with a registry key. However, a dictionary can only store *one* item for each key value. That is, dictionary keys must all be unique.

WSH Objects

Windows Script Host provides the following objects to scripts:

- The `Wscript` object, which provides access to core WSH operations.
- The `WshArguments` object, which provides access to command line arguments.
- The `WshNetwork` object, which provides access to network shares and information.
- The `WshShell` object, which provides access to miscellaneous system functions.
- The `WshEnvironment` object, which provides access to the system environment variables.
- The `WshShortcut` and `WshUrlShortcut` objects, which provide access to file system shortcuts.

The *Wscript* Object

The `Wscript` object provides access to core `WSH` information. This object is predefined by WSH for all scripts and does not need to be declared or created. The methods of the `Wscript` object have already been covered elsewhere. The `.CreateObject` and `.GetObject` methods were described in Chapter 6, "Introducing Objects," and the `.Echo` and `.Quit` methods were described in Chapter 2, "VBScript Language Essentials," as special "statements," although it should now be clear that these are actually object methods.

In addition to these methods, the `Wscript` object also has a number of properties:

- The `.FullName` property contains the full pathname of the WSH executable used to run the script.
- The `.Name` property contains the friendly name (title) of the WSH executable used to run the script.
- The `.Path` property contains the path (that is, folder name) of the WSH executable.
- The `.ScriptFullName` property contains full path to the script file.
- The `.ScriptName` property contains the full name of the script file, without the path.
- The `.Version` property contains the version of WSH as a string. Note that this is *not* the same as the version of VBScript that is recovered using the `ScriptEngineMajorVersion` and `ScriptEngineMinorVersion` functions. These functions return the version of VBScript (the script engine), while the `.Version` property returns the version of WSH (the script host). See the Introduction for a discussion of hosts and engines.

The `Wscript` object does not provide the folder name where the script file is located. However, this is easily derived from the `.ScriptFullName` property. For example:

```
g_sScriptPath = Wscript.ScriptFullName
g_sScriptName = Wscript.ScriptName
g_sScriptFolder = Left(g_sScriptPath, Len(g_sScriptPath) - Len(g_sScriptName))
```

The `.Sleep` method of the `Wscript` object causes script execution to pause for the specified number of milliseconds. For example:

```
Wscript.Sleep 5000
```

This pauses the script execution for 5 seconds. While script execution is paused, object events are still processed.

The *WshArguments* Object

The `WshArguments` object encapsulates the command line arguments provided to the script. This object has already been used extensively in examples, such as `ShowArgs1.vbs`. The `Wscript.Arguments` property of the `Wscript` object returns this object.

The `.Count` property returns a count of command line arguments, whereas the `.Item` property returns an individual argument by index. This is the default property for the `WshArguments` object.

When WSH parses a command line into arguments, it first removes those arguments that are processed directly by the WSH executable. The arguments all begin with a double slash character and are *not* passed to the script as part of the `WshArguments` object. Remaining arguments are then passed to the script via this object. Individual command line arguments are separated by one or more spaces. To include a space within an argument, enclose the argument in double quotes. The double quotes are *not* themselves included in the argument text returned by the `WshArguments` object.

The *WshNetwork* Object

The `WshNetwork` object provides methods to manipulate network printers and drive management. The ProgID for the object is `"Wscript.Network"`, and so the following example creates a `WshNetwork` object:

```
Dim oNet
Set oNet = CreateObject("Wscript.Network")
```

The `WshNetwork` object supports the following properties:

- The `.ComputerName` property returns the NetBIOS name of the computer.
- The `.UserDomain` property returns the domain name to which the user belongs.
- The `.UserName` property returns the name of the currently logged on user.

For example:

```
Dim oNet
Set oNet = CreateObject("Wscript.Network")
Wscript.Echo "User: " & oNet.UserDomain & "\" & oNet.UserName
```

The `WshNetwork` object can manage connections to remote computer shared directories. Use the `.MapNetworkDrive` method to map a network drive to a local drive letter. The first argument specifies the drive letter; the second argument specifies the UNC name of the network share to map. For example:

```
oNet.MapNetworkDrive "S:", "\\SERVER1\Setup"
oNet.MapNetworkDrive "L:", "\\SERVER1\Library"
```

The `.MapNetworkDrive` method supports up to three additional, optional, arguments. The first of these is specified if the drive mapping should be made persistent. The default value is `False`. If this argument is `True`, the drive mapping is recorded in the registry and restored the next time this user logs on. The final two arguments can specify an alternative user account and password to use when connecting to the specified share. For example:

```
oNet.MapNetworkDrive "P:", "\\Server2\BobConner", False, "MYDOMAIN\BConner", "secret"
```

This example maps a non-persistent share to local drive P:, using the specified domain account and password.

The `.RemoveNetworkDrive` method removes a network drive mapping. Specify the drive letter of the drive to remove. For example:

```
oNet.RemoveNetworkDrive "S:"
```

This method also supports two optional arguments. The first argument, if `True`, specifies that the drive mapping is removed even if it is currently in use. The default is not to remove the mapping if it is being used. The second argument, if `True`, specifies that the removal is persistent. That is, if the drive mapping was previously set up to be persistent, the registry data for this is removed.

The `.EnumNetworkDrives` method returns a `WshCollection` object that contains a list of all the current network drive mappings. Items in the `WshCollection` object are paired. The first item in the pair is the local drive letter; the second item is the UNC path. The collection also includes all network share connections made directly to shares without intermediate drive letters. For these connections, the drive letter string is empty. For example, this script substitutes "- -" in its output for drives without drive letters:

```
Dim oNet, oDrives, ix, sDrive, sUNCPath
Set oNet = CreateObject("Wscript.Network")
Set oDrives = oNet.EnumNetworkDrives
Wscript.Echo oDrives.Count / 2, "Network Connections"
For ix = 0 To oDrives.Count - 2 Step 2
    sDrive = oDrives(ix)
```

```
    sUNCPath = oDrives(ix+1)
    If sDrive = "" Then sDrive = "--"
    Wscript.Echo "Drive: " & sDrive, "UNC Path: " & sUNCPath
Next
```

The `WshNetwork` object can also manage network printer connections in a similar manner to the way it handles network share connections. The `.AddPrinterConnection` method adds a new printer connection. It uses the same arguments as the `.MapNetworkDrive` method, except that the first argument maps a printer port name. For example:

```
oNet.AddPrinterConnection "LPT1:", "\\PrintServer\HPLaser1"
```

The `.AddPrinterConnection` method also supports the same three optional arguments of the `.MapNetworkDrive` method.

The `.RemovePrinterConnection` method removes a network printer connection. It supports the same arguments as the `.RemoveNetworkDrive` method. The `.SetDefaultPrinter` method chooses a default printer. The printer name can be either a local printer name (such as `"LPT1:"`) or a share name (such as `"\\Server\HP100"`).

The `.EnumPrinterConnections` method enumerates printer connections in a manner similar to the `.EnumNetworkDrives` method. It returns a `WshCollection` object containing pairs of strings that specify the local printer name and the printer share name. For example:

```
Dim oNet, oPrinters, ix, sPrinter, sUNCPath
Set oNet = CreateObject("Wscript.Network")
Set oPrinters = oNet.EnumPrinterConnections
Wscript.Echo oPrinters.Count / 2, "Network Connections"
For ix = 0 To oPrinters.Count - 2 Step 2
    sPrinter = oPrinters(ix)
    sUNCPath = oPrinters(ix+1)
    If sPrinter = "" Then sPrinter = "--"
    Wscript.Echo "Printer: " & sPrinter, "UNC Path: " & sUNCPath
Next
```

Note

The printer connections managed by the `WshNetwork` *object are identical to those managed by the* `NET USE` *shell command. Windows NT and Windows 2000 computers do not always use printers mapped to local devices in this manner, and so not all active printers appear as printer connections.*

The *WshShell* Object

The `WshShell` object provides access to a number of system level facilities, including the registry, system environment variables, special folders, and shortcuts. The ProgID of the `WshShell` object is `"Wscript.Shell"`.

The `.SpecialFolders` property provides access to the various folders in the Windows environment that have special significance to the shell. These folders should never be accessed directly by name, because the name varies from locale to locale and the user might alter the name. Instead, use the `.SpecialFolders` property to access the folder information indirectly. This property returns a collection object that contains the names of all the special folders. These are then accessed indirectly by specifying the type of folder required. For example:

```
Dim oShell, oSpecialFolders
Set oShell = CreateObject("Wscript.Shell")
Set oSpecialFolders = oShell.SpecialFolders
Wscript.Echo "Your documents are stored in: " & oSpecialFolders("MyDocuments")
```

Table 7.1 lists the individual special folders that can be accessed via this collection.

Table 7.1 Special Folders

Folder Name	Meaning
`"AllUsersDesktop"`	Folder where items visible on all users desktops are stored
`"AllUsersStartMenu"`	Folder where items in Start menu for all users are stored
`"AllUsersPrograms"`	Folder where items in Start Programs menu for all users are stored
`"AllUsersStartup"`	Folder where items in Start Programs Startup menu for all users are stored
`"Desktop"`	Folder for this user's desktop items
`"Favorites"`	Folder for this user's Internet favorites
`"Fonts"`	Folder where fonts are stored
`"MyDocuments"`	Default folder where user stores documents
`"Programs"`	Folder where items in Start Programs menu for this user are stored
`"Recent"`	Folder where shortcuts to recently open documents for this user are stored
`"StartMenu"`	Folder where items in Start menu for this user are stored
`"Startup"`	Folder where items in Start Programs Startup menu for this user are stored

The `.Run` method of the `WshShell` object allows a script to execute any other application or command line. The method takes at least one argument, which specifies the command line to execute, including any command line arguments. For example:

```
Dim oShell
Set oShell = CreateObject("Wscript.Shell")
oShell.Run("notepad")
```

This example starts a copy of Windows Notepad. The `.Run` command accepts any command that can be typed at the Windows command shell prompt.

The `.Run` method accepts two optional arguments. The first argument specifies how any applications started by the `.Run` method should appear on the desktop, as follows:

- A value of 0 starts the application hidden. The user does not see the application on the desktop.
- A value of 1 (the default) starts the application in a normal window.
- A value of 2 starts the application minimized.
- A value of 3 starts the application maximized.
- A value of 10 starts the application in the same state as the script itself. For example, if the script is minimized, the application is also minimized.

The final argument to the `.Run` method determines if the script waits for the command to complete execution. If this argument is `False` (the default), the script continues executing immediately and does not wait for the command to complete. In this case, the `.Run` method always returns 0. If the argument is `True`, the script pauses execution until the command completes, and the return value from the `.Run` method is the exit code from the application. For example:

```
Dim oShell, nError
Set oShell = CreateObject("Wscript.Shell")
nError = oShell.Run("net start spooler", 1, True)
If nError = 0 Then Wscript.Echo "Spooler service started."
```

Registry Access Using the *WshShell* Object

The `WshShell` object provides three methods that provide basic access to the system registry:

- The `.RegDelete` method deletes a registry key or value.
- The `.RegRead` method reads a registry value.
- The `.RegWrite` method writes a registry value.

Note

Modifying the registry, though sometimes necessary, should be done with caution. Inadvertent changes to the registry may result in system instability or the inability to boot the operating system correctly. Always debug and validate scripts that modify the registry on test systems that do not contain live data and can be recovered in the event of catastrophe.

All the methods access the items in the registry by key name or value name. The name must begin with one of the predefined key names:

- HKEY_CURRENT_USER or HKCU to access the per-user information for the current user
- HKEY_LOCAL_MACHINE or HKLM to access the per-machine information
- HKEY_CLASSES_ROOT or HKCR to access the per-machine class information
- HKEY_USERS to access other users and the default user
- HKEY_CURRENT_CONFIG to access configuration data

Following the predefined key name are one or more key names separated by back-slash characters. A name that ends with a back-slash is assumed to specify a key name, otherwise the name is assumed to specify a value name.

Use the `.RegDelete` method to delete a key or value from the registry. Specify the name of the item to delete. For example:

```
Dim oShell
Set oShell = CreateObject("Wscript.Shell")
oShell.RegDelete "HKCU\Software\AcmeCorp\WindowSize"
oShell.RegDelete "HKCU\Software\AcmeCorp\"
```

Here, a registry value and then a key are deleted. The `.RegDelete` method cannot delete a key if it contains any subkeys, although it will delete a key that contains one or more values.

The `.RegRead` method reads a value from the registry. If the name specifies a key, the default value for that key is read, otherwise the specified value is read from the specified key. For example:

```
Wscript.Echo oShell.RegRead _
    "HKLM\CurrentControlSet\Control\ComputerName\ComputerName\ComputerName"
```

The `.RegWrite` method writes a value into the registry. If the name specifies a key, the default value for that key is written. Otherwise, the specified value is written. For example:

```
oShell.RegWrite "HKCU\Software\AcmeCorp\LastRunDate", Date
```

The `.RegWrite` method supports one optional argument that specifies the type of data to write to the registry. If can be one of:

- `"REG_SZ"` or `"REG_EXPAND_SZ"` to write a string value.
- `"REG_DWORD"` to write a 32-bit integer value.
- `"REG_BINARY"` to write a 32-bit binary value.

Application Control Using the *WshShell* Object

The `WshShell` object provides access to two methods that can be used to control Windows applications. These methods are used only with applications that are not COM based. COM applications and objects are manipulated using the object techniques described in Chapter 6.

For older legacy applications, the `WshShell` object provides two methods, `.AppActivate` and `.SendKeys`, that can be used to control the application.

The `.AppActivate` method is used to activate a running application and switch the input "focus" to that application. This method does *not* run an application; it only switches the focus to the application. To run an application, use the `.Run` method.

To activate an application, specify its window title (the text displayed at the top of the window) as a single argument. For example:

```
Dim oShell
Set oShell = CreateObject("Wscript.Shell")
oShell.AppActivate "Calculator"
```

Here, the application, named `Calculator` (the Windows calculator applet), is activated.

The `.AppActivate` method first tries to find a window with title text that exactly matches that supplied as an argument. If no match is found, the method looks for a window whose title *begins* with the text specified. Finally, if there is still no match, the method looks for a window whose title *ends* with the text specified. This allows `.AppActivate` to work with applications that add the document name to the window title text.

The second method provided to control legacy applications, `.SendKeys`, is used to send keystrokes to the application that currently has the focus. Thus, before using `.SendKeys`, the `.AppActivate` method is typically used to ensure that the correct application receives the keystrokes specified.

The `.SendKeys` method sends keystrokes to the application as if they had been typed at the system keyboard. Thus, by sending the correct sequence of keystrokes, the application can be driven by a script as if it were being used interactively.

To use `.SendKeys`, specify a sequence of keystrokes as a string argument. For example:

```
Dim oShell
Set oShell = CreateObject("Wscript.Shell")
oShell.AppActivate "Calculator"
oShell.SendKeys "1000"
```

Here, the calculator program is sent the value 1000.

Certain characters in the string argument to the `.SendKeys` method have special meanings. These are shown in Table 7.2.

Table 7.2 Special Characters in `.SendKeys` String

Characters	Meaning
`{BS}`	Sends Backspace key.
`{BREAK}`	Sends Break key.
`{CAPSLOCK}`	Sends Caps Lock key.
`{DEL}`	Sends Delete key.
`{DOWN}`	Sends down-arrow key.
`{END}`	Sends End key.
`{ENTER}` or `~`	Sends Enter key.
`{ESC}`	Sends Esc key.
`{HELP}`	Sends Help (F1) key.
`{HOME}`	Sends Home key.
`{INS}`	Sends Insert key.
`{LEFT}`	Sends left-arrow key.
`{NUMLOCK}`	Sends Num Lock key.
`{PGDN}`	Sends Page Down key.
`{PGUP}`	Sends Page Up key.
`{RIGHT}`	Sends right-arrow key.
`{SCROLLLOCK}`	Sends Scroll Lock key.
`{TAB}`	Sends Tab key.
`{UP}`	Sends up-arrow key.
`{Fn}`	Sends F*n* key (for example, `{F1}` sends F1, `{F10}` sends F10, and so on).
`{+}`	Sends + key.
`{^}`	Sends ^ key.
`{%}`	Sends % key.
`{~}`	Sends ~ key.
`{(}`	Sends open parenthesis key.

continues ▶

Characters	Meaning
`{)}`	Sends close parenthesis key.
`{{}`	Sends open brace key.
`{}}`	Sends close brace key.
`+key`	Sends *key* with the Shift key down.
`^key`	Sends *key* with the Ctrl key down.
`%key`	Sends *key* with the Alt key down.
`{key count}`	Sends *key* exactly *count* times.

In the `.SendKeys` string, characters with special meanings, such as `"+"` or `"~"`, must be enclosed in braces if they are to be sent literally. Otherwise, as shown in Table 7.2, they are used to modify the way characters are sent. For example, the string `"^S"` sends a single Ctrl+S keystroke to the application, whereas the string `"{^}S"` sends a carat character followed by an upper case S.

The `"+"`, `"^"`, and `"%"` characters can be used in combination. For example, the string `"+^A"` sends the Shift+Ctrl+A keystroke to the application.

To send a sequence of keys with a modifier key (Ctrl etc.) held down, enclose the keys in parentheses. For example, the string `"+(ABC)"` sends the three keys `"A"`, `"B"`, and `"C"` with the Shift key down.

To specify a repeated keystroke, specify the key and repeat count in braces. For example, the string `"{X 10}"` sends 10 `"X"` keys to the application.

Adding Events to the Event Log

The `WshShell` object provides a method, `.LogEvent`, to add an event to the system event log. On Windows NT and Windows 2000, this method adds an event to the application event log. On Windows 9x, this method adds the event to a file named `WSH.log` in the Windows directory.

The `.LogEvent` method takes three arguments. The first argument specifies the event type. Event types are shown in Table 7.3.

Table 7.3 Event Types

Code	Meaning
0	Success event. Indicates that an action was successful.
1	Error event. Indicates an error.
2	Warning event. Indicates a condition that should be corrected but was not fatal.
4	Information event. Provides general information.
8	Audit Success. An auditing event that succeeded.
16	Audit Failure. An auditing event that failed.

The second argument to the `.LogEvent` method specifies an arbitrary text string to be logged. This typically contains an informative message describing the event being logged.

The final argument, which is optional on Windows NT and Windows 2000 and ignored on Windows 9x, specifies the name of the computer where the event is to be logged. The default, if not specified, is to log the event on the local computer.

For example:

```
Dim oShell
Set oShell = CreateObject("Wscript.Shell")
oShell.LogEvent 1, "Script processing failed."
```

The *WshEnvironment* Object

The `WshShell` provides two ways to access the system environment strings. The `.ExpandEnvironmentStrings` method processes a string and replaces any references to environment variables with the values of those variables. Environment variables are enclosed in `"%"` signs as usual for command shell processing. For example:

```
Dim oShell
Set oShell = CreateObject("Wscript.Shell")
Wscript.Echo oShell.ExpandEnvironmentStrings("The temp dir is %TEMP%")
```

The `.Environment` property of the `WshShell` object returns a `WshEnvironment` object that can then access individual environment variables. The object returned can access environment variables in one of four sets by specifying a string argument as follows:

- `"System"` System environment variables that are stored in the HKEY_LOCAL_MACHINE portion of the registry.
- `"User"` User environment variables that are stored in the HKEY_CURRENT_USER portion of the registry.
- `"Volatile"` Volatile environment variables that are constructed on the fly during the system boot and logon process.
- `"Process"` Process environment variables. These include all the system, user, and volatile variables, and it also includes any variables created by the current process or the process that started the current script.

The `"Process"` set is typically used when reading variables. To make a change to a variable persistent, use either the `"System"` or the `"User"` sets.

Once the `WshEnvironment` object has been obtained, variables can be manipulated individually. The `WshEnvironment` is a collection object. For example:

```
Dim oShell, oEnv
Set oShell = CreateObject("Wscript.Shell")
Set oEnv = oShell.Environment("Process")
```

```
For Each sItem In oEnv
    Wscript.Echo sItem
Next
```

To change the value of an environment variable or add a new variable, specify the name of the item to change or add and assign it a value. For example:

```
oEnv("Path") = oEnv("Path") & ";c:\myapp"
```

This example adds an additional path name to the end of the PATH environment variable.

The `.Remove` method deletes an environment variable. For example:

```
oEnv.Remove "TempDir"
```

Note that changes to the process set of environment variables are local to the script process and any processes the script creates using the `WshShell.Run` method. They are *not* visible to other processes in the system.

The *WshShortcut* and *WshUrlShortcut* Objects

The `WshShell` object provides access to two distinct types of shortcuts: the file shortcut and the URL shortcut. Both are stored in small files. File shortcuts provide a link to a file in another location, whereas URL shortcuts provide a link to a Web site or Internet resource.

To create a shortcut, use the `.CreateShortcut` method. Specify the full pathname of the shortcut file to be created. This filename must end with a file type of either `.LNK` for regular file shortcuts or `.URL` for Internet URL shortcuts. For example:

```
Dim oShell, oSC, oURL
Set oShell = CreateObject("Wscript.Shell")
Set oSC = oShell.CreateShortcut("c:\MyDocs.LNK")
Set oURL = oShell.CreateShortcut("c:\MySite.URL")
```

After the shortcut object is created, set the properties of the shortcut and then use the `.Save` method to save the information in the shortcut file. Regular file shortcuts support the following properties:

- `.Arguments` Use this property to set additional arguments that are passed to the target application when the shortcut executes.
- `.Description` Use this property to add descriptive text to the shortcut.
- `.IconLocation` Use this property to specify the location of an icon for the shortcut. Specify a string containing a path name and icon index. If no icon is specified, the icon appropriate for the shortcut target is used.
- `.TargetPath` Use this property to specify the full pathname of the target application or document. Always specify a full path name, including a drive letter or UNC name.

- `.WorkingDirectory` Use this property to specify the directory to be used as the working directory when the shortcut executes. The default is the current working directory.
- `.WindowStyle` Use this property to specify the initial window location when the application starts. See the discussion of the `WshShell.Run` method earlier in this chapter for more information on window styles.

Internet URL shortcuts support the following properties:

- `.TargetPath` Use this property to specify the full URL to the internet location.

For example:

```
Dim oShell, oSC, oURL
Set oShell = CreateObject("Wscript.Shell")
oSC = oShell.CreateShortcut("c:\MyDocs.LNK")
oURL = oShell.CreateShortcut("c:\MySite.URL")
oSC.TargetPath = "e:\Users\Me\MyDocs"
oURL.TargetPath = "http://www.macmillantech.com"
oSC.Save
oURL.Save
```

Summary

The VBScript `Err`, `RegExp`, and `Dictionary` objects provide additional features to assist in the development of scripts. The `RegExp` object is particularly suitable for decoding and validating textual information. Dictionaries are useful when items of information must be stored and indexed by a text key.

The `Wscript` object provides access to various types of script-level information, such as the name of the script currently executing. The object also provides access to the `WshArguments` object, which encapsulates the script command-line arguments.

The `WshNetwork` object provides access to logon account information as well as to file and printer shares. The `WshShell` object provides access to several other internal objects, including objects to manipulate the system environment strings and system shortcuts. It also provides access to the system registry and various special folders.

8

File System Objects

All file and folder access in VBScript and WSH happens via a set of objects collectively referred to as *File System Objects*. The objects described in this chapter are:

- The `FileSystem` object, which is the root object in the file system object hierarchy.
- The `Drive` object and `Drives` collection, which represent logical and physical drives.
- The `Folder` object and `Folders` collection, which represent file system folders.
- The `File` object and `Files` collection, which represent files.
- The `TextStream` object, which provides access to text files and includes the special `StdIn`, `StdOut`, and `StrErr` text streams.

Note

As with all the sample scripts in this book, the scripts in this chapter should be run using the CSCRIPT host unless otherwise noted. The examples shown assume that CSCRIPT is the default WSH host. See Chapter 1, "Introducing WSH," for information on selecting the default WSH host. ◆

The *FileSystem* Object

The `FileSystem` object is the root object for all file-related objects. All other objects described in this chapter are accessed indirectly through this object. The ProgID for the `FileSystem` object is `"Scripting.FileSystemObject"`, and so the following code creates a `FileSystem` object reference:

```
Dim oFSO
Set oFSO = CreateObject("Scripting.FileSystemObject")
```

The other objects described in this chapter are accessed via the methods and properties of the `FileSystem` object. The examples in the rest of this chapter assume that a variable named `oFSO` has been declared and assigned a reference to this object using similar code.

The `FileSystem` object has a large number of methods and properties. These can be broken down into a number of distinct groups:

- Methods to manipulate path names
- Methods to manipulate files and folders
- Methods and properties to access related objects

The methods that access related objects are described in subsequent sections in this chapter. This section describes the methods that manipulate path names, files, and folders.

Constructing Path Names

All Microsoft operating systems support the familiar concept of a file path. A *path* is a text string that describes the location and name of a specific file or folder. A path is comprised of several distinct components, all of which are optional. The components, in order, are a drive name, one or more folder names, and a file name. The folder and file names are further broken down into a *name* part and an *extension* part. The complete syntax of a path name is:

```
[drive:] [\] [folder\ ...] [file ¦ folder]
```

The drive name is always a single letter followed by a colon character. If the drive is not present the *current drive* is assumed. The current drive for a script is the current drive of the process that executed the script, unless the script is started via a shortcut that specifies a working directory.

A path name might also be a *UNC name*, which specifies a network share instead of a drive name. A network share is always specified as follows:

```
\\computer\share
```

The *`computer`* is the name of the networked computer on which the share resides, and the *`share`* is the name of the share. The UNC name replaces the drive specification in the path. Almost all the `FileSystem` methods support UNC names.

Following the drive are zero or more folder names, separated by back-slash characters. If the list of folder names *begins* with a back-slash, the path name is called an *absolute* path name and always starts in the root directory of the specified drive. If the list of folders does *not* begin with a back-slash, the path name is a *relative* path name. In this case, the name is relative to the *current directory*. Like the current drive, the current directory is inherited from the process that started the script or from the working directory of the shortcut that invoked the script.

The final component of the path name is a file or folder name. If the last character of the path name is a back-slash character, the component before this character is assumed to be a folder name, and it is assumed that the entire path refers to a folder name. If the final component is a file or folder name (without a back-slash), the path refers to either a file or folder.

Finally, two special folder names are supported. The folder named `"."` always refers to the current directory at that point in the path, and the folder named `".."` always refers to the *parent* of the current directory at that point in the path.

The `FileSystem` object provides two methods that help construct file names:

- The `.GetAbsolutePathName` method converts a relative path name to an absolute path name. The method takes a path name string as an argument and returns an absolute path name string as a result. The current drive is added to the path name if necessary, and the current directory is also added. Finally, any relative folders names (that is, `"."` or `".."`) are converted to absolute names. This method does *not* validate the path name against files and folders stored on disk. Therefore, it is not guaranteed that the string returned by this method references a valid file, folder, or even drive.
- The `.BuildPath` method takes two arguments. The first is a path name, and the second is an additional path component (file or path name). The method appends the second argument to the first and returns the resulting string. If the first argument does *not* end with a back-slash character, the method places a back-slash between the two arguments in the return result. Otherwise, the return result is simply the two arguments concatenated.

The following simple script illustrates the use of the `.GetAbsolutePathName` and `.BuildPath` methods:

```
Dim oFSO, sArg1, sArg2, sResult
Set oFSO = CreateObject("Scripting.FileSystemObject")
If Wscript.Arguments.Count < 2 Then Wscript.Quit(1)
sArg1 = Wscript.Arguments(0)
sArg2 = Wscript.Arguments(1)
sResult = oFSO.BuildPath(sArg1, sArg2)
Wscript.Echo "Combined path:", sResult
Wscript.Echo "Absolute path:", oFSO.GetAbsolutePathName(sResult)
```

This example combines two command line arguments using the `.BuildPath` method and then converts the result to an absolute path using `.GetAbsolutePathName`. You can use this script to experiment with these methods by passing different combinations of drives, paths, and file names for each argument.

The .GetAbsolutePathName method also provides a way to access the current drive and directory. By definition, the path "." always refers to this directory, and the method converts this relative reference to an absolute one. For example:

```
Dim oFSO
Set oFSO = CreateObject("Scripting.FileSystemObject")
Wscript.Echo "The current directory is: " & oFSO.GetAbsolutePathName(".")
```

The FileSystem object also provides several methods to validate a path name against the file system, as follows:

- The .DriveExists method checks that the drive letter referenced in the path refers to a valid drive (either local or network). If the drive is valid, it returns True, otherwise it returns False.
- The .FileExists method returns True if the specified path refers to a file and the file exists at the location specified by the path.
- The .FolderExists method returns True if the specified path refers to a folder and the folder exists at the location specified by the path.

If both .FileExists and .FolderExists return False, either the path is malformed or the referenced file or folder does not exist. For example:

```
Dim oFSO, sPath
Set oFSO = CreateObject("Scripting.FileSystemObject")
If Wscript.Arguments.Count < 1 Then Wscript.Quit(1)
sPath = Wscript.Arguments(0)
If oFSO.FileExists(sPath) Then
    Wscript.Echo sPath, "is a file"
ElseIf oFSO.FolderExists(sPath) Then
    Wscript.Echo sPath, "is a folder"
Else
    Wscript.Echo sPath, "does not exist"
End If
```

Note

As previously noted, a path name that ends in a back-slash is always assumed to be a reference to a folder, not a file. A path name that ends in a name of a file or folder is ambiguous. It is not possible to determine, for example, if "c:\bin\myinfo" *refers to a folder or file without examining the contents of the* "c:\bin" *folder. The methods described here do not attempt to resolve these ambiguities. Instead, they assume that paths that end in a back-slash reference a folder, and paths that end in a file or folder name reference a file.*

Unfortunately, the .GetAbsolutePathName *method never returns a path name with a trailing back-slash, even if the path refers to a folder. Therefore, the only valid way to determine the type of the path name (file or folder) is to use the* .FileExists *or* .FolderExists *methods.* ◆

Decomposing Path Names

The `FileSystem` object also provides a set of decomposition methods that, given a path name as an argument, decompose the name into individual components. These methods do not attempt to validate the path name (for example, to see if a drive letter is valid or if a path exists); they simply decompose the path name based upon the syntax of the string. Therefore, these methods are best used with an absolute path name obtained with the `.GetAbsolutePathName` method. The methods are shown in Table 8.1.

Table 8.1 `FileSystem` *Object Decomposition Methods*

Method	Description
`.GetFileName`	Returns the file name portion of the path. This is always the *last component* of the path, even if the path ends in a back-slash character and is, in fact, a folder.
`.GetBaseName`	Returns the base name portion of the file name (that is, the name without the file extension). Like `.GetFileName`, this will return the base name of the last component of the path, even if it is a folder.
`.GetExtensionName`	Returns the file extension of the last component in the path if it has one.
`.GetParentFolderName`	Returns the path name of the parent folder. This is the path name passed as an argument with the last component removed.
`.GetDriveName`	Returns the drive name (including the `":"` character) or the UNC share name (in the form `"\\computer\share"`).

For example, the path name `"c:\bin\data\daily.dat"` decomposes as follows:

- The file name is `"daily.dat"`.
- The base name is `"daily"`.
- The extension name is `"dat"` (*without* the period).
- The parent folder name is `"c:\bin\data"`.
- The drive name is `"c:"`.

The previous decomposition will occur *regardless* of whether `"daily.dat"` is a folder name or a file name. The decomposition methods do not distinguish between files and folders; they simply assume that the last component of the name is a file name. This can be seen in the `SplitPath.vbs` script (Listing 8.1).

The `.GetParentFolderName` method can be applied repeatedly to extract each individual component of the path name, starting with the right-most and working back towards the root folder.

The `SplitPath.vbs` script illustrates the use of the various path manipulation methods. The script takes each command line argument, converts it to an absolute path, and then decomposes it into individual components.

Listing 8.1 *The `SplitPath.vbs` Script*

```
'//////////////////////////////////////////////////////////////////////////
' $Workfile: SplitPath.vbs $ $Revision: 1 $ $Date: 6/23/99 11:15a $
' $Archive: /Scripts/SplitPath.vbs $
' Copyright (c) 1999 Tim Hill. All Rights Reserved.
'//////////////////////////////////////////////////////////////////////////

' Decompose each argument as a path name

Option Explicit
Dim sArg, oFSO
Set oFSO = CreateObject("Scripting.FileSystemObject")


' Process each argument
For Each sArg In Wscript.Arguments
    ShowComponents sArg, 0
Next

Set oFSO = Nothing

'//////////////////////////////////////////////////////////////////////////
' ShowComponents
' Display individual components from passed path name
'
' sPath             Path name to decompose
' nLevel            Recursion level for indenting
'
Sub ShowComponents(sPath, nLevel)
    Dim sAbsPath, sIndent
    sIndent = Space(nLevel * 4)

    ' Stop recursion when path is empty
    If sPath = "" Then Exit Sub

    Wscript.Echo sIndent & "Decompose: " & Chr(34) & sPath & Chr(34)
    sAbsPath = oFSO.GetAbsolutePathName(sPath)
    Wscript.Echo sIndent & "    Absolute path: " & sAbsPath
    Wscript.Echo sIndent & "    Valid file   : " & CBool(oFSO.FileExists(sAbsPath))
    Wscript.Echo sIndent & "    Valid path   : " & CBool(oFSO.FolderExists(sAbsPath))
```

```
    Wscript.Echo sIndent & "    File name     : " & oFSO.GetFileName(sAbsPath)
    Wscript.Echo sIndent & "    Base name     : " & oFSO.GetBaseName(sAbsPath)
    Wscript.Echo sIndent & "    Extension     : " & oFSO.GetExtensionName(sAbsPath)
    Wscript.Echo sIndent & "    Drive name    : " & oFSO.GetDriveName(sAbsPath)
    Wscript.Echo

    ' Now recursively decompose the parent folder
    ShowComponents oFSO.GetParentFolderName(sAbsPath), nLevel + 1
End Sub

'//////////////////////////////////////////////////////////////////////////////
```

The `SplitPath.vbs` script simply takes each command line argument and passes it to the `ShowComponents` subroutine for display. Then, this subroutine converts the path to an absolute path name, and then it displays the results of applying this path to each of the decomposition methods of the `FileSystem` object.

The `ShowComponents` subroutine then uses recursion to display the components for the parent folder of the specified path. See Chapter 5, "User-Defined Procedures," for more information on recursion. Recursion is appropriate for manipulating paths because the parent folder of a path is itself a path. Therefore, the `ShowComponents` subroutine calls itself to display the components of the parent folder in the specified path. The `nLevel` value passed to the subroutine is used to indent the output by an additional amount each time a parent folder is decomposed.

File and Folder Operations

The `FileSystem` object supports several methods to manipulate files and folders. Some of the methods duplicate operations that can be accomplished through individual file and folder objects, but using these methods avoids the need to create an object just to invoke a single method.

Two methods are available to copy files and folders: The `.CopyFile` and `.CopyFolder` methods. Both methods take two mandatory arguments and one optional argument. The first argument specifies the source file or folder and the second argument specifies the destination file or folder. The third optional argument (which must be either `True` or `False`) specifies if files or folders with the same name in the destination folder are overwritten (the default is not to allow overwrites). For example:

```
oFSO.CopyFile "c:\db1\mydata.mdb", "a:\", True
```

This example copies the file `"mydata.mdb"` from the folder `"c:\db1"` to the root of drive A. If the file already exists in the root of drive A, the file is overwritten.

For the `.CopyFile` method, the source file can specify wildcards using normal command-shell wildcard syntax. For example, to copy all `.BAT` files in a folder, use:

```
oFSO.CopyFile "c:\scripts\*.bat", "d:\backup\scripts"
```

When copying individual files using the `.CopyFile` method, the destination argument can specify either a folder name or a file name. When copying multiple files (using a wildcard as the first argument), the destination must specify a folder name.

For the `.CopyFolder` method, the source folder can also specify wildcards. For example, to copy all folders that begin with `"backup"` from the `"d:\archive"` folder, use:

```
oFSO.CopyFolder "d:\archive\backup*.*", "\\offsite1\archive\backups\offline"
```

The destination argument for the `.CopyFolder` method must always specify a folder name. Unlike the `.CopyFile` method, which only copies one or more files in a single folder, the `.CopyFolder` method copies entire folders, *including* all the files in the folders and any folders and files in subfolders.

If the destination path specified for the `.CopyFolder` method ends in a `"\"` character, the source is copied into the folder specified by the destination. If the path does *not* end in a `"\"` character and the destination folder does not exist, the destination folder is *created* before the copy operation begins.

The `FileSystem` object also supports two similar methods for moving files and folders: The `.MoveFile` and `.MoveFolder` methods. These are essentially identical in operation to the `.CopyFile` and `.CopyFolder` methods except that they *move* the files and folders rather than *copy* them.

If an error occurs during any of the file copy or move operations, processing will terminate immediately. For example, if an attempt is made to copy over a read-only file, an error will occur and no more files will be copied, even if there are additional files that have not yet been copied.

Finally, the `FileSystem` objects supports two methods to delete files and folders: The `.DeleteFile` and `.DeleteFolder` methods.

The `.DeleteFile` method takes two arguments. The first is the name of the file to delete. Wildcards are allowed, and so multiple files can be deleted in one invocation of the method. The second argument, which is optional, specifies if the files should be deleted even if they are marked with the read-only attribute. If this argument is `True`, the files are deleted regardless of the argument. Otherwise, only read-write files are deleted.

The `.DeleteFolder` method also takes two arguments, which are identical to the arguments of the `.DeleteFile` method except that the first argument specifies a folder name and not a file name. As with the `.DeleteFile` argument, wildcards are allowed for the folder path name.

When the `.DeleteFolder` method deletes a folder, it also deletes all the files in that folder, and also any sub-folders and files in those sub-folders. Therefore, use some care when invoking the `.DeleteFolder` method. For example, the following trivial script deletes *all* the files on drive C, which is not typically desirable:

```
' DO NOT RUN THIS SCRIPT!!!!!!!!!!!
Dim oFSO, sPath
Set oFSO = CreateObject("Scripting.FileSystemObject")
oFS.DeleteFolder "c:\"
```

Note

The prior example is so dangerous that the script text contains a deliberate error to prevent anyone running it by mistake. If you do locate and correct this error, please take great care when using code such as this because it can result in a considerable loss of data. ◆

The *Drive* and *Drives* Objects

The `Drive` object provides access to the properties of a disk drive or UNC share. The `Drives` object is a collection object that enumerates all known drives (network and local).

Use the `Drives` property of the `FileSystem` object to get the `Drives` object. As is usual for collections, the `Drives` collection contains a `.Count` property that returns a count of the drives in the collection, and a default `.Item` property to return an individual drive. The individual items in the `Drives` collection are all `Drive` objects. For example:

```
Dim oFSO, oDrives, oDrive
Set oFSO = CreateObject("Scripting.FileSystemObject")
Set oDrives = oFSO.Drives
For Each oDrive In oDrives
    Wscript.Echo oDrive.Path
Next
```

The `.GetDrive` method of the `FileSystem` object is used to obtain a `Drive` object for a specified path. Specify a path name containing either a drive name or a UNC name. For example:

```
sPath = "c:"
Wscript.Echo "Free space on", sPath, "is", oFSO.GetDrive(sPath).FreeSpace
```

Here, the `.FreeSpace` property (described later) of the `Drive` object is used to obtain the free space on a specified drive. The path name supplied to the `.GetDrive` method can contain other elements (such as a file name), but these are ignored. Also, relative paths are not supported; therefore, always use the `.GetAbsolutePathName` method before passing a path name to the `.GetDrive` method.

The `Drive` object has no methods, and all the object's properties are read-only (they cannot be altered). The properties are listed in Table 8.2.

Table 8.2 `Drive` *Object Properties*

Property	Description
`.AvailableSpace`	Amount of space available, in bytes, on the drive for file storage. In systems that support per-user quotas, this might be less than the total free space on the drive.
`.DriveLetter`	Drive letter of the drive if the drive is a local drive or a mapped network drive. If the `Drive` object corresponds to a UNC name, this property will be an empty string.
`.DriveType`	Type of the drive (for example, fixed or CDROM), expressed as a numeric code. See "`DriveInfo.vbs` Script" for the meanings of each type code.
`.FileSystem`	Type of file system (for example, FAT or NTFS) used on this drive, as a string.
`.FreeSpace`	Total amount of free space, in bytes, on the drive. The actual space available for storage might be less if the system supports per-user quotas.
`.IsReady`	`True` if the drive is ready, or `False` if the drive is not ready. In general, a drive is ready unless it is a removable media drive and no media is currently inserted.
`.Path`	Full path name of the drive. For local and mapped drives, this is the drive letter plus a colon character. For UNC names, this is the UNC name.
`.RootFolder`	Returns a `Folder` object for the root folder on the drive.
`.SerialNumber`	Serial number of the drive. Serial numbers are assigned automatically when a drive is formatted and are displayed (in hexadecimal) as part of a `DIR` shell command.
`.ShareName`	For networked mapped drives and UNC names, this is the UNC share name. For local drives, this property is the empty string.
`.TotalSize`	Total size of the drive, in bytes.
`.VolumeName`	Volume label name of the drive, which is assigned either during formatting or by the `LABEL` shell command.

In systems that do not support per-user disk space quotas, the `.AvailableSpace` and `.FreeSpace` properties return the same value. In systems that support quotas, the `.AvailableSpace` property indicates the lesser of the free space and the space remaining for that user's quota, whereas the `.FreeSpace` property continues to show the true free space on the drive.

The `DriveInfo.vbs` script, shown in Listing 8.2, takes a drive name or UNC name from the command line and displays all the properties for the corresponding `Drive` object. It also decodes the individual drive type values returned by the `.DriveType` property. This script makes use of the `With` statement to simplify access to the many properties of the `Drive` object.

Listing 8.2 *`DriveInfo.vbs` Script*

```
'//////////////////////////////////////////////////////////////////////////////
' $Workfile: DriveInfo.vbs $ $Revision: 2 $ $Date: 7/04/99 12:33p $
' $Archive: /Scripts/DriveInfo.vbs $
' Copyright (c) 1999 Tim Hill. All Rights Reserved.
'//////////////////////////////////////////////////////////////////////////////

' Display info for specified drive

Option Explicit
Dim sArg, oFSO, sDriveName, sType
Set oFSO = CreateObject("Scripting.FileSystemObject")

' Get absolute path name from command line, then get drive name
If Wscript.Arguments.Count < 1 Then Wscript.Quit(1)
sArg = oFSO.GetAbsolutePathName(Wscript.Arguments(0))
sDriveName = oFSO.GetDriveName(sArg)

' Get drive object and display properties
With oFSO.GetDrive(sDriveName)
    Wscript.Echo "Total size of drive (KB):", .TotalSize / 1024
    Wscript.Echo "Available space (KB)    :", .AvailableSpace / 1024
    Wscript.Echo "Free space (KB)         :", .FreeSpace / 1024
    Wscript.Echo "Drive letter            :", .DriveLetter
    Wscript.Echo "UNC share name          :", .ShareName
    Wscript.Echo "Volume name             :", .VolumeName
    Wscript.Echo "Path                    :", .Path
    Wscript.Echo "Serial number           :", Hex(.SerialNumber)
    Wscript.Echo "File system             :", .FileSystem
    Wscript.Echo "Drive ready             :", CBool(.IsReady)
    Select Case .DriveType
        Case 1: sType = "Removable"
        Case 2: sType = "Fixed"
        Case 3: sType = "Network"
        Case 4: sType = "CDROM"
        Case 5: sType = "RAM Disk"
        Case Else sType = "Unknown"
```

continues ▶

Listing 8.2 *continued*

```
    End Select
    Wscript.Echo "Drive type                :", sType
End With
Set oFSO = Nothing

'//////////////////////////////////////////////////////////////////////////
```

The *Folder* and *Folders* Objects

The `Folder` object and `Folders` collection provide access to folders on a drive. There are several different ways to obtain `Folder` objects and `Folders` collections:

- The `.RootFolder` property of the `Drive` object returns a `Folder` object for the root folder on a drive.
- The `.GetFolder` method of the `FileSystem` object returns a `Folder` object for the specified folder path.
- The `.CreateFolder` method of the `FileSystem` object creates a new folder and returns a `Folder` object for that folder.
- The `.ParentFolder` property of the `File` and `Folder` objects returns a `Folder` object for the parent folder of the file or folder. (The parent folder is the folder that contains that file or folder.)
- The `.SubFolders` property of the `Folder` object returns a `Folders` collection that contains all the folders that are subfolders of the folder.
- The `.Add` method of the `Folders` collection returns a `Folder` object for a newly created subfolder.

As is usual for collections, the `Folders` collection contains a `.Count` property that returns a count of the folders in the collection. However, individual folder objects are only accessible using the `For Each` iterator statement—accessing individual folders using the `.Item` property of the collection is not supported. The individual items in the `Folders` collection are all `Folder` objects. In addition, the `Folders` collection has one method, `.Add`, which creates a new folder in the collection. This method takes one argument, the name of the folder to create. Another way to create folders uses the `.CreateFolder` method of the `FileSystem` object. For example:

```
Dim oFSO, oFolder
Set oFSO = CreateObject("Scripting.FileSystemObject")
Set oFolder = oFSO.CreateFolder("c:\xbin")
```

To process all the folders on a drive, use the `.RootFolder` method of the `Drive` object or the `.GetFolder` object of the `FileSystem` object to obtain a root `Folder` object, and then move down the folder tree using the `.SubFolders` property of each `Folder` object using a recursive procedure. For example:

```
Dim oFSO
Set oFSO = CreateObject("Scripting.FileSystemObject")
ShowTree oFSO.GetFolder("c:\")

Sub ShowTree(oFolder)
    Dim oSubFolder
    Wscript.Echo oFolder.Path
    For Each oSubFolder In oFolder.SubFolders
        ShowTree oSubFolder
    Next
End Sub
```

This example lists the full paths of all the folders on drive C.

Folder Object Properties

Table 8.3 lists the properties of the `Folder` object. All the properties are read-only except where noted.

Table 8.3 `Folder` *Object Properties*

Property	Description
`.Attributes`	Contains the folder attributes, packed one attribute per bit. Use the `And` operator and an appropriate mask constant to access individual attributes. See the `FolderInfo.vbs` script for individual attributes. This property is read-write: attributes can be read and written.
`.DateCreated`	Date the folder was created. Not all file systems support creation dates for folders; for those that do not, the system returns a fixed value for the creation date. This property is not valid for root folders.
`.DateLastAccessed`	Date the folder was last accessed. Not all file systems support last accessed dates for folders; for those that do not, the system returns a fixed value for the last accessed date. This property is not valid for root folders.
`.DateLastModified`	Date the folder was last modified. This property is not valid for root folders.
`.Drive`	Name of the drive on which the folder resides; this can be either a local drive, or a UNC share name.
`.Files`	Returns a collection that contains a file object for each file contained in the folder.

continues ▶

Property	Description
.IsRootFolder	True if the folder is the root folder on a drive or UNC share name.
.Name	Name of the folder. This property is read-write: changing the .Name property renames the folder.
.ParentFolder	Returns a Folder object for the folder that contains this folder. This property is not valid for root folders.
.Path	Full path name of the folder.
.ShortName	MS-DOS style name of the folder (limited to 8+3 upper case characters).
.ShortPath	MS-DOS style path for the folder (limited to 8+3 upper case characters for each element of the path).
.Size	Total size, in bytes, of all files contained in the folder including files in all subfolders of this folder. This can take some time to compute on folders with many files and subfolders.
.SubFolders	Returns a Folders collection that contains all the folders that are contained directly in this folder.
.Type	Type of the folder, which is a string that describes the folder type. For normal folders, this is always "File Folder".

The FolderInfo.vbs script, shown in Listing 8.3, takes a folder name from the command line and displays all the properties for the corresponding Folder object. It also decodes the folder attributes returned by the .Attributes property.

Listing 8.3 *FolderInfo.vbs Script*

```
'//////////////////////////////////////////////////////////////////////////
' $Workfile: FolderInfo.vbs $ $Revision: 1 $ $Date: 7/03/99 7:27p $
' $Archive: /Scripts/FolderInfo.vbs $
' Copyright (c) 1999 Tim Hill. All Rights Reserved.
'//////////////////////////////////////////////////////////////////////////

' Display info for specified folder

Option Explicit
Dim sArg, oFSO, oFolder, sAttr, nAttr
Set oFSO = CreateObject("Scripting.FileSystemObject")

' Get absolute path name from command line, then get drive name
If Wscript.Arguments.Count < 1 Then Wscript.Quit(1)
```

```
sArg = oFSO.GetAbsolutePathName(Wscript.Arguments(0))

' Get folder object and display properties
Set oFolder = oFSO.GetFolder(sArg)

Wscript.Echo "Drive containing folder :", oFolder.Drive
Wscript.Echo "Root folder?            :", oFolder.IsRootFolder
Wscript.Echo "Folder name             :", oFolder.Name
Wscript.Echo "Path                    :", oFolder.Path
Wscript.Echo "Short (MSDOS) name      :", oFolder.ShortName
Wscript.Echo "Short (MSDOS) path      :", oFolder.ShortPath
Wscript.Echo "Size (files+subfolders) :", oFolder.Size
Wscript.Echo "Folder type             :", oFolder.Type
If Not oFolder.IsRootFolder Then
    Wscript.Echo "Date created            :", oFolder.DateCreated
    Wscript.Echo "Date last accessed      :", oFolder.DateLastAccessed
    Wscript.Echo "Date last modified      :", oFolder.DateLastModified
    Wscript.Echo "Parent folder name      :", oFolder.ParentFolder.Name
End If
nAttr = oFolder.Attributes
Wscript.Echo "Attributes              :", Hex(nAttr)
sAttr = ""
If nAttr And 1 Then sAttr = sAttr & "Read-Only "
If nAttr And 2 Then sAttr = sAttr & "Hidden "
If nAttr And 4 Then sAttr = sAttr & "System "
If nAttr And 8 Then sAttr = sAttr & "Volume "
If nAttr And 16 Then sAttr = sAttr & "Folder "
If nAttr And 32 Then sAttr = sAttr & "Archive "
If nAttr And 64 Then sAttr = sAttr & "Alias "
If nAttr And 128 Then sAttr = sAttr & "Compressed "
Wscript.Echo "    " & sAttr

Set oFolder = Nothing
Set oFSO = Nothing

'//////////////////////////////////////////////////////////////////////////////
```

Folder Object Methods

The `Folder` object supports the following methods:

- `.Copy` This method is similar to the `.CopyFolder` method of the `FileSystem` object, but it uses the `Folder` object as the implicit source folder for the copy operation. Specify a destination folder name and an optional overwrite flag (either `True` or `False`).
- `.Move` This method is similar to the `.MoveFolder` method of the `FileSystem` object, but it uses the `Folder` object as the implicit source folder for the move operation. Specify a destination folder name and an optional overwrite flag (either `True` or `False`).

- `.Delete` This method is similar to the `.DeleteFolder` method of the `FileSystem` object, but it uses the `Folder` object as the implicit folder to delete. The method takes one optional argument that, if `True`, specifies that the folder is deleted even if it is marked as read-only.

As with the `.DeleteFolder` method of the `FileSystem` object, the `.Delete` method of the `Folder` object deletes the specified folder, all files in the folder, and all sub-folders and files. Thus, this method can delete the entire contents of a drive if invoked on the root folder of the drive.

The choice between the `FileSystem` and `Folder` versions of the `.Copy`, `.Move`, and `.Delete` methods is primarily convenience. If a `Folder` object exists, the `Folder` versions can be used. However, if the path name is known, it is simpler to use the `FileSystem` object and bypass the need to create a `Folder` object. For example:

```
Dim oFSO, oFolder
Set oFSO = CreateObject("Scripting.FileSystemObject")
oFSO.CopyFolder "c:\bin", "d:\bin"
Set oFolder = oFSO.GetFolder("c:\bin")
oFolder.Copy "d:\bin"
Set oFolder = Nothing
```

Here, the `.CopyFolder` method and the `.Copy` method both perform the same operation, but the `.CopyFolder` method does so without the need to create an intermediate `Folder` object.

The *VBTree.vbs* Script

Listing 8.4 shows the `VBTree.vbs` script, which provides a simple graphical representation of a folder tree. The script requires one argument, which specifies a folder to use as the root of the tree. The output of the script is similar to the output from the built-in `TREE` shell command.

Listing 8.4 *`VBTree.vbs` Script*

```
'////////////////////////////////////////////////////////////////////////////
' $Workfile: VBTree.vbs $ $Revision: 1 $ $Date: 7/03/99 6:49p $
' $Archive: /Scripts/VBTree.vbs $
' Copyright (c) 1999 Tim Hill. All Rights Reserved.
'////////////////////////////////////////////////////////////////////////////

' Show simple directory tree

Option Explicit
Dim sArg, oFSO
Set oFSO = CreateObject("Scripting.FileSystemObject")

' Get folder (default is current directory)
```

```
If Wscript.Arguments.Count > 0 Then
    sArg = Wscript.Arguments(0)
Else
    sArg = "."
End If
sArg = oFSO.GetAbsolutePathName(sArg)

' Process entire tree (if valid folder)
If oFSO.FolderExists(sArg) Then
    Wscript.Echo "Folder tree for:", sArg
    ShowTree "", oFSO.GetFolder(sArg)
End If

Set oFSO = Nothing
Wscript.Quit(0)

'//////////////////////////////////////////////////////////////////////////////
' ShowTree
' Show one level of folder tree
'
' sIndent           Indent string
' oFolder           Folder object for this level in tree
'
Sub ShowTree(sIndent, oFolder)
    Dim oSubFolder, ix
    ix = 1
    For Each oSubFolder In oFolder.SubFolders
        Wscript.Echo sIndent & "+-" & oSubFolder.Name
        If ix <> oFolder.SubFolders.Count Then
            ShowTree sIndent & "¦  ", oSubFolder
        Else
            ShowTree sIndent & "   ", oSubFolder
        End If
        ix = ix + 1
    Next
End Sub

'//////////////////////////////////////////////////////////////////////////////
```

The `VBTree.vbs` script uses a recursive procedure, `ShowTree`, to process each folder in the tree. Processing folder trees is a natural use of recursion because the folder structure on disk is recursive—each folder can contain a number of folders, which in turn, can contain additional folders.

The `ShowTree` procedure iterates each subfolder in the `Folder` object passed as an argument, and then it displays the name of each folder. The procedure is then called recursively to process all the subfolders of that folder. To produce an attractive layout for the tree, each level of subfolders is indented from the previous level. This is achieved by passing an indentation string as an argument to the `ShowTree` procedure, and then prefixing this string to the display of each folder's name. Each time the `ShowTree` argument is recursively invoked, the indent string is enlarged by adding an additional level of indenting text.

The *File* and *Files* Objects

The `File` object and the `Files` collection are similar to the `Folder` object and the `Folders` collection, except that they provide access to files instead of folders. `File` objects do not provide access to the *contents* of files, only to attributes of files. To access the contents of files, use text streams, which are described in "Text Stream Objects" later in this chapter.

There are two different ways to obtain `File` objects and `Files` collections:

- The `.GetFile` method of the `FileSystem` object returns a `File` object for the specified file path.
- The `.Files` property of the `Folder` object returns a `Files` collection that contains all the files within the folder.

As is usual for collections, the `Files` collection contains a `.Count` property that returns a count of the files in the collection. However, individual file objects are only accessible using the `For Each` iterator statement—accessing individual files using the `.Item` property of the collection is not supported. The individual items in the `Files` collection are all `File` objects.

To process all files in a folder, use the `.Files` property of the folder to obtain a `Files` collection and then iterate through the files using a `For Each` statement. This can be combined with the recursive folder processing described in "The Folder and Folders Objects" to process all files in a tree. For example:

```
Dim oFSO
Set oFSO = CreateObject("Scripting.FileSystemObject")
ShowAllFiles oFSO.GetFolder("c:\")

Sub ShowAllFiles(oFolder)
    Dim oSubFolder, oFile
    For Each oFile In oFolder.Files
        Wscript.Echo oFile.Path
    Next
    For Each oSubFolder In oFolder.SubFolders
        ShowAllFiles oSubFolder
    Next
End Sub
```

This example lists the full paths of all the files on drive C.

File Object Properties

Table 8.4 lists the properties of the `File` object. All the properties are read-only except where noted.

Table 8.4 `File` *Object Properties*

Property	Description
`.Attributes`	Contains the file attributes, packed one attribute per bit. Use the `And` operator and an appropriate mask constant to access individual attributes. See the `FileInfo.vbs` script for individual attributes. This property is read-write: attributes can be read and written.
`.DateCreated`	Date the file was created. Not all file systems support creation dates for files; for those that do not, the system returns a fixed value for the creation date.
`.DateLastAccessed`	Date the file was last accessed. Not all file systems support last accessed dates for files; for those that do not, the system returns a fixed value for the last accessed date.
`.DateLastModified`	Date the file was last modified.
`.Drive`	Name of the drive on which the file resides, which can be a local drive or a UNC share name.
`.Name`	Name of the file. This property is read-write: changing the `.Name` property renames the file.
`.ParentFolder`	Returns a `Folder` object for the folder that contains this file.
`.Path`	Full path name of the file.
`.ShortName`	MS-DOS style name of the file (limited to 8+3 upper case characters).
`.ShortPath`	MS-DOS style path for the file (limited to 8+3 upper case characters for each element of the path).
`.Size`	Size, in bytes, of the file.
`.Type`	Type of the file, which is a string that describes the file type. The type is obtained by looking up the file extension in the HKEY_CLASSES_ROOT in the system registry. Windows Explorer displays this same text when it lists files in Details view.

The `FileInfo.vbs` script, shown in Listing 8.5, takes a file name from the command line and displays all the properties for the corresponding `File` object. It also decodes the file attributes returned by the `.Attributes` property.

Listing 8.5 *FileInfo.vbs Script*

```
'//////////////////////////////////////////////////////////////////////////
' $Workfile: FileInfo.vbs $ $Revision: 1 $ $Date: 7/04/99 1:16p $
' $Archive: /Scripts/FileInfo.vbs $
' Copyright (c) 1999 Tim Hill. All Rights Reserved.
'//////////////////////////////////////////////////////////////////////////

' Display info for specified file

Option Explicit
Dim sArg, oFSO, oFile, sAttr, nAttr
Set oFSO = CreateObject("Scripting.FileSystemObject")

' Get absolute path name from command line, then get drive name
If Wscript.Arguments.Count < 1 Then Wscript.Quit(1)
sArg = oFSO.GetAbsolutePathName(Wscript.Arguments(0))

' Get file object and display properties
Set oFile = oFSO.GetFile(sArg)

Wscript.Echo "Drive containing file   :", oFile.Drive
Wscript.Echo "File name               :", oFile.Name
Wscript.Echo "Path                    :", oFile.Path
Wscript.Echo "Short (MSDOS) name      :", oFile.ShortName
Wscript.Echo "Short (MSDOS) path      :", oFile.ShortPath
Wscript.Echo "Size                    :", oFile.Size
Wscript.Echo "File type               :", oFile.Type
Wscript.Echo "Date created            :", oFile.DateCreated
Wscript.Echo "Date last accessed      :", oFile.DateLastAccessed
Wscript.Echo "Date last modified      :", oFile.DateLastModified
Wscript.Echo "Parent folder name      :", oFile.ParentFolder.Name
nAttr = oFile.Attributes
Wscript.Echo "Attributes              :", Hex(nAttr)
sAttr = ""
If nAttr And 1 Then sAttr = sAttr & "Read-Only "
If nAttr And 2 Then sAttr = sAttr & "Hidden "
If nAttr And 4 Then sAttr = sAttr & "System "
If nAttr And 8 Then sAttr = sAttr & "Volume "
If nAttr And 16 Then sAttr = sAttr & "Folder "
If nAttr And 32 Then sAttr = sAttr & "Archive "
If nAttr And 64 Then sAttr = sAttr & "Alias "
If nAttr And 128 Then sAttr = sAttr & "Compressed "
Wscript.Echo "    " & sAttr

Set oFile = Nothing
Set oFSO = Nothing

'//////////////////////////////////////////////////////////////////////////
```

File Object Methods

The `File` object supports the following methods:

- `.Copy` This method is similar to the `.CopyFile` method of the `FileSystem` object, but it uses the `File` object as the implicit source file for the copy operation. Specify a destination file name or folder name and an optional overwrite flag (either `True` or `False`). Unlike the `FileSystem` object method, this method can only copy a single file.
- `.Move` This method is similar to the `.MoveFile` method of the `FileSystem` object, but it uses the `File` object as the implicit source file for the move operation. Specify a destination folder name and an optional overwrite flag (either `True` or `False`). Unlike the `FileSystem` object method, this method can only move a single file.
- `.Delete` This method is similar to the `.DeleteFile` method of the `FileSystem` object, but it uses the `File` object as the implicit file to delete. The method takes one optional argument that, if `True`, specifies that the file is deleted even if it is marked as read-only.

TextStream Objects

The `FileSystem` object provides an object that allows a text file to be opened, read from or written to, and then closed. The object that provides access to the contents of a text file is called a `TextStream` object. `TextStream` objects do not provide access to binary files.

There are several different ways to create `TextStream` objects:

- The `.CreateTextFile` method of the `FileSystem` object creates a new text file and returns a `TextStream` object.
- The `.OpenTextFile` method of the `FileSystem` object opens an existing text file and returns a `TextStream` object.
- The `.CreateTextFile` method of the `Folder` object creates a new text file and returns a `TextStream` object.
- The `.OpenAsTextStream` method of the `File` object opens the file as a text file and returns a `TextStream` object.
- The `.StdIn`, `.StdOut`, and `.StdErr` properties of the `Wscript` object return predefined `TextStream` objects.

The `.CreateTextFile` methods of the `FileSystem` and `Folder` objects both create a new text file and open it for writing as a `TextStream` object. Both methods take up to three arguments. The first is the name of the file to create. For the `FileSystem` object, this is a full path name. For the `Folder` object, this is the name relative to that folder. The second argument is optional. If `True`, this argument specifies that any existing file can be over-written. The final argument is also optional. If `True`, the text file is created as a Unicode file. Otherwise the file is created as an ASCII file. For example:

```
Dim oFSO, oStream
Set oFSO = CreateObject("Scripting.FileSystemObject")
Set oStream = oFSO.CreateTextFile("c:\data.log", True)
```

This example creates a new file called `"c:\data.log"`, over-writing any existing file if necessary and opens it as a text stream.

The `.OpenTextFile` method of the `FileSystem` object takes up to four arguments; all but the first are optional. The first argument specifies the path of the file to open. The optional second argument specifies how the file is to be opened. It can take one of three values as follows:

- To open the file for reading, specify a value of 1. Write operations are not allowed. This is the default if the argument is not present.
- To open the file for writing, specify a value of 2. The existing contents of the file are lost and replaced by the new data written. Read operations are not allowed.
- To open the file for appending, specify a value of 8. The existing contents of the file are preserved, and new data is appended to the end of the file. Read operations are not allowed.

The optional third argument, if `True`, specifies that the file can be created if it does not already exist. The final optional argument specifies the character data format. It can be one of three values:

- 0 to read/write data as ASCII
- –1 to read/write data as Unicode
- –2 to read/write data in the system default (either ASCII or Unicode, depending upon the underlying operating system)

For example:

```
Dim oFSO, oStream
Set oFSO = CreateObject("Scripting.FileSystemObject")
Set oStream = oFSO.OpenTextFile("c:\data.log", 1)
```

This example opens the `"c:\data.log"` file for reading and specifies (by default) that the file must already exist.

The `.OpenAsTextStream` method of the `File` object opens the file as a text stream. The method takes up to two optional arguments. The first argument specifies how the file is to be opened, and it uses the same three values (1, 2, or 8) as are used for the `.OpenTextFile` method of the `FileSystem` object. The second argument specified the character data format, and it also uses the same values as the `.OpenTextFile` format. For example:

```
Dim oFSO, oStream, oFile
Set oFSO = CreateObject("Scripting.FileSystemObject")
Set oFile = oFSO.GetFile("c:\data.log")
Set oStream = oFile.OpenAsTextStream(2, -1)
```

This example opens the file ready for writing as a Unicode file.

After all file read and write operations are complete, the `.Close` method can be used to close the text stream object and flush all data to disk. This method is optional because text stream objects are automatically closed when the last object reference to them goes out of scope.

TextStream Object Properties

Table 8.5 lists the properties of the `TextStream` object. All the properties are read-only.

Table 8.5 `TextStream` *Object Properties*

Property	Description
`.AtEndOfLine`	`True` if the current location in the text stream is at the end of a line.
`.AtEndOfStream`	`True` if the current location in the text stream is at the end of the file.
`.Column`	The column number of the current location in the text stream. The first column is numbered 1.
`.Line`	The line number of the current location in the text stream. The first line is numbered 1.

All the `TextStream` properties reference an internal "current location." This hidden information tracks where, in the text stream, the next read or write operation occurs. When a text stream is opened for reading or writing, the current location is set at the start of the file. When a text stream is opened for appending, the current location is set at the end of the file. Subsequent read or write operations advance the current location through the file contents. The `.Column` and `.Line` properties retrieve the current location.

The `.AtEndOfStream` property is `True` if the current location is at the end of the text stream. This property is typically used to terminate processing of a text stream when the stream is being read.

The `.AtEndOfLine` property is `True` if the current location is at the end of a line. This property can be used to determine the location of line boundaries when the text stream is being read as a sequence of characters.

TextStream Object Methods

The `.ReadAll` method reads an entire text stream into a string variable. The text stream must have been opened for reading. The entire file contents, including line termination characters, are loaded into the string variable. For example:

```
Dim oFSO, oStream, sText
Set oFSO = CreateObject("Scripting.FileSystemObject")
Set oStream = oFSO.OpenTextFile(Wscript.Arguments(0), 1)
sText = oStream.ReadAll
Wscript.Echo sText
```

This example loads the text file specified by the first command line argument into the variable `sText`, and then displays the contents of the variable. The `.ReadAll` method is suited for processing smaller text files.

The `.ReadLine` method reads a single line from a text stream into a string variable. The line termination character at the end of the line is *not* included in the string variable. The text stream must have been opened for reading. The `.ReadLine` method is typically used to process text files on a line-by-line basis. The `.WriteLine` method writes a string variable to a text stream and appends a line termination character. The stream must have been opened for writing. The `.SkipLine` method reads a line from a text stream and then discards it. It is similar to the `.ReadLine` method, but instead it discards the line—no data is returned by the method. The `.WriteBlankLines` method writes one or more empty lines (that is, lines that consist only of a line termination character). Specify the number of blank lines to write as the only argument.

The `.ReadLine` and `.WriteLine` methods can be used to copy text data from one stream to another. For example:

```
Sub CopyStream(oInStream, oOutStream)
    Dim sLine
    Do Until oInStream.AtEndOfStream
        sLine = oInStream.ReadLine
        oOutStream.WriteLine sLine
    Loop
End Sub
```

This procedure copies the contents of the `oInStream` stream to the `oOutStream` stream.

The `.Read` method reads one or more characters from a text stream into a string variable. Specify the number of characters to read as the only argument. The method might return fewer than the specified number if the end of the stream is reached; therefore, always check the length of the string after invoking this method.

The `.Write` method writes a string to a text stream. Unlike the `.WriteLine` method, a line termination character is *not* appended to the write operation. The `.Skip` method skips ahead the specified number of characters in a stream. It is similar to the `.Read` method, but it does not return a text string.

The `ShowINFSection.vbs` script shown in Listing 8.6 uses a `TextStream` object and a `RegExp` object to extract a named section from an `.INF` file. `.INF` files are common in the Windows operating system. They are small text files that provide information for applications, such as Setup programs. The files are divided into sections by section headers that consist of a line containing only the section name enclosed in brackets.

The script takes two arguments. The first argument is the name of the section to display (without the brackets), and the second is the name of the `.INF` file to search. The script then displays the contents of the specified section if it is found.

Listing 8.6 *`ShowINFSection.vbs` Script*

```
'//////////////////////////////////////////////////////////////////////////
' $Workfile: ShowINFSection.vbs $ $Revision: 1 $ $Date: 7/04/99 3:13p $
' $Archive: /Scripts/ShowINFSection.vbs $
' Copyright (c) 1999 Tim Hill. All Rights Reserved.
'//////////////////////////////////////////////////////////////////////////

' Uses regular expressions to extract an INF section from an INF file

Option Explicit
Dim sArg, oFSO
Set oFSO = CreateObject("Scripting.FileSystemObject")

' If no arguments, show short usage
If Wscript.Arguments.Count < 2 Then
    Wscript.Echo "usage: showinfsection section-name INF-file"
    Wscript.Quit(0)
End If

' Prepare the regular expression objects
Dim oREStart, oREEnd
Set oREStart = new RegExp
Set oREEnd = new RegExp
oREStart.Pattern = "^\s*\[\s*" & Wscript.Arguments(0) & "\s*\]\s*$"
oREStart.IgnoreCase = True
oREEnd.Pattern = "^\s*\[.*\]\s*$"

' Prepare the input stream
Dim oStream, nState, sLine
Set oStream = oFSO.OpenTextFile(Wscript.Arguments(1))
```

continues ▶

Listing 8.6 *continued*

```
nState = 0
Do Until oStream.AtEndOfStream
    sLine = oStream.ReadLine
    Select Case nState
        Case 0:     ' State 0: Before section
            If oREStart.Test(sLine) Then nState = 1
        Case 1:     ' State 1: In section
            If oREEnd.Test(sLine) Then
                nState = 2
            Else
                Wscript.Echo sLine
            End If
        Case 2:     ' State 2: After section
    End Select
Loop
Set oStream = Nothing
Set oREStart = Nothing
Set oREEnd = Nothing

'//////////////////////////////////////////////////////////////////////////////
```

To function, the `ShowINFSection.vbs` script needs to break the `.INF` file into three divisions:

- All lines that occur *before* the target section
- All lines that occur *within* the target section
- All lines that occur *after* the target section

To accomplish this, the script uses a software construct known as a *state machine*. The state machine operates on each individual line of the `.INF` file. At any given line, the state machine records, in a variable, which division is currently being processed. The script then takes different actions depending upon the current state. State 0 represents the division before the specified section. In this state, the script simply searches for a section header that matches the required section. State 1 represents the division within the target section. In this state, the script displays the line of the section and checks to see if the beginning of the next section has been reached. State 2 represents the division after the specified section. In this state, the script does nothing.

To switch states, the script checks the current line to see if it matches the specified section header (in state 0) or to see if it matches any other section header (in state 1). These checks are performed by two regular expression objects. Matches against these objects indicate that the appropriate division boundary has been reached and the state is changed appropriately.

Note

State machines are frequently used in situations such as these. Another example of a state machine was given in Chapter 4, "Built-In Functions," in the `ParseArgs1.vbs` *script. The basic idea of a state machine always takes the same form. A program or script performs an operation on a data set (for example, lines of text in a file) one item at a time, usually in a loop. As the data is processed, the processing operation for the data item is controlled by a variable or variables that control the current state of the loop.* ♦

Predefined TextStream Objects

The `Wscript` object (described primarily in Chapter 7, "Built-In WSH and VBScript Objects") provides access to three predefined `TextStream` objects. These objects are *only* available when the CSCRIPT host is being used. They are not applicable to the WSCRIPT host. Refer to Chapter 2, "VBScript Language Essentials," for more information on the CSCRIPT and WSCRIPT hosts.

The three predefined text streams made available by the `Wscript` object correspond to the three standard text streams used with the Windows NT and Windows 2000 command shells. They are:

- *The* `StdIn` *stream* This read-only stream can be used to access the redirected input from the shell command line.
- *The* `StdOut` *stream* This write-only stream can be used to access the redirected output from the shell command line.
- *The* `StdErr` *stream* This write-only stream can be used to access the redirected error output from the shell command line.

By default, the `StdIn` stream corresponds to the console keyboard input; therefore, reading from this stream reads lines or characters from the console. The `StdOut` and `StdErr` streams correspond to the console window for the shell session, and so writing to these streams writes lines or characters to the console window.

The predefined streams are useful when writing text processing or filtering scripts. That is because the Windows NT and Windows 2000 command shells allow the streams to be *redirected* from the command line. Depending upon the command line syntax, the predefined streams can be redirected to or from a text file, or to or from another program (via a command shell pipe).

This simple script (from Chapter 1) always displays the `"Hello, world!"` text on the console:

```
Wscript.Echo "Hello, world!"
```

However, the following script displays the text, sends the text to a file, or sends the text to a command shell pipe, depending upon the command that invoked the script:

```
Wscript.StdOut.WriteLine "Hello, world!"
```

Assuming this one line script is placed in the file `Simple.vbs`, the following command writes the text to the console window:

```
C:\>simple
```

This command writes the text to the file `"hello.txt"`:

```
C:\>cscript simple >hello.txt
```

Finally, this command writes the text to the `MORE` filter via a command shell pipe:

```
C:\>cscript simple | more
```

Note

There is a bug in Windows NT that causes command redirection to fail with an error unless the WSH host is explicitly specified on the command line (regardless of default host selected). Therefore, always explicitly specify the CSCRIPT host when using i/o redirection or pipes with scripts. ◆

The `Tee.vbs` script, shown in Listing 8.7, shows one simple use of the predefined text streams. The operation of the script is simple: it reads the `StdIn` stream until it reaches the end of the stream. It then writes each line read to two places: the `StdOut` stream and another stream that corresponds to a text file named as the only command line argument.

Listing 8.7 `Tee.vbs` *Script*

```
'//////////////////////////////////////////////////////////////////////////
' $Workfile: SplitPath.vbs $ $Revision: 1 $ $Date: 6/23/99 11:15a $
' $Archive: /Scripts/SplitPath.vbs $
' Copyright (c) 1999 Tim Hill. All Rights Reserved.
'//////////////////////////////////////////////////////////////////////////

' "Tee" output to a file (as in a T-junction in plumbing)

Option Explicit
Dim sArg, oFSO, oStream, oStdIn, oStdOut, sLine
Set oFSO = CreateObject("Scripting.FileSystemObject")

' Setup oStream text stream from command line arg
If Wscript.Arguments.Count > 0 Then
    Set oStream = oFSO.CreateTextFile(Wscript.Arguments(0), True)
Else
    Set oStream = Nothing
End If
```

```
' Now copy StdIn to StdOut and oStream
Set oStdIn = Wscript.StdIn
Set oStdOut = Wscript.StdOut
Do Until oStdIn.AtEndOfStream
    sLine = oStdIn.ReadLine
    oStdOut.WriteLine sLine
    If Not oStream Is Nothing Then oStream.WriteLine sLine
Loop
Set oStdOut = Nothing
Set oStdIn = Nothing
Set oStream = Nothing
Wscript.Quit(0)

'//////////////////////////////////////////////////////////////////////////
```

The purpose of the `Tee.vbs` script (as the name obliquely suggests) is to branch a text stream into two flows. This is useful when processing command shell pipes. For example, the following command-shell command sorts the current directory and displays the result:

```
C:\>dir ¦ sort
```

The following command uses the `Tee.vbs` script to split the output of the `DIR` command and capture it to the file `dir.txt`, as well as displaying the result of the sort operation:

```
C:\>dir ¦ cscript tee dir.txt ¦ sort
```

The *VBGrep.vbs* Script

The `VBGrep.vbs` script, shown in Listing 8.8, provides a simple "grep" facility. Grep-like tools (the name comes from a Unix editor command) are used to filter text files for lines that match a regular expression pattern. Only the lines that match the pattern are passed through the filter to the output.

The `VBGrep.vbs` script uses at least one argument. This is a regular expression that is used as the match pattern. Any additional arguments are assumed to be folders that are then filtered by the regular expression. Lines that match the filter are passed through to the `StdOut` text stream. If no folders are supplied on the command line (that is, only a regular expression argument is supplied), the `StdIn` text stream is filtered instead.

Listing 8.8 `VBGrep.vbs` *Script*

```
'//////////////////////////////////////////////////////////////////////////
' $Workfile: SplitPath.vbs $ $Revision: 1 $ $Date: 6/23/99 11:15a $
' $Archive: /Scripts/SplitPath.vbs $
' Copyright (c) 1999 Tim Hill. All Rights Reserved.
'//////////////////////////////////////////////////////////////////////////

' Uses regular expressions to filter lines in one or more files
```

continues ▶

Listing 8.8 *continued*

```
Option Explicit
Dim sArg, oFSO
Set oFSO = CreateObject("Scripting.FileSystemObject")

' If no arguments, show short usage
If Wscript.Arguments.Count < 1 Then
    Wscript.Echo "usage: vbgrep reg-exp [folders]"
    Wscript.Echo "If no folders, reads stdin"
    Wscript.Quit(0)
End If

' Prepare the regular expression object
Dim oRE
Set oRE = new RegExp
oRE.Pattern = Wscript.Arguments(0)

' Now process the input
Dim nMatchCount, ix, oFolder, oFile, oStream
nMatchCount = 0
If Wscript.Arguments.Count < 2 Then
    nMatchCount = nMatchCount + GrepStream(Wscript.StdIn, oRE, Wscript.StdOut)
Else
    For ix = 1 To Wscript.Arguments.Count - 1
        sArg = Wscript.Arguments(ix)
        If oFSO.FolderExists(sArg) Then
            Set oFolder = oFSO.GetFolder(sArg)
            For Each oFile In oFolder.Files
                Set oStream = oFile.OpenAsTextStream(1)
                nMatchCount = nMatchCount + GrepStream(oStream, oRE, Wscript.StdOut)
                Set oStream = Nothing
            Next
            Set oFolder = Nothing
        Else
            Wscript.Echo sArg,"not found"
        End If
    Next
End If

Set oRE = Nothing
Set oFSO = Nothing
Wscript.Quit(nMatchCount)

'///////////////////////////////////////////////////////////////////////////
' GrepStream
' Filters a text stream based upon a regular expression object
'
' oStream           Text stream to filter
' oRE               Regular expression for filter
' oOutput           Output stream for results
' Returns           Number of matched lines
'
```

```
Function GrepStream(oStream, oRE, oOutput)
    Dim sLine, nCount

    'Process each line of input stream
    nCount = 0
    Do Until oStream.AtEndOfStream
        sLine = oStream.ReadLine
        ' If RE match, send line to output stream
        If oRE.Test(sLine) Then
            oOutput.WriteLine sLine
            nCount = nCount + 1
        End If
    Loop
    GrepStream = nCount
End Function

'//////////////////////////////////////////////////////////////////////////
```

The VBGrep.vbs script is actually quite simple. The heart of the script is the GrepStream function that takes three arguments. The first argument is an input text stream object, which is read one line at a time for text to filter. The second argument is a regular expression object that is used to filter the lines, and the third argument is an output text stream where matching lines are written. The function simply reads a line, matches it against the regular expression object, and then writes it if a match occurs. The function also counts the number of matched lines and returns this value, although the VBGrep.vbs script does not use this result.

The remainder of the VBGrep.vbs script handles the processing of the command line arguments and the preparation of the various objects to pass to the GrepStream function.

Summary

The FileSystem object provides all the properties, methods and objects that are necessary to manipulate drives, folders, and files from within scripts. The TextStream object provides convenient access to text files either line by line or character by character.

The three predefined text streams, StdIn, StdOut, and StdErr, allow a script to be constructed that can act as a command line filter or a text stream processor. This integrates well with the existing command shell syntax provided by Windows NT and Windows 2000.

9

Creating VBScript Classes

All the chapters in this book up to this point have focused on *using* objects supplied by other agents. This chapter, along with Chapter 10, "Windows Script Components," shows how VBScript and WSH can be used to define *new* objects. These new objects can then be used in script code in the same manner as the other objects described in Chapters 6, "Introducing Objects," 7, "Built-In WSH and VBScript Objects," and 8, "File System Objects."

This chapter focuses on creating *intra-script* objects. That is, objects that are used in the same script in which they are defined. Chapter 10 describes the Windows Script Components technology that facilitates the creation of *inter-script* objects, which can be accessed from many different scripts.

Note

As with all the sample scripts in this book, the scripts in this chapter should be run using the CSCRIPT host, unless otherwise noted. The examples shown assume that CSCRIPT is the default WSH host. (See Chapter 1, "Introducing WSH," for information on selecting the default WSH host.) ♦

Classes and Objects

Intra-script *objects* are not defined within a script. Instead an object *class* is defined in the script, and then one or more *instances* of that class are created and used in the script. Each instance of the class is an object, and each behaves in the same ways as the objects introduced in earlier chapters.

Classes are defined in a VBScript script using the `Class` statement, which has the following syntax:

```
Class name
    statements
End Class
```

The *name* item in the statement defines the name of the class. The *statements* define the behavior, methods, and properties of the class. Like procedures, Class statements can be placed anywhere in the script file—the *statements* in the class are only executed when an object of the class is created and manipulated.

Note

Although Class *statements must appear in the script file in which they are used, the* .WS *script file format (described in Chapter 1) does provide a way to "include" additional script* .VBS *files. This allows one or more classes to be defined in a single file and then referenced in many distinct scripts. See Chapter 1 for more details.* ◆

After a class has been defined using the Class statement, one or more distinct instances of that class can be created. Class instances are created using the New keyword. This keyword takes a class name and returns an object reference. For example:

```
Dim oObj1
Set oObj1 = New MyClass
```

Here, the variable oObj1 is assigned a reference to a new object instance of the class MyClass. As with all other object references, the Set statement is used to assign this reference, and apart from the use of the New keyword, working with class instances is essentially identical to working with other object types.

Simple Classes

Very simple classes just contain data. To create a class that contains data, define the class and place one or more Public statements within the class. Each Public statement declares one or more variables that hold data for the class. The syntax of a Public statement is identical to the syntax of the Dim statement, except that the keyword Public is used instead of Dim. For example:

```
Class Point
    Public x, y
End Class
```

This example defines a class called Point that contains two variable values, x and y. Variables declared in this manner, as part of a Class statement, are often called *member variables*.

Variables declared using the Public statement in a class become *properties* of the class, and they are accessed in the same manner as normal object properties. Continuing the previous example:

```
Dim oPoint
Set oPoint = New Point
```

```
oPoint.x = 10 : oPoint.y = 20
Wscript.Echo "x=", oPoint.x, "y=", oPoint.y
```

Each individual instance of a class has its own distinct set of `Public` variables. These are created (and initialized, as usual, to `Empty`) when the object is created by the `New` keyword, and they are destroyed when the last reference to the object is deleted. For example:

```
Dim oP1, oP2, oP3
Set oP1 = New Point
Set oP2 = New Point
Set oP3 = oP2
oP1.x = 10 : oP1.y = 10
oP2.x = oP1.x * 2 : oP2.y = oP1.y * 2
Set oP1 = Nothing
Set oP2 = Nothing
Set oP3 = Nothing
```

Here, two `Point` objects (that is, instances of the `Point` class) are created. The second object is referenced through both the `oP2` and `oP3` variables (that is, an *alias* to the object). Thus, two distinct sets of `x` and `y` properties exist, one accessible through the `oP1` object reference and the other through either the `oP2` or `oP3` object references.

The `Public` statement can also declare an array (either static or dynamic) as a class property. For example:

```
Class DataSet
    Public nData(100), nDataCount
End Class
```

As with simple `Public` variables, each instance of the `DataSet` class gets its own private array and variable. For example:

```
Dim oData1, oData2
Set oData1 = New DataSet
Set oData2 = New DataSet
oData1.nData(2) = 0
```

Here, two distinct objects each have a distinct `nData` array and a `nDataCount` variable. Individual elements of the array are accessed using normal array element syntax, as shown in the last line of the example.

Classes that contain only member variables effectively introduce new simple data types into VBScript. Chapter 3, "VBScript Data Storage," introduced the idea of using a dynamic array to represent a data structure. Classes are able to perform the same function but in a far more effective manner. Simply declare a class with each individual data item included as a `Public` variable. For example, the `Employee` array from Chapter 3 can be reconstructed as a class as follows:

```
Class Employee
    Public ID, Name, StartDate
End Class
```

Here, the `Employee` class contains all the information about an employee, including the employee ID, name, and date of employment.

The `TypeName` function (described in Chapter 4, "Built-In Functions") returns the name of the class given an object reference to that class. Continuing the `Employee` example:

```
Sub ShowEmployee(oEmp)
    If TypeName(oEmp) = "Employee" Then
        Wscript.Echo "ID=",oEmp.ID,"Name=",oEmp.Name,"Date=",oEmp.StartDate
    Else
        Wscript.Echo "Not an employee record"
    End If
End Sub
```

Class Methods

The `ShowEmployee` procedure in the previous example displays information about an `Employee` object. In the object-oriented paradigm, this procedure really belongs to the `Employee` class, and so it makes sense to convert this procedure to a method of the `Employee` class.

To add a method to a class, simply place a procedure definition within the `Class` statement. For example:

```
Class Employee
    Public ID, Name, StartDate

    Public Sub Show
        Wscript.Echo "ID=",ID,"Name=",Name,"Date=",StartDate
    End Sub
End Class
```

Here, the `Show` method defined in the `Employee` class has the same function as the previous `ShowEmployee` procedure. However, it has the following differences:

- The procedure definition (in this case, a subroutine) is preceded by the `Public` keyword. This makes the procedure available as a method of the class.
- Member variables are accessed directly by name, without any need to prefix the name with a period or any other special syntax.
- The method does not take any arguments. Access to member variables of the class is automatic; therefore, there is no need to pass an `Employee` reference to the method.

After a method is defined, it can be used like any other object method. For example:

```
Dim oEmp
Set oEmp = New Employee
oEmp.ID = 14567
oEmp.Name = "Simon Trevor"
```

```
oEmp.StartDate = #5/7/87#
oEmp.Show
```

Of course, methods can be defined that take one or more arguments, which are defined as usual. For example:

```
Class Employee
    Public ID, Name, StartDate

    Public Sub Show
        Wscript.Echo "ID=",ID,"Name=",Name,"Date=",StartDate
    End Sub

    Public Sub SetInfo(nID, sName, dStartDate)
        ID = nID
        Name = sName
        StartDate = dStartDate
    End Sub
End Class
```

Here, the `Employee` class is extended with a `SetInfo` method that sets all the properties of an employee in a single method invocation. It is sometimes convenient to define such a method, and in some cases it can be more efficient to set many properties at once with a single method invocation, rather than one at a time.

Calling methods with arguments follows the normal syntax for object method invocation:

```
Dim oEmp
Set oEmp = New Employee
oEmp.SetInfo 14567, "Simon Trevor", #5/7/87#
oEmp.Show
```

Class methods can also be functions. For example:

```
Class Employee
    Public ID, Name, StartDate

    Public Function DaysEmployed
        DaysEmployed = DateDiff("d", StartDate, Date)
    End Function

    [Rest of Employee class]
End Class
```

Here, the `DaysEmployed` function computes the number of days since the employee was hired. Notice that this function does not need any arguments. It already has access to the two items of information it needs: the start date of the employee is available in the `StartDate` property, and today's date is available via the `Date` function. It is common for class methods to have fewer arguments than required for stand-alone procedures because they can draw upon the member variables of the object for argument data.

As usual for functions, if a method function takes any arguments, they must be placed in parentheses following the method name. For example:

```
Class Employee
    Public ID, Name, StartDate, Salary

    Public Function PayRaise(nPercent)
        Salary = Salary + (Salary * (nPercent / 100))
        PayRaise = Salary
    End Function

    [Rest of Employee class]
End Class
```

Here, the `Employee` class is extended with a `Salary` property and a `PayRaise` method that raises the salary by a specified percentage and returns the new salary. For example:

```
Dim oEmp
Set oEmp = New Employee
oEmp.Salary = CCur("$10,000")
Wscript.Echo "New salary=", oEmp.PayRaise(25)
```

Here, the (fortunate) employee is given a 25 percent pay raise.

CountUNCNames Revisited

In Chapter 6, "Introducing Objects," a subroutine named `CountUNCNames` was converted to a hypothetical object that counted UNC path names. Here is the sample code from that chapter that used this hypothetical object:

```
Dim oOddCount, oEvenCount, sArg, ix
oOddCount.Reset : oEvenCount.Reset
For ix = 0 To Wscript.Arguments.Count - 1
    sArg = Wscript.Arguments(ix)
    If ix And 1 Then
        oOddCount.AddName sArg
    Else
        oEvenCount.AddName sArg
    End If
Next
Wscript.Echo oOddCount.Count, oEvenCount.Count
```

We can now complete this example by defining a `UNCCount` class that provides the necessary properties and methods. The `CountUNCNames.vbs` script, shown in Listing 9.1, demonstrates this simple class.

Listing 9.1 `CountUNCNames.vbs` *Script*

```
'//////////////////////////////////////////////////////////////////////////
' $Workfile: CountUNCNames.vbs $ $Revision: 1 $ $Date: 7/05/99 11:23a $
' $Archive: /Scripts/CountUNCNames.vbs $
' Copyright (c) 1999 Tim Hill. All Rights Reserved.
'//////////////////////////////////////////////////////////////////////////
```

```
' Count UNC names on command line, split between even and odd indexes

Option Explicit
Dim oOddCount, oEvenCount, sArg, ix

Set oOddCount = New UNCCount
Set oEvenCount = New UNCCount
oOddCount.Reset : oEvenCount.Reset
For ix = 0 To Wscript.Arguments.Count - 1
    sArg = Wscript.Arguments(ix)
    If ix And 1 Then
        oOddCount.AddName sArg
    Else
        oEvenCount.AddName sArg
    End If
Next
Wscript.Echo oOddCount.Count, oEvenCount.Count

'////////////////////////////////////////////////////////////////////////////
' UNC Counter class - counts UNC names
'
Class UNCCount
    Public Count

    ' Reset all properties
    Public Sub Reset
        Count = 0
    End Sub

    ' Add a name (if its a UNC name)
    Public Sub AddName(sName)
        If Left(sName, 2) = "\\" Then Count = Count + 1
    End Sub
End Class

'////////////////////////////////////////////////////////////////////////////
```

Variable Access in Methods

Chapter 5, "User-Defined Procedures," described the various scope and lifetime rules for global (per script) and local (per procedure) variables. Classes add a third scope: *class* scope. The member variables (properties) of a class all have class scope and lifetime. That is, they are created when an instance of that class is created, and they are destroyed when the instance is destroyed. A method in a class thus has access to three distinct sets of variables:

- *Local variables* Declared using `Dim` statements within the method.
- *Class variables* Declared using `Public` statements within the class in which the method is defined.
- *Global variables* Declared using `Dim` statements within the main script body.

As with local and global scope, a variable in local scope in a method shadows a variable in class or global scope of the same name. Similarly, a class variable shadows a global scope variable of the same name. For example:

```
Dim x
Class Test
    Public x
    Public Sub ShowX
        Wscript.Echo "x=", x
    End Sub
End Class

Sub ShowX
    Wscript.Echo "x=",x
End Sub

x = "Global x"
Dim oTest
Set oTest = New Test
oTest.x = "Class x"
ShowX
oTest.ShowX
```

Here, two distinct variables are named `x`. The first has global scope; the second has class scope in class `Test`. The `ShowX` method in the `Test` class displays the class scope variable, whereas the `ShowX` procedure displays the global scope variable.

This example also illustrates another important point. The namespace for a class is distinct from the global namespace of the script. This means that the `ShowX` method in the `Test` class and the `ShowX` procedure are both valid because they are in different namespaces. (See Chapter 5 for more information on namespaces.)

In VBScript, *each* class has its own namespace, just as each procedure has its own variable namespace. This allows each class to reuse the same names for properties and methods without any problems arising. This allows the designer of a class to freely use convenient names without any difficulties arising out of name collisions between classes.

Procedural Properties

Simple class properties can be expressed directly using `Public` member variables, as previously explained. However, some properties might be too complex to express as simple data. As described in Chapter 6, some properties are associated with code that executes when the property value is manipulated. These properties are sometimes known as *procedural properties*.

Procedural properties in a VBScript class are represented by three special types of procedures. Each type of procedure is associated with one of the three ways in which VBScript can access an object property:

- A `Property Get` procedure is used to obtain the value of a property from an object.
- A `Property Let` procedure is used to set a new value of a property in an object.
- A `Property Set` procedure is used to set a new value of a property in an object when the value is an object reference.

Each of these procedures is invoked implicitly when the specified property is referenced in script code. These implicit references occur as follows:

- When a procedural property is used as part of an expression, the `Property Get` procedure is invoked to fetch the current value of the property.
- When a procedural property is used as the target of an assignment statement (that is, on the left side of the `=` sign), the `Property Let` procedure is invoked to set the new value of the property.
- When a procedural property is used as the target of a `Set` statement (that is, on the left side of the `=` sign), the `Property Set` procedure is invoked to set the new object reference.

The syntax of a `Property Get` procedure is as follows:

```
Public Property Get name [(args)]
    statements
End Property
```

Apart from the slightly different syntax (the use of the `Property Get` keywords), a `Property Get` procedure is identical to a regular VBScript function. The *name* represents the name of the property. As with regular functions, a `Property Get` procedure can have zero or more arguments.

The return value from a `Property Get` procedure is used as the value of the property. As usual, if this value is an object reference, the `Set` statement must be used to assign the return value. The return value of the procedure defines the "value" of the property. How the procedure generates the return value is entirely dependent upon the underlying logic of the class in which the property resides. The procedure can simply return a constant value, or it can perform a complex computation.

Finally, a `Property Get` (and `Property Let` or `Property Set`) procedure can use the `Exit Property` statement to exit the procedure before reaching the procedure end statement. The syntax is:

```
Exit Property
```

The `Exit Property` statement is identical in operation to the `Exit Sub` statement described in Chapter 5.

Here is an example class with two `Property Get` procedures:

```
Class Rect
    Public Top, Left, Bottom, Right

    Public Property Get Width
        Width = Right - Left
    End Property

    Public Property Get Height
        Height = Bottom - Top
    End Property
End Class
```

Here, the `Rect` class defines a class that can store the coordinates of a rectangle as two (x,y) pairs: `Left+Top` and `Right+Bottom`. These four values are used as simple properties in the `Rect` class. In addition, the class defines `Width` and `Height` properties that are computed on the fly by `Property Get` procedures. The class can thus be used as follows:

```
Dim oRect
Set oRect = New Rect
oRect.Top = 5 : oRect.Left = 8
oRect.Bottom = 10 : oRect.Right = 40
Wscript.Echo "Width=", oRect.Width, "Height=", oRect.Height
```

The `Width` and `Height` properties in this example are *read-only* properties. This is because, although they have `Property Get` procedures, they have no `Property Let` or `Property Set` procedures. Thus, the `Width` and `Height` properties cannot be altered directly. In fact, thus far, the `Property Get` approach has no inherent advantage over using a class function to return the width or height.

To allow the `Width` and `Height` procedures to be altered, it is necessary to provide two `Property Let` procedures. The syntax of a `Property Let` procedure is as follows:

```
Public Property Let name (args, value)
    statements
End Property
```

A `Property Let` procedure is similar to a `Property Get` procedure except that it does not return a value. In addition, the `Property Let` procedure *always* has at least one argument. This argument is supplied automatically by VBScript, and is the new value to assign to the property. Additional arguments might be supplied, and if present they always precede the value argument (that is, the value argument is always the last argument to the procedure).

Properties that have a `Property Let` procedure and a `Property Get` procedure are *read-write* properties. Properties that only have a `Property Let` procedure are *write-only* properties.

A `Property Let` procedure is invoked when a property is used on the left side of the = sign in an assignment statement. VBScript first evaluates the expression on the right side of the = sign. Then, it invokes the `Property Let` procedure, passing it the expression result as the value (that is, the last argument to the procedure).

Here is the `Rect` class extended to support `Property Let` procedures for the `Width` and `Height` properties:

```
Class Rect
    Public Top, Left, Bottom, Right

    Public Property Get Width
        Width = Right - Left
    End Property

    Public Property Get Height
        Height = Bottom - Top
    End Property

    Public Property Let Width(nValue)
        Right = Left + nValue
    End Property

    Public Property Let Height(nValue)
        Bottom = Top + nValue
    End Property
End Class
```

Notice that the `Property Get` and `Property Let` procedures have the same names (`Width` and `Height`). This is the only case in VBScript where two items in the same scope can have the same name. VBScript allows `Property Get`, `Property Let`, and `Property Set` procedures in a class to all refer to the same property. This is because VBScript can always invoke the correct procedure based upon the context in which the property is used.

The new `Rect` class can be used as follows:

```
Dim oRect
Set oRect = New Rect
oRect.Top = 5 : oRect.Left = 8
oRect.Bottom = 10 : oRect.Right = 40
Wscript.Echo "Width=", oRect.Width, "Height=", oRect.Height
oRect.Width = 200
Wscript.Echo "Left=", oRect.Left, "Right=", oRect.Right, "Width=", oRect.Width
```

Here, the rectangle width is altered and, as expected, the `Right` property automatically adjusts to the new width.

Procedural properties are more common than the simple `Public` properties introduced at the start of this chapter. The reason for this is that, in most classes, changing a property has some additional effects that need to be taken into account by executing some procedural code, and procedural properties are what make this possible.

The final type of procedure property is the `Property Set` procedure. The syntax of this is:

```
Public Property Set name (args, reference)
    statements
End Property
```

The `Property Set` procedure is nearly identical to the `Property Let` procedure. The difference being that the procedure is invoked when the property is used on the left side of the `=` sign in a `Set` statement, and the value passed as the last argument is always an object reference. For example:

```
Class FileScan
    Public oRE

    Public Property Set RegExpr(oReg)
        Set oRE = oReg
    End Property
End Class
```

The `FileScan` class can be used as follows:

```
Dim oFS
Set oFS = New FileScan
Set oFS.RegExpr = New RegExp
```

Here, the first `Set` statement creates a new `FileScan` object. The second statement then assigns a new `RegExp` object to the `RegExpr` property of the `FileScan` object. Because this uses a `Set` statement, the `Property Set RegExpr` procedure in the `FileScan` class is invoked.

Advanced Classes

Many classes can be defined using the basic features of classes described thus far in this chapter. However, several additional features offered by VBScript can be used to enhance class functionality.

Private Class Information

As previously explained, any member variable declared using the `Public` keyword automatically becomes a class property. Sometimes, however, a class needs to maintain state information that is not available as properties. This information is only available *within* the class—it is not visible outside the class. Member variables that are not visible outside the class are called *private* member variables and are declared using the `Private` statement.

The syntax of the `Private` statement is identical to the `Dim` and the `Public` statements; follow the keyword by a list of one or more variable names. For example:

```
Class AnyClass
    Private ix, nTotal, oRegExp
End Class
```

Private variables are normally used by methods and property procedures to maintain the state of the object. Like properties, they are created when the object is created and destroyed when the object is destroyed. Unlike properties, however, they are not visible outside the class definition.

One common use of private variables is to maintain the state of read-only properties. Here is a simple class with a read-write property called `Count`:

```
Class Simple
    Public Count
End Class
```

To make the `Count` property read-only, it is necessary to do two things. First, the simple property variable must be replaced with a `Property Get` procedure. Because there is no corresponding `Property Let` procedure, the property is read-only. Second, the state that was maintained by the `Count` member variable must now be maintained by a private variable. The `Simple` class becomes:

```
Class Simple
    Private nCount

    Public Property Get Count
        Count = nCount
    End Property
End Class
```

The `Private` keyword can, in fact, be used anywhere the `Public` keyword has been used thus far in classes. Therefore, it is possible to have private methods and properties. For example:

```
Class Hidden
    Private Sub DoIt
    End Sub

    Private Property Get Password
    End Property
End Class
```

Here, the `Hidden` class contains a private method, `DoIt`, and a private read-only property `Password`.

Private methods are common inside more complex classes, and they are typically used to implement support functions and routines needed by the public methods and properties of the class. Private properties are far less common because the procedures in a class can access all private state information anyway.

Note

If a method or property is defined in a class without either the `Public` *or the* `Private` *keyword, the method or property is public by default. That is, the* `Public` *keyword is assumed. However, it is still a good idea to declare methods and properties explicitly as public because this clearly highlights in the script source code the script author's original intention.*

Default Class Properties

VBScript allows one `Property Get` property in each class definition to be designated as the *default* property. The default property is used when an object of the class is used in an expression without any explicit property. Default properties can only be defined by procedural properties—it is not possible to designate a simple public variable as the default property. In addition, the property must be a public property—it is not meaningful to declare a private property as the default property because this property is not visible outside the class itself.

To declare a `Property Get` procedure as the default property, add the `Default` keyword after the `Public` keyword. For example:

```
Class Simple
    Private nCount

    Public Default Property Get Count
        Count = nCount
    End Property

    Public Property Let Count
        nCount = Count
    End Property
End Class
```

Here, the `Simple` class described earlier has been enhanced by making the `.Count` property the default property. (A `Property Let` procedure has also been added.) The class can now be used as follows:

```
Dim oSimple
Set oSimple = New Simple
oSimple.Count = 400
Wscript.Echo oSimple.Count, oSimple
```

In this example, the `Wscript.Echo` statement displays the `Count` property twice—once by explicitly referencing the property, and once implicitly via the default property.

Only one `Property Get` procedure can be designated as the default property for any one class. Choosing which property (if any) to make the default depends upon the functionality of the class. Typically, it is the most frequently accessed or most important property in the class. In classes that act as collections (and have `.Count` and `.Item` properties) it is usually the `.Item` property.

VBScript does *not* support default properties for `Property Let` or `Property Set` property procedures. This is to avoid a syntactical ambiguity. Consider this example:

```
Dim oSimple
Set oSimple = New Simple
oSimple = 100
```

What does the last statement in the preceding code mean? Actually, it simply assigns the value 100 to the variable `oSimple`. The object reference in this variable is replaced by the simple integer value. However, if the `Simple` class supported a default `Property Let` property, this last statement could be interpreted to mean that the default property of the `oSimple` object should be set to 100. Thus, the meaning of such a statement would depend upon the definition of the `Simple` class. This would greatly diminish the readability of VBScript code, and so VBScript avoids this problem by not allowing default `Property Let` procedures.

Collections

Many of the objects discussed in earlier chapters have been *collection* objects. These objects' primary function is to contain a list of other data items. Sometimes these items are simple data values; sometimes they are, in turn, themselves objects.

It is possible to use classes to define collections, although with slight differences to the built-in collections offered by VBScript and other COM objects.

The following is an example collection class:

```
Class Coll
    Private nCount
    Private vData(100)

    Public Property Get Count
        nCount = CInt(Count)
    End Property

    Public Default Property Get Item(nIndex)
        Item = vData(nIndex)
    End Property

    Public Property Let Item(nIndex, vValue)
        vData(nIndex) = vValue
    End Property
```

```
    Public Function Add(vValue)
        Add = nCount
        vData(nCount) = vValue
        nCount = nCount + 1
    End Function
End Class
```

The `Coll` class has some interesting features, as follows:

- The count of items in the collection is maintained in the `nCount` private variable. This count is accessible as a read-only value via the `Count` property procedure.
- Individual items are accessible via the `Item` property. This is a read-write property (There is both a `Property Get` and a `Property Let` procedure.), and so individual items can be modified within the collection. Some collection classes might have items that are read-only; in which case, the `Property Let` procedure would not be present.
- The `vData` array holds the individual items. Because each element can hold data of any type (as can all VBScript variables), each item in the collection can be of any required type, even an object or another array. Refer to Chapter 3 for more information on data types.
- Items are accessed by numeric index, which is used directly as an array element index. However, other collection classes might use other indexing methods, such as a string key. It is even possible to define a single `Item` property that can fetch items by integer index or string name by using the `VarType` function to determine the type of data passed in the `nIndex` variable.
- New items are added to the collection via the `Add` method. As a convenience, this method returns the index of the item just added.
- When an object is created, VBScript initializes all the member variables (both public and private) to `Empty`. Retrieving the `Count` property on such a newly created object returns `Empty` rather than zero. Therefore, the `Property Get Count` procedure uses the `CInt` function to ensure that zero is returned even if the `nCount` variable is empty.

This final point is important. When designing a class, it is important that objects of that class should behave even when the object is newly created. Because all member variables contain `Empty` when the class is created, the `IsEmpty` function can be used to test the variable and act in a way that is appropriate for the class (by returning a default value for a property, for example).

The `Coll` class also contains a number of less desirable features:

- The data array used to store the items is of fixed size. This might be satisfactory for some classes, but in general, it is not a good idea to set arbitrary limits on the capacity of a collection. A better solution is to use some form of dynamic array.

- There is essentially no error checking. The index passed to the `Item` property procedures is not checked to see if it is in range (0 to `nCount - 1`). A bad index passed to the procedure will cause a run-time error. In addition, the `Add` procedure does not check to see if the array is full before adding the item.

Both of these issues (and others) are addressed in the `RDir.vbs` script described as follows.

Collection classes defined in VBScript are not quite as useful as the built-in collections, for two reasons:

- Because VBScript does not permit a class to have a default `Property Let`, the `Item` property of the collection must be explicitly referenced when used on the left side of the `=` sign in an assignment statement.
- Collection class objects cannot be used in `For Each` statements. Instead, a regular `For` loop must be used with an index value that is passed to the `Item` property. For example:

```
Dim oColl, ix
Set oColl = New Coll
For ix = 0 To oColl.Count - 1
    [process the item...]
Next
```

The *Me* Keyword

Sometimes, scripts are developed that contain several classes that interact to provide certain functionality. Consider this example:

```
Class Parent
    Public Function NewChild
        Dim oChild
        Set oChild = New Child
        Set NewChild = oChild
    End Function
End Class

Class Child
    Private oParent

    Public Property Get Parent
        Set Parent = oParent
    End Property
    Public Property Set Parent(oValue)
        Set oParent = oValue
    End Property
End Class
```

```
Dim oParent, oChild
Set oParent = New Parent
Set oChild = oParent.NewChild
Set oChild.Parent = oParent
```

Here, two classes, `Parent` and `Child`, are closely related. The `Parent` class contains a method called `NewChild` that creates a new `Child` object and returns it. The `Child` object has a special relationship to the parent (as implied by the name) in that it internally maintains an object reference back to the `Parent` object that created it (via the `oParent` private variable).

When a new `Child` object is created, the `Parent` property of the `Child` object is set to a reference to the `Parent` object. This allows the child to reference back to its parent (for example, to obtain properties from the parent or to invoke methods).

However, inter-connecting the parent to the child in the preceding example is done in the main body of the script outside of either the `Parent` or `Child` objects. It is far better to move the statement that sets the `Parent` property of the `Child` object into the `NewChild` method in the `Parent` object. That way, every child that is generated by the `NewChild` method is automatically set up with a reference back to its parent, and users of the `Parent` and `Child` objects do not have to remember to manually set the object reference for every child.

There is, however, a problem. What should the `NewChild` method set as the value of the object reference? In other words, what should the `???` in the revised `Parent` class code that follows become?

```
Class Parent
    Public Function NewChild
        Dim oChild
        Set oChild = New Child
        Set oChild.Parent = ???     ' What is this value?
        Set NewChild = oChild
    End Function
End Class
```

The problem is that *outside* of the class an object instance is always available because it is stored within the normal object variables, which are used to reference the object's methods and properties. That is why it is easy to set the parent/child link in the main script code. However, *within* the class there is no way to determine the object reference that is currently being used.

The fundamental question here is: What is the object reference used when invoking a method or property on a class instance? Fortunately, VBScript provides a built-in answer, the `Me` keyword. This special keyword acts like a read-only variable and, within a class, always contains the current object reference. Thus, the correct missing line in the `Parent` class is as follows:

```
Set oChild.Parent = Me
```

The `Me` keyword is not frequently used in scripts because it is only really necessary in scenarios where multiple objects interact and need to maintain mutual object references. For an example use of the `Me` keyword in a real script, see the `Animal.vbs` script in Chapter 14, "Miscellaneous Scripts."

Program Guide

More About *Me*

This explanation can be confusing. Don't forget that an object is an instance of a class. There can be many individual objects that all share the same class methods and properties. Each object, however, is unique because it has its own set of member variables. This set of member variables is accessed via the object reference. Outside of a class, each object is identified by a variable that contains the object reference. Inside the class, this variable is not accessible, but internally VBScript tracks which object is currently executing the class method or property, and makes this information available via the `Me` *keyword.* ◆

When classes contain object references to other objects, you should beware of a scenario known as a "deadly embrace." Consider this example:

```
Class A
    Public Ref
End Class

Class B
    Public Ref
End Class

Dim oA, oB
Set oA = New A
Set oB = New B
Set oA.Ref = oB
Set oB.Ref = oA
Set oA = Nothing
Set oB = Nothing
```

This example contains two classes, `A` and `B`, that each contain a single property called `Ref`. After creating an instance of `A` and `B`, the code sets the `Ref` property in each class to refer to the other object. Then, the object references are deleted by setting `oA` and `oB` to `Nothing`. When are the objects deleted? The answer is *never* (or at least not until the script terminates).

The reason is that an object is not deleted until all references to that object are deleted. Normally this means when the last variable containing a reference to the object is set to `Nothing` or goes out of scope. However, in this example, the `A` object won't be deleted because the `B` object holds a reference to `A`, and the `B` object won't be deleted because the `A` object holds a reference to *it*. Therefore, to delete object `A`, we must first delete object `B`, but to delete object `B`, we must first delete object `A`, which is impossible.

In fact, there is no easy solution to this problem except avoidance—don't design a set of interacting objects that hold mutual references to each other, unless you also provide a way to release those references.

The *RDir.vbs* Script

The `RDir.vbs` script, shown in Listing 9.2, illustrates many of the concepts described in this chapter. The script takes one or more arguments. The first argument is a regular expression (see Chapter 7, "Built-In WSH and VBScript Objects," for more information on regular expressions), and any additional arguments are assumed to be path names. If only one argument is supplied, the script uses the current path name as the default.

The script operates by providing a directory listing of all file names in the path that match the regular expression. All files in a given path are scanned, including files in subfolders, so supplying an argument of `"c:\"` as a path argument matches all files anywhere on drive C.

Files that match the regular expression are listed as the output of the script. Files that do not match the expression are skipped. For example, this command displays *all* the files on drive C because the regular expression `".*"` matches any sequence of characters:

```
C:\>rdir .* c:\
```

The following command displays all file names that contain spaces in their names:

```
C:\>rdir " +" c:\
```

Finally, the following command displays all file names that begin with the letter `"x"` and contain the text `".txt"`:

```
C:\>rdir "^x.*\.txt" c:\
```

The `RDir.vbs` script consists of two parts. The main script body processes the individual command line arguments, whereas a single class, `FileScan` provides all the core functionality.

Listing 9.2 *`RDir.vbs` Script*

```
'//////////////////////////////////////////////////////////////////////////
' $Workfile: RDir.vbs $ $Revision: 2 $ $Date: 7/07/99 9:28p $
' $Archive: /Scripts/RDir.vbs $
' Copyright (c) 1999 Tim Hill. All Rights Reserved.
'//////////////////////////////////////////////////////////////////////////

' Regular expression file search using FileScan class

Option Explicit
Dim oFileScan, oFSO, ix
Set oFSO = CreateObject("Scripting.FileSystemObject")
```

```
' Show usage if no arguments
If Wscript.Arguments.Count < 1 Then
    Wscript.Echo "usage: rdir reg-expr [path...]"
    Wscript.Quit(0)
End If

' Create the FileScan object and set the RE from cmd line
Set oFileScan = New FileScan
oFileScan.Expr = Wscript.Arguments(0)
oFileScan.ScanSubFolders = True

' Now process all arguments, or use current dir if none
If Wscript.Arguments.Count > 1 Then
    For ix = 1 To Wscript.Arguments.Count - 1
        oFileScan.Execute oFSO.GetAbsolutePathName(Wscript.Arguments(ix))
    Next
Else
    oFileScan.Execute oFSO.GetAbsolutePathName(".")
End If

' Display the results
For ix = 0 To oFileScan.Count
    Wscript.Echo oFileScan(ix)
Next

Wscript.Quit(oFileScan.Count)

'////////////////////////////////////////////////////////////////////////////
' FileScan
' File scan class, builds a collection of files based upon a regular expr
'
Class FileScan
    Public Expr                             ' Reg expr to match
    Public MatchFullPath                    ' True to match full path
    Public ScanSubFolders                   ' True to scan subfolders
    Private sFiles                          ' List of matching files
    Private nCount                          ' Count of matches

    ' Reset object (delete all file matches)
    Public Sub Reset
        nCount = 0                          ' Mark no files
        sFiles = Empty                      ' Empty the files array
    End Sub

    ' Return current file count (R/O)
    Public Property Get Count
        Count = CInt(nCount)                ' Just return count
    End Property

    ' Execute search (build file list)
    Public Sub Execute(sPath)
        Dim oFSO, oFolder, oRE
        Set oFSO = CreateObject("Scripting.FileSystemObject")
```

continues ▶

Listing 9.2 *continued*

```
        Set oFolder = oFSO.GetFolder(sPath)      ' Get folder path
        Set oRE = New RegExp
        oRE.Pattern = Expr                       ' Set match pattern
        oRE.IgnoreCase = True                    ' Ignore case
        MatchFiles oRE, oFolder                  ' Go match files here
    End Sub

    Private Sub MatchFiles(oRE, oFolder)         ' Match file in folder
        Dim oFile, oSubFolder
        For Each oFile In oFolder.Files          ' Scan all files
            If MatchFullPath Then
                If oRE.Test(oFile.Path) Then     ' Full path match
                    AddFile oFile.Path           ' Add if match
                End If
            Else
                If oRE.Test(oFile.Name) Then     ' Name match
                    AddFile oFile.Path           ' Add if match
                End If
            End If
        Next
        If ScanSubFolders Then                   ' If required..
            For Each oSubFolder In oFolder.SubFolders   ' Scan subs
                MatchFiles oRE, oSubFolder
            Next
        End If
    End Sub

    ' Get individual files (default property)
    Public Default Property Get Item(nIndex)     ' Get indexed item
        Dim ixMajor, ixMinor
        If (nIndex >= nCount) Or (nIndex >= 1024 * 4096) Then
            Item = ""                            ' Flag overflow
        Else
            ixMajor = nIndex / 4096              ' Compute major index
            ixMinor = nIndex And 4095            ' Compute minor index
            Item = sFiles(ixMajor)(ixMinor)      ' Get path name
        End If
    End Property

    ' Add new file item to dynamic array
    Private Sub AddFile(sPath)
        Dim ix, ixMajor, ixMinor, a              ' Array indices
        If IsEmpty(sFiles) Then                  ' If no array yet..
            ReDim sFiles(1023)                   ' Space for 1024 sets
        End If
        ix = nCount                              ' Get current index
        nCount = nCount + 1                      ' Bump counter
        If ix >= 1024 * 4096 Then Exit Sub       ' Exit if overflow!!
        ixMajor = ix / 4096                      ' Compute major index
        ixMinor = ix And 4095                    ' Compute minor index
        If IsEmpty(sFiles(ixMajor)) Then         ' If new array needed
```

```
            ReDim a(4095)                        ' Create temp array
            sFiles(ixMajor) = a                  ' Copy to populate
        End If
        sFiles(ixMajor)(ixMinor) = sPath         ' Add path to array
    End Sub
End Class
```

The `ScanFile` class has the following interface:

- An `.Expr` property (read-write), which defines the regular expression to be used when matching files.
- A `.MatchFullPath` property (read-write), which controls the match process. If this property is `False` (the default), the regular expression is matched against the file name text only. If this property is `True`, the regular expression is matched against the full path name of the file.
- A `.ScanSubFolders` property (read-write). If this property is `False` (the default), only files in the specified path are matched against the regular expression. If this property is `True`, files in subfolders are also matched.
- A `.Reset` method, which deletes existing file scan results and resets the object.
- A `.Count` property (read-only), which contains the count of files currently matched against the regular expression.
- An `.Execute` method, which performs the actual file match operation.
- An `.Item` property (read-only), which is the default property and which contains all the individual matched file path names, indexed from 0 to `.Count - 1`.

To use the `FileScan` class, proceed as follows:

1. Create a `FileScan` object.
2. Set the `.MatchFullPath` and `.ScanSubFolders` properties as desired.
3. Set the `.Expr` property to a regular expression string.
4. Invoke the `.Execute` method, passing a single argument that specifies a folder name to scan for files.
5. Repeat step 4 as necessary for additional folder names. Each `.Execute` invocation appends new files to the collection of files.
6. Use the `.Count` and `.Item` properties to recover the list of matched files.

For example:

```
Dim oFileScan, ix
Set oFileScan = New FileScan
oFileScan.ScanSubFolders = True
oFileScan.Expr = "^vb"
```

```
oFileScan.Execute "d:\"
For ix = 0 To oFileScan.Count - 1
    Wscript.Echo oFileScan(ix)
Next
```

This example lists all files that begin with the letters `"vb"` on drive D:.

The `FileScan` class brings together many of the class design techniques mentioned throughout this chapter:

- The `.Expr`, `.MatchFullPath`, and `.ScanSubFolders` properties are all simple public variables. The default values for these properties match an `Empty` variable. For example, an `Empty` variable always evaluates to `False` when used as a boolean value, and so the default value for `.MatchFullPath` is `False`.
- The `.Count` property is read-only, and so the actual count value is maintained in a private variable called `nCount`, which is only available via a `Property Get` procedure.
- The `.Item` property is also read-only. The `Property Get` procedure uses the passed index to recover one of the matched files. The procedure validates the index to ensure that it is within range, returning an empty string if the index is invalid.

The actual work of scanning files is handled in the `.Execute` method, which makes use of two additional private methods, `MatchFiles` and `AddFile` to handle most of the work.

The matched files are stored as path name strings in an array named `sFiles`. This array is later accessed by the `.Item` property to recover the matched files. However, the files array is not a simple array. Instead, the `FileScan` class uses a more sophisticated "split index" technique. This is used to avoid performance problems when large numbers of files are matched and stored.

One way to handle the storage of the file paths is to use a dynamic array and expand the array as necessary. Chapter 3 explained this technique and showed how enlarging the array in "chunks" of 100 elements could optimize the expansion of the array. However, when very large arrays are involved, even this method is too slow. Expanding a dynamic array from 100,000 elements to 100,100 elements might take several seconds if the `Preserve` keyword is used.

To avoid this overhead, the `FileScan` class uses a split index array. The split index array is implemented by the `AddFiles` private method as follows:

- The array is stored indirectly in a simple variable, named `sFiles`.
- When the first item is added to the array, a new dynamic array of exactly 1024 elements (0 to 1023) is created. This happens only once—the array is never enlarged.

- The array index is split into two sub-index values, a *major* index, and a *minor* index. The major index is the index divided by 4096, and the minor index is the index logically `And`ed with 4095. (See the next two bullets to find out why these numbers are used.)
- The major index is used as an index into the `sFiles` array. If the element of the array is empty, a new dynamic array of exactly 4096 elements is created and copied to this element.
- The path is stored in the dynamic array. The major index is used as an index into the `sFiles` array, whereas the minor index is used as an index into the dynamic array that is stored in this element.

The core of the split index technique is an array (`sFiles`) that contains dynamic arrays in each element. Thus, to access an individual path name in `sFiles`, it is necessary to provide two index values: an index into the `sFiles` array and an index into the dynamic array that is found at that element in `sFiles`. (See Chapter 3 for more information on arrays within arrays.) The reason this technique is used is that the dynamic arrays in each element of `sFiles` can be created only when necessary. In the `AddFile` method, each dynamic array holds 4096 individual path names; therefore, a new dynamic array is needed only every 4096 files. Furthermore, when the new array is created, it is simply added into the `sFiles` array—there is no need to use the `ReDim Preserve` statement anywhere because no arrays are being enlarged. This avoids the overhead associated with the `Preserve` keyword.

The only problem with this technique is that it requires two indices: one to access the `sFiles` array and another to access the dynamic array stored in the individual `sFiles` element. Fortunately, it's easy to derive both index values mathematically from a single index. To do this, the "master" index is split between a *major* value, used to access the `sFiles` array, and a *minor* value, used to access the dynamic array. This split is achieved by these two lines in `AddFile`:

```
ixMajor = ix / 4096
ixMinor = ix And 4095
```

Here is the value 4095 expressed as a 32-bit binary number:

```
        3         2         1
Bit:   10987654321098765432109876543210
Value: 00000000000000000000111111111111
```

Here is the value 4096 expressed as a 32-bit binary number:

```
        3         2         1
Bit:   10987654321098765432109876543210
Value: 00000000000000000001000000000000
```

Notice that 4096 is an exact power of 2 (only one binary bit is set in the number), and that 4095 is one less than this value. Thus, the minor index computed with the expression `ix And 4095` yields a value that cycles from 0 to 4095 repeatedly as `ix` is incremented. Whereas the expression `ix / 4096` yields a value that increments by 1 each time the minor index wraps around from 4095 back to 0.

When `AddFile` is first invoked, the `sFiles` array is empty. This causes the initial `If` statement to execute, and the `sFiles` array is created using a `ReDim` statement. (Thus, `sFiles` is itself a dynamic array although it is never resized.) The index, `ix`, which is 0, is then split into major and minor values, both of which are also 0 in this case.

Next, the individual `sFiles` element indexed by `ixMajor` (which is 0) is checked. This element is empty (the array has only just been created), and so the `If` statement executes and a new dynamic array is assigned to the element `sFiles(0)`. Finally, the path is stored in the new dynamic array, at location `sFiles(0)(0)`.

The next time `AddFile` is invoked, the index `ix` is 1. This splits into a major index of 0 and a minor index of 1. Because `sFiles(0)` is already populated with an array, no allocations are required, and the new path is immediately stored in `sFiles(0)(1)`. This also happens when `ix` is 2, when the path is stored in `sFiles(0)(2)`, and so on until `ix` is 4095, when the path is stored in `sFiles(0)(4095)`.

On the next invocation of `AddFile`, the index `ix` is 4096. This splits into a major index of 1 and a minor index of 0 (the minor index has “wrapped” from 4095 back to 0). Now, `sFiles(1)` is not yet populated with a dynamic array, and so a new array is assigned to this element. The path is then stored in `sFiles(1)(0)`.

This cycle repeats continuously, adding additional dynamic arrays to `sFiles` elements every 4096 files. The absolute limit in this example is 4193280 files, which fills all the elements in all 1024 dynamic arrays allocated.

The `AddFile` method is invoked from the `MatchFiles` method when a matched file is located. This method contains a simple loop, which checks each file’s name or path against the regular expression and adds the file if a match is found. The `MatchFiles` method also contains code to recursively process subfolders if the `ScanSubFolders` property is `True`.

Summary

User defined classes in VBScript are defined using the `Class` statement, which encloses one or more property and method definitions. Variables declared `Public` within the class definition become read-write properties of the class. Variables declared `Private` within the class are used for private-class state information visible only to the methods and properties of the class.

Instances of user-defined classes (objects) are created using the `New` keyword, and they are then accessed via object references stored in variables in the same manner as other built-in VBScript and COM objects.

Class methods are either `Sub` or `Function` procedures that are declared as `Public`. They have access to all the variables (both public and private) of the class, and they can manipulate the state of the class. Methods can also be declared `Private`, in which case they are only available within the class definition.

Property procedures allow a property within a class to be defined by a procedure rather than a simple variable. A read-only property is defined by a `Property Get` procedure, a write-only property by a `Property Let` procedure, a read-write property by both a `Property Get` and `Property Let` procedure. One (and only one) of the `Property Get` procedures for a class can be designated as the `Default` property for the class.

10

Windows Script Components

Chapter 9, "Creating VBScript Classes," provided details on how to define and create new object classes *within* a script. Although this is a useful facility, it does have some drawbacks. The most notable of these is that objects of the new class can be used only within the script in which the class is defined. That is, the classes are *local* to the individual script. This is quite different from the `FileSystem` object, for example, as described in Chapter 8, "File System Objects," which is available to *all* scripts.

One way to overcome this limitation is to use `.WS` script files, and then include the class definition script from a separate `.VBS` file using a `script` element, as described in Chapter 1, "Introducing WSH." The distinct `.VBS` file containing the class definition can be reused many times.

This chapter describes a WSH feature called *Windows Script Components (WSC)* that provides another way to make object classes available to multiple scripts. WSC allows a new object class (called a *component* in WSC) to be defined in a distinct `.WSC` script file. This file is then *registered*, using a process described later in this chapter. After it is registered, the component becomes available to *all* scripts in the system via the normal `CreateObject` function that accesses other objects (such as the `FileSystem` object).

In general, components and VBScript classes are similar. VBScript classes use the `New` keyword to create a new object, whereas components use the `CreateObject` function. However, in both cases the object that is created is an *instance* of the class or component, and the state information, stored in VBScript variables within the class or component, is maintained on a per-object basis. This state information is maintained only until the last reference to the object is deleted, and then it is destroyed.

Thus, there are three ways to use object class definitions within a script, each with advantages and disadvantages. These are summarized in Table 10.1.

Table 10.1 Class Definition Methods

Method	Advantages	Disadvantages
`Class` statement within script file.	Simple to create. Class will always be available to script.	Class is only available to one script. Class is not available to other `.VBS` scripts.
`Class` statement in distinct `.VBS` file.	Simple to create. Class is available to all `.WS` scripts.	Requires placing path to `.VBS` file in `script` element, which makes maintenance difficult.
Windows Script Component	Component is available to *all* scripts, both `.WS` and `.VBS`. Component is available as COM object to all COM clients. Scripts do not need to know path to `.WSC` file.	Harder to create. Requires registration and installation on each machine where the component is used.

The focus of this chapter is Windows Script Components. However, when creating a class, always take a moment to consider which class definition method best suits your needs.

Note

As with all the sample scripts in this book, the scripts in this chapter should be run using the CSCRIPT host unless otherwise noted. The examples shown assume that CSCRIPT is the default WSH host. (See Chapter 1 for information on selecting the default WSH host.) ◆

Creating a Windows Script Component

Windows Script Component files can be created in two ways:

- Manually using a text editor
- Automatically using the Windows Script Component Wizard

See Appendix A, "Installing Script Components" and Appendix B, "Other Scripting Resources," for more information on using the Windows Script Component Wizard, which builds a prototype `.WSC` file. This chapter focuses on creating a `.WSC` file manually. The wizard provides a fast way to create an initial `.WSC` file, but it does require an understanding of the required contents of the file before it can be used effectively.

Creating and using a Windows Script Component involves the following steps:

1. Create a .wsc file that contains one or more component definitions.
2. Deploy that file on all the computers that will run scripts that reference the components.
3. Register the components on each computer.
4. In a script, create an object of the component class using the CreateObject function.
5. Use the object to access the methods and properties of the class.

A .wsc file is a text file that is similar in format to a .ws script file. It contains XML elements that define the components and VBScript code to define the methods and properties of the components. Listing 10.1 shows a simple .wsc file, Simple.wsc. The details underlying the structure of this file are described in "Creating .wsc Files."

Listing 10.1 *Simple.wsc Component*

```
<!--
////////////////////////////////////////////////////////////////////////
$Workfile: Simple.wsc $ $Revision: 2 $ $Date: 11/10/98 4:09p $
$Archive: /Scripts/Simple.wsc $
Copyright (c) 1998 Tim Hill. All Rights Reserved.
////////////////////////////////////////////////////////////////////////
-->

<component id="Simple">
    <registration
        description="Simple"
        progid="Simple.WSC"
        version="1.00"
        classid="{91c38ef2-37bb-11d3-a228-0080c74acb6f}"
    />

    <public>
        <method name="Hello"/>
    </public>

<script language="VBScript">
    Function Hello()
        Hello = "Hello, world!"
    End Function
</script>
</component>
```

Before a Windows Script Component can be used, the .wsc file containing the component must be *registered* on the computer where it will be used. Deploying and registering components in large-scale installations can be automated using logon scripts, as described in Chapter 12, "Logon Scripts." Registration is described in detail in "Component Registration." The easiest way to register a component is via Windows Explorer. Locate the `Simple.wsc` component, and right-click it. Then select the **Register** option from the pop-up menu. This registers the component on the computer.

After a component is created and registered, it is used within a script in the same way that any other system-supplied object is used: An object is created using `CreateObject`, and then the methods and properties of that object are used. From the viewpoint of a script, a WSC component and a normal system object are identical. Listing 10.2 shows the `UseSimple.vbs` script, which uses the `Simple.wsc` component.

Listing 10.2 *`UseSimple.vbs` Script*

```
'//////////////////////////////////////////////////////////////////////////
' $Workfile: UseSimple.vbs $ $Revision: 1 $ $Date: 7/13/99 9:57a $
' $Archive: /Scripts/UseSimple.vbs $
' Copyright (c) 1998 Tim Hill. All Rights Reserved.
'//////////////////////////////////////////////////////////////////////////

' Simple "Hello World!" WSH Sample

Option Explicit
Dim oSimple
Set oSimple = CreateObject("Simple.WSC")
Wscript.Echo oSimple.Hello
Set oSimple = Nothing

'//////////////////////////////////////////////////////////////////////////
```

Executing the `UseSimple.vbs` script displays the message `"Hello, world!"`. This text is obtained from the `.Hello` method of the `Simple` component. When the `Wscript.Echo` statement in `UseSimple.vbs` executes, the expression containing `oSimple.Hello` is evaluated. This results in the `.Hello` method on the `Simple` component being invoked.

The remainder of this chapter examines the details surrounding creating and using Windows Script Components.

Creating *.WSC* Files

Windows Script Component files are similar to `.WS` script files introduced in Chapter 1. They are composed of a series of XML elements that define the component. The primary element used to define a component is the `component` element. The syntax of this element is:

```
<component [id="name"]>
    [component definition]
</component>
```

The component definition is contained entirely within the `component`. The `id` attribute, if present, assigns a unique id to the component. However, the `id` is not mandatory, and this attribute is only used internally—it does *not* define the component name when accessed from the `CreateObject` function.

Within the `component` element, additional elements define the component. Although there can be many different elements that define the component, the three most common elements are the `registration`, `public`, and `script` elements. These typically appear in order in the `component` element. Therefore, a component definition typically looks like this:

```
<component>
    <registration [registration info] />

    <public>
        [publication information]
    </public>

    <script language="VBScript">
        [script code for component]
    </script>
</component>
```

The `script` element contains VBScript source code that defines the component. This is similar to the `Class` statement described in Chapter 9 with the following differences:

- The code in the `script` element is *not* enclosed in a `Class` statement.
- Variables are declared using the `Dim` statement, not the `Public` or `Private` statements.
- Procedures are defined using the `Sub` or `Function` statements without any preceding `Public` or `Private` keyword.
- Procedural properties are *not* defined using the `Property Get`, `Property Let`, or `Property Set` keywords.

Thus, the script code within a `script` element simply consists of `Dim` statements, and procedure (subroutine and function) definitions. (There can also be executable statements that are *not* contained in procedures. See "Advanced Component Features" for more information.)

There can be multiple `script` elements within a component. Thus, like `.WS` files, a `.WSC` file can contain script code in many different script languages.

The `public` element is responsible for declaring, or *publishing*, the interface to the component. Only properties and methods published by this element are available to users of the component. Thus, the `public` element defines the interface to the component, whereas the `script` element defines the implementation of the component.

The *registration* Element

The `registration` element contains the information necessary to register a component on a computer. The registration process, described later in "Component Registration," uses this information to register the component with the operating system. After the registration is complete, objects that reference the component can be instantiated using the `CreateObject` function. The `registration` element contains the following information:

- *The ProgID of the component.* ProgIDs were described in Chapter 6, "Introducing Objects." The ProgID specified in the `registration` element is used in the `CreateObject` function to instantiate an object reference to the component. The ProgID is the "glue" that binds the component to a script that uses the component.
- *The GUID of the component.* Every component must specify a unique value known as a GUID (pronounced "goo-id").
- *A description of the component.* This is stored during registration, and it is used to provide a "friendly" description of the component.
- *The version of the component.* This is a string describing the component version, for example, "1.0."

Each of these items is specified in an attribute of the `registration` element. Table 10.2 shows each of these attributes:

Table 10.2 `registration` *Element Attributes*

Attribute	Meaning
`progid`	ProgID of the component
`classid`	GUID of the component
`description`	Description of the component
`version`	Version of the component

Thus, a simple `registration` element appears as:

```
<registration
    progid="Acme.SuperComponent"
    description="Acme Inc Super Component"
    classid="{B6660E65-3725-11d3-A228-0080C74ACB6F}"
    version="1.0"
/>
```

Choosing ProgID and GUID Values

The ProgID value chosen for a component will be used in the `CreateObject` function to access the component. It is, therefore, sensible to choose a ProgID that has mnemonic significance. However, ProgID values are global on a given computer. That is, every component, regardless of the source, must have a unique ProgID. So, choosing a common ProgID, such as `"SpellChecker"`, is not a good idea because it is quite possible someone else will use the same name.

One way to avoid collisions of ProgID names is to use a format like *`"company.component"`*, that is, prefix the component name with the company name.

The GUID also has the same constraints as the ProgID. It must be unique on the computer. In fact, the GUID must be unique *in the whole world*. To achieve this, Microsoft supplies special tools that generate a GUID, which is (statistically) guaranteed to be globally unique. Tools that generate GUIDs include:

- `UUIDGEN.EXE` This is a command line tool that generates a GUID upon demand, and it is available as part of Visual C++ and the Platform SDK products.
- `GUIDGEN.EXE` This is a GUI tool that generates a GUID upon demand, and it is available as part of Visual Basic, Visual C++, and the Platform SDK products.
- *The Windows Script Component Wizard* If you do not have access to either of the preceding tools, the WSC wizard will generate a GUID when it builds a prototype `.wsc` file.

Simple Properties

Like VBScript classes defined using the `Class` statement, simple properties in components are defined using variables. To define a simple property in a component, declare a variable using a `Dim` statement in the `script` element, and then publish the property using a `property` element in the `public` element. For example:

```
<component>
   <registration
      description="Test"
      progid="Test.WSC"
      version="1.00"
      classid="{342BB9A6-3729-11d3-A228-0080C74ACB6F}"
   />

   <public>
      <property name="Fish"/>
   </public>

<script language="VBScript">
   Dim Fish
</script>
</component>
```

Here, a component with a ProgID of "Test.WSC" contains a single simple property called .Fish. The variable to store the property value is declared using a Dim statement in the script element. The property element within the public element is what makes this variable a property of the component.

The property element is used to specify simple properties. Place all property elements within the public element. Each property element defines a single VBScript variable as a property. The name attribute of the property element defines the *external* name of the property. That is, the name that is used to reference the property from scripts that use the component. Typically (as in this example), the *internal* name of the property, that is the name of the VBScript variable, is the same as the external name. However, it is possible to associate a property with a variable of a different name. For example:

```
<component>
    <registration
        description="Test"
        progid="Test.WSC"
        version="1.00"
        classid="{342BB9A7-3729-11d3-A228-0080C74ACB6F}"
    />

    <public>
        <property name="Fish" internalname="nDataValue"/>
    </public>

<script language="VBScript">
    Dim nDataValue
</script>
</component>
```

Here, the name of the variable has been changed from Fish to nDataValue. To associate this variable with the .Fish property, the internalname attribute has been added to the property element. This attribute specifies the name of the VBScript variable if it is different from the external property name.

Using the internalname attribute does *not* alter the interface to the component. Scripts still access the property using the same .Fish name and are unaware that, internally, this references a variable named nDataValue.

Methods

Like VBScript classes defined using the Class statement, component methods are defined using procedures. Either subroutines or functions can be used. Defining a method in a component is similar to the technique used to define a simple property: the code for the method is placed in a script element and the method is then published in the public element. For methods, the method element publishes the method. For example:

```
<component>
    <registration
        description="Test"
        progid="Test.WSC"
        version="1.00"
        classid="{342BB9A8-3729-11d3-A228-0080C74ACB6F}"
    />

    <public>
        <property name="Fish" internalname="nDataValue"/>
        <method name="Cod">
            <parameter name="nValue"/>
        </method>
    </public>

<script language="VBScript">
    Dim nDataValue

    Sub Cod(nValue)
        nDataValue = nValue * 2
    End Sub
</script>
</component>
```

Here, the previous example has been extended with a method named `.Cod`. The method is implemented using the `Cod` subroutine in the `script` element and published using the `method` element.

Like the `property` element, the `method` element uses a `name` attribute to specify the external name of the method (that is, the name that users of the component specify to access the method). The `method` element also supports the `internalname` attribute if the external method name is different from the internal procedure name.

If a method takes one or more arguments, each argument must also be published using one `parameter` element per argument. These elements are placed in the body of the `method` element, as shown in the previous example. Each `parameter` element requires a `name` attribute that specifies the name of the argument.

Methods can also correspond to functions within the `script` element. The publication method is identical to that used for subroutines. The return value from a function does *not* need to be published in the `public` element.

Procedural Properties

Components also support procedural properties. Like procedural properties in VBScript classes, component procedural properties associate a property with executable script code.

Procedural properties in components are slightly different from VBScript class procedural properties:

- There is no equivalent of the `Property Set` VBScript procedural property.
- The VBScript `Property Get` procedural property corresponds to a "get" function defined in the `script` element.
- The VBScript `Property Let` procedural property corresponds to a "put" subroutine defined in the `script` element.

In VBScript classes, the `get`/`set`/`let` procedures for a property were distinguished with the appropriate `Property` *`xxx`* keywords. In components, the `get` and `put` procedures are distinguished using arbitrarily named procedures. To publish a procedural property, extend the `property` element with a `get` element and/or a `put` element. For example:

```
<component>
    <registration
        description="Test"
        progid="Test.WSC"
        version="1.00"
        classid="{342BB9A9-3729-11d3-A228-0080C74ACB6F}"
    />

    <public>
        <property name="Fish" internalname="nDataValue"/>
        <method name="Cod">
            <parameter name="nValue"/>
        </method>
        <property name="Salmon">
            <get internalname="GetSalmon"/>
        </property>
        <property name="Trout">
            <get/>
            <put/>
        </property>
    </public>

<script language="VBScript">
    Dim nDataValue
    Dim nTroutValue

    Sub Cod(nValue)
        nDataValue = nValue * 2
    End Sub

    Function GetSalmon
        GetSalmon = nDataValue + 1000
    End Function
```

```
    Function get_Trout
        get_Trout = nTroutValue
    End Function

    Sub put_Trout(nValue)
        MsgBox "About to set Trout to " & nValue
        nTroutValue = nValue
    End Sub
</script>
</component>
```

Here, the (rather fishy) component now has two new properties, and both of them are procedural. The first, `.Salmon`, is a read-only property implemented by the `GetSalmon` procedure. The corresponding `property` element now contains a `get` element. This element uses an `internalname` attribute to connect the property to the function that returns the value of the property. Because there is no `put` element, the property is read-only.

The second new property, `.Trout`, is a read-write property because it has both `get` and `put` elements within the corresponding `property` element. In this case, however, there is no `internalname` attribute. If the `internalname` attribute is not present in a `get` or `put` element, a procedure name is synthesized using the property external name and the prefix `"get_"` for the get property and `"put_"` for the put property.

Here is a simple VBScript script that uses the `Test` component shown in the last example:

```
Dim oTest
Set oTest = CreateObject("Test.WSC")
oTest.Fish = 1000
Wscript.Echo oTest.Fish
oTest.Cod 100
Wscript.Echo oTest.Salmon
oTest.Trout = 3.14
Wscript.Echo oTest.Trout
```

To experiment with this simple example, save the example component in a file (for example, `Test.wsc`), and then register the component by right clicking on it in Explorer and selecting **Register** from the menu. Then, save the example script previously shown (as `Test.vbs`, for example) and execute it.

Note

Do not place `Wscript.Echo` *statements in a component. The* `Wscript` *object is not available to components (unless it is passed as an argument to a method), and so this statement is not available in components. To trace execution within a component, use the* `MsgBox` *function from Chapter 4, "Built-In Functions." This is shown in the example* `Test` *component in the* `put_Trout` *procedure.* ◆

Default Properties

Like VBScript classes, it is possible to designate one (and only one) property in a component as the *default* property. The default property is accessed whenever an object variable is used in script code without an explicit property or method name.

To designate a property as the default property, add the special attribute `dispid="0"` to the desired `property` element. For example:

```
<component>
    .
    .

    <public>
        <property name="Salmon" dispid="0">
            <get internalname="GetSalmon"/>
        </property>
    </public>

<script language="VBScript">
    Dim nDataValue

    Function GetSalmon
        GetSalmon = nDataValue + 1000
    End Function
</script>
</component>
```

Here, the `.Salmon` property is designated as the default property.

Component Registration

Before a component is used, it must be *registered*. Registration adds the component to the database of components maintained by Windows on the computer. This database is stored in the system registry under the HKEY_CLASSES_ROOT key. The information registered allows the `CreateObject` function in VBScript to locate and load the component when needed. For more information on how `CreateObject` locates objects, see Chapter 6.

Two keys are created for a registered component. The first key, which has the same name as the ProgID of the component, contains additional keys that reference the GUID. The second key, which has the same name as the GUID of the component, contains the information needed to load and instantiate an object that references the component.

Components can be registered in either of two ways:

- Interactively via Windows Explorer
- From the command line using the REGSVR32 utility

To register a component interactively, right-click on the `.wsc` file in Windows Explorer and select the **Register** command from the pop-up menu. The component is registered and a dialog box appears to confirm this. The `.wsc` file is scanned for syntax errors at registration time, and so it is possible that one or more error dialogs can appear and registration can fail if the `.wsc` file contains errors.

To register a component from the command line, use the REGSVR32 utility. Specify the full path name to the `.wsc` file *as an Internet style URL*. For example:

```
C:\>regsvr32 file:c:\scripts\simple.wsc
```

Here, the `file:` syntax specifies that this URL references a local disk file.

It is also possible to specify a UNC name when registering a component. For example:

```
C:\>regsvr32 file:\\mycomputer\share\simple.wsc
```

Components can also be *unregistered* using similar methods. Unregistration removes the component information from the system registry.

To unregister a component interactively, right-click on the `.wsc` file in Windows Explorer, and select the **Unregister** command from the pop-up menu.

To unregister a component from the command line, use the REGSVR32 utility with the `/u` switch. For example:

```
C:\>regsvr32 /u file:c:\scripts\simple.wsc
```

The ProgID can be specified instead of the `.wsc` file name when unregistering. For example:

```
C:\>regsvr32 /u Simple.WSC
```

The *FileScan.wsc* Component

To illustrate the use of components, the `RDir.vbs` script from the last chapter can be broken up into two parts: a component in the `FileScan.wsc` file and a small client script in the `RDir2.vbs` file.

Listing 10.3 shows the `FileScan.wsc` component.

Listing 10.3 `FileScan.wsc` *Component*

```
<?xml version="1.0"?>
<?component error="true"?>
<!--
////////////////////////////////////////////////////////////////////////////
$Workfile: FileScan.wsc $ $Revision: 1 $ $Date: 11/10/98 4:09p $
$Archive: /Scripts/FileScan.wsc $
Copyright (c) 1998 Tim Hill. All Rights Reserved.
////////////////////////////////////////////////////////////////////////////
-->
```

continues ▶

Listing 10.3 *continued*

```
<component id="FileScan">
    <registration
        description="File Scanning Component"
        progid="FileScan.WSC"
        version="1.00"
        classid="{91c38ef1-37bb-11d3-a228-0080c74acb6f}"
    />

    <public>
        <property name="Expr"/>
        <property name="MatchFullPath"/>
        <property name="ScanSubFolders"/>
        <method name="Reset"/>
        <property name="Count">
            <get internalname="Count"/>
        </property>
        <method name="Execute">
            <parameter name="sPath"/>
        </method>
        <property name="Item" dispid="0">
            <get internalname="Item">
                <parameter name="nIndex"/>
            </get>
        </property>
    </public>

<script language="VBScript">
<![CDATA[
    Dim Expr                                    ' Reg expr to match
    Dim MatchFullPath                           ' True to match full path
    Dim ScanSubFolders                          ' True to scan subfolders
    Dim sFiles                                  ' List of matching files
    Dim nCount                                  ' Count of matches

    ' Reset object (delete all file matches)
    Sub Reset
        nCount = 0                              ' Mark no files
        sFiles = Empty                          ' Empty the files array
    End Sub

    ' Return current file count (R/O)
    Function Count
        Count = CInt(nCount)                    ' Just return count
    End Function

    ' Execute search (build file list)
    Sub Execute(sPath)
        Dim oFSO, oFolder, oRE
        Set oFSO = CreateObject("Scripting.FileSystemObject")
        Set oFolder = oFSO.GetFolder(sPath)     ' Get folder path
        Set oRE = New RegExp
        oRE.Pattern = Expr                      ' Set match pattern
        oRE.IgnoreCase = True                   ' Ignore case
        MatchFiles oRE, oFolder                 ' Go match files here
    End Sub
```

```
    Sub MatchFiles(oRE, oFolder)                    ' Match file in folder
        Dim oFile, oSubFolder
        For Each oFile In oFolder.Files             ' Scan all files
            If MatchFullPath Then
                If oRE.Test(oFile.Path) Then        ' Full path match
                    AddFile oFile.Path              ' Add if match
                End If
            Else
                If oRE.Test(oFile.Name) Then        ' Name match
                    AddFile oFile.Path              ' Add if match
                End If
            End If
        Next
        If ScanSubFolders Then                      ' If required..
            For Each oSubFolder In oFolder.SubFolders   ' Scan subs
                MatchFiles oRE, oSubFolder
            Next
        End If
    End Sub

    ' Get individual files (default property)
    Function Item(nIndex)                           ' Get indexed item
        Dim ixMajor, ixMinor
        If (nIndex >= nCount) Or (nIndex >= 1024 * 4096) Then
            Item = ""                               ' Flag overflow
        Else
            ixMajor = nIndex / 4096                 ' Compute major index
            ixMinor = nIndex And 4095               ' Compute minor index
            Item = sFiles(ixMajor)(ixMinor)         ' Get path name
        End If
    End Function

    ' Add new file item to dynamic array
    Sub AddFile(sPath)
        Dim ix, ixMajor, ixMinor, a                 ' Array indices
        If IsEmpty(sFiles) Then                     ' If no array yet..
            ReDim sFiles(1023)                      ' Space for 1024 sets
        End If
        ix = nCount                                 ' Get current index
        nCount = nCount + 1                         ' Bump counter
        If ix >= 1024 * 4096 Then Exit Sub          ' Exit if overflow!!
        ixMajor = ix / 4096                         ' Compute major index
        ixMinor = ix And 4095                       ' Compute minor index
        If IsEmpty(sFiles(ixMajor)) Then            ' If new array needed
            ReDim a(4095)                           ' Create temp array
            sFiles(ixMajor) = a                     ' Copy to populate
        End If
        sFiles(ixMajor)(ixMinor) = sPath            ' Add path to array
    End Sub
]]>
</script>
</component>
```

The FileScan component is adapted directly from the FileScan class of Chapter 9. The component has the same methods and properties as the class. All the differences are related to packaging the functionality as a component. First and most significant is that the FileScan component now lives in a file of its own, instead of being part of the RDir.vbs file. This is, of course, the main advantage of components—they are independent of the script files that use them and are available for use by any script that knows the ProgID of the component.

The remaining changes account for the different syntax used in components:

- The Property Get and Property Let procedural properties are replaced with normal subroutines and functions.
- The Public and Private variable declarations are replaced with Dim declarations.
- The Public and Private keywords before procedure declarations are removed.
- The entire component is enclosed in a component element.
- All the VBScript code is enclosed in a script element.
- The methods and properties of the component are published in a public component, and they are linked to the procedures and variables in the script element.
- Registration information for the component is supplied by the registration element.

Apart from these changes, however, all the functional script code remains unchanged. The component is used by the RDir2.vbs script, which is shown in Listing 10.4.

Listing 10.4 *Rdir2.vbs Script*

```
'//////////////////////////////////////////////////////////////////////////////
' $Workfile: RDir2.vbs $ $Revision: 1 $ $Date: 7/13/99 9:57a $
' $Archive: /Scripts/RDir2.vbs $
' Copyright (c) 1999 Tim Hill. All Rights Reserved.
'//////////////////////////////////////////////////////////////////////////////

' Regular expression file search using FileScan class

Option Explicit
Dim oFileScan, oFSO, ix
Set oFSO = CreateObject("Scripting.FileSystemObject")

' Show usage if no arguments
If Wscript.Arguments.Count < 1 Then
    Wscript.Echo "usage: filescan reg-expr [path...]"
    Wscript.Quit(0)
End If
```

```
' Create the FileScan object and set the RE from cmd line
Set oFileScan = CreateObject("FileScan.WSC")
oFileScan.Expr = Wscript.Arguments(0)
oFileScan.ScanSubFolders = True

' Now process all arguments, or use current dir if none
If Wscript.Arguments.Count > 1 Then
    For ix = 1 To Wscript.Arguments.Count - 1
        oFileScan.Execute oFSO.GetAbsolutePathName(Wscript.Arguments(ix))
    Next
Else
    oFileScan.Execute oFSO.GetAbsolutePathName(".")
End If

' Display the results
For ix = 0 To oFileScan.Count
    Wscript.Echo oFileScan(ix)
Next

Wscript.Quit(oFileScan.Count)
```

The `RDir2.vbs` script is changed even less than the `FileScan` component. The biggest change is the deletion of the `FileScan` class because this functionality is now handled by the `FileScan` component. The only other change is to alter the way in which the object is created. In `RDir.vbs`, the `oFileScan` object was created as follows:

```
Set oFileScan = New FileScan
```

In `RDir2.vbs`, the `oFileScan` object is created as follows:

```
Set oFileScan = CreateObject("FileScan.WSC")
```

This is the *only* code change made to this script. Because both `oFileScan` objects support the same interface, the remaining code works unaltered with either the class or component versions of `FileScan`.

Advanced Component Features

Components offer several additional features not available via VBScript classes. These are described in this section.

Initializing an Object's State

In VBScript classes, all the variables (both `Public` and `Private`) that compose the state of the object are initialized to `Empty`. This means that methods and properties of the object must account for the possibility that state information is not yet initialized by testing to see if a state variable is empty before using its value. This can be inconvenient when there are many state variables or a large number of references to them.

In this respect, components are superior to VBScript classes, in that a component can execute *initialization* code *when the object is created*. This script code executes during the invocation of the `CreateObject` function that creates the object, and therefore, it executes *before* the methods or properties of the object are accessed. This gives the component an opportunity to initialize the state variables to any desired default values. In addition, it typically allows much of the special empty testing associated with classes to be removed because the methods and properties can rely on the state information being valid.

To add initialization code to a component, simply include it within the `script` element, but place it *outside* of any procedure. The code is then executed once for each object that is created, when the object is created. For example:

```
<component>
    <registration
        description="Test2"
        progid="Test2.WSC"
        version="1.00"
        classid="{342BB9A7-3729-11d3-A228-0080C74ACB6F}"
    />

    <public>
        <property name="Fish"/>
    </public>

<script language="VBScript">
    Dim Fish
    Fish = "halibut"            ' Initialize the Fish property
    MsgBox "Object Initialized"
</script>
</component>
```

Here is a script that uses this object:

```
Dim oFish
MsgBox "Starting"
Set oFish = CreateObject("Test2.WSC")
MsgBox "Done. Fish=" & oFish.Fish
```

If the `Test2` component is registered and the example script executed, three dialog boxes will appear. The first will say `Starting`. The second, which comes from the component, will say `Object Initialized`. The final dialog box will say `Fish=halibut`. This is the value of the `.Fish` property for a newly created `Test2` object because the `Fish` variable in the object is initialized with this value by the assignment statement in the `script` element.

Placing Multiple Components in a Single File

It is possible, and frequently desirable, to place more than one component in a single `.wsc` file. This allows several related components to be packaged together. To place more than one component in a file, place multiple `component` elements inside a single `package` element. For example:

```
<package>
    <component id="component1">
        [definition of component1]
    </component>

    <component id="component2">
        [definition of component2]
    </component>
</package>
```

Components packaged together like this are identical to components that are placed by themselves in a file. The only difference is that when a file containing multiple components is registered (either using Windows Explorer or the REGSVR32 utility), *all* the components in the package are registered at once. Similarly, when a file is unregistered, all the components are unregistered.

Although there is no limit to the number of components that can be placed in a single file, there is some overhead associated with processing large files. VBScript preprocesses all script code before execution, and if the script is *very* big, this processing can take a noticeable amount of time. A good rule of thumb is to try to keep the size of `.wsc` files to less than 5000 lines of code.

Accessing Components via *GetObject*

The normal (and recommended) way to access a component is via the `CreateObject` function. However, WSC also supports an alternative access to components via the `GetObject` function and the `script` moniker.

The primary advantage of the `GetObject` access method is that it does not require the component to be registered. The disadvantage, however, is that it requires that the full path name of the `.wsc` file is known. (Contrast this to the `CreateObject` function, where only the ProgID needs to be known.) Therefore, extensive use of the `GetObject` function to access components can lead to scripts becoming dependent on a fixed path and folder structure, making the scripts non-portable from installation to installation.

To use the `GetObject` function to access a component, supply the path name to the component prefixed by the `"script:"` moniker. For example:

```
Dim oLog
Set oLog = GetObject("script:c:\scripts\log.wsc")
```

Here, the component in the `log.wsc` file is instantiated to create an object reference stored in the `oLog` variable.

If a `.WSC` file contains multiple components, the specific component to instantiate can be specified by following the path name with the component ID. Separate the two items with a `#` character. For example:

```
Dim oLog
Set oLog = GetObject("script:c:\scripts\log.wsc#readlog")
```

Here, the `readlog` component in the `log.wsc` file is explicitly instantiated. The component ID is named in the `.WSC` file using the `id` attribute of the `component` element. See "Placing Multiple Components in a Single File" for more information.

If a `.WSC` file contains multiple components and if a component ID is not explicitly specified, the first component in the file is instantiated.

The path specified for the `"script:"` moniker can also be a URL, so it is possible to load a component from a Web server. For example:

```
Dim oLog
Set oLog = GetObject("script:http://scriptserver/log.wsc")
```

Here, the `log.wsc` component is located on a remote Web server.

Running Code During Registration

The registration process described in "Component Registration" places information in the system registry, which allows a component to be instantiated using a ProgID. Sometimes it is necessary for the component itself to participate in the registration process. For example, the component could display a copyright message, or initialize some additional registry keys with default values. To enable this kind of activity, it is possible to execute script code during the registration process.

To specify the script to execute during registration, include a `script` element *within* the `registration` element. Then, within the `script` element, define a function named `Register`. Similarly, define a function in this element named `Unregister` to execute code when the component is unregistered on the computer. For example:

```
<component>
    <registration
        description="Test"
        progid="Test.WSC"
        version="1.00"
        classid="{342BB9A8-3729-11d3-A228-0080C74ACB6F}"
    >
        <script language="VBScript">
            Function Register
                MsgBox "Registering component."
            End Function
```

```
        Function Unregister
            MsgBox "Unregistering component."
        End Function
    </script>
  </registration>

  [rest of component]
</component>
```

Both the `Register` and `Unregister` functions must be supplied. Supplying one without the other will cause registration or unregistration to fail.

Note

Note the subtle change to the preceding `registration` *element. Up until this point, all* `registration` *elements have been empty elements, and so they have been composed of the usual XML empty element syntax:*

```
<registration attributes />
```

To place a `script` *element inside the* `registration` *element, the element is no longer empty. Therefore, it must be broken into the usual open/close element pair:*

```
<registration attributes>
</registration>
```

The change at the end of the opening element, from `/>` *to* `>`*, is easy to miss.* ◆

Using Well-Formed XML

Windows Script Component files (`.wsc` files) and WSH 2.0 script files (`.ws` files) use XML syntax and XML elements to delimit the file structure. However, by default WSH uses a *relaxed* form of XML that is less demanding than the more strict rules of formal XML syntax. It is also possible to specify that the syntax of a `.wsc` or `.ws` file conform to the strict syntax of the XML specification. To do this, add the special XML processing instruction *at the very start* of the file. This instruction is formatted as follows:

```
<?xml version="1.0"?>
```

If this special instruction is placed at the start of the file, the stricter rules of XML formatting are applied. This has the following effects:

- Element names and attribute names are case-sensitive. Therefore, the `script` element is valid, whereas the `Script` element is not. All the examples in this chapter use the strictly correct case for element and attribute names.
- All attribute values must be enclosed in double quotes. This is true regardless of the type of the attribute—even numeric values must be quoted. For example, the attribute `dispid=0` is invalid, whereas `dispid="0"` is valid.

- The characters "<", "&" and ">" have special meaning and must be escaped. If any of these characters are used as literal text within an element, they must be replaced by their quoted equivalents, "<", "&" and ">".

The last rule is awkward. It means that the characters "<", "&" and ">" must be replaced with the ugly XML escapes "<", "&" and ">" in the body of every element, *including* script elements. Unfortunately, these are common characters in VBScript, and so expressions like "a < b" must be replaced by "a < b".

Fortunately, XML has a mechanism to avoid this difficulty—the CDATA section. The CDATA section is a pair of special enclosing markers that delimit text that is *not* XML conformant and that can contain any characters, even the three special characters previously noted.

The CDATA section markers are "<![CDATA[" to start a CDATA section and "]]>" to end a section. To use these markers, place them within a script element, but surround the entire body of VBScript code with the markers. For example:

```
<?xml version="1.0"?>
<component>
    [registration etc information]

<script language="VBScript">
<![CDATA[
    [place all VBScript code here, within markers]
]]>
</script>
</component>
```

Other Component XML Elements

.WSC files support many additional, less used XML elements that are described here.

The ?component? processing instruction is used to control error handling in the component. Place this instruction directly after the ?xml? processing instruction in the file. The instruction supports two attributes: error and debug, which can be set to either true or false.

- If error is true, detailed error messages are generated if errors are found in the component file during registration or execution.
- If debug is true, debugging of the script in the component is enabled.

For example:

```
<?xml version="1.0"?>
<?component error="true"?>
```

The `comment` element can be used to add comments to a `.WSC` file. It can be placed anywhere in a `component` element. For example:

```
<component>
    <comment>This is a comment</comment>
</component>
```

The `object` element provides an alternative way to the `CreateObject` function to create objects *within* a component. Typically, objects needed within a component are created using the `CreateObject` function. However, if an object is used globally by the component, it can be created once using the `object` element. Place this element within the `component` element. The `object` element requires two attributes: the `id` attribute specifies the name of the object, and the `progid` attribute specifies the ProgID for the object. For example:

```
<component>
    [registration info etc]
    <object id="oFSO" progid="Scripting.FileSystemObject"/>

<script language="VBScript">
    Sub GetFile
        Dim oFile
        Set oFile = oFSO.GetFile("c:\mydata.log")
    End Sub
</script>
</component>
```

The `resource` element provides a mechanism to define resources for the component. A *resource* is an arbitrary item of string data that is defined outside of the script code. Resources are available regardless of the script language, and they have the advantage of being gathered in one place outside of the actual script code. This can often make script maintenance easier.

Individual `resource` elements use a single attribute, `id`, to name the resource. The element content is the resource value. To access a resource within a script, use the `GetResource` function, and supply the resource name as an argument. For example:

```
<component>
    [registration info etc]
    <resource id="copyright">Copyright  1999 Macmillan</resource>

<script language="VBScript">
    Sub ShowCopyright
        MsgBox GetResource("copyright")
    End Sub
</script>
</component>
```

Summary

Windows Script Components provide an effective means to encapsulate script functionality as a COM object. Component objects can be created and manipulated using the normal object access mechanisms of VBScript, such as `CreateObject`.

Because a component is defined in a distinct script file and accessed only via a ProgID, many scripts can use the same component, thus allowing script code inside a component to be reused in many different script projects. The only disadvantage of components is that each one must be registered on each computer where it is used.

Part III

Sample Script Solutions

11

A Script Developer's Toolkit

This chapter and the remaining chapters of this book, focus on using the information and techniques from the first two parts of the book to present a series of ready-to-use sample scripts. These scripts can be used either "as-is" or modified to suit local requirements.

The scripts in this chapter provide a toolkit that is used by the scripts in the remaining chapters; these tools also can be used by your own custom scripts. The scripts presented in this chapter are:

- The `Template.vbs` script, which provides a skeleton script that can be used as a starting point when developing a new script.
- The `MTPLib.wsc` component library, which provides several useful component objects that can be used in other scripts.

Note

As with all the sample scripts in this book, the scripts in this chapter should be run using the CSCRIPT host unless otherwise noted. The examples shown assume that CSCRIPT is the default WSH host. (See Chapter 1, "Introducing WSH," for information on selecting the default WSH host.) ◆

The *Template.vbs* Script

The `Template.vbs` script is a skeleton script that can be used as the starting point for new script projects. The template is designed for scripts that are run from the command line (that is, scripts that use the CSCRIPT host). To use this script:

1. Copy the `Template.vbs` script to a new name with a `.VBS` file type.
2. Edit the `ShowHelpMessage` procedure to add a brief help message.
3. Edit the `Main` procedure to provide the script functionality.

4. Edit the `g_sVersion` variable declaration at the start of the script to reflect the version number of the script.
5. Add any additional procedures and classes required by the `Main` procedure.

Scripts based on the `Template.vbs` script have the following built-in functionality:

- They check for and handle help requests via the `"/?"`, `"/help"`, `"-?"`, or `"-help"` command line argument.
- They automatically display a simple sign-on banner.
- The return value from the `Main` function is passed back to the command shell as the process exit code (where it can be checked using the `%ERRORLEVEL%` shell variable or `IF ERRORLEVEL` shell command).
- Script tracing can be enabled by setting the shell environment variable `WSHTRACE` to a trace level before the script executes.
- Several global objects are predefined: `g_oFSO` contains a `FileSystem` object reference, and `g_oShell` contains a `WshShell` object reference.
- Several global variables are predefined: `g_sScriptPath` contains the script path, `g_sScriptName` contains the script name (no path), `g_sScriptFolder` contains the script folder (that is, the folder containing the `.VBS` file), and `g_sVersion` contains the version number of the script.

When a script based on `Template.vbs` executes, it initializes the predefined global variables and objects, and then checks for a help command-line argument (for example, `"/?"`, and so forth). If this is found, the `ShowHelpMessage` procedure is called to display help, and the script terminates. Otherwise, the `Main` procedure is called. The return value from this procedure is then used as the exit value from the script.

The `Template.vbs` script is shown in Listing 11.1.

Listing 11.1 *`Template.vbs` Script*

```
'//////////////////////////////////////////////////////////////////////////////
' $Workfile: Template.vbs $ $Revision: 1 $ $Date: 7/18/99 10:42p $
' $Archive: /Scripts/Template.vbs $
' Copyright (c) 1998 Tim Hill. All Rights Reserved.
'//////////////////////////////////////////////////////////////////////////////

' Template for creating scripts

' Explicit variable declaration and standard globals
Option Explicit
Dim g_sScriptPath, g_sScriptName, g_sScriptFolder, g_sVersion
Dim g_nTraceLevel
```

```
Dim g_oShell, g_oFSO
Dim s, ix, i

' Set standard globals and create global objects
g_sVersion = "1.0"
g_sScriptPath = Wscript.ScriptFullName
g_sScriptName = Wscript.ScriptName
g_sScriptFolder = Left(g_sScriptPath, Len(g_sScriptPath) - Len(g_sScriptName))
Set g_oShell = CreateObject("Wscript.Shell")
Set g_oFSO = CreateObject("Scripting.FileSystemObject")

' Setup trace control from WSHTRACE environment variable
i = g_oShell.Environment("Process").Item("WSHTRACE")
If IsNumeric(i) Then g_nTraceLevel = CInt(i) Else g_nTraceLevel = 0

' Check for -help, -? etc help request on command line
If Wscript.Arguments.Count > 0 Then
    s = LCase(Wscript.Arguments(0))
    If (s = "-help") Or (s = "-?") Or (s = "/help") Or (s = "/?") Then
        ShowHelpMessage
        Wscript.Quit(1)
    End If
End If

' Show signon banner, then call Main function
ix = Instr(g_sScriptName, ".")
If ix <> 0 Then s = Left(g_sScriptName, ix - 1) Else s = g_sScriptName
Wscript.Echo s & " version " & g_sVersion & vbCRLF
i = Main

' Release standard global objects, then exit script
Set g_oFSO = Nothing
Set g_oShell = Nothing
Wscript.Quit(i)

'//////////////////////////////////////////////////////////////////////////////
' Main
' Main function called to embody primary script logic
'
' Returns           Exit code from script
'
Function Main
    Trace 1, "+++Main"

    ' Return value is passed to Wscript.Quit as script exit code
    Main = 0
End Function

'//////////////////////////////////////////////////////////////////////////////
' ShowHelpMessage
' Display help message
'
```

continues ▶

Listing 11.1 *continued*

```
Sub ShowHelpMessage
    Trace 1, "+++ShowHelpMessage"
    Wscript.Echo "Place help text here."
End Sub

'////////////////////////////////////////////////////////////////////////////
' Trace
' Debug trace output controlled by g_nTraceLevel and WSHTRACE env var
'
' nLevel          Trace level. Only display if <= WSHTRACE env var
' sText           Text to display
'
Sub Trace(nLevel, sText)
    if g_nTraceLevel >= nLevel Then Wscript.Echo sText
End Sub

'////////////////////////////////////////////////////////////////////////////
```

Template.vbs Implementation Details

The implementation of `Template.vbs` is quite straightforward. The various global variables and objects previously mentioned are initialized first. The `g_sScriptFolder` variable is easily derived from the `g_sScriptPath` and `g_sScriptName` variables as follows:

```
g_sScriptFolder = Left(g_sScriptPath, Len(g_sScriptPath) - Len(g_sScriptName))
```

By definition, the script folder name is the script path name with the actual script name discarded from the end. The number of characters to discard is, therefore, `Len(g_sScriptName)`, and so the required number of characters is the difference between this and the length of the full path. This count is then used with the `Left` function to derive the folder name.

Help request processing is equally trivial, except that the script uses the `LCase` function to ensure that both `"/help"` and `"/HELP"` are acceptable.

The trace facility in `Template.vbs` is more interesting. Tracing allows a complex script with a large number of internal facilities to be monitored. Each procedure name is displayed as the procedure is invoked, allowing script execution to be viewed. This can often assist in script debugging.

The `Trace` procedure provides core trace facilities. Each procedure that is to be traced invokes this procedure, passing two arguments: a "trace level" (explained later) and a trace string. For example:

```
Trace 1, "+++Main"
```

By convention, trace strings start with the string `"+++"` so that they can be distinguished in the output from the normal output of the script. The trace string can also include the values of arguments and local variables, so that internal program values can be viewed. For example:

```
Trace 1, "+++DumpData " & CStr(nDataLevel)
```

The first argument to the `Trace` procedure specifies the *trace level*. The trace level controls the amount of detail output by the `Trace` procedure. The global variable `g_nTraceLevel` specifies the trace level for the script, and only those trace requests with a trace level *less than or equal to* this value are displayed. Thus, if `g_nTraceLevel` is 2, only trace requests at levels 1 and 2 are displayed. The trace level thus controls the verbosity of the tracing. If `g_nTraceLevel` is 1, only basic trace output appears, if `g_nTraceLevel` is 2, more trace output appears, and so on. A trace level of 0 suppresses all trace output. This assumes that the script calls the `Trace` function with the trace level set appropriately. Typically, a script calls `Trace` with a trace level of 1 for procedure invocation tracing, a level of 2 to show major data within a procedure, and a level of 3 to show internal procedure details, but these are only guidelines.

What makes the trace facility useful is the way in which the `g_nTraceLevel` global variable is set. This variable is set by reading the `WSHTRACE` environment variable, as follows:

```
i = g_oShell.Environment("Process").Item("WSHTRACE")
If IsNumeric(i) Then g_nTraceLevel = CInt(i) Else g_nTraceLevel = 0
```

The `g_nTraceLevel` variable is set to 0 if the environment variable does not exist.

Thus tracing can be controlled *outside* the script without editing the script text in any way. To control script tracing, simply open a Command Prompt window, enter a `Set` shell command, and then run the script. For example:

```
C:\>Set WSHTRACE=2
C:\>Template /help
```

In summary, the `WSHTRACE` environment variable is loaded into the `g_nTraceLevel` variable at script start-up. The `Trace` procedure is invoked with a trace level and a trace string. If the trace level is greater than that specified by `g_nTraceLevel`, the trace string is displayed.

Note

For compatibility with older WSH versions, the example `Trace` *function uses the* `Wscript.Echo` *statement to display trace information. However, tracing is more useful if the trace output can be captured in a log file. This can be easily implemented by changing the* `Trace` *function to write the trace strings to a text stream.*

To do this, create and initialize a new global object at the start of the script to manage the text stream, and then use this object in the `Trace` *procedure. For example:*

```
Set g_oTraceStream = g_oFSO.CreateTextFile(g_sScriptPath & ".Log", True)
```

Here is the revised Trace procedure:

```
Sub Trace(nLevel, sText)
    if g_nTraceLevel > nLevel Then g_oTraceStream.WriteLine sText
End Sub
```

Another possible variant is to send all trace output to the `StdErr` *predefined stream.* ◆

Using *Template.vbs* with WSCRIPT

As previously noted, `Template.vbs` is designed for use with scripts that use the CSCRIPT host. However, with a few alterations, `Template.vbs` can be used as the basis of scripts that use the WSCRIPT host. The changes required are:

- The `ShowHelpMessage` script should create a single string containing help information and then display it using the `MsgBox` function.
- Tracing *must* be modified to output to a text stream. If this is not done, every trace message will pop up a dialog box, which is distracting.

These changes are not difficult and are left as an exercise for the reader.

The *MTPLib.wsc* Component Library

The `MTPLib.wsc` script is a component library containing a small set of useful components. These components are used by several of the sample scripts presented in subsequent chapters. As with all `.WSC` components, this script must be registered on each computer where it is used. See Chapter 10, "Windows Script Components," for more information on component registration, and Chapter 12, "Logon Scripts," for techniques on automating component registration using logon scripts.

The components provided by the `MTPLib.wsc` library are:

- The `MTP.Info` component, which allows scripts to validate the version of the library
- The `MTP.CmdArg` and `MTP.CmdArgs` components, which provide a robust and flexible command-line parsing facility
- The `MTP.BinaryTreeNode` and `MTP.BinaryTree` components, which provide a generic binary tree facility that can sort object collections based upon user-supplied criteria

The `MTPLib.wsc` component is shown in Listing 11.2.

Listing 11.2 *MTPLib.wsc Component Library*

```
<?xml version="1.0"?>
<?component error="true"?>
<!--
////////////////////////////////////////////////////////////////////////////////
$Workfile: MTPLib.wsc $ $Revision: 1 $ $Date: 11/10/98 4:09p $
$Archive: /Scripts/MTPLib.wsc $
Copyright (c) 1998-99 Tim Hill. All Rights Reserved.
////////////////////////////////////////////////////////////////////////////////
-->

<package>

<!-- MTP.Info Component -->
<!-- Provides basic information on current MTPLib version -->
<component id="MTP.Info">
    <!-- Registration -->
    <registration
        description="MTP Library Info Component"
        progid="MTP.Info"
        version="1.0"
        classid="{91c38ef0-37bb-11d3-a228-0080c74acb6f}"
    />

    <!-- Resources -->
    <resource id="name">MTP Library</resource>
    <resource id="copyright">Copyright (c) 1998-99 Tim Hill. All Rights Reserved.</resource>
    <resource id="version">1.0</resource>

    <!-- Public Interface -->
    <public>
        <!-- Library name (RO) -->
        <property name="Name" dispid="0">
            <get/>
        </property>
         <!-- Copyright notice (RO) -->
         <property name="Copyright">
            <get/>
        </property>
        <!-- Library version (RO) -->
        <property name="Version">
            <get/>
        </property>
    </public>

<!-- Implementation -->
<script language="VBScript">
<![CDATA[
    ' Name Property (RO)
    Function get_Name
        get_Name = GetResource("name")
    End Function
```

continues ▶

Listing 11.2 *continued*

```
    ' Copyright property (RO)
    Function get_Copyright
        get_Copyright = GetResource("copyright")
    End Function

    ' Version property (RO)
    Function get_Version
        get_Version = GetResource("version")
    End Function
]]>
</script>
</component>


<!-- MTP.CmdArg Component -->
<!-- Encapsulates and parses a single command-line argument -->
<component id="MTP.CmdArg">
    <!-- Registration -->
    <registration
        description="MTP Command Line Argument"
        progid="MTP.CmdArg"
        version="1.0"
        classid="{91c38ef3-37bb-11d3-a228-0080c74acb6f}"
    />

    <!-- Public Interface -->
    <public>
        <!-- Text contains raw argument text (default, RW) -->
        <property name="Text" dispid="0"><get/><put/></property>
        <!-- Delims contains switch prefix delimiter set (RW) -->
        <property name="Delims"><get/><put/></property>
        <!-- Argument type properties (RO) -->
        <property name="IsNormal"><get/></property>
        <property name="IsSwitch"><get/></property>
        <property name="IsMacro"><get/></property>
        <!-- Parse results: type, delim, name and value (RO) -->
        <property name="ArgType"><get/></property>
        <property name="Delim"><get/></property>
        <property name="Name"><get/></property>
        <property name="Value"><get/></property>
        <!-- Index property is for CmdArgs use only -->
        <property name="Index"/>
    </public>

<!-- Implementation -->
<script language="VBScript">
<![CDATA[
    Const cNormal = 1                           ' Normal type
    Const cSwitch = 2                           ' Switch type
    Const cMacro = 4                            ' Macro type
    Dim sDelims                                 ' Delimiter set
    Dim sText                                   ' Actual arg text (R/W)
```

```
Dim nType                                ' Type mask (1,2,4)
Dim sDelim                               ' Switch delim text or ""
Dim sName                                ' Switch/macro name
Dim sValue                               ' Switch/macro value
Dim Index                                ' For CmdArgs use only
Dim bDirty                               ' Text needs reparse

' Set default values for properties
sDelims = "" : sText = "" : bDirty = True

' Get/set argument text (force reparse)
Function get_Text
    get_Text = CStr(sText)               ' Get current text
End Function
Sub put_Text(sValue)
    sText = CStr(sValue)                 ' Set new text
    bDirty = True                        ' Request reparse
End Sub

' Get/set delimiters (force reparse)
Function get_Delims                      ' Get current delims
    get_Delims = CStr(sDelims)
End Function
Sub put_Delims(sValue)
    sDelims = CStr(sValue)               ' New delimiters
    bDirty = True                        ' Request reparse
End Sub

' Get argument type
Function get_IsNormal
    If bDirty = True Then Parse          ' Parse if needed
    get_IsNormal = (nType And cNormal) <> 0 ' True if normal
End Function
Function get_IsSwitch
    If bDirty = True Then Parse          ' Parse if needed
    get_IsSwitch = (nType And cSwitch) <> 0 ' True if switch
End Function
Function get_IsMacro
    If bDirty = True Then Parse          ' Parse if needed
    get_IsMacro = (nType And cMacro) <> 0   ' True if macro
End Function

' Get parse results: type, delim, name and value
Function get_ArgType                     ' Get type
    If bDirty = True Then Parse          ' Parse if needed
    get_ArgType = nType                  ' Return the type
End Function
Function get_Delim                       ' Get delimiter
    If bDirty = True Then Parse          ' Parse if needed
    get_Delim = sDelim                   ' Return the delim
End Function
Function get_Name                        ' Get name
    If bDirty = True Then Parse          ' Parse if needed
    get_Name = sName
```

continues ▶

Listing 11.2 *continued*

```
    End Function
    Function get_Value                               ' Get value
        If bDirty = True Then Parse                  ' Parse if needed
        get_Value = sValue
    End Function

    ' Parse or reparse argument
    Sub Parse
        Dim oRE
        bDirty = False                               ' Mark done parsing
        nType = cNormal                              ' Set default results
        sDelim = "" : sName = sText : sValue = ""
        If sText = "" Then Exit Sub                  ' Empty: all done
        Set oRE = New RegExp                         ' Get RE object
        If sDelims = "" Then
            oRE.Pattern = "^\s*([/+-])([^:=]+)([:=](.*)¦)"
        Else
            oRE.Pattern = "^\s*([" & sDelims & "])([^:=]+)([:=](.*)¦)"
        End If
        If oRE.Test(sText) Then                      ' If switch..
            nType = cSwitch                          ' Set switch type
            sDelim = oRE.Replace(sText, "$1")        ' Get delimiter
            sName = oRE.Replace(sText, "$2")         ' .. and name
            sValue = oRE.Replace(sText, "$4")        ' .. and value
            Exit Sub                                 ' .. and all done
        End If
        oRE.Pattern = "([^=]+)=(.*)"
        If oRE.Test(sText) Then                      ' If macro..
            nType = cMacro                           ' Set macro type
            sDelim = "="                             ' Fixed delim
            sName = oRE.Replace(sText, "$1")         ' Get name
            sValue = oRE.Replace(sText, "$2")        ' .. and value
            Exit Sub                                 ' .. and all done
        End If
    End Sub
]]>
</script>
</component>


<!-- MTP.CmdArgs Component -->
<!-- Encapsulates a complete command-line(s) of args (collection) -->
<component id="MTP.CmdArgs">
    <!-- Registration -->
    <registration
        description="MTP Command Line Arguments"
        progid="MTP.CmdArgs"
        version="1.0"
        classid="{91c38ef4-37bb-11d3-a228-0080c74acb6f}"
    />
```

```
<!-- Public Interface -->
<public>
    <!-- Delims contains default switch delimiters (RW) -->
    <property name="Delims"/>
    <!-- Reset clears object of all content -->
    <method name="Reset"/>
    <!-- Count returns count of args in object (RO) -->
    <property name="Count"><get/></property>
    <!-- Access as single command line string (RW) -->
    <property name="CmdLine"><get/><put/></property>
    <!-- Append arguments from collection -->
    <method name="FromCollection">
        <parameter name="oArgs"/>
    </method>
    <!-- Append arguments from text stream -->
    <method name="FromStream">
        <parameter name="oStream"/>
    </method>
    <!-- Append arguments from text string -->
    <method name="Add">
        <parameter name="sCmdLine"/>
    </method>
    <!-- Get individual argument items (default, RO) -->
    <property name="Item" dispid="0">
        <get>
            <parameter name="nIndex"/>
        </get>
    </property>
    <!-- Find argument by type and name -->
    <method name="FindArg">
        <parameter name="nMask"/>
        <parameter name="sName"/>
        <parameter name="nIndex"/>
    </method>
    <!-- Test for switch found -->
    <method name="TestSwitch">
        <parameter name="sName"/>
    </method>
    <!-- Get named switch argument or default -->
    <method name="GetSwitch">
        <parameter name="sName"/>
        <parameter name="sDefValue"/>
    </method>
    <!-- TypedCount gets count of arg type (RO) -->
    <property name="TypedCount">
        <get>
            <parameter name="nMask"/>
        </get>
    </property>
    <!-- TypedItem gets arg item by type (RO) -->
    <property name="TypedItem">
        <get>
```

continues ▶

Listing 11.2 *continued*

```
                <parameter name="nMask"/>
                <parameter name="nIndex"/>
            </get>
        </property>
    </public>

<!-- Implementation -->
<script language="VBScript">
<![CDATA[
    Dim Delims                                  ' Default delimiter set
    Dim nCount                                  ' Count of arguments
    Dim oArgs                                   ' Actual argument objects

    ' Initialize default values for properties
    Delims = "" : nCount = 0 : oArgs = Empty

    ' Reset object (delete all args)
    Sub Reset
        nCount = 0                              ' Mark no args
        oArgs = Empty                           ' Empty the arg array
    End Sub

    ' Return current argument count (R/O)
    Function get_Count
        get_Count = CInt(nCount)                ' Just return count
    End Function

    ' Get/set arguments as single command line string
    Function get_CmdLine
        Dim bFirst, oArg, sArg
        get_CmdLine = "" : bFirst = True        ' Init cmd line
        If IsEmpty(oArgs) Then Exit Function    ' End if no args
        For Each oArg in oArgs                  ' For each argument..
            sArg = oArg.Text                    ' Get arg text
            If Instr(sArg, " ") <> 0 Then       ' If contains spaces
                sArg = Chr(34) & sArg & Chr(34) ' ..quote the arg
            End If
            if Not bFirst Then
                get_CmdLine = get_CmdLine & " " & sArg  ' Separator + arg              Else
                get_CmdLine = sArg              ' First arg copied
            End If
            bFirst = False
        Next
    End Function
    Sub put_CmdLine(sCmdLine)
        Reset                                   ' Clear existing args
        Add(sCmdLine)                           ' Add this command line
    End Sub

    ' Get arguments from collection (typically Wscript.Arguments)
    Sub FromCollection(oArgs)
        Dim sArg
```

```
    For Each sArg in oArgs
        AddArg CStr(sArg)                   ' Add new argument
    Next
End Sub

' Get arguments from stream
Sub FromStream(oStream)
    Do Until oStream.AtEndOfStream          ' Until all stream read
        Add(oStream.ReadLine)               ' Add to arguments
    Loop
End Sub

' Append string of arguments
Sub Add(sCmdLine)                           ' Add additional arguments
    Dim oRE, oMatches, oMatch, ix
    Set oRE = New RegExp                    ' Prepare RE object
    oRE.Global = True
    oRE.Pattern = "((\S*""[^""]*"")+\S*)|(\S+)" ' Locates args
    Set oMatches = oRE.Execute(CStr(sCmdLine))  ' Locate all args
    For Each oMatch In oMatches             ' For each arg..
        AddArg Replace(oMatch.Value, Chr(34), "")
    Next
End Sub

' Get individual arguments (default property)
Function get_Item(nIndex)                   ' Get indexed item
    If nIndex < nCount Then                 ' If in range..
        Set get_Item = oArgs(nIndex)        ' Get arg object
    Else
        Set get_Item = Nothing              ' Get no object
    End If
End Function

' Compute count of arguments of specific type
Function get_TypedCount(nMask)
    Dim ix

    get_TypedCount = 0                      ' Clear counter
    For ix = 0 To nCount - 1                ' For each argument..
        If oArgs(ix).ArgType And nMask Then ' If mask match
            get_TypedCount = get_TypedCount + 1 ' Bump counter
        End If
    Next
End Function

' Return typed item by index
Function get_TypedItem(nMask, nIndex)
    Dim ix, iy

    iy = nIndex                             ' Set index
    For ix = 0 To nCount - 1
        If oArgs(ix).ArgType And nMask Then ' If correct type..
            If iy = 0 Then                  ' .. and index..
                Set get_TypedItem = oArgs(ix)
```

continues ▶

Listing 11.2 *continued*

```
                Exit Function
            Else
                iy = iy - 1
            End If
        End If
    Next
    Set get_TypedItem = Nothing             ' Item not found
End Function

' Locate argument by name and type
Function FindArg(nMask, sName, nIndex)
    Dim ix
    Set FindArg = Nothing                   ' Default if not found
    ix = nIndex                             ' Set start index
    Do While ix < nCount                    ' Until out of range
        If (oArgs(ix).ArgType And nMask) And StrComp(oArgs(ix).Name, sName, vbTextCompare) =
        0 Then
            Set FindArg = oArgs(ix)         ' Return arg object
            Exit Function
        End If
        ix = ix + 1                         ' Bump index
    Loop
End Function

' Test for switch present
Function TestSwitch(sName)
    Dim oArg
    Set oArg = FindArg(2, sName, 0)         ' Locate the argument
    TestSwitch = Not oArg Is Nothing        ' True if found
End Function

' Get switch argument (with default value)
Function GetSwitch(sName, sDefValue)        ' Get switch w/default value
    Dim oArg
    Set oArg = FindArg(2, sName, 0)         ' Locate the argument
    If Not oArg Is Nothing Then             ' If found..
        GetSwitch = oArg.Value              ' .. get value
    Else
        GetSwitch = sDefValue               ' Use default value
    End If
End Function

' Add argument text to arg array
Sub AddArg(sText)
    Dim ix
    ix = CInt(nCount)                       ' Get arg index
    nCount = ix + 1                         ' Bump arg counter
    If IsEmpty(oArgs) Then ReDim oArgs(20)  ' Init array if needed
    If ix > UBound(oArgs) Then              ' If required..
        ReDim Preserve oArgs(nCount + 20)   ' Extend the args array
    End If
    Set oArgs(ix) = CreateObject("MTP.CmdArg")  ' Create new object
```

```
        oArgs(ix).Index = ix                        ' Record index
        oArgs(ix).Delims = Delims                   ' Set default delims
        oArgs(ix).Text = sText                      ' Install new arg text
    End Sub
]]>
</script>
</component>

<!-- MTP.BinaryTreeNode -->
<!-- Encapsulates a single node in the binary tree -->
<component id="MTP.BinaryTreeNode">
    <!-- Registration -->
    <registration
        description="MTP Binary Tree Node"
        progid="MTP.BinaryTreeNode"
        version="1.0"
        classid="{91c38ef5-37bb-11d3-a228-0080c74acb6f}"
    />
    <!-- Public Interface -->
    <public>
        <!-- Left and right subnodes (RW) -->
        <property name="oLeft"/>
        <property name="oRight"/>
        <!-- Object property contains object reference (default, RW) -->
        <property name="oObject" dispid="0"/>
    </public>

<!-- Implementation -->
<script language="VBScript">
<![CDATA[
    Dim oLeft, oRight                               ' Left/right object refs
    Dim oObject                                     ' Object reference
]]>
</script>
</component>

<!-- MTP.BinaryTree -->
<!-- Generic binary tree to sort items in order -->
<component id="MTP.BinaryTree">
    <!-- Registration -->
    <registration
        description="MTP Binary Tree"
        progid="MTP.BinaryTree"
        version="1.0"
        classid="{91c38ef6-37bb-11d3-a228-0080c74acb6f}"
    />
    <!-- Public Interface -->
    <public>
        <!-- Count property (# of items) (RO) -->
        <property name="Count"><get/></property>
        <!-- Reset tree (clear all nodes) -->
        <method name="Reset"/>
```

continues ▶

Listing 11.2 *continued*

```
        <!-- Add a new object to the tree -->
        <method name="Add">
            <parameter name="oObj"/>
        </method>
        <!-- Visit all the objects in order -->
        <method name="VisitAll"/>
    </public>

<!-- Implementation -->
<script language="VBScript">
<![CDATA[
    Dim oRoot                                       ' Root object
    Dim nCount                                      ' Count of items

    ' Initialize default values for state
    Set oRoot = Nothing                             ' No tree yet
    nCount = 0

    ' Reset tree (delete all nodes)
    Sub Reset
        Set oRoot = Nothing                         ' VBScript will cleanup
        nCount = 0                                  ' No nodes now
    End Sub

    ' Return current object count
    Function get_Count
        get_Count = CInt(nCount)                    ' Just return count
    End Function

    ' Add new node to tree
    Sub Add(oObj)
        Dim oNode, oPtr, oPtrNext
        nCount = nCount + 1                         ' Bump node counter

        ' Create new node
        Set oNode = CreateObject("MTP.BinaryTreeNode")
        Set oNode.oLeft = Nothing
        Set oNode.oRight = Nothing
        Set oNode.oObject = oObj

        ' Insert node into tree
        If oRoot Is Nothing Then                    ' If empty tree
            Set oRoot = oNode                       ' Store node at root
        Else
            Set oPtrNext = oRoot                    ' Start at tree root
            Do Until oPtrNext Is Nothing
                Set oPtr = oPtrNext                 ' Get current node
                If oObj.Compare(oPtr.oObject) < 0 Then  ' Choose l/r
                    Set oPtrNext = oPtr.oLeft
                Else
                    Set oPtrNext = oPtr.oRight
                End If
```

```
        Loop
        If oObj.Compare(oPtr.oObject) < 0 Then  ' Choose l/r
            Set oPtr.oLeft = oNode          ' Insert at left
        Else
            Set oPtr.oRight = oNode         ' Insert at right
        End If

    End If
End Sub

' Visit all nodes in sorted order
Sub VisitAll
    Visit oRoot                             ' Visit the entire tree
End Sub

Sub Visit(oNode)
    If Not oNode Is Nothing Then            ' If not empty node..
        Visit oNode.oLeft                   ' Do left sub-tree
        oNode.oObject.Visit                 ' Visit this node
        Visit oNode.oRight                  ' Do right sub-tree
    End If
End Sub
]]>
</script>
</component>
</package>
```

Using the *MTP.Info* Component

The ProgID for this component is `"MTP.Info"`, and so create an object using code such as the following:

```
Dim oInfo
Set oInfo = CreateObject("MTP.Info")
```

This component has no methods and three read-only properties, as follows:

- The `.Name` property returns the name of the library. This is the default property.
- The `.Copyright` property returns copyright information as a string.
- The `.Version` property returns the version number of the MTP library.

Using the *MTP.CmdArgs* Component

The ProgID for this component is `"MTP.CmdArgs"`. Individual command line arguments are stored in component objects with a ProgID of `"MTP.CmdArg"`.

The `MTP.CmdArgs` component encapsulates the task of command-line parsing. Consider this hypothetical command line:

```
C:\>myscript params=12,8 "f:\dst file" /auto:off /v /comment:"Auto Copy #1"
```

Here, there are five arguments. As usual for command lines, individual arguments are separated by one or more spaces. Arguments that contain spaces must be enclosed either wholly (like the second argument in the preceding code) or partially (like the last argument) in double quotes. Individual arguments are classified into three distinct types:

- Switches are arguments that begin with a delimiter character, such as `"/"`. A switch can also optionally have a *value*, which is separated from the switch *name* with a colon or equal sign character. For example, the `"/auto:off"` switch shown in the preceding code has a name of `"auto"` and a value of `"off"`.
- Macros are arguments that take the form *name=value*. The preceding example contains one macro, `"params=12,8"` with a name of `"params"` and a value of `"12,8"`.
- Normal arguments are all arguments that are not switches or macros.

The `MTP.CmdArgs` component provides facilities to parse command lines like the one previously shown. It can split a command-line into a set of arguments or re-combine those arguments back into a single command-line string. Each individual command-line argument can then be further analyzed as to its type and content using the related `MTP.CmdArg` component. Thus, the `MTP.CmdArgs` component encapsulates a complete command line, whereas the `MTP.CmdArg` component encapsulates a single command-line argument. The `MTP.CmdArgs` component has the following properties:

- The `.Delims` property (read-write) sets the default delimiters for command-line switches. Multiple delimiters can be supplied in the string. The default delimiter set is `"/+-"`, which is compatible with standard Windows shell conventions. The `.Delims` property should be set *before* command line data is added to the object.
- The `.Count` property (read-only) returns a count of arguments in the current command line.
- The `.CmdLine` property (read-write) contains the current command line as a single text string. When read, this property contains all the arguments in a single string. When written, this property replaces any existing command line with the new command line specified. To append, rather than replace, a command line uses one of the following methods.
- The `.Item` property (read-only) returns an individual command line argument by index (starting at zero). The return value is an object of type `MTP.CmdArg`. This is the default property.
- The `.TypedCount` (read-only) property returns the count of arguments that match the supplied type mask (described later).
- The `.TypedItem` (read-only) property returns an individual command line argument by index (starting at zero) that matches the supplied type mask. Like the `.Item` property, this property returns an object of type `MTP.CmdArg`.

The `MTP.CmdArgs` component has the following methods:

- The `.Reset` method resets the component and deletes any existing command line arguments. This allows an object of this type to be reused multiple times.
- The `.FromCollection` method appends additional arguments onto the current command line from a collection object or string array. The method takes a single argument that must be either an object, that can be iterated to obtain a list of argument strings, or a string array. This is typically used with the `Wscript.Arguments` object to initialize the component from the script command line arguments.
- The `.FromStream` method appends additional arguments onto the current command line from a text stream. All lines of the text stream are read and appended to the command line. The method takes a single argument, which must be a text stream object.
- The `.Add` method appends additional arguments onto the current command line from a string.
- The `.FindArg` method locates an argument by name and type mask. The first argument specifies the type mask (described later), the second argument is the name of the command line argument to be located, and the third argument is the starting index for the search. To find the first matching argument, specify 0 for the start index. To find subsequent matches, specify an index that is one greater than the index of the last match. The return value is either `Nothing`, if no argument is found, or a `MTP.CmdArg` object.

The `.CmdLine` property and the `.FromStream` and `.Add` methods all accept command lines in the form of text strings. In all cases, the command line is automatically parsed into individual arguments.

The `.CmdLine` property provides access to the complete command line as a single string. When read, each argument is separated from the next by a single space, and arguments containing spaces are enclosed in double quotes. This property can be written to replace the existing command line with a new command line. To append, rather than replace, the command line uses one of the `.FromCollection`, `.FromStream`, or `.Add` methods. For example:

```
Dim oCmdArgs, oStream, ix
Set oCmdArgs = CreateObject("MTP.CmdArgs")
Set oStream = CreateObject("Scrpting.FileSystemObject").OpenTextFile("c:\args.txt")
oCmdArgs.Reset
oCmdArgs.FromCollection(Wscript.Arguments)
oCmdArgs.FromStream(oStream)
oCmdArgs.Add("/default:none /data")
Wscript.Echo "There are " & oCmdArgs.Count & " total arguments."
For ix = 0 To oCmdArgs.Count
    Wscript.Echo "Arg " & ix & ": " & oCmdArgs(ix).Text
Next
```

This example composes a single command line from three sources. First, the command line arguments from `Wscript.Arguments`, then a text file `"c:\args.txt"`, and finally two additional explicit arguments `"/default:none"` and `"/data"`.

The `.Item` property, which is the default property, returns an object of type `MTP.CmdArg`, which encapsulates a single argument. Objects of this type are also returned by the `.TypedItem` property and `.FindArg` method. Objects of type `MTP.CmdArg` encapsulate a single command line argument. These objects have no methods and the following properties:

- The `.Text` property (read-write) contains the complete text of the argument. This is the default property.
- The `.Delims` property (read-write) contains the delimiters used to identify a switch argument. A switch argument is defined as an argument whose first character is any of the characters in the `.Delims` string. The default value for this property is taken from the `.Delims` property of the `MTP.CmdArgs` component.
- The `.ArgType` property (read-only) identifies the type of argument. This can be 1 for a normal argument, 2 for a switch argument, and 4 for a macro argument.
- The `.IsNormal`, `.IsSwitch` and `.IsMacro` properties (read-only) return `True` if the argument is of the specified type.
- The `.Delim` property (read-only) returns the actual delimiter located at the start of the argument if the argument is a switch argument.
- The `.Name` property (read-only) returns the name of the argument. For switches and macros, this is the *name* portion of the switch or macro as previously described. For normal arguments, this is the complete argument text.
- The `.Value` property (read-only) returns the value of the argument. For switches and macros, this is the *value* portion of the switch or macro as previously described. For normal arguments, this property is always empty.
- The `.Index` property contains the item index. It is used internally by the `MTP.CmdArgs` component.

For example:

```
Dim oCmdArgs, ix, oCmd
Set oCmdArgs = CreateObject("MTP.CmdArgs")
oCmdArgs.FromCollection(Wscript.Arguments)
For ix = 0 To oCmdArgs.Count
    Set oCmd = oCmdArgs(ix)
    If oCmd.IsSwitch Then
        Wscript.Echo "Switch: delim=" & oCmd.Delim, "name= & oCmd.Name
    End If
Next
```

The `.Text` property of `MTP.CmdArg` objects is read-write. Thus, a new argument can be written to the object and the type, name, and value retrieved. There are several different ways to process the arguments in a command line encapsulated in a `MTP.CmdArgs` object:

- Use the `.Count` and `.Item` properties to enumerate the entire list of arguments, processing each individually.
- Use the `.TypedCount` and `.TypedItem` properties to enumerate only arguments of a specified type or types, and then process these individually.
- Use the `.FindArg` method to locate an argument by type and name.

Enumerating all the arguments is straightforward, and it is shown in the prior examples. The `.TypedCount` and `.TypedItem` properties provide an alternative enumeration where only arguments of a specified type are enumerated. The type is specified as a *type mask*, which is the sum of the individual types desired. So, for example, to enumerate only switches, use a type mask of `2`. To enumerate normal and macro arguments, use a type mask of `1+4`. For example:

```
Dim oCmdArgs, ix, oCmd
Set oCmdArgs = CreateObject("MTP.CmdArgs")
oCmdArgs.FromCollection(Wscript.Arguments)
For ix = 0 To oCmdArgs.TypedCount(1+4)
    Set oCmd = oCmdArgs.TypedItem(1+4, ix)
    Wscript.Echo "Arg: " & oCmd.Text
Next
```

The `.FindArg` method provides a convenient way to locate a specific argument by name and type mask. For example, to locate the `"/auto:off"` argument in the example command line shown at the start of this section:

```
Dim oCmdArgs, oCmd
Set oCmdArgs = CreateObject("MTP.CmdArgs")
oCmdArgs.FromCollection(Wscript.Arguments)
Set oCmd = oCmdArgs.FindArg(2, "auto", 0)
If Not oCmd Is Nothing Then Wscript.Echo "Found: " & oCmd.Text
```

The final argument to `.FindArg` allows multiple arguments of the same name to be located. The argument specifies which instance to locate, starting at zero.

Using the *MTP.BinaryTree* Component

A *binary tree* is a data structure that contains a list of elements, similar to an array. However, unlike an array, the binary tree maintains the elements in sorted order. Elements are sorted incrementally as they are added to the tree—they are not re-sorted if their values later change.

The `MTP.BinaryTree` component implements a simple generic binary tree. This implementation is interesting in that it provides a simple form of polymorphism. *Polymorphism* is an object-oriented technique that allows one object to use another without being aware of the exact identity of that object.

In this case, the `MTP.BinaryTree` component can sort objects of any type, as long as that object supplies two methods:

- A `.Compare` method that can compare this object to another object of the same class. This method takes one argument, which is a reference to the other object for the comparison. This method should return a negative number if the object is less than the one passed as an argument, zero if the two objects are equal, and a positive number if the object is greater than the one passed as an argument.
- A `.Visit` method that is used when the objects are enumerated in sorted order.

To use the `MTP.BinaryTree` object, proceed as follows:

1. Define the objects that are to be stored and sorted by the tree object. These can be defined as VBScript `Class` objects or Windows Script Components. In either case, the object must provide the two methods previously noted.
2. Create a `MTP.BinaryTree` object.
3. Add one or more user-defined objects to the tree using the `.Add` method.
4. Visit the user-defined objects in order using the `.VisitAll` method.

Here is an example VBScript `Class` that can be used with the `MTP.BinaryTree` component:

```
Class Node
    Public sData

    Public Function Compare(oNode)
        Compare = StrComp(sData, oNode.sData, vbTextCompare)
    End Function

    Public Sub Visit
        Wscript.Echo "Visit: " & sData
    End Sub
End Class
```

This simple example encapsulates a simple text string. It provides the two required methods. In this example, the `.Compare` method performs a textual comparison between the current object's data and the data in the object passed as an argument. The `.Visit` method just displays the value of the data.

Here is an example of the `MTP.BinaryTree` in action, using the class previously defined:

```
Dim sArg, oTree, oObj
Set oTree = CreateObject("MTP.BinaryTree")
For Each sArg In Wscript.Arguments
    Set oObj = New Node
    oObj.sData = sArg
    oTree.Add oObj
Next
Wscript.Echo oTree.Count, "nodes"
oTree.VisitAll
```

This example creates a new `Node` object for each command line argument and then adds this object to the tree. The `.VisitAll` method is then invoked. This results in the `.Visit` method in each object in the tree being invoked once in sorted order. Therefore, this results in each command line argument being listed, in alphabetical order.

Note

The user-defined object defines the order in which the objects are sorted. In the previous example, the `.Compare` *method compared the two string values. However, it could just as easily have compared the lengths of the strings, in which case, the arguments would be sorted by length. This is really the heart of polymorphism. As a user, you have no idea how the* `MTP.BinaryTree` *component works and it, in turn, has no idea about the sort order. However, as long as your object has a* `.Compare` *and* `.Visit` *method, you can use the* `MTP.BinaryTree` *component to sort the items in any way desired.* ◆

MTP.CmdArgs Implementation Details

Although quite long, the `MTP.CmdArgs` and `MTP.CmdArg` components are not complex, although they make some sophisticated use of the `RegExp` object to perform most of the parsing functionality.

The *MTP.CmdArg* Component

The `MTP.CmdArg` component encapsulates a single command line argument. Apart from the `.Index` property, which is a simple variable, all the properties are implemented as procedures. The component stores the full text of the argument in the `sText` variable and the delimiter set (used to identify the argument as a switch) in the `sDelims` variable.

The primary function of the `MTP.CmdArg` component is to categorize the argument as a switch, macro, or normal argument and further decompose switches and macros into `name` and `value` parts. The primary issue here is *when* this processing should take place:

- The component could perform this as soon as the `.Text` property changes value. This is known as *early evaluation*. In this case, the component also has to re-process the argument text if the `.Delims` property changes.
- The component could perform the processing each time one of the read-only properties is accessed (for example, `.IsNormal` and `.Name`). This is known as *late evaluation*. This must be performed when *any* of the read-only properties is accessed.

Both techniques have advantages and disadvantages. Early evaluation is inefficient if the `.Text` property is changed many times but the read-only properties are accessed only a few times. For example:

```
Dim oCmd
Set oCmd = CreateObject("MTP.CmdArg")
oCmd.Text = "/auto:on"
oCmd.Delims = "/-"
Wscript.Echo oCmd.Name
```

Here, early evaluation means that the object must process the argument twice. Once when the `.Text` property is set, and once when the `.Delims` property is set. This doubles the overhead of using the component, which can be significant if thousands of arguments are being processed.

Late evaluation suffers from exactly the opposite problem. For example:

```
Dim oCmd
Set oCmd = CreateObject("MTP.CmdArg")
oCmd.Text = "/auto:on"
Wscript.Echo oCmd.Delim, oCmd.Name, oCmd.Value
```

Here, late evaluation means that the object must process the argument three times, once for each of the properties accessed in the `Wscript.Echo` statement.

Thus, neither approach is perfect for all cases. To overcome this problem, the `MTP.CmdArg` component uses an alternative technique called *lazy evaluation*. Lazy evaluation provides the advantages of both the other evaluation methods but none of the disadvantages.

Lazy evaluation works by breaking up the internal state of the `MTP.CmdArg` component into two distinct sets: *input* state and *output* state. The input state comprises the properties that can be changed (in this case, the `.Text` and `.Delims` properties), and the output state comprises the properties that cannot be changed (`.Name`, `.Value`, and so on). A single function, in this case the `Parse` procedure inside the component, then processes the input state and saves it in the output state.

The "trick" with lazy evaluation is how and when this function is called. Here, in outline, is how this works:

- The component adds a new variable, called `bDirty`. This is initialized to `True`.
- Whenever any of the input state properties (that is, `.Text` or `.Delims`) are altered, the `bDirty` variable is set to `True`.
- Whenever any of the output state properties are read (for example, `.Name`), the `bDirty` variable is examined. If the variable is `True`, the `Parse` procedure is called, and then the property value is returned. If the `bDirty` variable is `False`, the property value is immediately returned.
- The `Parse` procedure sets the `bDirty` variable to `False`.

When an output state property is read for the first time, the `bDirty` flag is `True`. Thus, the `Parse` procedure is called to set the output state properties, and they can then be returned safely. However, the `Parse` procedure *clears* the `bDirty` flag, so subsequent accesses to output state properties do not cause a re-parse to occur. Thus, access to output state properties is efficient, since parsing occurs once only.

When an input state property is changed, the only action is to save the new value and set the `bDirty` flag. This is quick and efficient. Each change to the input state is equally efficient. Only when the output state is referenced is the `Parse` procedure invoked.

It should be clear why the `bDirty` flag is thus named: It indicates that the input state is dirty and needs to be cleaned by updating the output state. This update only occurs, however, when the output state is actually needed. This is why this technique is known as lazy evaluation.

Here is a synthetic example that illustrates the advantages of lazy evaluation:

```
Dim oCmd, ix, sName
Set oCmd = CreateObject("MTP.CmdArg")
For ix = 0 To 10000
    oCmd.Text = "/auto:on"
    oCmd.Delims = "/-"
Next
For ix = 0 To 10000
    SName = oCmd.Name
Next
Wscript.Echo sName
```

If the `MTP.CmdArg` component used early evaluation, this example would invoke the internal `Parse` procedure 20,000 times (twice each time around the first `For` loop). If the object used late evaluation, the `Parse` procedure would be invoked 10,000 times (once for each time around the second `For` loop). Using lazy evaluation, the `Parse` procedure is invoked just *once*—the first time the `.Name` property is accessed.

Argument Parsing In *MTP.CmdArg*

The `Parse` procedure in the `MTP.CmdArg` component actually parses an individual argument. It first checks to see if the argument is a switch, then a macro, and if it is neither of these, it is assumed to be a normal argument. The procedure uses the `sText` and `sDelims` variables as inputs, and it updates the `sDelim`, `sName`, `sValue`, and `nType` variables as output.

All the parsing work is done by regular expression objects (see Chapter 7, "Built-In WSH and VBScript Objects"). The expressions themselves are complex. For example, here is the regular expression used to determine if an argument is a switch:

```
^\s*([/+-])([^:=]+)([:=](.*)¦)
```

This can be interpreted as follows: A switch is any leading whitespace (`"^\s*"`), followed by a switch delimiter character (`"[/+-]"`), followed by one or more characters other than colon or equals (`"[^:=]+"`), followed by either (a) a colon or equals and then any other text, or (b) nothing (`"[:=](.*)¦"`).

The parentheses around various parts of the expression are present so that the `.Replace` method of the `RegExp` object can be used to extract the various parts of the argument. For example:

```
sName = oRE.Replace(sText, "$2")
```

Here, the switch name is extracted from the argument text.

The *MTP.CmdArgs* Component

The `MTP.CmdArgs` component encapsulates an entire command line. This component is actually simple. The command line itself is stored as an array of individual `MTP.CmdArg` objects in `oArgs`, with the number of arguments stored in `nCount`.

New arguments are added to the array using the internal `AddArg` procedure. This procedure allocates a new `MTP.CmdArg` object to hold the argument and then adds this object, after initialization, to the `oArgs` array. The array is actually a dynamic array that is grown in groups of 20 elements using the usual `ReDim Preserve` statement. This number was chosen because typical command lines are small. However, if this component is used to parse large numbers of arguments, this value could be increased to (say) 200 to improve performance.

When read, the `.CmdLine` property must assemble the `oArgs` array into a single command line string. This is easily done by concatenating the text of each argument, separating each with a single space. The argument is also checked to see if it contains one or more space characters. If it does, it is first enclosed in double quotes.

The `.FromCollection` method adds a set of command arguments from a collection. This simply requires that the collection is iterated and the `AddArg` procedure called for each one. The other methods to add arguments (`.FromStream` and `.Add`) as well as the `.CmdLine` property are more complex because they must decompose a string into individual arguments.

This decomposition is performed using a `RegExp` object. The match string matches individual arguments (and correctly processes quoted arguments with spaces). Then, the `AddArg` procedure is called for each individual match.

MTP.BinaryTree Implementation Details

The `MTP.BinaryTree` component uses a helper component, `MTP.BinaryTreeNode`, to assist in its operation. This helper component represents a single node in the binary tree. The binary tree component itself simply stores the root of the tree in the `oRoot` variable.

Each node in the tree stores three items of information. The first item, `oObject`, stores a reference to the user-defined object. The second two items, `oLeft` and `oRight`, store references to additional nodes in the tree. The tree is arranged so that all objects that are less than or equal to the current node (as defined by the user-defined object) are stored in the left branch, whereas all objects that are greater than the current node are stored in the right branch. This is true throughout the entire tree. Therefore, by definition, the "smallest" object (as defined by the user-defined object) is the left-most node in the tree, whereas the "largest" object is the right-most node in the tree.

Thus, to visit each object in sorted order, it is necessary to work through the nodes in the tree in left to right order. This is done by the `Visit` procedure, which is invoked by the `.VisitAll` method. This recursive procedure walks down the tree to the left, then visits that node, then continues walking along the tree toward the right, visiting each node in turn.

A full understanding of tree and graph theory is beyond the scope of this book, but this component illustrates one point quite clearly: It is not necessary to understand *how* the binary tree works to use it. This is, of course, one of the advantages of the separation of interface and implementation discussed in Part II, "Objects and Classes."

12

Logon Scripts

Probably the most obvious use of WSH in medium and large networks is for *logon scripts*. It is actually nearly impossible to construct a truly generic logon script because the requirements of these scripts vary so much from installation to installation. Therefore, this chapter concentrates on some of the more typical issues surrounding these scripts, and it provides sample scripts that can be used as starting points for a fully custom logon script.

This chapter focuses on the specific issues surrounding WSH as used in logon scripts. It does *not* provide general-purpose information on deploying logon scripts in Windows NT and Windows 2000.

Note

As with all the sample scripts in this book, the scripts in this chapter should be run using the CSCRIPT host unless otherwise noted. The examples shown assume that CSCRIPT is the default WSH host. (See Chapter 1, "Introducing WSH," for information on selecting the default WSH host.)

Logon Script Issues

A logon script executes when a user logs onto a Windows NT or Windows 2000 domain. The script to execute is specified by the account information associated with the user account. However, typically only the *name* of the script is specified. The script is always located in the `NETLOGON` share of the domain controller handling the logon for that account (this can vary from session to session).

Although logon scripts are located on a domain controller, they are *executed* on the machine where the user is logging on. Thus, they can execute on a number of different operating systems, including:

- Windows 2000
- Windows NT
- Windows 95 and 98

- Windows for Workgroups 3.x (that is, 16-bit Windows)
- MS-DOS

Thus, a truly generic logon script needs to be able to execute successfully on any of these platforms. The requirement for MS-DOS might seem unnecessary, but many system administrators begin configuration of a computer by booting an MS-DOS floppy disk and then use that to connect to the network. Thus, the logon script should at least provide minimal functionality for MS-DOS connections.

An additional complication is that only Windows 2000 recognizes a `.VBS` file as a valid logon script. The other operating systems previously listed can only execute `.BAT` or (in some cases) `.EXE` files as logon scripts.

Finally, WSH only comes pre-installed on Windows 98 and Windows 2000. Therefore, WSH might not even be available on some computers when the script executes.

Two-Phase Logon Scripts

To overcome several of these problems, a *two-phase* logon script is used. A traditional shell `.BAT` batch file drives the first phase, and a `.VBS` script drives the second phase. This overcomes the previously noted problem noted in which only `.BAT` files are allowed as logon scripts with some operating systems.

The simplest `.BAT` file logon script is actually just one line:

```
cscript //i //nologo %0\..\mtplogon.vbs
```

This single line executes the `MTPLogon.vbs` script using the CSCRIPT host.

Logon scripts cannot make assumptions about the environment in which they execute. For example, it is *not* safe to assume that the user has selected the CSCRIPT host as the default WSH host. That is why the preceding example explicitly uses the CSCRIPT host to execute the `MTPLogon.vbs` script. For the same reason, the `//i` and `//nologo` switches are used to explicitly state exactly how the script is executed.

The path name of the `MTPLogon.vbs` script in the preceding example is unusual. It is designed to overcome one problem with the two-phase approach. Where is the second phase script located? The initial `.BAT` script executes from the `NETLOGON` share on the domain controller but *which* domain controller? On Windows NT and Windows 2000, this information is available in an environment variable, but this is not true for Windows 95. Fortunately, the `%0` parameter of the logon script contains the full path name to the current script. On Windows NT and Windows 2000, this is the UNC name of the `NETLOGON` share. On other systems, this is a local drive (typically Z:) used temporarily for logon purposes. In either case, the text `"%0\..\"` is the parent folder containing the logon script, and this is, therefore, the correct location from which to access additional scripts (and even additional executables if necessary).

The "%0" path can be viewed explicitly using the following batch script:

```
echo %%0=%0
cscript //i //nologo %0\..\mtplogon.vbs
pause
```

The first phase of the two-phase script can also check that the operating system is capable of supporting WSH. There is no direct test for this condition, but this can be checked indirectly by performing two tests:

1. Verify that the %windir% environment variable exists.
2. Verify that the file KERNEL32.DLL exists at that location in the SYSTEM or SYSTEM32 folders.

These two tests pass for Windows 9x, Windows NT, and Windows 2000, but fail for MS-DOS and 16-bit Windows. The following batch script illustrates this:

```
echo %%0=%0
if "%windir%"=="" goto :NOWSH
if exist %windir%\system\kernel32.dll goto :WSHOK
if exist %windir%\system32\kernel32.dll goto :WSHOK
goto :NOWSH
:WSHOK
cscript //i //nologo %0\..\mtplogon.vbs
goto :EXIT
:NOWSH
call %0\..\doslogon.bat
:EXIT
```

In this example, the .VBS logon script is only executed on platforms that support WSH. Otherwise, execution branches to the label :NOWSH and some form of non-WSH based logon can occur. In this example, the script simply invokes an additional .BAT script, called DOSLOGON.BAT. (Actually, despite the name, this script will also execute on 16-bit Windows platforms because this platform also cannot support WSH.)

Automatic Installation of WSH

The last example solved two of the previously noted problems: the lack of WSH support in MS-DOS and 16-bit Windows and the inability of Windows 9x and Windows NT to execute a .VBS script directly. However, this example fails if run on a Windows NT or Windows 95 installation where WSH is not yet installed.

To overcome this problem, the phase-one script (the .BAT phase) should check to see if WSH is installed, and automatically install it if required *before* executing the .VBS script to start the second phase.

This automatic installation should be applied to the three fundamental WSH components: WSH itself, VBScript, and ADSI (ADSI is described in Chapter 13, "System Management Scripts"). In each case, installation is detected by testing for the presence of an essential file in a known location. Table 12.1 lists these files and locations.

Table 12.1 *Key File Locations*

Component	Key File	Locations
Windows Script Host	CSCRIPT.EXE	%windir%\command
		%windir%\system
		%windir%\system32
VBScript	VBSCRIPT.DLL	%windir%\system
		%windir%\system32
ADSI	ADSNT.DLL	%windir%\system
		%windir%\system32

To detect if a component is installed, check for the essential file specified in Table 12.1 in all the locations listed. If the component is not found, it must be installed. For example:

```
if exist %windir%\command\cscript.exe goto :WSHFOUND
if exist %windir%\system\cscript.exe goto :WSHFOUND
if exist %windir%\system32\cscript.exe goto :WSHFOUND
[install WSH component]
:WSHFOUND
```

The same basic batch script code can be used to check for the other components listed in Table 12.1.

To install the component (such as WSH), invoke the appropriate self-installing executable (see Appendix A, "Installing Script Components," for more information). For example:

```
%0\..\wsh20en /q
```

This example assumes that the executable is located in the same folder as the logon scripts.

Note

Depending upon local policy, installation of WSH and other components could require administrative access on the local computer. If so, the automatic installation technique presented here might not be appropriate. In this case, a logon script that checks and fails to find WSH might have to fail (and perhaps log an error).

One alternative to this technique is to automate deployment using other tools, such as System Management Server (SMS). ◆

Version Checking

Checking for key executable files correctly indicates if a component is installed or not. However, it does not check the *version* of that component. For example, Windows 98 ships with WSH 1.0, and so the tests previously described detect WSH as already installed. However, this book assumes that WSH 2.0 is installed, and so many of the sample scripts will not work unless this newer version is installed.

The easiest way to version check WSH and VBScript is to execute a short .VBS script and let the script validate and return version information. Obviously, this requires *some* version of WSH and VBScript to be available, and so this additional check must be performed after the key file check is performed.

Here is a script, `CheckVBSVersion.vbs`, which checks the version of VBScript against that passed as a command-line argument. For simplicity, the version is passed as an integer value, where `"510"` means version 5.10.

```
Dim nVersion
nVersion = (ScriptEngineMajorVersion * 100) + ScriptEngineMinorVersion
If nVersion < CInt(Wscript.Arguments(0)) Then
    Wscript.Quit(1)
Else
    Wscript.Quit(0)
End If
```

Here is a similar script, `CheckWSHVersion.vbs`, which checks the version of WSH:

```
Dim nVersion
nVersion = Wscript.Version * 100
If nVersion < CInt(Wscript.Arguments(0)) Then
    Wscript.Quit(1)
Else
    Wscript.Quit(0)
End If
```

In both cases, the script returns 0 if the version number is correct, or 1 if the current version is older than that specified (that is, it needs upgrading). Here is the batch script to process this:

```
cscript //i //nologo %0\..\checkwshversion.vbs 510
if errorlevel 1 %0\..\wsh20en /q
```

In this example, the error level is checked to determine the exit code from the `CheckWSHVersion.vbs` script. If necessary, the batch script invokes the self-installing executable to install the latest version of WSH.

Local Environment Set Up

The final task of the phase one logon script is to set up local scripts. This is a purely optional task, but it is quite frequently necessary. Typically, a central library of scripts should be distributed to client computers. This library of scripts might include .BAT batch files, .VBS scripts, and .WSC components. Although these scripts can be executed from a network share, it is more common to copy the scripts so that they are available even when the computer is not connected to the network (this is particularly important with laptops).

The following batch script code copies all files from a central location to the local C:\Scripts folder:

```
if not exist c:\Scripts\*.* md c:\Scripts
xcopy %0\..\LocalScripts c:\Scripts /i /r
```

The local C:\Scripts folder is created if necessary, and then the contents of the LocalScripts folder are copied into it. In this example, the LocalScripts folder is copied from the NETLOGON share, although this could be changed to a specific UNC name depending upon local requirements. One advantage of placing this folder in the NETLOGON share is that it automatically benefits from the replication and load balancing features of Windows NT and Windows 2000 domains.

.VBS and .WS scripts are available for execution immediately after copying to a local script folder. However, .WSC components must be *registered* before they can be used on a computer. This registration process can also be automated in the phase one script, as follows:

```
for %%i in (c:\scripts\*.wsc) do regsvr32 /s /c file:%%i
```

This batch script command uses a FOR command to enumerate all the .WSC files in the local scripts folder, and then registers the component using the REGSVR32 command. The /S switch requests silent operation, and the /C switch directs any output to the console.

The previously shown command assumes that the latest version of REGSVR32 is available on the client computer. As previously noted, this is not a safe assumption in a logon script. Instead, a slightly different version of the command can be used which is compatible with all versions of REGSVR32:

```
for %%i in (c:\scripts\*.wsc) do regsvr32 /s /c scrobj.dll /n /i:file:%%i
```

Phase Two Script

The phase two script in the two-phase scheme is the portion processed by the .VBS script. This phase is run by the phase one shell batch script using a command such as this:

```
cscript //i //nologo %0\..\mtplogon.vbs
```

The phase two script is free to perform any actions required to complete the logon. Typically, these actions include the following:

- Setting the local computer time from a timeserver
- Mapping network drives to standard shares
- Mapping network drives based upon group membership
- Mapping network printers
- Install or validate special applications, such as virus checkers

Some operations, such as setting the system time, are most easily accomplished using shell commands. To do this, execute the command using the `.Run` method of the `WshShell` object. To use this correctly, it is necessary to invoke the command using the command shell appropriate to the local operating system, either `COMMAND.COM` for Windows 9x or `CMD.EXE` for Windows NT and Windows 2000.

This function executes a shell command using the correct platform:

```
Sub RunCmd(sCmd)
    Dim sShell, oShell
    Set oShell = CreateObject("Wscript.Shell")
    sShell = oShell.Environment("Process").Item("COMSPEC")
    g_oShell.Run sShell & " /c " & sCmd, &H20000000, True
End Sub
```

Here, the shell name is determined using the `COMSPEC` environment variable, which contains the name of the shell to use, regardless of the operating system. The actual command text is then executed by that shell using the `"/c"` switch.

Most of the other operations previously noted use the `WshNetwork` object (described in Chapter 7, "Built-In WSH and VBScript Objects") to map or remap a network connection. For example:

```
Dim oNet
Set oNet = CreateObject("Wscript.Network")
oNet.MapNetworkDrive "S:", "\\Server4\System"
```

Performing operations based upon group membership (a common requirement for logon scripts) requires the use of ADSI to access the list of groups for the current user. ADSI is covered in Chapter 13. This simple `IsMember` function uses ADSI to check group membership for the current user:

```
Function IsMember(sGroup)
    Dim sAdsPath, oUser, oGroup, oNet
    Set oNet = CreateObject("Wscript.Network")
    sAdsPath = oNet.UserDomain & "/" & oNet.UserName
    Set oUser = GetObject("WinNT://" & sAdsPath & ",user")
    For Each oGroup In oUser.Groups
        If StrComp(sGroup, oGroup.Name, vbTextCompare) = 0 Then
            IsMember = True : Exit Function
        End If
    Next
    IsMember = False
End Function
```

The `MTPLogon.vbs` sample script (described later) demonstrates a more efficient way to test for group membership using ADSI.

Sample Logon Scripts

The four sample scripts in this chapter build upon the issues previously discussed to provide a complete, functional, two-phase logon script. The script is compatible with Windows 9x, Windows NT, and Windows 2000, and the phase one script supports MS-DOS and 16-bit Windows via a distinct `DOSLOGON.BAT` script (not shown).

The *MTPLogon.bat* Script

The `MTPLogon.bat` batch script, shown in Listing 12.1, drives the first phase of the two-phase logon. This script is specified as the logon script in the users account information.

Listing 12.1 *`MTPLogon.bat` Script*

```
@echo OFF
if not "%ECHO%"=="" echo %ECHO%
rem $Workfile: MTPLogon.bat $ $Revision: 1 $ $Date: 7/25/99 12:59p $
rem Copyright (c) 1998 Tim Hill. All Rights Reserved.
set MTPLOGONVER=$Revision: 1 $
set WSHVERSION=510
set VBSVERSION=500
set WSHINSTALL=%0\..\WSH20EN.EXE /Q
set VBSINSTALL=%0\..\STE50EN.EXE /Q
set SCRIPTDIR=c:\Scripts
set SRCDIR=%0\..\LocalScripts
echo %%0=%0

rem Branch based upon OS platform (WSH or non-WSH)
if "%windir%"=="" goto :NOWSH
if exist %windir%\system\kernel32.dll goto :WSHOK
if exist %windir%\system32\kernel32.dll goto :WSHOK
goto :NOWSH
:WSHOK
echo Executing WSH script...

rem Install WSH if not found...
if exist %windir%\command\cscript.exe goto :WSHFOUND
if exist %windir%\system\cscript.exe goto :WSHFOUND
if exist %windir%\system32\cscript.exe goto :WSHFOUND
%WSHINSTALL%
:WSHFOUND

rem Install VBScript if not found...
if exist %windir%\system\vbscript.dll goto :VBSFOUND
if exist %windir%\system32\vbscript.dll goto :VBSFOUND
%VBSINSTALL%
:VBSFOUND
```

```
rem Upgrade WSH if required...
cscript //i //nologo %0\..\checkwshversion.vbs %WSHVERSION%
if errorlevel 1 %WSHINSTALL%

rem Upgrade VBScript if required...
cscript //i //nologo %0\..\checkvbsversion.vbs %VBSVERSION%
if errorlevel 1 %VBSINSTALL%

rem Install local scripts and register them
if not exist %SCRIPTDIR%\*.* md %SCRIPTDIR%
attrib -r -s -h %SCRIPTDIR%
rem del %SCRIPTDIR%\*.*
copy %SRCDIR% %SCRIPTDIR%
for %%i in (%SCRIPTDIR%\*.wsc) do regsvr32 /s /c scrobj.dll /n /i:file:%%i

rem Now execute the phase 2 logon script...
cscript //i //nologo %0\..\mtplogon.vbs
goto :EXIT

rem We get here if we are running on a non-WSH platform
:NOWSH
echo Executing non-WSH script...
if exist %0\..\doslogon.bat call %0\..\doslogon.bat
goto :EXIT

rem Special fix for buggy logon script end
:EXIT
if exist c:\windows\*.* echo . >c:\windows\lmscript.$$$
if exist c:\win95\*.* echo . >c:\win95\lmscript.$$$
if exist c:\win98\*.* echo . >c:\win98\lmscript.$$$
```

All the items in the script that typically vary from one installation to another are controlled by environment variables that are set near the start of the script. The rest of the script uses these variables to control script execution. The variables are:

- `WSHVERSION` This variable specifies the current version of WSH. In this case, the value `510` means 5.10. This is used to control automatic upgrading of WSH during logon.
- `VBSVERSION` This variable specifies the current version of VBScript, and it is used like `WSHVERSION` to control automatic upgrading of VBScript during logon.
- `WSHINSTALL` This variable specifies the full command to execute and install the most recent version of WSH, including the full path and any command-line switches required.
- `VBSINSTALL` This variable specifies the full command to execute and install the most recent version of VBScript.

- `SCRIPTDIR` This is the local directory (folder) into which to copy standard scripts during logon.
- `SRCDIR` This is the network path from which to copy standard scripts during logon.

After these variables are set, the `MTPLogon.bat` batch script performs the following steps:

1. If the operating system is MS-DOS or 16-bit Windows, the script branches to the label `:NOWSH` that executes the alternate `DOSLOGON.BAT` script.
2. If WSH is not installed, it is installed automatically.
3. If VBScript is not installed, it is installed automatically.
4. If the installed version of WSH is older than the current version, it is upgraded.
5. If the installed version of VBScript is older than the current version, it is upgraded.
6. Standard scripts are copied from the network onto the local computer.
7. All Windows Script Components copied in step 6 are registered.
8. The phase two script, `MTPLogon.vbs`, is executed.
9. The dummy `LMSCRIPT.$$$` file is created in the Windows directory. This works around a bug in some versions of Windows not detecting the end of the logon script correctly.

Steps 4 and 5 in the preceding list use the `CheckWSHVersion.vbs` and `CheckVBSVersion.vbs` scripts, which are shown in Listing 12.2 and Listing 12.3, respectively.

Listing 12.2 *`CheckWSHVersion.vbs` Script*

```
'//////////////////////////////////////////////////////////////////////////
' $Workfile: CheckWSHVersion.vbs $ $Revision: 1 $ $Date: 7/25/99 12:59p $
' $Archive: /Scripts/CheckWSHVersion.vbs $
' Copyright (c) 1998 Tim Hill. All Rights Reserved.
'//////////////////////////////////////////////////////////////////////////

' Check WSH version and return 0 if ok, non-zero if it needs updating

Dim nVersion
nVersion = CInt(Wscript.Version * 100)
Wscript.Echo "This is version: " & nVersion

If Wscript.Arguments.Count < 1 Then
    Wscript.Echo "usage: checkwshversion <vers>"
```

```
    Wscript.Echo "<vers> should be 120 for version 1.20 etc."
    Wscript.Echo "Returns 0 if ok, 1 if version needs updating"
    Wscript.Quit(0)
End If

If nVersion < CInt(Wscript.Arguments(0)) Then
    Wscript.Quit(1)
Else
    Wscript.Quit(0)
End If
```

Listing 12.3 *`CheckVBSVersion.vbs` Script*

```
'//////////////////////////////////////////////////////////////////////
' $Workfile: CheckVBSVersion.vbs $ $Revision: 1 $ $Date: 7/25/99 12:59p $
' $Archive: /Scripts/CheckVBSVersion.vbs $
' Copyright (c) 1998 Tim Hill. All Rights Reserved.
'//////////////////////////////////////////////////////////////////////

' Check VBScript version and return 0 if ok, non-zero if needs updating

Dim nVersion
nVersion = CInt((ScriptEngineMajorVersion * 100) + ScriptEngineMinorVersion)
Wscript.Echo "This is version: " & nVersion

If Wscript.Arguments.Count < 1 Then
    Wscript.Echo "usage: checkvbsversion <vers>"
    Wscript.Echo "<vers> should be 120 for version 1.20 etc."
    Wscript.Echo "Returns 0 if ok, 1 if version needs updating"
    Wscript.Quit(0)
End If

If nVersion < CInt(Wscript.Arguments(0)) Then
    Wscript.Quit(1)
Else
    Wscript.Quit(0)
End If
```

Both `CheckWSHVersion.vbs` and `CheckVBSVersion.vbs` are trivial scripts. The only minor complication is the use of the `CInt` function when computing version information to ensure that versions are correctly matched if they are exactly equal.

The *MTPLogon.vbs* Script

The `MTPLogon.vbs` script handles all the phase two logon script processing. It is executed by the `MTPLogon.bat` batch script after the operating system and versions of WSH and VBScript have been verified. The script is shown in Listing 12.4.

Listing 12.4 *MTPLogon.vbs Script*

```
'//////////////////////////////////////////////////////////////////////////////
' $Workfile: MTPLogon.vbs $ $Revision: 4 $ $Date: 7/25/99 3:17p $
' $Archive: /Scripts/MTPLogon.vbs $
' Copyright (c) 1998 Tim Hill. All Rights Reserved.
'//////////////////////////////////////////////////////////////////////////////

' Phase 2 logon script

' Explicit variable declaration and standard globals
Option Explicit
Dim g_oShell, g_oFSO, g_oNet, g_oGroupDict
Set g_oShell = CreateObject("Wscript.Shell")
Set g_oFSO = CreateObject("Scripting.FileSystemObject")
Set g_oNet = CreateObject("Wscript.Network")

' A drive map is comprised "<drive>,<UNCshare>"
' Use * in either field for the home drive or directory
Dim g_sDriveMap(25)
g_sDriveMap(0) = "J:,\\K140\JAZDRIVE"
g_sDriveMap(1) = "L:,\\K140\LIBRARY"
g_sDriveMap(2) = "S:,\\K140\SETUP"
g_sDriveMap(3) = "P:,*"
g_sDriveMap(4) = "K:,\\K140\COMMON"
g_sDriveMap(5) = "R:,\\K140\C$"

' Map drives based upon drive mapping table
Dim sMap, bResult, sItems
For Each sMap In g_sDriveMap
    If Not IsEmpty(sMap) Then
        sItems = Split(sMap, ",")
        bResult = MapDrive(sItems(0), sItems(1))
        If Not bResult Then Wscript.Echo "*** FAILED"
    End If
Next

'Map drives based upon group membership
If IsMember("Domain Admins") Then
    bResult = MapDrive("W:", "\\K140\NetApps")
    If Not bResult Then Wscript.Echo "*** FAILED"
End If

Wscript.Quit(0)

'//////////////////////////////////////////////////////////////////////////////
' IsMember
' Test to see if user if member of specified group
'
' sGroup            Name of group
' Returns           True if user is group member
'
Function IsMember(sGroup)
    Dim sAdsPath, oUser, oGroup
```

```
    ' Populate dictionary if not yet created
    If IsEmpty(g_oGroupDict) Then
        Set g_oGroupDict = CreateObject("Scripting.Dictionary")
        g_oGroupDict.CompareMode = vbTextCompare
        sAdsPath = g_oNet.UserDomain & "/" & g_oNet.UserName
        Set oUser = GetObject("WinNT://" & sAdsPath & ",user")
        For Each oGroup In oUser.Groups
            g_oGroupDict.Add oGroup.Name, "-"
        Next
        Set oUser = Nothing
    End If
    IsMember = CBool(g_oGroupDict.Exists(sGroup))
End Function

'////////////////////////////////////////////////////////////////////////////
' MapDrive
' Map a network drive as specified
'
' g_oFSO            FileSystem object
' g_oNet            WshNetwork object
' sPath             Path name for drive or * (can be relative)
' sUNCPath          UNC path to share or * for home (\\computer\sharename)
' Returns           True if drive mapped ok, else error
'
Function MapDrive(ByVal sPath, ByVal sUNCPath)
    Dim nExit, sAdsPath, oAdsObj, sComputer, sShare, x, sDrive, sLocalPath
    ' If required, get home dir or drive
    If sPath = "*" Or sUNCPath = "*" Then
        sAdsPath = g_oNet.UserDomain & "/" & g_oNet.UserName
        Set oAdsObj = GetObject("WinNT://" & sAdsPath & ",user")
        If sPath = "*" Then sPath = oAdsObj.HomeDirDrive
        If sUNCPath = "*" Then sUNCPath = oAdsObj.HomeDirectory
        Set oAdsObj = Nothing
    End If
    ' Validate the parameters, then parse the UNC name
    If sPath = "" Or sUNCPath = "" Then
        MapDrive = False : Exit Function
    End If
    x = Split(sUNCPath, "\")
    If UBound(x) < 3 Then
        MapDrive = False : Exit Function
    End If
    sComputer = x(2) : sShare = x(3)
    sDrive = GetDriveName(sPath)
    Wscript.Echo "Map: " & sDrive & " -> " & sUNCPath
    ' Try to unmap or unSUBST the drive
    UnmapDrive(sDrive)
    ' Cannot map local drives
    If IsLocalDrive(sDrive) Then
        MapDrive = False : Exit Function
    End If
    ' If possible, use SUBST as this is faster than local loopback
```

continues ▶

Listing 12.4 *continued*

```
    If IsWinNT And StrComp(sComputer, g_oNet.ComputerName, vbTextCompare) = 0 Then
        sAdsPath = sComputer & "/lanmanserver/" & sShare
        Set oAdsObj = GetObject("WinNT://" & sAdsPath & ",fileshare")
        sLocalPath = oAdsObj.Path
        Set oAdsObj = Nothing
        nExit = RunCmd("subst " & sDrive & " " & sLocalPath)
        ' All done if good SUBST mapping
        If nExit = 0 Then
            MapDrive = True : Exit Function
        End If
    End If
    ' Map the network drive and return result
    g_oNet.MapNetworkDrive sDrive, sUNCPath
    MapDrive = IsNetworkDrive(sDrive)
End Function

'///////////////////////////////////////////////////////////////////////////////
' UnmapDrive
' Unmap a network drive (or a SUBST drive on WinNT)
'
' g_oFSO            FileSystem object
' g_oNet            WshNetwork object
' sPath             Path name for drive (can be relative)
'
Sub UnmapDrive(sPath)
    Dim nExit, sDrive
    sDrive = GetDriveName(sPath)
    ' On WinNT, SUBST drives appear as local
    If IsWinNT And IsLocalDrive(sDrive) Then
        nExit = RunCmd("subst " & sDrive & " /d")
    End If
    ' Can only unmap network drives
    If IsNetworkDrive(sDrive) Then
        g_oNet.RemoveNetworkDrive sDrive, True, True
    End If
End Sub

'///////////////////////////////////////////////////////////////////////////////
' IsNetworkDrive
' Tests to see if a drive is a networked drive
'
' g_oFSO            FileSystem object
' sPath             Path name for drive (can be relative)
' Returns           True if drive is networked, False otherwise
Function IsNetworkDrive(sPath)
    Dim oDrive
    Set oDrive = GetDriveObject(sPath)
    ' Test type if valid drive
    If Not oDrive Is Nothing Then
        IsNetworkDrive = CBool(oDrive.DriveType = 3)
    Else
```

```
        IsNetworkDrive = False
    End If
End Function

'//////////////////////////////////////////////////////////////////////////
' IsLocalDrive
' Tests to see if a drive is a local drive (any type)
'
' g_oFSO            FileSystem object
' sPath             Path name for drive (can be relative)
' Returns           True if drive is local, False otherwise
'
Function IsLocalDrive(sPath)
    Dim oDrive
    Set oDrive = GetDriveObject(sPath)
    ' Test type if valid drive
    If Not oDrive Is Nothing Then
        IsLocalDrive = CBool(oDrive.DriveType <> 3)
    Else
        IsLocalDrive = False
    End If
End Function

'//////////////////////////////////////////////////////////////////////////
' GetDriveObject
' Get FSO drive object with error checking
'
' g_oFSO            FileSystem object
' sPath             Path name for drive (can be relative)
' Returns           Drive object or Nothing if drive does not exist
'
Function GetDriveObject(sPath)
    On Error Resume Next
    Set GetDriveObject = Nothing
    Set GetDriveObject = g_oFSO.GetDrive(GetDriveName(sPath))
    If Err.Number <> 0 Then Set GetDriveObject = Nothing
End Function

'//////////////////////////////////////////////////////////////////////////
' GetDriveName
' Get drive name from path name
'
' g_oFSO            FileSystem object
' sPath             Path name for drive (can be relative)
' Returns           Drive name from path
'
Function GetDriveName(sPath)
    GetDriveName = g_oFSO.GetDriveName(g_oFSO.GetAbsolutePathName(sPath)) End Function

'//////////////////////////////////////////////////////////////////////////
' RunCmd
' Run a shell command
'
```

continues ▶

Listing 12.4 *continued*

```
' g_oShell          WshShell object
' sCmd              Command to execute
' Returns           Exit code from application
'
Function RunCmd(sCmd)
    Dim sShell
    ' Get name of command processor
    sShell = g_oShell.Environment("Process").Item("COMSPEC")
    If sShell = "" Then
        If IsWinNT Then sShell = "cmd" Else sShell = "command"
    End If
    ' Run command via "COMSPEC /c command"
    WScript.Echo "Run: " & sCmd
    RunCmd = g_oShell.Run(sShell & " /c " & sCmd, &H20000000, True)
End Function

'//////////////////////////////////////////////////////////////////////////////
' IsWinNT
' Tests for Windows NT or Windows 2000
'
' g_oShell          WshShell object
' Returns           True on NT or Win2K, False otherwise
'
Function IsWinNT
    Dim sOS
    sOS = g_oShell.Environment("Process").Item("OS")
    IsWinNT = CBool(sOS = "Windows_NT")
End Function

'//////////////////////////////////////////////////////////////////////////////
```

The `MTPLogon.vbs` script begins by initializing some global variables. These contain some standard objects that are used throughout the rest of the script, including a `WshShell`, `FileSystem`, and `WshNetwork` object.

The rest of the `MTPLogon.vbs` script is best understood by reading the script backwards from the lowest level procedures to the higher levels that then use these procedures.

The `IsWinNT` function is used to distinguish between operating systems, such as Windows NT, Windows 2000, and Windows 9x. The function returns `True` on Windows NT and Windows 2000, and `False` on other platforms. The function works by checking the value of the `OS` environment variable.

The `RunCmd` function is a variation on the `RunCmd` procedure previously shown. This version is a function that returns the exit code of the shell command.

The `GetDriveName` function is a trivial function that extracts the drive name from any path name (even a relative path name). This is used by the `GetDriveObject` function to get a `Drive` object for any specified path. This function returns either the `Drive` object or `Nothing` if the drive does not exist.

The `IsLocalDrive` and `IsNetworkDrive` functions return `True` if the specified drive is a local or network drive, respectively. The functions first get a drive object using `GetDriveObject` and then test the drive type. Note that both functions return `False` if the drive is not valid.

The `UnmapDrive` and `MapDrive` functions perform network drive mapping for the logon script. They are essentially a wrapper for the `.MapNetworkDrive` and `.RemoveNetworkDrive` methods of the `WshNetwork` object, but they perform additional error checking and optimization.

The primary optimization performed is the replacement of network mapping with `SUBST` commands on Windows NT and Windows 2000 computers when the drive mapping references a local computer in the UNC name. In this case, drive access via a `SUBST` command is much more efficient than access via the network stack.

The `UnmapDrive` function un-maps a drive if the drive is a networked drive. It also attempts to un-`SUBST` a locally mapped drive by executing the appropriate `SUBST` command.

Most of the work of the `MTPLogon.vbs` script happens inside the `MapDrive` function. This function performs the following actions:

1. If the drive name is a single asterisk, this is replaced with the home drive as specified in the users account information.
2. If the UNC path is a single asterisk, this is replaced with the home directory as specified in the users account information.
3. The UNC name is broken into computer name and share name components.
4. The specified drive is unmapped from any pre-existing drive mappings using the `UnmapDrive` function.
5. If the drive is still a local drive, it is not possible to map the drive, and `MapDrive` returns with an error.
6. If the local computer (the one running the logon script) is the same as the computer specified in the UNC share name *and* the operating system is Windows NT, the function uses a `SUBST` command to map the drive to the share.
7. Otherwise, the function uses the `.MapNetworkDrive` method of the `WshNetwork` object to map the drive to the remote computer share.

The use of the single asterisk convention in steps 1 and 2 allows the specification of the user's home drive and home directory. For example:

```
Dim bResult
bResult = MapDrive("H:", "*")
```

This maps the user's home directory to drive H:.

To achieve this mapping, the `MapDrive` function needs to obtain the users home directory. It does this by looking up the users account information using ADSI. First, it creates an ADSI object corresponding to the users account:

```
sAdsPath = g_oNet.UserDomain & "/" & g_oNet.UserName
Set oAdsObj = GetObject("WinNT://" & sAdsPath & ",user")
```

This object is then used to obtain the home directory and drive. For more information on ADSI, see Chapter 13.

ADSI is also used if the `MapDrive` function determines that the share is a local share (that is, on the same computer). In this case, as previously noted, a `SUBST` command is used instead of a network drive mapping. To do this, the function must obtain the *local path* that corresponds to the share name. Again, ADSI is used to obtain an object that represents the share, and the local path is extracted for use in the `SUBST` command.

The only other significant function in `MTPLogon.vbs` is the `IsMember` function. This function takes the name of a Windows NT group and returns `True` if the user logging on is a member of that group. This function is similar to the `IsMember` function presented in the *Phase Two Script* shown earlier. However, it contains an optimization that allows it to work more efficiently than the earlier version.

Specifically, the set of groups to which the user belongs is fetched from ADSI only *once*. This information is then used to set up a dictionary object. Each key in the dictionary object contains the name of one group. Therefore, testing group membership simply involves testing for the existence of a dictionary key:

```
IsMember = CBool(g_oGroupDict.Exists(sGroup))
```

This is much faster than the `For` loop used in the earlier version of the `IsMember` function.

The only additional work is setting up the dictionary. This is done the first time the `IsMember` function is called. The function detects this condition by checking the global `g_oGroupDict`. If this variable is empty, then the function has not been called before. A new dictionary object is created and populated with group names. These names are obtained from ADSI via a user account object.

Finally, the `MapDrive` and `IsMember` functions are called from the main body of the `MTPLogon.vbs` script to map the required drives. In this example script, the individual mappings are placed in an array, and a `For Each` loop is used to process each entry in the array.

Summary

When used as part of a two-phase logon script, WSH gives logon scripts access to the power and flexibility of VBScript. This allows the script to be much "smarter" about logon issues than simple batch scripts. This intelligence also lets a logon script move beyond simple tasks and perform an intelligent initialization of each system as a user logs on.

13

System Management Scripts

This chapter focuses on a specific technology called *Active Directory Service Interface*, or *ADSI*. This technology is available as a download from Microsoft. See Appendix A, "Installing Script Components," and Appendix B, "Other Scripting Resources," for more information.

The ADSI technology provides an interface to various *directories*, such as the Windows NT user account database or the Windows 2000 Active Directory. The information stored in these directories is made available as a series of objects. Manipulating these objects allows manipulation of the underlying directory information. For example, ADSI can be used for the following tasks on Windows NT or Windows 2000:

- Enumerate all computers, users, and groups in a Windows NT domain.
- Create new users and groups, and check or change group membership.
- Enumerate all installed services on a Windows NT or Windows 2000 computer.
- Start, stop, and manipulate installed services.
- Enumerate, create and delete file shares, print queues and user logon sessions.

ADSI is a comprehensive directory solution, and therefore the documentation is extensive and quite complex. A complete description of all the ADSI features is beyond the scope of this book. However, the sample scripts in this chapter (particularly the `ADSIExplore.vbs` script) and the "Reading the ADSI Documentation," section should help to provide a basic understanding of the way ADSI is used.

The scripts presented in this chapter are:

- The `ADSIExplore.vbs` script, which provides a generic mechanism to explore the ADSI namespace. It can also help in understanding the structure of the ADSI directory schema.

- The `DumpUsers.vbs` script, which generates an Excel spreadsheet containing user account information for a specified computer or domain.
- The `NewUser.vbs` script, which creates a new user account on a computer or domain.

Note

As with all the sample scripts in this book, the scripts in this chapter should be run using the CSCRIPT host unless otherwise noted. The examples shown assume that CSCRIPT is the default WSH host. (See Chapter 1, "Introducing WSH," for information on selecting the default WSH host.) ♦

The *ADSIExplore.vbs* Script

ADSI presents almost all its features and facilities through one or more COM objects. Each of these objects represents an item in the directory that can be manipulated. For example, there are objects for domains, computers, users, and groups.

ADSI objects can be accessed in one of two ways:

- By using the `GetObject` function to create a new object from an ADSI *path*
- By referencing properties or invoking methods of other ADSI objects

The first method, invoking `GetObject`, requires that the function be supplied with a string identifying the ADSI *path*. The path specifies which object to fetch. Each directory supported by ADSI has a different path prefix. For Windows NT domains, it is `"WinNT:"`. Table 13.1 lists some example ADSI paths and the type of object located.

For example, to access a computer named ACCESS10 in the domain DATA1, use the following code:

```
Dim oComputer
Set oComputer = GetObject("WinNT://ACCESS10/DATA1,Computer")
```

In fact, ADSI is quite flexible in its use of paths, and it will attempt to resolve a path as best it can, although this might take some time. For example, it is possible to skip the domain name in the preceding path, as follows:

```
Dim oComputer
Set oComputer = GetObject("WinNT://DATA1,Computer")
```

It is also possible to omit the trailing `",Computer"` information. This is known as the *object class*, and it is used as a hint to assist ADSI when locating an object. In general, try to provide as much information as possible in a path, including the domain and class, to improve performance.

Table 13.1 *Example ADSI Paths*

Path	Meaning
`WinNT://`*`mydomain`*`,Domain`	Access domain *`mydomain`*
`WinNT://`*`mydomain/mycomputer`*`, Computer`	Access computer *`mycomputer`* in domain *`mydomain`*
`WinNT://`*`mydomain/username`*`,User`	Access *`username`* user account in domain *`mydomain`*
`WinNT://`*`mydomain/groupname`*`,Group`	Access *`groupname`* group in domain *`mydomain`*
`WinNT://`*`mycomputer/username`*`,User`	Access *`username`* user account on computer *`mycomputer`*
`WinNT://`*`mycomputer/groupname`*`,Group`	Access *`groupname`* group on computer *`mycomputer`*
`WinNT://`*`mycomputer/servicename`*`, Service`	Access *`servicename`* service on computer *`mycomputer`*
`WinNT://`*`mycomputer`*`/lanmanserver, FileService`	Access *`fileservice`* information on *`mycomputer`*
`WinNT://`*`mycomputer`*`/lanmanserver/`*`sharename`*`,FileShare`	Access *`sharename`* share on *`mycomputer`*

After an object has been obtained using `GetObject`, the object's methods and properties are available for access. All ADSI objects support several basic properties, as follows:

```
Dim oUser
Set oUser = GetObject("WinNT://DATA1/Fred,User")
Wscript.Echo "Object name : " & oUser.Name
Wscript.Echo "Object class: " & oUser.Class
Wscript.Echo "ADSI path   : " & oUser.AdsPath
Wscript.Echo "Parent path : " & oUser.Parent
```

- The `.Name` property is the name of the object. For a user object, this is the user account name, and for a computer object, this is the computer name.
- The `.Class` property is the class name. Class names are the optional names that can be appended to the end of the ADSI path to distinguish the type of object required, for example `"User"` for user objects.
- The `.AdsPath` property contains the full ADSI path of the object, without the class appended.
- The `.Parent` property contains the full ADSI path of this object's parent object. For example, a user object will have either a domain or a computer object as its parent.
- The `.Schema` property contains the full ADSI path of the schema object that provides class information for this object.

All ADSI objects support a generic set of operations on an internal *property cache*. This cache contains all the properties associated with an object. The `.Get` method is used to retrieve a property from the cache, and the `.Put` method is used to alter a property in the cache. For example:

```
Dim oUser
Set oUser = GetObject("WinNT://DATA1/Fred,User")
Wscript.Echo oUser.Get("Description")
oUser.Put "FullName", "Fred Brown"
oUser.SetInfo
```

Here, the `"Description"` property is read from a user object, and the `"FullName"` property updated. The properties that are maintained by each object are held in a temporary cache and are *only* updated in the object (and hence the underlying directory) when the `.SetInfo` method is called. Therefore, always call the `.SetInfo` method after changing one or more properties in an object. There is a corresponding `.GetInfo` method to load the cache, but this is done automatically when a property is fetched using the `.Get` method, and so this method is seldom used.

Many cached properties can also be accessed directly as regular VBScript object properties. The previous example can be re-written as:

```
Dim oUser
Set oUser = GetObject("WinNT://DATA1/Fred,User")
Wscript.Echo oUser.Description
oUser.FullName = "Fred Brown"
oUser.SetInfo
```

Properties can also be enumerated, as follows:

```
Dim oUser, oPropEntry, ix
Set oUser = GetObject("WinNT://DATA1/Fred,User")
For ix = 0 To oUser.PropertyCount
    Set oPropEntry = oUser.Item(ix)
    Wscript.Echo oPropEntry.Name & "=" & oUser.Get(oPropEntry.Name)
Next
```

Here, each property item is retrieved using the `.Item` property. Individual items are *property entry* objects, which support a `.Name` property that specifies the name of the property.

Many objects in ADSI also act as *containers* for other objects. For example, computer objects contain user, group, and service objects. These contained items can be enumerated using a normal `For Each` statement. This is shown in the `ADSIExplore.vbs` script in Listing 13.1.

In addition to the standard methods and properties already described and the properties accessible in the property cache, each ADSI object can also have additional methods and properties that are specific to that object. For example, the user account object supports the `.SetPassword` method to set a password for a user account and the `.Groups` property that returns a group collection.

The `ADSIExplore.vbs` script provides a way to explore the ADSI object space and understand how objects are related. The script takes a single argument that is assumed to be an ADSI Path, and then it dumps information about that object. For example:

```
C:\>adsiexplore WinNT://poorman,Computer
```

This command will dump information about the computer POORMAN. The `ADSIExplore.vbs` script is shown in Listing 13.1.

Listing 13.1 *`ADSIExplore.vbs` Script*

```
'//////////////////////////////////////////////////////////////////////
' $Workfile: ADSIExplore.vbs $ $Revision: 1 $ $Date: 7/18/99 10:42p $
' $Archive: /Scripts/ADSIExplore.vbs $
' Copyright (c) 1998 Tim Hill. All Rights Reserved.
'//////////////////////////////////////////////////////////////////////

' Enumerate all ADSI objects on the specified computer

' Explicit variable declaration and standard globals
Option Explicit
Dim g_sScriptPath, g_sScriptName, g_sScriptFolder, g_sVersion
Dim g_nTraceLevel
Dim g_oShell, g_oFSO
Dim s, ix, i

' Set standard globals and create global objects
g_sVersion = "1.0"
g_sScriptPath = Wscript.ScriptFullName
g_sScriptName = Wscript.ScriptName
g_sScriptFolder = Left(g_sScriptPath, Len(g_sScriptPath) - Len(g_sScriptName))
Set g_oShell = CreateObject("Wscript.Shell")
Set g_oFSO = CreateObject("Scripting.FileSystemObject")

' Setup trace control from WSHTRACE environment variable
i = g_oShell.Environment("Process").Item("WSHTRACE")
If IsNumeric(i) Then g_nTraceLevel = CInt(i) Else g_nTraceLevel = 0

' Check for -help, -? etc help request on command line
If Wscript.Arguments.Count > 0 Then
    s = LCase(Wscript.Arguments(0))
    If (s = "-help") Or (s = "-?") Or (s = "/help") Or (s = "/?") Then
        ShowHelpMessage
        Wscript.Quit(1)
    End If
End If

' Globals used by Main etc
Dim g_bSubObjSwitch, g_bVerboseSwitch, g_aFilters

' Show signon banner, then call Main function
```

continues ▶

Listing 13.1 *continued*

```
ix = Instr(g_sScriptName, ".")
If ix <> 0 Then s = Left(g_sScriptName, ix - 1) Else s = g_sScriptName
Wscript.Echo s & " version " & g_sVersion & vbCRLF
i = Main

' Release standard global objects, then exit script
Set g_oFSO = Nothing
Set g_oShell = Nothing
Wscript.Quit(i)

'//////////////////////////////////////////////////////////////////////////////
' Main
' Main function called to embody primary script logic
'
' Returns          Exit code from script
'
Function Main
    Trace 1, "+++Main"
    Dim sAdsPath, oAdsObj, nCount, oArgs, oArg

    ' Parse command line into globals
    Set oArgs = CreateObject("MTP.CmdArgs")
    oArgs.FromCollection(Wscript.Arguments)      ' Get command line
    If oArgs.TypedCount(1+4) < 1 Then            ' If missing path..
        ShowHelpMessage
        Wscript.Quit(0)
    End If
    sAdsPath = oArgs.TypedItem(1+4, 0).Text      ' Get ADSI path name
    g_bSubObjSwitch = oArgs.TestSwitch("c") Or oArgs.TestSwitch("s")
    g_bVerboseSwitch = oArgs.TestSwitch("v")
    ReDim g_aFilters(100) : ix = 0 : nCount = 0
    Do
        Set oArg = oArgs.FindArg(2, "f", ix)     ' Find /f switch
        If Not oArg Is Nothing Then
            ix = oArg.Index + 1                  ' Ready for next
            g_aFilters(nCount) = oArg.Value      ' Get filter value
            nCount = nCount + 1
        End if
    Loop Until oArg Is Nothing
    If nCount > 0 Then
        ReDim Preserve g_aFilters(nCount - 1)    ' Trim array
    Else
        g_aFilters = Empty                       ' Delete array
    End If
    Set oArgs = Nothing

    ' Prepare the ADSI object
    On Error Resume Next
    Set oAdsObj = GetObject(sAdsPath)
    If Err.Number <> 0 Then
        Wscript.Echo sAdsPath & ": not found (0x" & Hex(Err.Number) & ")"
```

```
        Wscript.Quit(Err.Number)
    End If
    On Error Goto 0

    ' Display heading, then dump primary object and contained
    Wscript.StdOut.WriteLine "ADSI Dump of: " & sAdsPath
    Wscript.StdOut.WriteLine
    If g_bVerboseSwitch Then
        DumpSchema "", oAdsObj
        Wscript.StdOut.WriteLine
    End If
    DumpAll "", oAdsObj

    ' Return value is passed to Wscript.Quit as script exit code
    Main = 0
End Function

'////////////////////////////////////////////////////////////////////////////////
' DumpSchema
' Dump the schema for the specified ADSI object
'
' sPrefix          Spaces prefix for indenting
' oAdsObj          Object to dump
'
Sub DumpSchema(sPrefix, oAdsObj)
    Trace 1, "+++DumpSchema"
    Dim sData, oClass, sList

    ' Get the class object for the ADSI object
    Set oClass = GetObject(oAdsObj.Schema)

    ' Dump the class contents (objects)
    Wscript.StdOut.WriteLine sPrefix & "Schema for class: " & oClass.Name
    If oClass.Container Then
        Wscript.StdOut.WriteLine sPrefix & "    Contained objects:"
        sList = ""
        For Each sData In oClass.Containment
            If sList = "" Then
                sList = sData
            Else
                sList = sList & ", " & sData
            End If
        Next
        Wscript.StdOut.WriteLine sPrefix & "        " & sList
    End If

    ' Dump the class properties
    Wscript.StdOut.WriteLine sPrefix & "    Properties (O=optional, M=mandatory):"
    For Each sData In oClass.MandatoryProperties
        Wscript.StdOut.WriteLine sPrefix & "        (M) " & sData
    Next
    For Each sData in oClass.OptionalProperties
```

continues ▶

Listing 13.1 *continued*

```
        Wscript.StdOut.WriteLine sPrefix & "        (0) " & sData
    Next
End Sub

'//////////////////////////////////////////////////////////////////////////////
' DumpAll
' Dump object and any objects it contains, recursively
'
' sPrefix           Spaces prefix for indenting
' oAdsObj           Object to dump
'
Sub DumpAll(sPrefix, oAdsObj)
    Trace 2, "+++DumpAll"
    Dim oSubObj

    ' Dump the object itself
    DumpObject sPrefix, oAdsObj
    Wscript.StdOut.WriteLine

    ' If object is a container, enumerate all contained objects
    If g_bSubObjSwitch And GetObject(oAdsObj.Schema).Container = True Then
        If Not IsEmpty(g_aFilters) Then
            oAdsObj.Filter = g_aFilters         ' Setup filters
        End If
        For Each oSubObj In oAdsObj
            DumpAll sPrefix & "    ", oSubObj
        Next
    End If
End Sub

'//////////////////////////////////////////////////////////////////////////////
' DumpObject
' Dump individual ADSI object (also dumps related object info)
'
' sPrefix           Spaces prefix for indenting
' oAdsObj           Object to dump
'
Sub DumpObject(sPrefix, oAdsObj)
    Trace 3, "+++DumpObject"
    Dim nPropCount, ix, sName, vData, sType, oPropEntry

    ' Show basic object information
    Wscript.StdOut.WriteLine sPrefix & "*** " & oAdsObj.Class & ": " & oAdsObj.Name
    Wscript.StdOut.WriteLine sPrefix & "AdsPath: " & oAdsObj.AdsPath & "," & oAdsObj.Class

    ' Load the property cache and get property count
    oAdsObj.GetInfo
    On Error Resume Next
    nPropCount = oAdsObj.PropertyCount
    If Err.Number <> 0 Then nPropCount = 0
    On Error Goto 0
```

```
    ' Process any class-specific information
    Select Case oAdsObj.Class
        Case "Group", "LocalGroup"
            Wscript.StdOut.WriteLine sPrefix & "Members:"
            Wscript.StdOut.WriteLine sPrefix & "    " & GetList(oAdsObj.Members)
        Case "User"
            Wscript.StdOut.WriteLine sPrefix & "Groups:"
            Wscript.StdOut.WriteLine sPrefix & "    " & GetList(oAdsObj.Groups)
        Case "Service"
            Wscript.StdOut.WriteLine sPrefix & "Status=" & oAdsObj.Status
        Case "FileService"
            Wscript.StdOut.WriteLine sPrefix & "Sessions:"
            Wscript.StdOut.WriteLine sPrefix & "    " & GetList(oAdsObj.Sessions)
    End Select

    ' Dump the property list (if verbose)
    If nPropCount <> 0 And g_bVerboseSwitch Then
        Wscript.StdOut.WriteLine sPrefix & "Properties (" & nPropCount & "):"
        For ix = 0 To nPropCount - 1
            Set oPropEntry = oAdsObj.Item(ix)
            If oPropEntry.AdsType <> 0 Then
                vData = oAdsObj.Get(oPropEntry.Name)
                sType = oPropEntry.AdsType & "," & TypeName(vData)
                sName = oPropEntry.Name & "[" & sType & "]="
                Wscript.StdOut.WriteLine sPrefix & "    " & sName & CStr(vData)
            End If
        Next
    End If
End Sub

' Build comma delimited name list
Function GetList(oColl)
    Dim oObj

    GetList = ""
    For Each oObj In oColl                      ' For each object
        If GetList = "" Then                    ' if first item..
            GetList = oObj.Name
        Else
            GetList = GetList & ", " & oObj.Name
        End If
    Next
End Function

'//////////////////////////////////////////////////////////////////////////////
' ShowHelpMessage
' Display help message
'
Sub ShowHelpMessage
    Trace 1, "+++ShowHelpMessage"
    Wscript.Echo "usage: adsiexplore <ADSI-path> [<switches>]"
```

continues ▶

Listing 13.1 *continued*

```
    Wscript.Echo "    /c      Dump contained (child) objects"
    Wscript.Echo "    /s      Same as /c"
    Wscript.Echo "    /f:cls  Filter for specified class (def: all)"
    Wscript.Echo "            (Multiple /f switches are allowed)"
    Wscript.Echo "    /v      Verbose output (schema and other details)"
    Wscript.Echo ""
    Wscript.Echo "Enumerates all ADSI properties in the WinNT space for"
    Wscript.Echo "the specified ADSI path (e.g. WinNT://computer,computer)."
End Sub

'////////////////////////////////////////////////////////////////////////////
' Trace
' Debug trace output controlled by g_nTraceLevel and WSHTRACE env var
'
' nLevel            Trace level. Only display if >= WSHTRACE env var
' sText             Text to display
'
Sub Trace(nLevel, sText)
    if g_nTraceLevel > nLevel Then Wscript.Echo sText
End Sub

'////////////////////////////////////////////////////////////////////////////
```

Using the *ADSIExplore.vbs* Script

The basic output of `ADSIExplore.vbs` displays the name of the object (from the `.Name` property) and the full ADSI path of the object (from the `.AdsPath` and `.Class` properties). This is useful in showing how ADSI resolves ADSI paths.

Use the `/v` switch to enable verbose output mode. In verbose mode, the script also dumps the following additional information for the specified object:

- *The* schema *for the object.* This describes the class of the object in detail, including the classes of object (if any) which are contained in objects of this class, and which properties are supported for this object.
- *All the properties for the object, their types, and their values.* The type information is shown as both ADSI type data and the equivalent VBScript type data from the `TypeName` function.

Use the `/c` switch to also dump all *contained* objects. For example, this will dump the local account database (users and groups) for a computer and any print queues or installed services. The combination of the `/v` and `/c` switches produces the most comprehensive output. For example:

```
C:\>adsiexplore WinNT://poorman,Computer /v /c
```

Implementation Details

The `ADSIExplore.vbs` script is based upon the `Template.vbs` script from Chapter 11, "A Script Developer's Toolkit," and so execution begins at the `Main` procedure. This uses the `MTP.CmdArgs` component to parse the command line and extract the ADSI path name and switches. The ADSI object is then obtained using the `GetObject` function.

If the verbose switch (`/v`) is specified, the `DumpSchema` procedure is called to dump the schema for the object. The `.Schema` property is used to obtain a new schema object, and the contents of this object are then dumped. Schema objects have a `.Containment` property that returns a string array containing the class names of each object type that can be contained by objects of this class. They also have two other properties, `.MandatoryProperties` and `.OptionalProperties`, which list the individual properties that the objects of this class might have.

The `DumpObject` procedure performs the work of actually dumping the object contents. This procedure operates as follows:

- The basic object properties (name and so on) are displayed first.
- The property cache is loaded and a count of properties fetched from the `.PropertyCount` property. Because some objects do not support this property, the code is protected from errors with an `On Error Resume Next` statement.
- Next, the object class is checked and any special, per-class properties are displayed.
- Finally, if required, each of the properties of the object is displayed. The property name, data type, and value are displayed.

The *DumpUsers.vbs* Script

The `DumpUsers.vbs` script makes use of ADSI to enumerate all user accounts on a computer. The information in these accounts is then extracted and placed into an Excel spreadsheet.

The `DumpUsers.vbs` script is shown in Listing 13.2.

Listing 13.2 `DumpUsers.vbs` *Script*

```
'//////////////////////////////////////////////////////////////////////
' $Workfile: DumpUsers.vbs $ $Revision: 1 $ $Date: 7/18/99 10:42p $
' $Archive: /Scripts/DumpUsers.vbs $
' Copyright (c) 1998 Tim Hill. All Rights Reserved.
'//////////////////////////////////////////////////////////////////////

' Dump user accounts to an Excel spreadsheet
```

continues ▶

Listing 13.2 *continued*

```
' Explicit variable declaration and standard globals
Option Explicit
Dim g_sScriptPath, g_sScriptName, g_sScriptFolder, g_sVersion
Dim g_nTraceLevel
Dim g_oShell, g_oFSO
Dim s, ix, i

' Set standard globals and create global objects
g_sVersion = "1.0"
g_sScriptPath = Wscript.ScriptFullName
g_sScriptName = Wscript.ScriptName
g_sScriptFolder = Left(g_sScriptPath, Len(g_sScriptPath) - Len(g_sScriptName))
Set g_oShell = CreateObject("Wscript.Shell")
Set g_oFSO = CreateObject("Scripting.FileSystemObject")

' Setup trace control from WSHTRACE environment variable
i = g_oShell.Environment("Process").Item("WSHTRACE")
If IsNumeric(i) Then g_nTraceLevel = CInt(i) Else g_nTraceLevel = 0

' Check for -help, -? etc help request on command line
If Wscript.Arguments.Count > 0 Then
    s = LCase(Wscript.Arguments(0))
    If (s = "-help") Or (s = "-?") Or (s = "/help") Or (s = "/?") Then
        ShowHelpMessage
        Wscript.Quit(1)
    End If
End If

' Show signon banner, then call Main function
ix = Instr(g_sScriptName, ".")
If ix <> 0 Then s = Left(g_sScriptName, ix - 1) Else s = g_sScriptName
Wscript.Echo s & " version " & g_sVersion & vbCRLF
i = Main

' Release standard global objects, then exit script
Set g_oFSO = Nothing
Set g_oShell = Nothing
Wscript.Quit(i)

'////////////////////////////////////////////////////////////////////////////
' Main
' Main function called to embody primary script logic
'
' Returns          Exit code from script
'
Function Main
    Trace 1, "+++Main"
    Dim sAdsPath, sExcelPath, oSheet, oExcel, oUser, oAdsObj

    ' Validate command line and get args
    If Wscript.Arguments.Count < 2 Then
        ShowHelpMessage
```

```
        Wscript.Quit(1)
    End If
    sAdsPath =  "WinNT://" & Wscript.Arguments(0)
    sExcelPath = g_oFSO.GetAbsolutePathName(Wscript.Arguments(1))

    ' Prepare ADSI computer/domain object
    On Error Resume Next
    Set oAdsObj = GetObject(sAdsPath)
    If Err.Number <> 0 Then
        Wscript.Echo sAdsPath & ": not found (0x" & Hex(Err.Number) & ")"
        Wscript.Quit(Err.Number)
    End If
    On Error Goto 0

    ' Prepare spreadsheet
    Set oExcel = CreateObject("Excel.Application")
    oExcel.Workbooks.Add
    oExcel.ActiveWorkbook.Worksheets.Add
    Set oSheet = oExcel.ActiveWorkbook.Worksheets(1)
    oSheet.Cells.Font.Size = 8
    oSheet.Name = "User Dump"
    oSheet.Cells(1,1).Value = "Dump of User Accounts on: " & Wscript.Arguments(0)
    oSheet.Cells(1,1).Font.Bold = True
    oSheet.Cells(1,1).Font.Size = 10
    oSheet.Range("A3:I3").Font.Bold = True
    oSheet.Range("A3:I3").Interior.Color = RGB(192,192,192)
    SetupCol oSheet, 3, 1,  12, "Name"
    SetupCol oSheet, 3, 2,  18, "Full Name"
    SetupCol oSheet, 3, 3,  10, "Home Drive"
    SetupCol oSheet, 3, 4,  12, "Home Dir"
    SetupCol oSheet, 3, 5,  12, "Login Script"
    SetupCol oSheet, 3, 6,  8, "User Flags"
    SetupCol oSheet, 3, 7,  12, "Profile"
    SetupCol oSheet, 3, 8,  36, "Description"
    SetupCol oSheet, 3, 9,  36, "Groups"

    ' Enumerate all users in the computer/domain
    oAdsObj.Filter = Array("User")              ' Filter user accounts only
    ix = 0
    For Each oUser In oAdsObj                   ' For each user account..
        DumpAccount oSheet, ix, oUser           ' Go add to sheet
        ix = ix + 1                             ' Bump index
    Next

    ' Save spreadsheet and close
    oExcel.ActiveWorkbook.SaveAs sExcelPath
    oExcel.ActiveWorkbook.Close
    Set oSheet = Nothing
    Set oExcel = Nothing
    Set oAdsObj = Nothing

    ' Return value is passed to Wscript.Quit as script exit code
    Main = 0
End Function
```

continues ▶

Listing 13.2 *continued*

```
Sub SetupCol(oSheet, nRow, nCol, nWidth, sTitle)
    oSheet.Cells(nRow, nCol).Value = sTitle
    oSheet.Cells(nRow, nCol).ColumnWidth = nWidth
End Sub

'////////////////////////////////////////////////////////////////////////////
' DumpAccount
' Dump user accounts
'
' oSheet            Spreadsheet object
' ix                Account index
' oUser             User account object
'
Sub DumpAccount(oSheet, ix, oUser)
    Dim oObj, sList

    ' Build group list
    sList = ""
    For Each oObj In oUser.Groups
        If sList = "" Then
            sList = oObj.Name
        Else
            sList = sList & ", " & oObj.Name
        End If
    Next

    ' Setup cell values
    oSheet.Cells(4 + ix,  1).Value = oUser.Name
    oSheet.Cells(4 + ix,  2).Value = oUser.FullName
    oSheet.Cells(4 + ix,  3).Value = oUser.HomeDirDrive
    oSheet.Cells(4 + ix,  4).Value = oUser.HomeDirectory
    oSheet.Cells(4 + ix,  5).Value = oUser.LoginScript
    oSheet.Cells(4 + ix,  6).Value = "0x" & Hex(oUser.UserFlags)
    oSheet.Cells(4 + ix,  7).Value = oUser.Profile
    oSheet.Cells(4 + ix,  8).Value = oUser.Description
    oSheet.Cells(4 + ix,  9).Value = sList
End Sub

'////////////////////////////////////////////////////////////////////////////
' ShowHelpMessage
' Display help message
'
Sub ShowHelpMessage
    Trace 1, "+++ShowHelpMessage"
    Wscript.Echo "usage: dumpusers <computer¦domain> <xls-file>"
    Wscript.Echo
    Wscript.Echo "Dumps user account information into the specified Excel"
    Wscript.Echo "spreadsheet file. Specify either a computer name or a"
    Wscript.Echo "domain name. To improve performance, append "",computer"""
    Wscript.Echo "to computer names and "",domain"" to domains name."
    Wscript.Echo "For example:"
    Wscript.Echo
```

```
    Wscript.Echo "    dumpusers mydomain,domain mydomain.xls"
    Wscript.Echo
    Wscript.Echo "This will dump users in the domain MYDOMAIN to MYDOMAIN.XLS"
End Sub

'//////////////////////////////////////////////////////////////////////////////
' Trace
' Debug trace output controlled by g_nTraceLevel and WSHTRACE env var
'
' nLevel            Trace level. Only display if >= WSHTRACE env var
' sText             Text to display
'
Sub Trace(nLevel, sText)
    if g_nTraceLevel > nLevel Then Wscript.Echo sText
End Sub

'//////////////////////////////////////////////////////////////////////////////
```

Using the *DumpUsers.vbs* Script

To use `DumpUsers.vbs`, specify two arguments. The first argument gives the computer or domain name from which to extract the user list, and the second argument is the path name for the Excel spreadsheet that is created by the script. For example:

```
C:\>dumpusers nyoffice4 c:\dumps\NewYorkOffice.xls
```

To assist ADSI (and improve performance), the class name can be specified as part of the computer or domain name. For example:

```
C:\>dumpusers backup4,computer c:\dumps\backup4.xls
```

Implementation Details

The `DumpUsers.vbs` script uses ADSI to access user account information and Excel to generate the spreadsheet file. After validating the command line, the script then prepares an ADSI path name and an Excel path name as follows:

```
sAdsPath =  "WinNT://" & Wscript.Arguments(0)
sExcelPath = g_oFSO.GetAbsolutePathName(Wscript.Arguments(1))
```

The ADSI object corresponding to this path (either a computer or a domain) is then obtained using `GetObject`.

Preparing the Excel spreadsheet is slightly more complex as both an Excel application object and a spreadsheet object must be created. This is done as follows:

```
Set oExcel = CreateObject("Excel.Application")
oExcel.Workbooks.Add
oExcel.ActiveWorkbook.Worksheets.Add
Set oSheet = oExcel.ActiveWorkbook.Worksheets(1)
```

After the oSheet spreadsheet object is available, some initial formatting work and cell headings are prepared.

The main work of the script is done in a small For Each loop that enumerates all the ADSI user objects contained in the computer or domain object, as follows:

```
oAdsObj.Filter = Array("User")
ix = 0
For Each oUser In oAdsObj
    DumpAccount oSheet, ix, oUser
    ix = ix + 1
Next
```

Because the computer/domain object can contain objects other than user objects, it is necessary to set up an ADSI *filter*, which restricts the object to enumerate only specified classes of objects. This is the purpose of the .Filter property, which is set to an array of strings, each of which specifies a single object class. After this is set, the For Each loop enumerates each individual ADSI user object and passes it to the DumpAccount procedure for processing.

The DumpAccount procedure is straightforward. It simply installs various properties from the ADSI user object into spreadsheet cells. One of the arguments, ix, is used to indicate which row to use in the spreadsheet. The only extra processing is an additional simple For Each loop to accumulate all the individual groups for the account into a comma-delimited list.

The *NewUser.vbs* Script

The NewUser.vbs script creates a new user account either on a computer or in a domain (assuming the user of the script has sufficient access rights to perform this operation). In addition to creating the account, the script also performs several other tasks traditionally associated with new accounts:

- The account is made a member of one or more groups.
- Optionally, a new share on a server is created for the user's home directory.
- Optionally, the new share is populated with a set of prototype files and folders.

The NewUser.vbs script is shown in Listing 13.3.

Listing 13.3 *NewUser.vbs Script*

```
'//////////////////////////////////////////////////////////////////////////////
' $Workfile: NewUser.vbs $ $Revision: 1 $ $Date: 7/18/99 10:42p $
' $Archive: /Scripts/NewUser.vbs $
' Copyright (c) 1998 Tim Hill. All Rights Reserved.
'//////////////////////////////////////////////////////////////////////////////
```

```
' Create a new user in the specified computer or domain

' Explicit variable declaration and standard globals
Option Explicit
Dim g_sScriptPath, g_sScriptName, g_sScriptFolder, g_sVersion
Dim g_nTraceLevel
Dim g_oShell, g_oFSO
Dim s, ix, i

' Set standard globals and create global objects
g_sVersion = "1.0"
g_sScriptPath = Wscript.ScriptFullName
g_sScriptName = Wscript.ScriptName
g_sScriptFolder = Left(g_sScriptPath, Len(g_sScriptPath) - Len(g_sScriptName))
Set g_oShell = CreateObject("Wscript.Shell")
Set g_oFSO = CreateObject("Scripting.FileSystemObject")

' Setup trace control from WSHTRACE environment variable
i = g_oShell.Environment("Process").Item("WSHTRACE")
If IsNumeric(i) Then g_nTraceLevel = CInt(i) Else g_nTraceLevel = 0

' Check for -help, -? etc help request on command line
If Wscript.Arguments.Count > 0 Then
    s = LCase(Wscript.Arguments(0))
    If (s = "-help") Or (s = "-?") Or (s = "/help") Or (s = "/?") Then
        ShowHelpMessage
        Wscript.Quit(1)
    End If
End If

' Globals used by Main etc
Dim g_bDomainSwitch, g_sFullNameSwitch, g_sDescriptionSwitch
Dim g_sLoginScriptSwitch, g_sHomeDirSwitch, g_sHomeDriveSwitch
Dim g_aGroupList, g_sHomeComputerSwitch, g_sProtoFilesSwitch
Dim g_sPasswordSwitch, g_sComputerName, g_sUserName

' Show signon banner, then call Main function
ix = Instr(g_sScriptName, ".")
If ix <> 0 Then s = Left(g_sScriptName, ix - 1) Else s = g_sScriptName
Wscript.Echo s & " version " & g_sVersion & vbCRLF
i = Main

' Release standard global objects, then exit script
Set g_oFSO = Nothing
Set g_oShell = Nothing
Wscript.Quit(i)

'//////////////////////////////////////////////////////////////////////////////
' Main
' Main function called to embody primary script logic
'
' Returns           Exit code from script
'
```

continues ▶

Listing 13.3 *continued*

```
Function Main
    Trace 1, "+++Main"
    Dim oArgs, oArg, ix, nCount, sAdsPath, oAdsObj
    Dim oUser, oGroup, sGroup

    ' Get command line and parse into globals
    Set oArgs = CreateObject("MTP.CmdArgs")
    oArgs.FromCollection(Wscript.Arguments)      ' Get command line
    If oArgs.TypedCount(1+4) < 2 Then            ' Must have comp+user
        ShowHelpMessage
        Wscript.Quit(0)
    End If
    g_sComputerName = oArgs.TypedItem(1+4, 0)    ' Get computer name
    g_sUserName = oArgs.TypedItem(1+4, 1)        ' .. and user name
    g_bDomainSwitch = oArgs.TestSwitch("Domain")
    g_sFullNameSwitch = oArgs.GetSwitch("FullName", "")
    g_sDescriptionSwitch = oArgs.GetSwitch("Description", "")
    g_sLoginScriptSwitch = oArgs.GetSwitch("LoginScript", "")
    g_sHomeDirSwitch = oArgs.GetSwitch("HomeDir", "")
    g_sHomeDriveSwitch = oArgs.GetSwitch("HomeDrive", "")
    g_sHomeComputerSwitch = oArgs.GetSwitch("HomeComputer", "")
    g_sProtoFilesSwitch = oArgs.GetSwitch("ProtoFiles", "")
    g_sPasswordSwitch = oArgs.GetSwitch("Password", "")
    ix = 0 : nCount = 0 : ReDim g_aGroupList(100)
    Do
        Set oArg = oArgs.FindArg(2, "Group", ix) ' Get Group arg..
        If Not oArg Is Nothing Then
            ix = oArg.Index + 1                  ' Set search index
            g_aGroupList(nCount) = oArg.Value    ' Get group name
            nCount = nCount + 1                  ' Bump counter
        End If
    Loop Until oArg Is Nothing
    If nCount > 0 Then                           ' If some groups..
        ReDim Preserve g_aGroupList(nCount - 1) ' Trim array
    Else
        g_aGroupList = Empty                     ' Mark no groups
    End If
    Set oArgs = Nothing

    ' Prepare the ADSI object
    sAdsPath = "WinNT://" & g_sComputerName      ' Basic path
    If g_bDomainSwitch Then                      ' If its a domain..
        sAdsPath = sAdsPath & ",domain"
    Else
        sAdsPath = sAdsPath & ",computer"
    End If
    Set oAdsObj = GetObject(sAdsPath)

    ' If /HomeComputer specified, create the share and edit the home dir
    If g_sHomeComputerSwitch <> "" And g_sHomeDirSwitch <> "" Then
        g_sHomeDirSwitch = CreateHomeShare(g_sHomeComputerSwitch, g_sUserName, g_sHomeDirSwitch)
    End If
```

```
    ' Create the basic account
    Set oUser = oAdsObj.Create("user", g_sUserName)
    oUser.FullName = g_sFullNameSwitch          ' Set users full name
    oUser.Description = g_sDescriptionSwitch    ' .. and description
    oUser.LoginScript = g_sLoginScriptSwitch    ' Login script name
    oUser.HomeDirectory = g_sHomeDirSwitch      ' Home directory
    oUser.HomeDirDrive = g_sHomeDriveSwitch     ' .. and drive
    oUser.SetInfo                               ' Update the object
    If g_sPasswordSwitch <> "" Then
        oUser.SetPassword = g_sPasswordSwitch   ' Set the password
    End If
    oUser.SetInfo                               ' Update the object

    ' Add the new account to any required groups
    If Not IsEmpty(g_aGroupList) Then           ' If some specified..
        For Each sGroup In g_aGroupList         ' For each group..
            Set oGroup = GetObject(oAdsObj.AdsPath & "/" & sGroup & ",group")
            oGroup.Add oUser.AdsPath            ' Add the user
            Set oGroup = Nothing
        Next
    End If
    Set oUser = Nothing

    ' Copy the prototype tree to the new home directory
    If g_sProtoFilesSwitch <> "" And g_sHomeDirSwitch <> "" Then
        Wscript.Echo "Copy: " & g_sProtoFilesSwitch & " To: " & g_sHomeDirSwitch
        g_oFSO.CopyFolder g_sProtoFilesSwitch, g_sHomeDirSwitch & "\", False
    End If

    ' Return value is passed to Wscript.Quit as script exit code
    Main = 0
End Function

'//////////////////////////////////////////////////////////////////////////////
' CreateHomeShare
' Create a new share on the specified computer
'
' sComputer         Target computer (where to create share)
' sUserName         Name of user account for share
' sPath             Path to share on computer (local path)
' Returns           UNC path to the new share
'
Function CreateHomeShare(sComputer, sUserName, sPath)
    Trace 1, "+++ShowHelpMessage"
    Dim oAdsObj, sAdsPath, oShare

    sAdsPath = "WinNT://" & sComputer & "/lanmanserver,fileservice"
    Set oAdsObj = GetObject(sAdsPath)           ' Get service path
    Set oShare = oAdsObj.Create("fileshare", sUserName & "$")   ' Create share
    oShare.Path = sPath                         ' Set local path of share
    oShare.SetInfo                              ' Save the new share
    Set oShare = Nothing
```

continues ▶

Listing 13.3 *continued*

```
    Set oAdsObj = Nothing
    CreateHomeShare = "\\" & sComputer & "\" & sUserName & "$"
End Function

'//////////////////////////////////////////////////////////////////////////////
' ShowHelpMessage
' Display help message
'
Sub ShowHelpMessage
    Trace 1, "+++ShowHelpMessage"
    Wscript.Echo "usage: newuser <computer> <username> [<switches>]"
    Wscript.Echo
    Wscript.Echo "Creates a new user account on the computer or domain"
    Wscript.Echo "specified as the first argument. The following switches"
    Wscript.Echo "are supported:"
    Wscript.Echo "    /Domain             Creates the account in a domain"
    Wscript.Echo "    /FullName:name      Users full name"
    Wscript.Echo "    /Description:text   Descriptive text for account"
    Wscript.Echo "    /LoginScript:name   Login script name"
    Wscript.Echo "    /HomeDir:path       Path to home directory"
    Wscript.Echo "    /HomeDrive:name     Drive to map to home directory"
    Wscript.Echo "    /Group:name         Make user a member of group"
    Wscript.Echo "    /HomeComputer:name  Computer for username$ share"
    Wscript.Echo "    /ProtoFiles:path    Source of prototype files"
    Wscript.Echo "    /Password:pwd       Initial password"
    Wscript.Echo "Multiple /Group switches are allowed. If the"
    Wscript.Echo "/HomeComputer is specified, a new share named username$"
    Wscript.Echo "will be created on the computer at the location in"
    Wscript.Echo "/HomeDir. The actual home dir for the account will then"
    Wscript.Echo "reference this share."
End Sub

'//////////////////////////////////////////////////////////////////////////////
' Trace
' Debug trace output controlled by g_nTraceLevel and WSHTRACE env var
'
' nLevel            Trace level. Only display if >= WSHTRACE env var
' sText             Text to display
'
Sub Trace(nLevel, sText)
    if g_nTraceLevel > nLevel Then Wscript.Echo sText
End Sub

'//////////////////////////////////////////////////////////////////////////////
```

Using the *NewUser.vbs* Script

To use the `NewUser.vbs` script, specify a computer name and the new account name as arguments. For example:

```
C:\>newuser mycomputer fredbrown
```

This command creates the `fredbrown` account on `mycomputer`. To create an account in a domain, specify a domain name and add the `/Domain` switch. For example:

```
C:\>newuser mydomain fredbrown /domain
```

Additional switches can be used to specify account attributes, as follows:

- `/FullName:`*`name`* The full name of the user is set to *`name`*. Place name in double quotes if it contains spaces.
- `/Description:`*`text`* The description for the account is set to *`text`*. Place text in double quotes if it contains spaces.
- `/LoginScript:`*`name`* The name of the login script is set to *`name`*.
- `/HomeDir:`*`path`* The home directory path is set to *`path`*.
- `/HomeDrive:`*`name`* The home drive (the drive mapped to the home directory) is set to *`name`*.
- `/Group:`*`name`* The new user is made a member of the specified group. Multiple `/Group` switches can be used.
- `/HomeComputer:`*`name`* A new home directory share is created on the specified computer.
- `/ProtoFiles:`*`path`* A prototype set of files is copied to the home directory from the specified *`path`*.
- `/Password:`*`pwd`* The account password is set to *`pwd`*.

If the `/HomeComputer` switch is *not* specified, the contents of the `/HomeDir` switch is used "as-is," as the home directory for the new user account. However, if the `/HomeComputer` switch is present, the script performs additional processing as follows:

- A new file share, named *`username`*`$`, is created on the specified home computer. The path for the share is set to the path specified by the `/HomeDir` switch. In this case, the path is specified relative to the home computer (that is, the path `"c:\users\bob"` refers to drive C: on the remote computer).
- The home directory for the user is changed to `\\`*`computer`*`\`*`username`*`$`; the computer name comes from the computer specified by the `/HomeComputer` switch.

Implementation Details

The script uses the `MTP.CmdArgs` component to perform all the command line parsing. All the various switches are loaded into global variables, along with the computer/domain name and the new user account name. The `/Group` switches are accumulated into an array named g_aGroupList, with one group name per element.

The initial ADSI object is prepared. The ADSI path is composed from the computer name and either ",domain" or ",computer" depending upon the presence of the /Domain switch.

If the /HomeComputer switch is specified, the CreateHomeShare function is invoked to create a new share for the user home directory. This directory is passed the target computer name (from the /HomeComputer switch), the user name, and the path for the share (from the /HomeDir switch). The function returns the UNC name of the newly created share.

To create the share, the CreateHomeShare function first creates a new ADSI object. This object is a FileService object that refers to the lanmanserver service, the service in Windows that manages file shares. The .Add method on this object is then used to create a new share, and the .Path property on the new share is set to the path of the share.

After the home share is created by the CreateHomeShare function, the new user account is created. This is done using the .Create method of the ADSI computer or domain object. This method requires two arguments. The first specifies the class of ADSI object to create (in this case, "user"), and the second specifies the object name. For example:

```
Set oUser = oAdsObj.Create("user", g_sUserName)
```

After the new user account object is created, the various account properties are set from the command-line arguments and the .SetInfo method is used to flush the cache. This also creates the new object in the Windows domain. After the object is created, the password (if specified) is set.

Next, the NewUser.vbs script adds the newly created account to each group specified with a /Group switch, as follows:

```
For Each sGroup In g_aGroupList
    Set oGroup = GetObject(oAdsObj.AdsPath & "/" & sGroup & ",group")
    oGroup.Add oUser.AdsPath
    Set oGroup = Nothing
Next
```

For each /Group switch (and hence each element in the g_aGroupList array), an ADSI group object is created and the .Add method is invoked to add the user to the group. This method requires an ADSI path to specify the user (rather than a simple user name), and this is obtained from the .AdsPath property of the oUser object. The ADSI path to the group object is itself composed of the ADSI path of the computer or domain, the group name, and the ",group" class string.

Finally, the `NewUser.vbs` script copies any prototype file tree specified using the `/ProtoFiles` switch to the new home directory (which might now be a UNC share name if the `/HomeComputer` switch was specified). This is achieved using the `.CopyFolder` method of the `FileSystem` object.

There is currently very little error checking in the `NewUser.vbs` script. Specifically, the script will fail if the specified account already exists, if the computer name is invalid, or if one of the groups does not exist. A more robust version of the script should check all these conditions (and others) before starting account creation.

Reading the ADSI Documentation

The scripts in this chapter provide an introduction to using ADSI for directory management. Full information on ADSI is available from Microsoft, but the documentation is primarily aimed at C++ and Visual Basic programmers. Translating this information into scripting terms is sometimes difficult.

First, like all COM objects, the ADSI objects provide multiple *interfaces*. An interface is a packaged set of APIs that the object makes available. C++ and Visual Basic are able to access these interfaces directly. VBScript can only access the interfaces indirectly via a process known as *late binding*. Late binding occurs either through a special interface named `IDispatch` or through any other interface that is known as a *dual interface*. Automation and dual interfaces are easy to identify because they always support a method called `Invoke`.

Visual Basic can work directly with individual interfaces. To do this, object reference variables are set to reference specific interfaces by specifying the interface name in the `Dim` statement. For example:

```
Dim oContainer as IADsContainer
```

This binds the `oContainer` object directly to the `IADsContainer` interface.

This technique is not available to VBScript scripts. Consequently, all the available properties and methods on *all* interfaces that can be accessed via late binding are available via the single object variable that references the ADSI object.

This means, for example, that an ADSI object representing a user has access to the `IADs`, `IADsUser`, and `IADsPropertyList` interfaces present in this object. The `IADs` interface is responsible for the `.Name`, `.Class`, and other core properties of the object, whereas the `IADsPropertyList` interface is responsible for enumerating the properties of the object. Finally, the `IADsUser` interface provides properties and methods that are specific to the user account class of objects.

Therefore, to understand what features of an object are available from VBScript, first locate all the interfaces on the object. Then identify those interfaces that support a `.Invoke` method. The methods and properties of each of these interfaces are then available for access from VBScript.

Finally, interfaces only support procedural properties. Therefore, just like the Windows Script Components described in Chapter 10, "Windows Script Components," each property is defined by a pair of methods named `.get_Xxx` and `.put_Xxx` for a read-write property, and `.get_Xxx` only for a read-only property.

14

Miscellaneous Scripts

This chapter presents four additional scripts that either are useful in their own right or present additional useful scripting techniques. In addition, because this is the last chapter in the book, the final script is of a more whimsical nature.

The scripts presented in this chapter are:

- The `XMLDir.vbs` script, which generates an XML file containing information about a specified directory.
- The `VBSToWS.vbs` Script, which generates a WSH 2.0 style `.WS` script from one or more WSH 1.0 style `.VBS` scripts.
- The `FindMovedFiles.vbs` script, which assists in directory tree synchronization and replication by locating moved files.
- The `Animal.vbs` script, which plays the classic animal guessing game.

Note

As with all the sample scripts in this book, the scripts in this chapter should be run using the CSCRIPT host unless otherwise noted. The examples shown assume that CSCRIPT is the default WSH host. (See Chapter 1, "Introducing WSH," for information on selecting the default WSH host.)

The *XMLDir.vbs* Script

The `XMLDir.vbs` script, as its name suggests, generates a directory listing as an XML file. The XML generated by this script is well formed, but not valid because the script does not generate or reference a DTD (document type definition) for the XML. However, the XML schema used is simple, and the generation of such a schema is a simple task.

Here is sample output from the `XMLDir.vbs` script:

```
<?xml verion="1.0"?>
<!-- XML Directory of P:\Scripts\x -->
```

```
<DIRECTORY path="P:\Scripts\x">
    <FILE>
        <NAME>AutoRevise.vbs</NAME>
        <DATECREATED>7/17/99 4:40:50 PM</DATECREATED>
        <DATELASTACCESSED>7/17/99 4:40:50 PM</DATELASTACCESSED>
        <DATELASTMODIFIED>7/17/99 4:40:50 PM</DATELASTMODIFIED>
        <SIZE>348</SIZE>
        <ATTR>-----A</ATTR>
    </FILE>
    <FOLDER>
        <NAME>Revisions</NAME>
        <DATECREATED>7/17/99 4:40:58 PM</DATECREATED>
        <DATELASTACCESSED>7/17/99 4:40:58 PM</DATELASTACCESSED>
        <DATELASTMODIFIED>7/17/99 4:40:58 PM</DATELASTMODIFIED>
        <ATTR>----D-</ATTR>
    </FOLDER>
</DIRECTORY>
```

The `XMLDir.vbs` script is shown in Listing 14.1.

Listing 14.1 *`XMLDir.vbs` Script*

```
'//////////////////////////////////////////////////////////////////////////
' $Workfile: XMLDir.vbs $ $Revision: 1 $ $Date: 7/18/99 10:42p $
' $Archive: /Scripts/XMLDir.vbs $
' Copyright (c) 1998 Tim Hill. All Rights Reserved.
'//////////////////////////////////////////////////////////////////////////

' Generate an XML representation of a directory

' Explicit variable declaration and standard globals
Option Explicit
Dim g_sScriptPath, g_sScriptName, g_sScriptFolder, g_sVersion
Dim g_nTraceLevel
Dim g_oShell, g_oFSO
Dim s, ix, i

' Set standard globals and create global objects
g_sVersion = "1.0"
g_sScriptPath = Wscript.ScriptFullName
g_sScriptName = Wscript.ScriptName
g_sScriptFolder = Left(g_sScriptPath, Len(g_sScriptPath) - Len(g_sScriptName))
Set g_oShell = CreateObject("Wscript.Shell")
Set g_oFSO = CreateObject("Scripting.FileSystemObject")

' Setup trace control from WSHTRACE environment variable
i = g_oShell.Environment("Process").Item("WSHTRACE")
If IsNumeric(i) Then g_nTraceLevel = CInt(i) Else g_nTraceLevel = 0

' Check for -help, -? etc help request on command line
If Wscript.Arguments.Count > 0 Then
    s = LCase(Wscript.Arguments(0))
    If (s = "-help") Or (s = "-?") Or (s = "/help") Or (s = "/?") Then
        ShowHelpMessage
```

```
        Wscript.Quit(1)
    End If
End If

' Show signon banner, then call Main function
ix = Instr(g_sScriptName, ".")
If ix <> 0 Then s = Left(g_sScriptName, ix - 1) Else s = g_sScriptName
Wscript.Echo s & " version " & g_sVersion & vbCRLF
i = Main

' Release standard global objects, then exit script
Set g_oFSO = Nothing
Set g_oShell = Nothing
Wscript.Quit(i)

'////////////////////////////////////////////////////////////////////////////
' Main
' Main function called to embody primary script logic
'
' Returns          Exit code from script
'
Function Main
    Trace 1, "+++Main"
    Dim sPath, oFolder, oFile, oSubFolder

    ' Get the absolute path name of the directory
    If Wscript.Arguments.Count < 1 Then
        sPath = "."                               ' Use this directory
    Else
        sPath = Wscript.Arguments(0)
    End If
    sPath = g_oFSO.GetAbsolutePathName(sPath)   ' Make absolute
    Set oFolder = g_oFSO.GetFolder(sPath)       ' Get the folder

    ' Emit the preamble
    Wscript.StdOut.WriteLine "<?xml verion=""1.0""?>"       ' Special XML header
    Wscript.StdOut.WriteLine "<!-- XML Directory of " & sPath & " -->"
    Wscript.StdOut.WriteLine
    Wscript.StdOut.WriteLine "<DIRECTORY path=" & MakeQXML(sPath) & ">"

    ' Emit individual file and folder elements
    For Each oFile In oFolder.Files             ' For each file..
        EmitFile "    ", oFile                  ' Emit the XML
    Next
    For Each oSubFolder In oFolder.SubFolders   ' For each folder
        EmitFolder "    ", oSubFolder           ' Emit the XML
    Next

    ' Emit the postamble
    Wscript.StdOut.WriteLine "</DIRECTORY>"
    Set oFolder = Nothing
```

continues ▶

Listing 14.1 *continued*

```
    ' Return value is passed to Wscript.Quit as script exit code
    Main = 0
End Function

'//////////////////////////////////////////////////////////////////////////////
' EmitFile
' Emit file object as XML
'
Sub EmitFile(sPrefix, oFile)
    Wscript.StdOut.WriteLine sPrefix & "<FILE>"             ' Start element
    EmitElement sPrefix & "    ", "NAME", oFile.Name
    EmitElement sPrefix & "    ", "DATECREATED", oFile.DateCreated
    EmitElement sPrefix & "    ", "DATELASTACCESSED", oFile.DateLastAccessed
    EmitElement sPrefix & "    ", "DATELASTMODIFIED", oFile.DateLastModified
    EmitElement sPrefix & "    ", "SIZE", oFile.Size
    EmitElement sPrefix & "    ", "ATTR", GetAttrString(oFile.Attributes)
    Wscript.StdOut.WriteLine sPrefix & "</FILE>"            ' Close element
End Sub

'//////////////////////////////////////////////////////////////////////////////
' EmitFolder
' Emit folder object as XML
'
Sub EmitFolder(sPrefix, oFolder)
    Wscript.StdOut.WriteLine sPrefix & "<FOLDER>"               ' Start element
    EmitElement sPrefix & "    ", "NAME", oFolder.Name
    EmitElement sPrefix & "    ", "DATECREATED", oFolder.DateCreated
    EmitElement sPrefix & "    ", "DATELASTACCESSED", oFolder.DateLastAccessed
    EmitElement sPrefix & "    ", "DATELASTMODIFIED", oFolder.DateLastModified
    EmitElement sPrefix & "    ", "ATTR", GetAttrString(oFolder.Attributes)
    Wscript.StdOut.WriteLine sPrefix & "</FOLDER>"          ' Close element
End Sub

'//////////////////////////////////////////////////////////////////////////////
' GetAttrString
' Get string form of attributes
'
Function GetAttrString(nAttr)
    Dim sAttr
    GetAttrString = ""
    If nAttr And 1 Then sAttr = "R" Else sAttr = "-"
    GetAttrString = GetAttrString & sAttr
    If nAttr And 2 Then sAttr = "H" Else sAttr = "-"
    GetAttrString = GetAttrString & sAttr
    If nAttr And 4 Then sAttr = "S" Else sAttr = "-"
    GetAttrString = GetAttrString & sAttr
    If nAttr And 8 Then sAttr = "V" Else sAttr = "-"
    GetAttrString = GetAttrString & sAttr
    If nAttr And 16 Then sAttr = "D" Else sAttr = "-"
    GetAttrString = GetAttrString & sAttr
```

```
    If nAttr And 32 Then sAttr = "A" Else sAttr = "-"
    GetAttrString = GetAttrString & sAttr
End Function

'//////////////////////////////////////////////////////////////////////////////
' EmitElement
' Emit individual XML element
'

Sub EmitElement(sPrefix, sName, sValue)
    Dim sElement

    sElement = "<" & sName & ">" & MakeXML(sValue) & "</" & sName & ">"
    Wscript.StdOut.WriteLine sPrefix & sElement
End Sub

'//////////////////////////////////////////////////////////////////////////////
' MakeXML and MakeQXML
' Make a string valid for XML use (converts reserved chars to entities)
'
' sString          String to convert
'

Function MakeXML(sString)
    ' Replace reserved characters with entities
    MakeXML = sString                            ' Get replacement string
    MakeXML = Replace(MakeXML, "&", "&amp;")     ' MUST BE FIRST!!
    MakeXML = Replace(MakeXML, "<", "&lt;")      ' Less than
    MakeXML = Replace(MakeXML, ">", "&gt;")      ' Greater than
    MakeXML = Replace(MakeXML, "'", "&apos;")    ' Apostrophe
    MakeXML = Replace(MakeXML, Chr(34), "&quot;")    ' Double quote
End Function

Function MakeQXML(sString)
    MakeQXML = Chr(34) & MakeXML(sString) & Chr(34)
End Function

'//////////////////////////////////////////////////////////////////////////////
' ShowHelpMessage
' Display help message
'

Sub ShowHelpMessage
    Trace 1, "+++ShowHelpMessage"
    Wscript.Echo "usage: xmldir [<path>]"
    Wscript.Echo
    Wscript.Echo "Generates an XML file to StdOut containing a well-formed"
    Wscript.Echo "XML file (w/o a DTD) the describes the contents of the"
    Wscript.Echo "specified directory, or the current directory if none is"
    Wscript.Echo "specified."
End Sub

'//////////////////////////////////////////////////////////////////////////////
```

continues ▶

Listing 14.1 *continued*

```
' Trace
' Debug trace output controlled by g_nTraceLevel and WSHTRACE env var
'
' nLevel            Trace level. Only display if >= WSHTRACE env var
' sText             Text to display
'
Sub Trace(nLevel, sText)
    if g_nTraceLevel > nLevel Then Wscript.Echo sText
End Sub

'///////////////////////////////////////////////////////////////////////////
```

Using the *XMLDir.vbs* Script

To use the `XMLDir.vbs` script, specify the directory for the listing as a single command-line argument. If no arguments are supplied, the current directory is listed.

The output of the `XMLDir.vbs` script is written to `Wscript.StdOut`, which means that normal command-line redirection can be used to capture the output to a file. For example:

```
C:/>cscript xmldir.vbs c:\ >dir.xml
```

Implementation Details

The implementation of the `XMLDir.vbs` script is simple. The XML generation can be split into four stages:

1. Generation of XML preamble
2. Generation of per-file elements
3. Generation of per-folder elements
4. Generation of XML post-amble

The preamble and post-amble phases simply generate the required XML instructions and elements and then write them to the output stream as strings. Two `For Each` loops then handle generation of the file and folder elements (one per file and folder, respectively). These invoke the `EmitFile` and `EmitFolder` procedures to output the actual XML elements. As a convenience, the attributes on files and folders are converted from numeric form to a text representation by the `GetAttrString` function before they are output.

The `EmitElement` procedure is used as a helper routine. It emits a complete XML element, including a name and a value.

The XML generated by `XMLDir.vbs` is well formed. In well-formed XML, certain characters are reserved for use in describing the structure of the XML file. These are:

```
& < > ' "
```

Because these characters might appear in the contents of some of the elements, it is necessary to convert the characters into their normal "entity" form, such as `&` for the ampersand character. This conversion is handled by the `MakeXML` function, which takes a plain-text string as input and returns that string with all the reserved characters replaced with their equivalent entities.

Note

The `MakeXML` *function has one wrinkle. Because entities begin with an ampersand themselves, it is necessary to convert the ampersand characters first. Otherwise, ampersands that delimit entities would also be converted.*

The *VBSToWS.vbs* Script

Chapter 1 described the two primary forms of a WSH script: The WSH 1.0 style script that is used throughout this book and the WSH 2.0 style script that uses XML elements to delimit the script code. As noted in Chapter 1, a WSH 2.0 script can contain multiple independent scripts contained within distinct `job` elements.

The `VBSToWS.vbs` script converts one or more `.VBS` scripts into a single `.WS` script containing one job for each `.VBS` input script. This enables libraries of `.VBS` scripts to be quickly packaged as `.WS` scripts.

The `VBSToWS.vbs` script is shown in Listing 14.2.

Listing 14.2 `VBSToWS.vbs` *Script*

```
'////////////////////////////////////////////////////////////////////////////
' $Workfile: VBSToWS.vbs $ $Revision: 1 $ $Date: 7/18/99 10:42p $
' $Archive: /Scripts/VBSToWS.vbs $
' Copyright (c) 1998 Tim Hill. All Rights Reserved.
'////////////////////////////////////////////////////////////////////////////

' Converts a .VBS script into a .WS script

' Explicit variable declaration and standard globals
Option Explicit
Dim g_sScriptPath, g_sScriptName, g_sScriptFolder, g_sVersion
Dim g_nTraceLevel
Dim g_oShell, g_oFSO
Dim s, ix, i

' Set standard globals and create global objects
g_sVersion = "1.0"
g_sScriptPath = Wscript.ScriptFullName
g_sScriptName = Wscript.ScriptName
```

continues ▶

Listing 14.2 *continued*

```
g_sScriptFolder = Left(g_sScriptPath, Len(g_sScriptPath) - Len(g_sScriptName))
Set g_oShell = CreateObject("Wscript.Shell")
Set g_oFSO = CreateObject("Scripting.FileSystemObject")

' Setup trace control from WSHTRACE environment variable
i = g_oShell.Environment("Process").Item("WSHTRACE")
If IsNumeric(i) Then g_nTraceLevel = CInt(i) Else g_nTraceLevel = 0

' Check for -help, -? etc help request on command line
If Wscript.Arguments.Count > 0 Then
    s = LCase(Wscript.Arguments(0))
    If (s = "-help") Or (s = "-?") Or (s = "/help") Or (s = "/?") Then
        ShowHelpMessage
        Wscript.Quit(1)
    End If
End If

' Show signon banner, then call Main function
ix = Instr(g_sScriptName, ".")
If ix <> 0 Then s = Left(g_sScriptName, ix - 1) Else s = g_sScriptName
Wscript.Echo s & " version " & g_sVersion & vbCRLF
i = Main

' Release standard global objects, then exit script
Set g_oFSO = Nothing
Set g_oShell = Nothing
Wscript.Quit(i)

'//////////////////////////////////////////////////////////////////////////////
' Main
' Main function called to embody primary script logic
'
' Returns          Exit code from script
'
Function Main
    Trace 1, "+++Main"
    Dim sDstPath, oDstStream, sSrcPath, oSrcStream, ix, sLine, sID

    ' The LAST argument is the .WS output file, others are .VBS i/p files
    If Wscript.Arguments.Count < 2 Then
        ShowHelpMessage
        Wscript.Quit(1)
    End If
    sDstPath = Wscript.Arguments(Wscript.Arguments.Count - 1)
    If sDstPath <> "-" Then
        sDstPath = g_oFSO.GetAbsolutePathName(sDstPath)
        Set oDstStream = g_oFSO.CreateTextFile(sDstPath, True)
    Else
        Set oDstStream = Wscript.StdOut
    End If
```

```
    ' Emit the preamble
    oDstStream.WriteLine "<?xml verion=""1.0""?>"   ' Special XML header
    oDstStream.WriteLine "<!-- Created by VBStoWS Script -->"
    oDstStream.WriteLine
    If Wscript.Arguments.Count > 2 Then         ' If multiple .VBS files
        oDstStream.WriteLine "<package>"
        oDstStream.WriteLine
    End If

    ' Process each individual .VBS file
    For ix = 0 To Wscript.Arguments.Count - 2
        sSrcPath = g_oFSO.GetAbsolutePathName(Wscript.Arguments(ix))
        sID = g_oFSO.GetBaseName(sSrcPath)

        ' Emit the file preamble
        oDstStream.WriteLine "<!-- " & sSrcPath & " -->"
        oDstStream.WriteLine "<job id=" & MakeQXML(sID) & ">"
        oDstStream.WriteLine "<script language=""VBScript"">"
        oDstStream.WriteLine "<![CDATA["

        ' Copy the .VBS file to the .WS file
        Set oSrcStream = g_oFSO.OpenTextFile(sSrcPath)
        Do Until oSrcStream.AtEndOfStream
            sLine = oSrcStream.ReadLine
            oDstStream.WriteLine sLine
        Loop
        oSrcStream.Close
        Set oSrcStream = Nothing

        ' Emit the file postamble
        oDstStream.WriteLine "]]>"
        oDstStream.WriteLine "</script>"
        oDstStream.WriteLine "</job>"
        oDstStream.WriteLine
    Next

    ' Emit the postamble and close the dest stream
    If Wscript.Arguments.Count > 2 Then         ' If multiple .VBS files
        oDstStream.WriteLine "</package>"
    End If
    oDstStream.Close
    Set oDstStream = Nothing

    ' Return value is passed to Wscript.Quit as script exit code
    Main = 0
End Function

'//////////////////////////////////////////////////////////////////////////////
' MakeXML and MakeQXML
' Make a string valid for XML use (converts reserved chars to entities)
'
' sString          String to convert
'
```

continues ▶

Listing 14.2 *continued*

```
Function MakeXML(sString)
    ' Replace reserved characters with entities
    MakeXML = sString                            ' Get replacement string
    MakeXML = Replace(MakeXML, "&", "&amp;")     ' MUST BE FIRST!!
    MakeXML = Replace(MakeXML, "<", "&lt;")      ' Less than
    MakeXML = Replace(MakeXML, ">", "&gt;")      ' Greater than
    MakeXML = Replace(MakeXML, "'", "&apos;")    ' Apostrophe
    MakeXML = Replace(MakeXML, Chr(34), "&quot;")    ' Double quote
End Function

Function MakeQXML(sString)
    MakeQXML = Chr(34) & MakeXML(sString) & Chr(34)
End Function

'//////////////////////////////////////////////////////////////////////////////
' ShowHelpMessage
' Display help message
'
Sub ShowHelpMessage
    Trace 1, "+++ShowHelpMessage"
    Wscript.Echo "usage: vbstows <vbs-file> ... <ws-file>"
    Wscript.Echo
    Wscript.Echo "Converts one or more WSH 1.0 style .VBS scripts into a"
    Wscript.Echo "single WSH 2.0 .WS script by adding the necessary XML"
    Wscript.Echo "elements. The last arguments specifies the <ws-file> to"
    Wscript.Echo "use for output. Each .VBS file is written to the .WS file as"
    Wscript.Echo "a single job element. If the <ws-file> is ""-"", the"
    Wscript.Echo "output is written to StdOut."
End Sub

'//////////////////////////////////////////////////////////////////////////////
' Trace
' Debug trace output controlled by g_nTraceLevel and WSHTRACE env var
'
' nLevel            Trace level. Only display if >= WSHTRACE env var
' sText             Text to display
'
Sub Trace(nLevel, sText)
    if g_nTraceLevel > nLevel Then Wscript.Echo sText
End Sub

'//////////////////////////////////////////////////////////////////////////////
```

Using the *VBSToWS.vbs* Script

To use the `VBSToWS.vbs` script, list the script `.VBS` script files to convert on the command line. Place the output `.WS` script file name last on the command line. For example:

```
C:\>vbstows one.vbs two.vbs three.vbs numbers.ws
```

This command converts the three .VBS files, one.vbs, two.vbs, and three.vbs, into three jobs in the numbers.ws script.

The VBSToWS.vbs script also enables the output .WS script file name to be "-". In this case, the output script is written to the Wscript.StdOut stream. This enables the script output to be viewed on screen or captured using normal command-shell redirection.

Implementation Details

The implementation of the VBSToWS.vbs script is similar to the XMLDir.vbs script. One slight wrinkle is that the output file is the *last* command-line argument, so this must be extracted first, as follows:

```
sDstPath = Wscript.Arguments(Wscript.Arguments.Count - 1)
```

All other command-line arguments are assumed to be input files (.VBS scripts). The script simply iterates each file one by one using a For loop. Because the last argument is the output file, the last argument must *not* be processed in this way. This yields the following loop:

```
For ix = 0 To Wscript.Arguments.Count - 2
    sSrcPath = g_oFSO.GetAbsolutePathName(Wscript.Arguments(ix))
    [process this source file]
Next
```

Each individual .VBS input script is written into its own job element with a unique job ID attribute derived from the base name of the script file. If there is more than one input script file, the entire set of job elements is enclosed in a package element. Package elements are explained in Chapter 1.

Like the XMLDir.vbs script, the output of the VBSToWS.vbs script is well formed XML. This means that the same restrictions for the reserved XML characters apply. However, rather than converting all these characters to entities, the script places the entire script file contents within a CDATA section. See Chapter 10, "Windows Script Components," for more information about CDATA sections.

The *FindMovedFiles.vbs* Script

There are a number of tools available to compare and synchronize two directory trees. One of the most popular is the ROBOCOPY tool from the Windows NT Resource Kit, but there are many others; some are GUI based and others are command-line based. All these tools replicate a directory tree from one location to another, much like the XCOPY shell command. However, unlike XCOPY, these tools are generally "smart." They compare the source tree to the destination tree and only perform the minimum work to make the destination tree a replica of the source tree. This minimalist approach is particularly important if the replication occurs over a slow WAN link (such as a dial-up connection).

However, almost all these replication tools suffer from one problem. They typically cannot identify *moved* files. For example, suppose you have two directory trees, `C:\Master` and `D:\Slave` that are perfectly in sync. As implied by the names, the `D:\Slave` tree is a replica of the `C:\Master` tree, and at periodic intervals, it is updated so that its contents match the master tree, `C:\Master`. If, for example, a file in the `C:\Master` tree is moved from the `C:\Master\Basic` folder to the `C:\Master\Extra` folder, the replicator software will not detect this as a moved file. Instead it will interpret this as a *deleted* file in `C:\Master\Basic` and a *new* file in `C:\Master\Extra`. Then, when replication occurs, it will delete the file in `D:\Slave\Basic` and copy the file from `C:\Master\Extra` to `D:\Slave\Extra`.

This delete and copy action correctly synchronizes the two trees, *but* it is much slower than simply moving the file from `D:\Slave\Basic` to `D:\Slave\Extra`, an operation that is equivalent to the delete/copy sequence but does not involve sending data. If the connection is a 56K modem and the file in question is large, the move operation can take one or two seconds, whereas the delete/copy operation can take hours.

The `FindMovedFiles.vbs` script is a "helper" script that attempts to expedite this situation by identifying opportunities to use the fast move operation. Thus, `FindMovedFiles.vbs` can be used as a pre-processing step before the synchronization tool is used.

The `FindMovedFiles.vbs` script is shown in Listing 14.3.

Listing 14.3 *`FindMovedFiles.vbs` Script*

```
'//////////////////////////////////////////////////////////////////////////////
' $Workfile: FindMovedFiles.vbs $ $Revision: 1 $ $Date: 7/18/99 10:42p $
' $Archive: /Scripts/FindMovedFiles.vbs $
' Copyright (c) 1998 Tim Hill. All Rights Reserved.
'//////////////////////////////////////////////////////////////////////////////

' Find all files moved in a tree

' Explicit variable declaration and standard globals
Option Explicit
Dim g_sScriptPath, g_sScriptName, g_sScriptFolder, g_sVersion
Dim g_nTraceLevel
Dim g_oShell, g_oFSO
Dim s, ix, i

' Set standard globals and create global objects
g_sVersion = "1.0"
g_sScriptPath = Wscript.ScriptFullName
g_sScriptName = Wscript.ScriptName
```

```
g_sScriptFolder = Left(g_sScriptPath, Len(g_sScriptPath) - Len(g_sScriptName))
Set g_oShell = CreateObject("Wscript.Shell")
Set g_oFSO = CreateObject("Scripting.FileSystemObject")

' Setup trace control from WSHTRACE environment variable
i = g_oShell.Environment("Process").Item("WSHTRACE")
If IsNumeric(i) Then g_nTraceLevel = CInt(i) Else g_nTraceLevel = 0

' Check for -help, -? etc help request on command line
If Wscript.Arguments.Count > 0 Then
    s = LCase(Wscript.Arguments(0))
    If (s = "-help") Or (s = "-?") Or (s = "/help") Or (s = "/?") Then
        ShowHelpMessage
        Wscript.Quit(1)
    End If
End If

' Show signon banner, then call Main function
ix = Instr(g_sScriptName, ".")
If ix <> 0 Then s = Left(g_sScriptName, ix - 1) Else s = g_sScriptName
Wscript.Echo s & " version " & g_sVersion & vbCRLF
i = Main

' Release standard global objects, then exit script
Set g_oFSO = Nothing
Set g_oShell = Nothing
Wscript.Quit(i)

'///////////////////////////////////////////////////////////////////////////////
' Main
' Main function called to embody primary script logic
'
' Returns          Exit code from script
'
Function Main
    Trace 1, "+++Main"
    Dim sSrcPath, sDstPath, oSrcDict, oDstDict, oSrcRoot, oDstRoot, nCount

    ' Validate arguments (must be at least two, and both must be valid dirs)
    If Wscript.Arguments.Count < 2 Then ShowHelpMessage : Wscript.Quit(0)
    sSrcPath = g_oFSO.BuildPath(Wscript.Arguments(0), ".")
    If Not g_oFSO.FolderExists(sSrcPath) Then
        Wscript.Echo Wscript.Arguments(0) & " does not exist"
        Wscript.Quit(0)
    End If
    sDstPath = g_oFSO.BuildPath(Wscript.Arguments(1), ".")
    If Not g_oFSO.FolderExists(sDstPath) Then
        Wscript.Echo Wscript.Arguments(1) & " does not exist"
        Wscript.Quit(0)
    End If
    sSrcPath = g_oFSO.GetAbsolutePathName(g_oFSO.GetParentFolderName(sSrcPath))
    sDstPath = g_oFSO.GetAbsolutePathname(g_oFSO.GetParentFolderName(sDstPath))
```

continues ▶

Listing 14.3 *continued*

```
    ' Build the src and dst dictionaries
    Set oSrcDict = BuildDictionary(sSrcPath)
    Set oDstDict = BuildDictionary(sDstPath)

    ' Locate all orphaned source files and find moved file in destination
    Set oSrcRoot = g_oFSO.GetFolder(sSrcPath)
    Set oDstRoot = g_oFSO.GetFolder(sDstPath)
    nCount = FindMovedFiles(oSrcRoot, oDstRoot, oSrcDict, oDstDict, oSrcRoot)

    ' Return value is passed to Wscript.Quit as script exit code
    Main = nCount
End Function

'//////////////////////////////////////////////////////////////////////////////
' BuildDictionary
' Build a dictionary object containing signatures for all files in tree
'
' sPath             Path of folder at root of tree
' Returns           Created dictionary object
'
Function BuildDictionary(sPath)
    Trace 1, "+++BuildDictionary: " & sPath
    Dim oDict, oFolder
    Set oDict = CreateObject("Scripting.Dictionary")
    oDict.CompareMode = vbTextCompare           ' Ignore case
    Set oFolder = g_oFSO.GetFolder(sPath)
    AddFiles oDict, oFolder                     ' Recursively add files
    Set BuildDictionary = oDict
End Function

Sub AddFiles(ByVal oDict, ByVal oFolder)
    Trace 2, "+++AddFiles: " & oFolder.Path
    Dim oFile, sSig, oSubFolder

    ' Add each file in this folder
    For Each oFile In oFolder.Files             ' For each file..
        sSig = GetSignature(oFile)              ' Get signature
        If oDict.Exists(sSig) Then              ' If it exists..
            oDict.Item(sSig) = oDict.Item(sSig) & ";" & oFile.Path
        Else
            oDict.Add sSig, oFile.Path          ' Add new item
        End If
    Next

    ' Add subfolder files recursively
    For Each oSubFolder in oFolder.SubFolders   ' For each subfolder..
        AddFiles oDict, oSubFolder              ' ..add more files
    Next
End Sub

'//////////////////////////////////////////////////////////////////////////////
```

```
' FindMovedFiles
' Finds all moved files by comparing src to dst
'
' oSrcRoot          Source root folder
' oDstRoot          Destination root folder
' oSrcDict          Source file signature dictionary
' oDstDict          Destination file signature dictionary
' oFolder           Current folder to scan (recursively)
' Returns           Count of moved files located
'
Function FindMovedFiles(oSrcRoot, oDstRoot, oSrcDict, oDstDict, oFolder)
     Trace 2, "+++FindMovedFiles: " & oFolder.Path
    Dim nCount, oFile, oSubFolder, sSig, sCmd, sCmd1, sCmd2
    Dim sSrcPath, sDstPath, sSrcRelPath, sDstRelPath
    nCount = 0

    ' Process each file in this folder
    For Each oFile In oFolder.Files
        sSig = GetSignature(oFile)              ' Get file signature
        ' Signature must exist in src and dst trees
        If oSrcDict.Exists(sSig) And oDstDict.Exists(sSig) Then
            ' There must be only one src and dst file
            If Instr(oSrcDict.Item(sSig), ";") = 0 Then
                If Instr(oDstDict.Item(sSig), ";") = 0 Then
                    ' Src/dst relative paths must be different
                    sSrcPath = oSrcDict.Item(sSig)
                    sDstPath = oDstDict.Item(sSig)
                    sSrcRelPath = Mid(sSrcPath, Len(oSrcRoot.Path) + 1)
                    sDstRelPath = Mid(sDstPath, Len(oDstRoot.Path) + 1)
                    If StrComp(sSrcRelPath, sDstRelPath, vbTextCompare) <> 0 Then
                        sCmd1 = g_oFSO.BuildPath(oDstRoot.Path, sDstRelPath)
                        sCmd2 = g_oFSO.GetParentFolderName(g_oFSO.BuildPath(oDstRoot.Path,
                        sSrcRelPath))
                        sCmd = "MOVE " & sCmd1 & " " & sCmd2
                        Wscript.StdOut.WriteLine sCmd
                        ' Uncomment the next line to perform the actual MOVE operations
                        'g_oFSO.MoveFile sCmd1, sCmd2
                    End If
                End If
            End If
        End If
    Next

    ' Process subfolders recursively
    For Each oSubFolder In oFolder.SubFolders
        nCount = nCount + FindMovedFiles(oSrcRoot, oDstRoot, oSrcDict, oDstDict, oSubFolder)
    Next

    FindMovedFiles = nCount                     ' Return move count
End Function

'/////////////////////////////////////////////////////////////////////////////
```

continues ▶

Listing 14.3 *continued*

```
' GetSignature
' Compute signature for a file object
'
' oFile           File object
' Returns         Signature string for file
'
Function GetSignature(oFile)
    Trace 3, "+++GetSignature: " & oFile.Name
    Dim nAttr
    nAttr = oFile.Attributes And Not (32+64+2048)
    GetSignature = oFile.Name & ";" & CStr(oFile.DateCreated)
    GetSignature = GetSignature & ";" & CStr(oFile.DateLastModified)
    GetSignature = GetSignature & ";" & CStr(oFile.Size) & ";" & CStr(nAttr)
End Function

'//////////////////////////////////////////////////////////////////////////////
' ShowHelpMessage
' Display help message
'
Sub ShowHelpMessage
    Trace 1, "+++ShowHelpMessage"
    Wscript.Echo "usage: findmovedfiles <src-path> <dst-path>"
    Wscript.Echo "The trees located at src-path and dst-path are compared"
    Wscript.Echo "and files that are at a different location in dst-path"
    Wscript.Echo "(i.e. have been moved) are identified. The output"
    Wscript.Echo "is a list of these files expressed as a series of"
    Wscript.Echo "MOVE commands, which can be captured to a file and"
    Wscript.Echo "executed as a batch script."
End Sub

'//////////////////////////////////////////////////////////////////////////////
' Trace
' Debug trace output controlled by g_nTraceLevel and WSHTRACE env var
'
' nLevel          Trace level. Only display if >= WSHTRACE env var
' sText           Text to display
'
Sub Trace(nLevel, sText)
    if g_nTraceLevel > nLevel Then Wscript.Echo sText
End Sub

'//////////////////////////////////////////////////////////////////////////////
```

Using the *FindMovedFiles.vbs* Script

To use the `FindMovedFiles.vbs` script, specify two folder names as command-line arguments. The first folder is the source or *master* folder; the second is the destination or *slave* folder. For example:

```
C:\>findmovedfiles c:\master d:\slave
```

The script will analyze the master and slave trees (including sub-folders), searching for opportunities where a move operation on the slave tree will re-synchronize the tree contents. For each opportunity identified the script outputs (to the `Wscript.Stdout` stream) a command shell `MOVE` command that will perform the required move operation. Note that the script does not actually *execute* this command. However, it is a trivial matter to capture the output of the script to a shell batch script and then execute that script. For example:

```
C:\>cscript findmovedfiles.vbs c:\master d:\slave >movelist.bat
C:\>movelist
```

The criteria for locating a candidate file to move are as follows:

- The file must exist in the master tree, but must *not* exist in the corresponding location in the slave tree.
- The file must exist at a different location in the slave tree.
- The file in the master tree and the file in the slave tree must have the same name, size, attributes, and time stamps.
- The file must exist at only one location in the master and slave trees.

The last criterion avoids ambiguities. If multiple copies of the same file exist, it is not possible to reconcile which to move.

Implementation Details

The fundamental problem that must be solved by this script is locating two identical files that are in different locations in the master and slave trees. One simple way to do this is to process each file in the master tree one by one and, for each file, search the slave tree for matches. If both trees contained 5,000 files, this would require 25,000,000 file comparison operations and would probably take far longer than the copy operation that the script is supposed to replace.

Therefore, the script takes a different approach and uses a *dictionary* to rapidly reconcile files in the master and the slave trees. See Chapter 7, "Built-In WSH and VBScript Objects," for more information on dictionary objects.

The script operates by building two dictionaries, one for the master tree and one for the slave tree. The master tree is then traversed and information in the dictionaries is used to rapidly locate corresponding files in the slave tree. If the previously listed criteria are met, a `MOVE` shell command is generated.

`MOVE` commands are only generated for files that are considered *identical*. Here, identical means that the files have the same name, size, attributes, and time stamps. To locate identical files, the `FindMovedFiles.vbs` script generates and uses file *signatures*. A signature is simply a concatenation of the name, size, and so on into a single string. Therefore, by definition, two files are identical if their signatures are identical. Note that the path name of the file is *not* part of the signature because we are trying to find files that might exist in different folders. The `GetSignature` function creates a signature string for a file, given a `File` object as an argument.

The dictionaries for the master and slave trees use signatures as keys. The value for each key is the path name where the file is located in the tree. If multiple identical files exist in a tree, the paths to all the copies are stored in the value of the key, separated by semi-colon characters.

Given a `File` object named `oFile` and a dictionary named `oDict`, it is easy to see if an identical file already exists, as follows:

```
Dim sSig
sSig = GetSignature(oFile)
If oDict.Exists(sSig) Then Wscript.Echo "File exists at path: " & oDict.Item(sSig)
```

The `BuildDictionary` function builds a complete dictionary object from a tree. The file tree is traversed using a recursive function, `AddFiles`, which processes all files and folders in the entire tree. For each file, the signature is generated. The dictionary is then checked to see if the signature already exists. If it does not, a new key is created and the value is set as the path to the file. If a key already exists, the path of the current file is appended to the value, separated by a semi-colon.

The core of the `FindMovedFiles.vbs` script is a single recursive procedure, `FindMovedFiles`, which traverses the master tree looking for file move opportunities. Candidate files are identified using the dictionary information previously built using the `BuildDictionary` functions as follows:

1. The signature of the current file is generated.
2. The master and slave dictionaries are checked to see that the file exists somewhere in both the master and slave trees.
3. The dictionaries are checked to ensure that only one copy of the file exists in the master and slave trees. (This is done by checking for a semi-colon in the path name, which would indicate multiple paths.)
4. The relative paths in the master and slave trees are compared. If they are the same, the files are *already* in the same relative location, and no move command is required.

If all the criteria pass, a `MOVE` command is generated. The move command that is generated moves the slave file in the slave tree from its current location to a location in the slave tree that corresponds to the location of the master file in the master tree.

As it currently exists, `FindMovedFiles.vbs` is incomplete. For example, it does not detect moved *folders*, only moved *files*. It also cannot handle the case where a file is moved into a *new* folder. However, even in its current form it can improve the efficiency of many tree replication operations.

Also, the script does not actually move the files; it only emits the necessary shell commands to do so. Changing the script to perform the move is trivial, however, and the necessary script code, a single line, is included in the `FindMovedFiles.vbs` script hidden as a comment in the `FindMovedFiles` procedure.

The *Animal.vbs* Script

The `Animal.vbs` script is a re-implementation of the `Animal.bat` shell script that accompanied the book *Windows NT Shell Scripting* (published by Macmillan Technical Publishing). Thanks to the far more sophisticated facilities available in VBScript, the `Animal.vbs` script is far more approachable than it's command shell counterpart. However, they do share the same data file format, and so they can be used interchangeably. For reference, the `Animal.bat` script is also included in the sample scripts in electronic form.

Although the game is trivial, the `Animal.vbs` script illustrates several advanced uses of objects, including the use of *cursor* objects and the `Me` keyword.

The script plays the classic ANIMAL computer game, which was originally developed during the 1970's as a simple demonstration of artificial intelligence. ANIMAL is a simple but surprisingly challenging game. The computer maintains a database of animal species and an additional database of yes/no answer questions. The game begins by the (human) player thinking of an animal. The computer then asks a series of yes/no questions until either it correctly guesses the animal or it runs out of questions. What makes the game interesting is that the computer then asks what animal you are thinking of, and it also asks for a *new* yes/no question so it can distinguish this animal from its best guess. This information is then added to the database maintained by the game. This database is stored in a data file, and so each time the computer plays the game, it increases its knowledge of fauna. Eventually, it can become quite challenging to think of an animal that the computer cannot guess. Many years ago, one of the computers at MIT was rumored to have amassed a database of several thousand animals, and prizes were offered to anyone who could think of an animal not known to the computer.

The `Animal.vbs` script is shown in Listing 14.4.

Listing 14.4 *Animal.vbs Script*

```
'////////////////////////////////////////////////////////////////////////////
' $Workfile: Animal.vbs $ $Revision: 1 $ $Date: 7/18/99 10:42p $
' $Archive: /Scripts/Animal.vbs $
' Copyright (c) 1998 Tim Hill. All Rights Reserved.
'////////////////////////////////////////////////////////////////////////////

' Plays the ancient Animal computer game

Option Explicit
Dim oAnimals, sDatabase, n

' Form data file path name
sDatabase = Wscript.ScriptFullName
sDatabase = Left(sDatabase, InStrRev(sDatabase, ".") - 1) & ".dat"

' Load database and play game, then save if database is dirty
Set oAnimals = New AnimalSet
oAnimals.Reset
oAnimals.Load sDatabase
If PlayGame(oAnimals) Then
    oAnimals.Save sDatabase
End If
Set oAnimals = Nothing
Wscript.Quit(0)

'////////////////////////////////////////////////////////////////////////////
' PlayGame
' Plays the actual animal game
'
' oAnimals          Ref to AnimalSet object ready to play the game
' Returns           True if the set has changed (new animals)
'
Function PlayGame(ByRef oAnimals)
    Dim sMsg, nComputer, nHuman
    nComputer = 0 : nHuman = 0
    sMsg = ""
    PlayGame = False                            ' Not dirty yet
    Dim oCursor, n, sAnimal, sQuestion, bYesForNew
    Do While True
        Set oCursor = oAnimals.GetCursor        ' Get the game cursor
        n = MsgBox(sMsg & "Computer: " & nComputer & vbCRLF & "Human: " & nHuman & vbCRLF &
"Think of an animal, then click OK to play or Cancel to end the game.", vbOKCancel, "Animal")
        If n = vbCancel Then Exit Do
        Do While oCursor.IsQuestion
            n = MsgBox(oCursor.Text, vbYesNo, "Animal")
            If n = vbYes Then
                oCursor.FollowYes
            Else
                oCursor.FollowNo
            End If
        Loop
```

```
        n = MsgBox("Is it a " & oCursor.Text & "?", vbYesNo, "Animal")
        If n = vbYes Then
            sMsg = "I won!! Let's play again." & vbCRLF
            nComputer = nComputer + 1
        Else
            sAnimal = InputBox("You won!! What animal were you thinking of?", "Animal")
            sAnimal = Trim(sAnimal)
            If sAnimal = "" Then Wscript.Quit(1)
            Do
                sQuestion = InputBox("Please type a yes/no question to distinguish a " & sAnimal
& " from a " & oCursor.Text & ".", "Animal")
                sQuestion = Trim(sQuestion)
                If Instr(sQuestion, "?") = 0 Then
                    n = MsgBox("Please type a question (with a ""?"" at the end)!", vbOK,
"Animal")
                    sQuestion = ""
                End If
            Loop While sQuestion = ""
            n = MsgBox("The question is: """ & sQuestion & """" & vbCRLF & "For a " & sAnimal & "
the answer would be?", vbYesNo, "Animal")
            If n = vbYes Then
                oCursor.AddNewAnimal sAnimal, sQuestion, True
            Else
                oCursor.AddNewAnimal sAnimal, sQuestion, False
            End If
            PlayGame = True
            sMsg = "I want revenge!" & vbCRLF
            nHuman = nHuman + 1
        End If
        Set oCursor = Nothing                       ' Release the cursor
    Loop
End Function

'//////////////////////////////////////////////////////////////////////////
' IsValidObject
' Checks to see if a variable is a non-nothing object
'
' oObj              Object reference to check
' Returns           True if the var contains a valid object
'
Function IsValidObject(ByRef oObj)
    IsValidObject = False
    If IsObject(oObj) Then
        If Not oObj Is Nothing Then
            IsValidObject = True
        End If
    End If
End Function

'//////////////////////////////////////////////////////////////////////////
' AnimalCursor class
' Manages an animal game by traversing the animal tree
'
```

continues ▶

Listing 14.4 *continued*

```
Class AnimalCursor
    Private m_oTree                              ' Tree we are attached to
    Private m_oNode                              ' Current node in tree

    ' Attach/detach to/from a tree
    Public Sub Attach(ByRef oTree, ByRef oNode) ' Attach cursor to tree
        Set m_oTree = oTree
        Set m_oNode = oNode
    End Sub

    Public Sub Detach                            ' Detach cursor from tree
        Set m_oTree = Nothing
        Set m_oNode = Nothing
    End Sub

    ' IsAnimal and IsQuestion tests
    Public Property Get IsAnimal
        If IsValidObject(m_oNode) Then
            If IsValidObject(m_oNode.Yes) Then
                IsAnimal = False                 ' Animals are leaves
            Else
                IsAnimal = True
            End If
        Else
            IsAnimal = False
        End If
    End Property

    Public Property Get IsQuestion
        If IsValidObject(m_oNode) Then
            IsQuestion = Not IsAnimal            ' Questions are interior nodes
        Else
            IsQuestion = False
        End If
    End Property

    ' Traverse to next node
    Public Sub FollowYes
        If IsValidObject(m_oNode.Yes) Then       ' Only if valid
            Set m_oNode = m_oNode.Yes
        End If
    End Sub

    Public Sub FollowNo
        If IsValidObject(m_oNode.No) Then        ' Only if valid
            Set m_oNode = m_oNode.No
        End If
    End Sub

    Public Property Get Text
        Text = m_oNode.Text                      ' Current node text
    End Property
```

```
    ' Add new animal to tree (at end of game)
    Public Sub AddNewAnimal(sAnimal, sQuestion, bYesForNew)
        Dim oYesNode, oNoNode
        If IsValidObject(m_oNode) Then          ' Only if valid cursor
            Set oYesNode = m_oTree.NewNode(sAnimal, Nothing, Nothing)
            Set oNoNode = m_oTree.NewNode(m_oNode.Text, Nothing, Nothing)
            m_oNode.Text = sQuestion            ' New interior node
            If bYesForNew Then                  ' Link in correct way
                Set m_oNode.Yes = oYesNode
                Set m_oNode.No = oNoNode
            Else
                Set m_oNode.Yes = oNoNode
                Set m_oNode.No = oYesNode
            End If
        End If
    End Sub
End Class

'//////////////////////////////////////////////////////////////////////////////
' AnimalNode class
' Stores data for a single node in the animal tree
'
Class AnimalNode
    Public Text                                 ' Current node text
    Public Yes                                  ' Yes answer node ref
    Public No                                   ' No answer node ref
    Public Index                                ' Used when saving
End Class

'//////////////////////////////////////////////////////////////////////////////
' AnimalSet class
' Stores the complete set of animal nodes (leaves are animals)
'
Class AnimalSet
    Private m_oRoot                             ' Animal tree root
    Private m_nIndex                            ' Used when numbering nodes

    ' Reset the tree (delete all nodes)
    Public Sub Reset
        DeleteNode m_oRoot                      ' Delete entire tree
    End Sub

    Private Sub DeleteNode(ByRef oNode)
        If IsValidObject(oNode) Then            ' If valid node..
            DeleteNode oNode.Yes                ' Delete Yes sub-tree
            DeleteNode oNode.No                 ' Delete No sub-tree
        End If
        Set oNode = Nothing                     ' Delete the node itself
    End Sub
```

continues ▶

Listing 14.4 *continued*

```
' Load the tree from a file
Public Sub Load(sFilename)
    Dim oFSO, oFile, nLastNode, nNodeSize
    Dim sLine, vData, oNode, ix, oNodes()
    Reset
    Set oFSO = CreateObject("Scripting.FileSystemObject")
    If Not oFSO.FileExists(sFilename) Then
        LoadBuiltin                         ' Load the builtin DB
        Set oFSO = Nothing
        Exit Sub                            ' .. and done
    End If
    Set oFile = oFSO.OpenTextFile(sFilename, 1)
    nLastNode = 0 : nNodeSize = 0
    Do While Not oFile.AtEndOfStream
        sLine = Trim(oFile.ReadLine)
        If Len(sLine) > 0 And Left(sLine, 1) <> ";" Then
            vData = Split(sLine, ",", 3)
            Set oNode = NewNode(vData(2), vData(0), vData(1))
            nLastNode = nLastNode + 1
            If nLastNode > nNodeSize Then
                nNodeSize = nLastNode + 100
                ReDim Preserve oNodes(nNodeSize)
            End If
            Set oNodes(nLastNode) = oNode
            Set oNode = Nothing
        End If
    Loop
    Set oFile = Nothing
    For ix = 1 To nLastNode
        n = oNodes(ix).Yes
        If n <> 0 Then
            Set oNodes(ix).Yes = oNodes(n)
        Else
            Set oNodes(ix).Yes = Nothing
        End If
        n = oNodes(ix).No
        If n <> 0 Then
            Set oNodes(ix).No = oNodes(n)
        Else
            Set oNodes(ix).No = Nothing
        End If
    Next
    Set m_oRoot = oNodes(1)                 ' Set root node
    Erase oNodes
End Sub

' Load the builtin animal database
Public Sub LoadBuiltin
    Reset
    Set m_oRoot = NewNode("Does it live in the sea?", Nothing, Nothing)
```

```
    Set m_oRoot.No = NewNode("dog", Nothing, Nothing)
    Set m_oRoot.Yes = NewNode("fish", Nothing, Nothing)
End Sub

' Save the tree to a file
Public Sub Save(sFilename)
    Dim oFSO, oFile
    m_nIndex = 1                            ' Start index
    NumberNodes m_oRoot                     ' Number all nodes
    Set oFSO = CreateObject("Scripting.FileSystemObject")
    Set oFile = oFSO.CreateTextFile(sFilename, True)
    oFile.WriteLine ";ANIMAL data (" & m_nIndex - 1 & ")"
    SaveTree oFile, m_oRoot
    oFile.Close
    Set oFile = Nothing
    Set oFSO = Nothing
End Sub

Private Sub SaveTree(ByRef oFile, ByRef oNode)
    Dim nYes, nNo
    If IsValidObject(oNode) Then
        If IsValidObject(oNode.Yes) Then
            nYes = oNode.Yes.Index
        Else
            nYes = 0
        End If
        If IsValidObject(oNode.No) Then
            nNo = oNode.No.Index
        Else
            nNo = 0
        End If
        oFile.WriteLine nYes & "," & nNo & "," & oNode.Text
        SaveTree oFile, oNode.Yes
        SaveTree oFile, oNode.No
    End If
End Sub

Private Sub NumberNodes(ByRef oNode)
    If IsValidObject(oNode) Then
        oNode.Index = m_nIndex              ' Number this node
        m_nIndex = m_nIndex + 1             ' Bump the index
        NumberNodes oNode.Yes               ' Number yes tree
        NumberNodes oNode.No                ' .. and no tree
    End If
End Sub

' Get a cursor
Public Function GetCursor
    Set GetCursor = New AnimalCursor        ' Create a new cursor
    GetCursor.Attach Me, m_oRoot            ' Attach to this tree
End Function
```

continues ▶

Listing 14.4 *continued*

```
    ' Create a new node
    Public Function NewNode(sText, ByRef oYes, ByRef oNo)
        Set NewNode = New AnimalNode            ' Create new node
        NewNode.Text = sText
        If IsObject(oYes) Then
            Set NewNode.Yes = oYes
            Set NewNode.No = oNo
        Else
            NewNode.Yes = oYes
            NewNode.No = oNo
        End If
    End Function
End Class

'//////////////////////////////////////////////////////////////////////////////
```

Using the *Animal.vbs* Script

To play the game, simply execute the script. All interaction occurs through message and dialog boxes. The script stores its database of animals in the file `Animal.dat`, which it locates in the same folder as the script itself. This file is updated at the end of the game if one or more new animals are added. Therefore, place the script in a folder with read/write access before playing.

If no `Animal.dat` file is located, the script will start a new game with a built-in database of two animals: dog and fish.

Implementation Details

The game logic in the script is divided between one procedure, `PlayGame`, and three interacting classes, `AnimalCursor`, `AnimalNode`, and `AnimalSet`.

The database of animal information is maintained in a binary tree structure that is comprised of one or more nodes. Each node is implemented as an `AnimalNode` object. The node contains four properties, which are all simple variables: `.Text`, which contains the node text, `.Yes` and `.No`, which contain references to other nodes in the tree, and `.Index`, which is only used when saving the tree to the database file at the end of a game session. Each node in the tree is one of two types:

- *Leaf nodes* Leaf nodes are at the edges of the tree. A leaf node is indicated by both the `.Left` and `.Right` properties being empty. Leaf nodes represent animals, and the animal names are stored in the `.Text` property.
- *Branch nodes* Branch nodes are on the interior of the tree. A branch node is indicated by having valid `AnimalNode` object references in both the `.Left` and `.Right` properties. Branch nodes represent questions, and the questions are stored in the `.Text` property.

The game play logic is simple:

1. The game begins at the root node in the tree.
2. The node is examined. If the node is a leaf node, game play continues at step 6.
3. The node is a branch node and contains a question. The script displays the question with yes/no buttons and waits for user input.
4. If the user clicks the Yes button, the script uses the `.Yes` property of the current node to move down the tree to the next node. Otherwise, it moves down the tree using the `.No` property.
5. Play continues using the new node at step 2.
6. The game has reached an animal node. The script displays a dialog asking if the animal is correct. If it is, game play ends.
7. If the script guessed the wrong animal, a series of dialogs are displayed to gather the name of the animal, and a yes/no question (with answer) about the animal. This information is then used to extend the tree.
8. To extend the tree, two new nodes are created and attached to the `.Yes` and `.No` properties of the current node, thus converting the current node to a branch node. The branch node is then populated with the new question, and the two new leaf nodes are populated with the animal names: one new, the other from the old leaf node that is now a branch node.

The `AnimalSet` class contains the core code to manage the tree. The root of the tree (that is, a reference to the first `AnimalNode` object) is contained in the `m_oRoot` variable. The class also contains `.Load` and `.Save` methods that save or load the tree to/from the `Animal.dat` file.

However, the `AnimalSet` class does not contain any logic to play the actual game. Instead, this logic is handled by the `PlayGame` procedure and a special class, the `AnimalCursor` class.

The `AnimalCursor` class encapsulates an abstract entity known as a *cursor*. The `AnimalSet` class maintains a tree of animal nodes, and the `AnimalCursor` class maintains information about the *current node* in that tree. Cursors are always used in this manner—a cursor is an object that is related to a collection object, and it contains a reference to a specific item in that object's collection. In this case, the `AnimalCursor` contains a reference to a specific node in the collection of `AnimalNode` objects maintained by the `AnimalSet` class.

Objects of the `AnimalCursor` class are created using the `.GetCursor` method of the `AnimalSet` class. The new cursor object is prepared by the `AnimalSet.GetCursor` method so that it is ready to use. The cursor is preset to reference the root node in the tree. The `AnimalCursor` class has the following methods and properties:

- The `.IsAnimal` property returns `True` if the current node is a leaf (that is, animal) node. The `.IsQuestion` property returns the opposite of this.
- The `.Text` property contains the contents of the `.Text` property of the current node. This is sometimes called a *pass-through* property because the cursor passes through the corresponding property from the object that the cursor is currently referencing.
- The `.FollowYes` and `.FollowNo` methods move the current node referenced by the cursor to either the node referenced by the `.Yes` or `.No` properties or the current node.
- The `.AddNewAnimal` method adds a new animal at the current leaf node.

Therefore, in outline, this is the logic of the animal game:

```
Dim oAnimalSet, oCursor
Set oAnimalSet = New AnimalSet
oAnimalSet.Load(sAnimalFileName)
Set oCursor = oAnimalSet.GetCursor
Do While oCursor.IsAnimal
    [ask yes/no question obtained from the .Text property of the cursor]
    If [answer was yes] Then
        oCursor.FollowYes
    Else
        oCursor.FollowNo
    End If
Loop
[ask "is it a..." obtained from the .Text property of the cursor]
[if wrong, get new animal information, and then use oCursor.AddNewAnimal to add new
animal]
```

The advantage of the cursor technique is that the program logic shown in the preceding code does not need to know about nodes or trees or any of the underlying details about *how* the `AnimalSet` implements all the state information in the collection. All it knows is how to obtain a cursor object, and then how to use that object to play the game.

A Final Word

The system scripting technologies described in this book form a powerful foundation for automating complex, mundane, and repetitive system tasks. When combined with the additional resources and facilities described in Appendix B, "Other Scripting Resources," there is, quite literally, no limit to the uses to which system scripts can be put. Almost all the new technologies being deployed today (and tomorrow) on Windows platforms are scriptable, which means that each day new ways to deploy and manage systems are made available. The techniques and technologies presented in this book should enable you to create and deploy timesaving script solutions to the problems that you face on a day-to-day basis.

Happy Scripting!

Part IV

Appendixes

Installing Windows Script Host

The technologies described in this book, primarily WSH and VBScript, are each compatible with all 32-bit versions of Windows, including Windows 95, Windows 98, Windows NT and Windows 2000. Some of these operating systems ship with WSH, whereas others do not, as follows:

- *Windows 95* This does not ship with WSH, and so the latest WSH run-time and script engines must be installed before scripts are run on this platform.
- *Windows 98* This ships with WSH 1.0, but the newer WSH 2.0 run-time should be installed, as should the latest script engines.
- *Windows NT* This does not ship with WSH, although WSH 1.0 is available in the Option Pack. Again, the newer WSH 2.0 should be installed, as should the latest script engines.
- *Windows 2000* This ships with WSH 2.0 and the latest script engines and is, therefore, up to date as of the publication date of this book.

Fortunately, the most recent WSH run-time and script engine downloads are compatible with all the previously listed operating systems. Using the most recent release on all platforms ensures that scripts developed on one platform will operate on all the others.

Note

For some reason, WSH 1.0 includes script hosts that sign-on with a version number of 5.0, and WSH 2.0 includes script hosts that sign-on with a version of 5.1. ◆

The latest versions of WSH and the VBScript script engine are available from the main Microsoft script web site at:

`http://msdn.microsoft.com/scripting`

The WSH run-time (including the `CSCRIPT.EXE` and `WSCRIPT.EXE` hosts) is packaged as a self-installing archive named `WSH20EN.EXE` for the V2.0 English edition. To install the run-time, simply double-click on the archive file. The archive also accepts several command-line switches:

- Use `/Q` to install quietly with the minimum number of dialogs (typically none).
- Use `/C` to extract the files but not install. The `/T` switch must also be supplied in this case.
- Use `/T:`*`path`* to use *`path`* as the temporary file directory during install. This is also the target directory when the `/C` switch is used.

The VBScript script engine (which also includes the JScript engine) is also packaged as a self-installing archive. The archive file is `STE50EN.EXE` for the V5.0 English edition. To install the engines, simply double-click on the archive file. The archive accepts the same switches as the WSH run-time archive.

Microsoft ships the VBScript engine with many other products, including Internet Explorer. It is, therefore, quite possible that a computer will already have the latest script engines already installed.

Other additional tools and technologies that can be useful for script developers are described in Appendix B, "Other Scripting Resources."

B

Other Scripting Resources

In addition to the core technologies described in this book, there are numerous additional resources available to enhance and extend WSH in various ways. Many of these resources are free, whereas others carry a nominal charge. This appendix provides a brief listing of some of the resources investigated by the author. Note that the inclusion of a resource in this list is *not* an endorsement of the product or service. As always, you should exercise your judgment when evaluating a technology.

Online Scripting Resources

The following online resources provide additional materials on WSH, VBScript, or both. As with all Web sites, the following URLs might be updated over time.

Microsoft Scripting Web Site

`http://msdn.microsoft.com/scripting`

The Microsoft site is of course the primary location for new script technologies, articles, and updates.

Clarence Washington Scripting Web Site

`http://cwashington.netreach.net`

This site, maintained by Clarence Washington, contains numerous third party sample scripts in many different script languages. Clarence is also active on many of the scripting newsgroups.

Ian Morrish Scripting Web Site

`http://wsh.glazier.co.nz/frame.htm`

Another independent script site, maintained by Ian Morrish.

Steven Bondi Scripting Web Site

`http://homepages.go.com/~sbondi/powerscripting`

This page, maintained by Steven Bondi, is less focused on WSH, but it still has some useful script information and links.

Microsoft Public Newsgroups

`news:msnews.microsoft.com`

The Microsoft sponsored newsgroups contain several newsgroups dedicated to various scripting technologies. Look for newsgroups named `microsoft.public.scripting.*`

Additional Scriptable Technologies

ADSI

The full ADSI (Active Directory Service Interface) documentation can be found in the MSDN portion of the Microsoft Web site at:

`http://msdn.microsoft.com/isapi/msdnlib.idc?theURL=/library/sdkdoc/adsi/ds2intro_53ud.htm`

This documentation is also available for download. For more information on ADSI see Chapter 13, "System Management Scripts."

WMI

WMI stands for *Windows Management Instrumentation*, and it is the Microsoft implementation of a new industry standard called *WBEM (Web Based Enterprise Management)*. WMI is an enterprise management technology that is similar in many ways to ADSI but much larger in scope. Whereas ADSI only manages directories, WMI manages almost all resources on a Windows NT or Windows 2000 computer, including the operating system, hardware and device drivers, the system registry, and event logs. WMI is also extensible through the provision of additional *providers*, which add additional management capabilities.

Like ADSI, WMI is scriptable through a series of objects. For more information, see the following Web sites:

`http://msdn.microsoft.com/isapi/msdnlib.idc?theURL=/library/sdkdoc/wmi/wmi.html`

`http://www.microsoft.com/NTServer/management/Techdetails/ProdArchitect/WMIScripting.asp`

Windows Explorer Shell

The Windows Explorer desktop shell is itself scriptable via a series of COM objects. For information on these objects and on how to use the shell, see the following Web site:

`http://msdn.microsoft.com/library/sdkdoc/shellcc/Shell/Objects/Objects.htm`

ADO

ADO (ActiveX Data Objects) is a scriptable set of objects that provide generic access to local and remote databases, including Microsoft Access and SQL Server. ADO is part of MDAC, which can be obtained from:

`http://www.microsoft.com/data`

CDO

CDO (Collaboration Data Objects) is a scriptable technology to allow scripts to interact with mail servers such as Microsoft Exchange. Documentation on CDO can be found in the MSDN Library or online at:

`http://msdn.Microsoft.com`

Microsoft Office 2000

All the components of Office 2000 are scriptable, including Excel, Word, and Outlook. Documentation on the objects, methods, and properties is available in the Office 2000 Developer Edition and in online help that ships with the Office 2000 product.

Microsoft Internet Explorer

MSIE is fully scriptable, and it acts as an ActiveX script host, allowing VBScript's scripts to execute within a Web page. More information on scripting IE is available in the Internet SDK and the Internet Explorer Resource Kit. These kits are available from MS Press or through computer bookstores.

Microsoft XML Control

The MSXML ActiveX control is a scriptable control that parses conformant XML files. The control is part of Internet Explorer 5, and documentation can be found at:

`http://msdn.Microsoft.com/xml`

Development Tools

XRay

The Microsoft IIS (Internet Information Server) Resource Kit contains a useful tool called XRay that displays the properties and methods of COM objects. This kit is available from MS Press or through computer bookstores.

Script Debugger

Microsoft has a free script debugger available at the scripting site previously listed. This debugger provides facilities to set breakpoints, monitor global and local variables, and step through a script one statement at a time.

Script Encoder Tool

In addition to the script debugger, Microsoft also offers for download a script encoder tool that obfuscates script source code. The purpose of the tool is to make it more difficult for users to view and edit scripts. The encoding is simple, and it should not be viewed as a security device, although it will probably prevent casual users from "improving" a script. The tool is available on the main Microsoft scripting site previously noted.

Windows Script Component Wizard

This is another technology available from the main Microsoft scripting Web site. The wizard automates the development of a `.wsc` file and generates the appropriate skeleton of XML elements.

OLEView Tool

The OLEView tool is a part of the Microsoft Platform SDK, Visual C++, or it can be downloaded from the Microsoft Web site. The tool allows all the COM objects installed on a computer to be inspected, although the details generated can be overwhelming.

PrimalScript

This excellent scripting IDE is available from Sapien Technologies at:

`http://www.sapien.com`

CodeMagic

Another scripting IDE, with an unbeatable price, is available from:

`http://www.petes-place.com/codemagic.html (full IDE)`

Index

A

B

C

D

E

F

G-H

L

M

N

O

P

Q-R

S

T

W-Z

New Riders Professional Library

Michael Masterson, Herman Knief, Scott Vinick, and Eric Roul: ***Windows NT DNS***
(ISBN: 1-56205-943-2)

Sandra Osborne: ***Windows NT Registry***
(ISBN: 1-56205-941-6)

Mark Edmead and Paul Hinsburg: ***Windows NT Performance Monitoring, Benchmarking, and Tuning***
(ISBN: 1-56205-942-4)

Karanjit Siyan: ***Windows NT TCP/IP***
(ISBN: 1-56205-887-8)

Ted Harwood: ***Windows NT Terminal Server and Citrix MetaFrame***
(ISBN: 1-56205-944-0)

Anil Desai: ***Windows NT Network Management: Reducing Total Cost of Ownership***
(ISBN: 1-56205-946-7)

Eric K. Cone, Jon Boggs, and Sergio Perez: ***Planning for Windows 2000***
(ISBN: 0-7357-0048-6)

Doug Hauger, Marywynne Leon, and William C. Wade III: ***Implementing Exchange Server***
(ISBN: 1-56205-931-9)

Janice Rice Howd: ***Exchange System Administration***
(ISBN: 0-7357-0081-8)

Sean Baird and Chris Miller: ***SQL Server Administration***
(ISBN: 1-56205-955-6)